Grover Hudson

Language Acquisition

Language Acquisition

JILL G. de VILLIERS

PETER A. de VILLIERS

Harvard University Press

Cambridge, Massachusetts, and London, England · 1978

Library of Congress Cataloging in Publication Data

De Villiers, Jill G   1948–
    Language acquisition.

    Bibliography: p.
    Includes index.
        1. Children—Language.   2. Psycholinguistics.
3. Speech disorders in children.   I. De Villiers,
Peter A., 1946–   joint author.   II. Title.
P118.D4   401'.9   77-22132
ISBN 0-674-50931-5

To our parents,

and to Nicholas, who was conceived with this book

but who learned to speak despite it

Acknowledgments

To Roger Brown, for stimulating our interest in child language in the first place, and for his longhand comments that threatened to exceed the chapters in length and to surpass them in quality. To Eric Wanner, for his friendship, encouragement, and guidance; he unwittingly became the personification of our collective superego. To Susan Carey, for many helpful suggestions on the semantics chapter, and for showing us more where we thought it was all just tiv. To Helen Tager-Flusberg and Kenji Hakuta, who deserve particular mention among the students from whom we stole ideas. To Jean Berko Gleason, for critically reading an early draft and saving us from some unmentionable slips of the mind. To Harry Foster, a splendid editor whom we recommend most highly for experiments on the detection of ambiguity. To Virginia Koster, Peggy Burlet, and Mari Tavitian, for all the last-minute typing and yet still smiling when they see us.

To the following authors and publishers for permission to reprint material: P. 15, Figure 2: from P. C. Delattre, A. M. Liberman, and F. S. Cooper, "Acoustic loci and transitional cues for consonants," *J. Acoust. Soc. Amer.* (1955) 27: 769–773; by permission of the American Institute of Physics and A. M. Liberman. P. 21, "The Lama" (copyright 1931 by Ogden Nash), from *The face is familiar* by Ogden Nash; reprinted by permission of Little, Brown and Company. P. 22, Table 2: from R. W. Brown, *Social psychology,* copyright 1965 Macmillan Publishing Company; reprinted by permission of the publisher and R. W. Brown. P. 26, Figures 3 and 4: from R. W. Brown, *Social psychology,* copyright 1965 Macmillan Publishing Company; reprinted by permission of the publisher and R. W. Brown (adapted from A. M. Liberman, K. S. Harris, H. S.

Contents

Language Acquisition

1

Introduction

The tiny sixteen-month-old child toddles off down the garden path, her diaper trailing down around her knees. Close behind her follow two adults. She pauses, looks around, and says meaningfully: "Windy." The adults scribble furiously in their Woolworth's notepads. A heavy truck trundles by on the highway near the garden. "Noisy lorry . . . naughty lorry!" says the child. Again the adults scribble, one writing down the words, the other making notes on the context.

This was how we spent most of a brief vacation in the south of England in the summer of 1971, following our little niece wherever she toddled and faithfully recording every word she said—like two naturalists observing some exotic species in a suburban garden. Such consuming interest in the statements of a rather average English child with nothing more momentous to tell us than endless repetitions of "noisy _____," "naughty _____," "oh dear me," and "pardon," may seem a trifle odd to the uninitiated reader. But ponder the fact that this scene is being repeated over and over again in gardens, homes, and playrooms from rural African huts to American university laboratories. We are but two of a large and rapidly increasing group of psychologists and linguists from many different countries who spend hours and days tape recording, videotaping, transcribing, and submitting to sophisticated linguistic and acoustic analysis the seemingly trivial early sentences of children. What could possibly generate all this interest or justify all of this effort? We at least had the excuse that Elizabeth was our first niece, and it is true that linguists' children are recorded more than any others. Yet, surely familial pride alone cannot explain all the time and energy (not to mention the federal funds) expended on child language research.

1

Language acquisition research is important for our understanding of man in general and of the intellectual development of the child in particular; it addresses major questions about the nature of man, questions that have generated a great deal of lively and often acrimonious debate over the centuries amongst philosophers and psychologists. Here we will briefly consider four such themes; in the course of the book we hope to show how they are addressed and illuminated by the research on language acquisition.

MAN VERSUS ANIMAL

Throughout history, man has tried to establish which aspects of his behavior and thought make him unique amongst the world's creatures. Language has been the aspect most frequently chosen. Writers point to the importance of language in man's socialization and adaptation to his environment. Man can pass on his accumulated knowledge of the world and his culture to his offspring by means of oral and written words, making first-hand experience unnecessary. Linguistic symbols also provide us with a powerful and flexible tool for thought. Indeed, the child's understanding and use of language often provides us with the best, and sometimes the only, window on the development of his thought and reasoning.

Nevertheless, the degree to which human language is qualitatively different from, as opposed to just more complex than, other animal communication systems continues to dominate much of the theoretical debate in the study of language. For example, honey bees perform an intricate dance that serves to indicate to the other bees the direction and distance from the hive of a source of nectar. What particular properties distinguish this communication from human language? The most passionate disagreement and the greatest media attention have been aroused by recent efforts to teach chimpanzees a form of language. In Chapter 7 we shall consider several claims about the uniqueness of human language and examine what chimps have to tell us about this issue. The question of the continuity of man and animal also takes another form in accounts of child language. To what degree can principles and theories of learning derived from studies of lower animals in controlled laboratory experiments account for the child's acquisition of language?

NATURE VERSUS NURTURE

Another recurring question is, What does the child bring into the world with him by way of inherited knowledge or behavior, and what is the product of experience? Psychologists often dismiss this problem as insoluble or poorly formulated, pointing out that clearly both nature (genetics) and nurture (experience) are important in the acquisition of knowledge, but they interact in such complex ways that it is impossible to tease them apart. Nevertheless, the issue, often cleverly disguised, recurs constantly in psychology and continues to arouse heated discussion.

One form it takes in the study of language acquisition concerns the possible innate basis of the child's linguistic knowledge. Does the child come to the language learning task with any innate concept of what sentences are (McNeill, 1970) or with a bias towards acquiring a particular kind of linguistic system? Another version of the nature versus nurture controversy considers the influence of biological maturation on the course of language acquisition. It is known from neurophysiological studies that the brain of the child takes some years to mature completely. While there appear to be certain basic environmental conditions, such as minimal levels of nutrition and sensory stimulation, that must be fulfilled for brain development to take place, under a normal range of environments the biological maturation of the child is influenced little by experience. The physical development of the child's brain, as opposed to the quality of his experience with language, may be a major determinant of several aspects of his language development, including the ages at which he begins to babble speech sounds, begins to combine words, and masters certain complex sentence forms.

A particularly influential argument for biological determination posits a critical period for language learning based on the maturity of the child's brain. On this view a first language must be acquired during the years in which the brain is developing. Language acquisition is not possible before the brain of the child has reached a certain level of development, and is difficult, if not impossible, once that development is complete.

ACTIVE VERSUS PASSIVE LEARNING

Is the child an active participant in the learning process, trying to make sense of the world about him, or is his behavior passively shaped by the environment? In the study of child language this issue is illustrated by an opposition between two accounts of acquisition. One account stresses the way children develop their own grammar or phonological rule system and views the child as an active contributor who adopts strategies, forms hypotheses, and searches for evidence to confirm or deny them. An extreme version of this approach suggests that language is not *learned* by the child, it is *created*. The other approach points to the structured environment of the child, the simplified language he hears from his parents, and their responses to his attempts at speech, and emphasizes their role in his learning of the language. Questions of the child's contribution to the

learning process and the effects of his linguistic and nonlinguistic environment will be addressed throughout the book, particularly in Chapters 7
and 8.

For each of these issues, there are sharply contrasting poles of
opinion. Behavioral psychologists who wish to extend theories of learning
from animals to human cognition and language typically emphasize biological continuity, the role of the environment, and the shaping of the
child's linguistic behavior by others (Skinner, 1957). Many linguists, on
the other hand, stress the uniqueness of language, the creativity of the
child, and innate determinants of the course of acquisition (Chomsky,
1959, 1965). Clearly, a continuum of opinion exists between the two extremes, and each emphasis supplies us with insights into the nature of language acquisition as well as providing a healthy counterbalance to the ex-
cesses of the other extreme.

NORMAL VERSUS ABNORMAL BEHAVIOR
AND THOUGHT

Over the years one of the major tasks of psychology has been to provide
an adequate account of abnormal behavior and thought, an account that
distinguishes it from normal behavior, explains its origins, and suggests
possible treatments or prevention. Deviant or delayed language development accompanies many childhood disorders, amongst them sensory deficits, psychotic syndromes, and general mental retardation. In some cases
the language disability may reflect the basic problem of the child better
than other symptoms do. Study of normal language acquisition provides a
standard with which to compare the specific language difficulties of the
disordered child, frequently bringing greater insight into the nature of the
disorder as well as suggesting guidelines for treatment programs. In
Chapter 9 we shall use what we know about normal acquisition to explore
the language disabilities that accompany four major childhood disorders:
hearing loss, developmental aphasia, mental retardation, and infantile autism.

In short, language acquisition fascinates because psychology fascinates. Human behavior and its explanation have a universal appeal as
subjects of speculation or study, yet its scientific description is often elu-
sive. We are fortunate in the case of language that there is a branch of science devoted to its precise description, namely linguistics.

LINGUISTICS AND CHILD LANGUAGE

A fertile but often tempestuous union exists between linguistics and psychology in the study of child language. As in many productive marriages,
the union of the two disciplines leads to the growth and strengthening of

each, but there remains some disagreement as to the respective roles of the partners in the joint enterprise.

Linguistics provides the child-language researcher with carefully defined concepts and units of analysis for the investigation of language, as well as formal descriptions of the adult's knowledge of language, the end point of the child's development. Linguists consider an idealization of the speech that is actually produced by ordinary persons as pertinent to their theories: incomplete sentences or other departures from grammar are attributed to memory lapses, wandering attention, or some other disruption of the speaker's train of thought. A distinction is made between the *competence,* or underlying linguistic knowledge of the speaker-hearer, and his actual *performance*. This distinction can be made for adult informants because samples of speech can be supplemented by judgment and reflection; we can ask each other: "Did you really mean to say that?," or: "Which is better, *I do* or *I does*?" It is much more difficult in the case of the young child to distinguish between a lack of underlying knowledge and mere errors of use; first of all, because self-reflection is a late-blooming skill and children cannot respond appropriately to meta-linguistic interrogation until age four or five (see Chapter 6). Several different grammars can describe any given sample of child speech, but which best captures the knowledge of the child? For the adult we can test these alternative rules by asking, "Would you say X or would you say Y?" For young children, however, not only is linguistic intuition lacking but the sentences are often incomplete and elliptical and do not provide the critical information needed to decide among possible grammars.

Some changes in the child's speech and understanding reflect the growth of linguistic knowledge, others reflect the development of memory capacity, attention span, or reasoning ability. How to determine the appropriate description of the child's linguistic knowledge at each stage of development will concern us in several chapters. Psychology plays a vital role in these decisions by contributing information about the child's conceptual development, ability to use contextual and social cues to meaning, and powers of abstraction. A full account of the acquisition of language thus depends critically on the survival of the marriage—of the disciplines, that is.

2

From Sound
to Meaning

In *Alice in Wonderland,* the duchess says to Alice: "And the moral of all *that* is—Take care of the sense, and the sounds will take care of themselves." Children in the early stages of language acquisition seem to have taken the advice of the duchess to heart, for they are much more concerned with the sense of an utterance than with the correctness of its form (de Villiers and de Villiers, 1972; also Chapter 6). Nevertheless, in order to understand others and to be understood, the child must acquire the ability to hear and produce the sounds of his language as the adults around him do, and that is no small task. Sounds are far more crucial for sense than the duchess thought.

For a start, the child must distinguish between speech sounds and other sounds in his environment, especially between speech and the other noises produced by the people around him. For example, most of the wheezes, grunts, clicks, and cooing sounds that may accompany the English spoken to the child are not relevant to its meaning, although some of them may be important in other languages (for example, the click sounds in many African dialects). As we shall see later in this chapter, evidence is rapidly accumulating that the ability to discriminate speech sounds from nonspeech sounds develops very early in infancy, and may even be innate.

Once he has separated speech from other noises, what aspects of the sound system of his language must the child learn about? We shall describe five features of speech that linguists have explored and then turn to their development in young children. Our linguistic description will use English as an example, since it is the acquisition of that language that will concern us most in this chapter, but ways in which other languages differ from English will also be noted.

6

The features we examine are:

1. *Phones,* the separate speech sounds that are produced by speakers of English, and how they are articulated.
2. *Phonemes,* the sound types that function in the language to distinguish between different words.
3. *Distinctive features,* articulatory or acoustic properties that serve to distinguish between different phonemes.
4. *Phonological rules,* by which the sounds are combined into words, and which account for systematic variations in the form of word endings in different phonetic contexts.
5. *Intonation,* changes in stress and pitch throughout a sentence that signal differences in its meaning.

PRODUCING AND PERCEIVING SPEECH SOUNDS

The child must know how to produce and discriminate those particular sounds used as speech elements in his language. Phonetics provides us with a description of how speech sounds in any language are produced by the various organs of the vocal tract (*articulatory phonetics*) and a description of the sound waves themselves (*acoustic phonetics*). The transcription systems developed by phoneticians enable us to represent the types of speech sounds we produce, a task for which our usual alphabets are inadequate. For example, the English alphabet has twenty-six letters, but there are over forty basic speech sounds in English. Some words that are identical in written form sound different, for example, a courtly *bow* versus a *bow* and arrow, while others that sound identical are written differently, for example, the *bough* of a tree and the *bow* of a courtier. Phonetic symbols enable the linguist to indicate these differences and similarities by assigning a different symbol to each sound type. A phonetic transcription is thus an important tool for studying the acquisition of speech, since we can represent the differences in articulation among individual children, between children and adults, and among different stages of development for any particular child in a clear and unambiguous way.

Articulatory Phonetics

How, then, are the speech sounds of English articulated by adults? Like all other languages, English has two major classes of speech sounds, consonants and vowels.

Consonants

The consonants of English are produced by impeding or cutting off a stream of air expelled from the lungs as it passes through the throat and mouth, sometimes diverting it through the nose. This sets up waves or disturbances in the air that are heard as sounds. The traditional phonetic classification of consonant sounds specifies three variables: (1) their manner of articulation, (2) their place of articulation, and (3) whether or not they are accompanied by vibration of the vocal cords.

Manner of articulation describes the nature of the interference with the stream of air. For *stop* consonants such as [b][1] the air is fully stopped at the point of articulation and then suddenly released in a burst—hence they are also called *plosives*. The English consonants [b], [p], [d], [t], [g], and [k] all share this manner of articulation. When the air is merely constricted while passing through the mouth, as in the initial sounds of *that* (symbolized by [ð]) and *thin* [θ], the consonant is called a *fricative*. These include [f], [v], and [h], plus the *sibilants or s*-sounds: [s], [z], the initial sound of *shed* [š], and the *s*-sound in *pleasure* [ž]. Some consonants in English combine stop and fricative modes of articulation. For the initial sounds of *cheese* [č] and *juice* [ǰ] the air stream is first stopped and then slowly released with friction. Called *affricates,* these consonants can be represented as a blend of [t] + [š] and [d] + [ž]. A rare mode of articulation in English is that of *flaps,* like the [ř] in the British *very,* where the tongue is brought against the roof of the mouth for only a brief period of time and then taken sharply away again.

Other modes of articulation cause less friction or constriction of the air flow, and the characteristic sound results from the shape and resonant qualities of the oral or nasal cavity. These include *lateral* consonants, [l] sounds, in which the tongue is placed against the roof of the mouth but the air passes by on one or both sides of it; and *nasal* consonants, such as [m], [n], and the final sound in *song* [ŋ], in which the oral cavity is closed at some point but the air passes through the nose.

These different ways of articulating the consonants of English far from exhaust the modes of articulation used by speakers of other languages. Some have *trilled* consonants, in which a flexible articulator like the tongue is set briefly into vibration so that a rapid series of sounds is heard. In the initial [ř] in Italian (*risotto*) and Spanish (*rio*) the tip of the tongue is trilled against the ridge of gum behind the upper teeth. Other languages have *implosive* stop consonants, produced by sucking the air in when the consonant is released, as if sucking on a pipe. Zulu, a language spoken in South Africa, has a "hard" [b] in *bheka* (to look) and *bhala* (to write), produced like our plosive [b]; and a "soft" [b] in *beka* (to put) and *bala* (to count), pronounced at the same point in the mouth but with implosion. Finally, several African languages, including Zulu, use *click consonants,* made by drawing the tongue downward to create a vacuum and then releasing it sharply.

---

[1] The symbols for phonetic transcriptions of speech sound types are placed in square brackets [   ]; phonemes are placed between slashes /   /.

Place of articulation is defined by the point of maximum constriction in the mouth or upper throat, the location at which the complete or partial stoppage of the air flow is effected. For example, among the English stop consonants, [b] and [p] are produced with the lips initially touching, [d] and [t] with the tip of the tongue placed on the ridge of gum just behind the upper teeth, and [g] and [k] with the back of the tongue against the soft back of the palate. These and other places of articulation combine with the different modes to give the full set of English consonants.

Most of the consonant types come in pairs, one accompanied by *voicing,* the vibration of the vocal cords, the other *voiceless.* For example, of the different types of stop consonants, [b], [d], and [g] are voiced; [p], [t], and [k] are voiceless. Table 1 shows the common consonants of English, classified according to their place and manner of articulation and the presence or absence of voicing.

English clearly does not use all possible combinations of the three articulatory variables; there are many gaps in the table. Yet some of the missing ones are easy enough to produce and do occur in other languages or English dialects. The Scots use a fricative produced at the velum (the back of the palate), as in the final sound of *loch* and *pibroch* (music for the bagpipes), a sound that also occurs in German, as in *Nacht* (night). Welsh uses a voiceless nasal [m] in *mhen* ("my head"). Every child must learn to produce the appropriate consonant sounds for his own language community. Later in this chapter we shall evaluate the claim that children in the period of babbling prior to intelligible speech actually produce a much wider range of speech sounds than those used in the language they will acquire.

There remain three types of sounds called *semivowels.* Linguists classify these sounds, [w], [y], and [r], with the consonants, since they occur in consonantal positions in words and are of very brief duration. When they occur at the beginning of a word some friction or turbulence is created in the air stream, as in the production of a consonant, but if they follow vowels they seem merely to alter (or "color") the sound of the vowel. Compare *real* with *earl.*

Vowels

Vowels are produced by the air expelled from the lungs flowing through the vocal cords and then passing freely through the mouth and sometimes through the nose. If the vocal cords are stretched with the right tension, they vibrate as the air passes through them, causing sound waves. These sound waves are modified, primarily by the height and location of the tongue in the mouth and by the shape of the lips, to form the different vowels. For example, the vowel sound in *Pete* is produced with the tongue raised near the front of the mouth, so it is called a *high front vowel.* The vowel in *pool* is produced with the tongue raised near the back

Table 1. Classification of the consonants of English

Manner of articulation	Place of articulation													
	Bilabial (lower lip, upper lip)		Labio-dental (lower lip, upper teeth)		Apico-dental (tip of tongue, upper teeth)		Apico-alveolar (tip of tongue, alveolae[a])		Fronto-palatal (front of tongue, palate)		Dorso-velar (back of tongue, velum[b])		Glottal (vocal cords)	
	+V[c]	−V[d]	+V	−V	+V	−V	+V	−V	+V	−V	+V	−V	+V	−V
Stops	b	p					d	t			g	k		ʔ[e]
Fricatives			v	f	ð (this)	θ (thin)							ɦ (ahead)	h (hymn)
Silibants							z	s	ž (leisure)	š (shed)				
Affricates							ǰ (judge)	č (chin)						
Flaps							ř (very)							
Nasals	m						n				ŋ (song)			
Laterals							l (lip)	ł (pill)						
Semivowels	w						r		y					

[a] the ridge of gum behind the teeth.
[b] the soft back of the palate.
[c] voiced.
[d] voiceless.
[e] the sound that replaces [t] in *mountain* in many American dialects.

of the mouth, so it is a *high back vowel*. Similarly, the vowel sound in *pat* is a *low front vowel*—the tongue is in roughly the same forward position as for *Pete,* but now it is kept down low. As you produce the series *Pete, pit, pate, pat, pot,* the tongue drops lower and lower in the mouth as the vowel is produced. Pursing your lips while producing the vowel also changes its sound. For *rounded* vowels, as in *pool,* the lips are somewhat pursed and protruded; for *unrounded* vowels, as in *Pete,* they are relaxed and somewhat spread. The reader can readily verify this by watching his lips in a mirror while pronouncing these two words. In most standard dialects of English, all back vowels are rounded and all front and central vowels unrounded, but rounded front and unrounded back vowels occur in several languages. The vowels in the French *feu* (fire) and *cru* (growth) and the German *Hölle* (hell) and *Hütte* (hut) are examples of rounded front vowels, while Turkish uses an unrounded high back vowel. Phoneticians usually classify English vowels in terms of these basic attributes: the elevation of the tongue (from high to low), the location of the highest portion of the tongue in the mouth (front, central, or back), and the amount of rounding or spreading of the lips.

Vowels vary along several other dimensions besides these three, however. They can be *nasalized* by diverting part of the air stream through the nasal passage. This is true of several French vowels and also gives the twang of some southern American accents. Vowels differ in *length,* in *pitch,* and in the *tenseness* of the articulators during their production. Finally, they can be almost *voiceless,* produced without much vibration of the vocal cords, as when they are whispered. A full phonetic transcription provides symbols that indicate the value of each attribute in the pronunciation of the vowel.

The various vowels of English are frequently pronounced as *diphthongs,* combinations of two sounds. Speech sounds do not occur as separate, individual units in ongoing speech, but are joined together in a continuous flow of sound. So at junctures where they meet, they blend into each other. When we pronounce the word *toot,* the two consonant sounds are articulated at the teeth, but the vowel is a high back vowel, so the tongue moves back and forth during the word. There is bound to be some transitional sound produced between the consonants and the vowel. Most of the time these transitional sounds go by so rapidly that we don't hear them, but sometimes they are distinct enough to be noted in the phonetic description of the word. The nucleus of the vowel in these cases often consists of a stressed first part in a particular vowel position followed by a transition to another vowel position that is clear enough to be heard. The vowel nucleus is then transcribed as a diphthong of the two vowels.

There are a great many regional dialects of English that differ primarily in the pronunciation of vowels. In *Pygmalion,* George Bernard

Shaw has Professor Higgins, a phonetician, claim to be able to "place any man within six miles . . . within two miles in London. Sometimes within two streets." For each dialect, a phonetic description in terms of the three basic variables, plus the others we have noted, will capture the way speakers articulate the vowels.

Children acquire the characteristic pronunciation of the community in which they are raised. Should they move to a different region or country, there seems to be a period of particular sensitivity prior to puberty during which they readily adopt the dialect of their new peers. Their parents, on the other hand, are usually stuck with their accents: as soon as they open their mouths to speak they reveal their roots in New England, the Deep South, or the Midwest, or even more specifically in a particular state or city—who could mistake a Boston or a Brooklyn accent? Once we reach adulthood it takes a great deal more conscious effort either to lose the habits of articulation of our childhood or to acquire a new dialect or language with the appropriate accent; frequently it proves impossible (see Chapter 8).

Acoustic Phonetics

The preceding discussion of consonants and vowels summarizes most of the basic articulatory patterns that the child must master in order to speak English. But he must also be able to discriminate and identify those sound patterns in the speech that he hears, and that is no easy task. Speech is not like a pure tone or a simple musical note; the complex sounds pro-

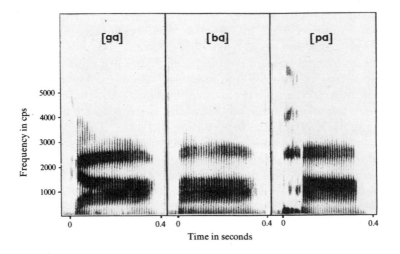

Figure 1.   Spectrograms of the syllables [ga], [ba], and [pa], showing transitions and vowel formants.

duced by the vocal tract include sounds at a large number of different frequencies (pitches) and intensities simultaneously. Furthermore, the flow of speech is continuous, so that the individual speech sounds blend into each other.

The complex stream of speech can be dissected into its various components in order to establish the distinctive elements of each type of speech sound. One method of achieving this is the sound spectrograph, a machine that transforms speech sounds into a pictorial pattern on paper—a spectrogram (see Figure 1). The spectrogram depicts changes in the frequency and loudness of the sound as time passes. The vertical axes of the spectrograms in Figure 1 represent increasing sound wave frequencies; the higher the pitch of the sound, the higher up the paper it will be marked. The intensity, or loudness, of any particular sound frequency is represented by the darkness of the markings on the paper at the level corresponding to that frequency.

Vowels

Vowels are typically made up of several major frequencies of sound, shown by the dark horizontal bands on the spectrograms in Figure 1. These bands of sound are called *formants*. For a particular speaker the different vowels are primarily distinguished by the sound frequency of the first and second formants, the lowest two bands of sound. In general, the higher the tongue is when the vowel is articulated, the lower the frequency of the first formant; the further back in the mouth it is, the lower the second formant. Thus, for the high front vowel of *bit* [ı], the first two formants are widely separated in frequency, but for the lower-mid back vowel of *bought* [ɔ], they are close together; so these two vowels are easily discriminable (see Figure 2). But our recognition of vowel sounds cannot be based on just the placement of these two formants, since there is no simple correspondence between their frequency and the vowels we perceive. We hear an [a] as an [a] regardless of whether it is pronounced in a deep bass voice or in a high soprano, by a man, a woman, or a child; yet the frequencies of the formants vary considerably from voice to voice. In addition, the sound pattern of a vowel can be influenced by the phonetic context in which it appears, especially by the place of articulation of any preceding or following consonants. Front vowels following a consonant produced at the back of the mouth ([g] or [k]) tend to be articulated further back than when they are said in isolation, with a corresponding drop in the frequency of the second formant.

In order to identify vowels, we therefore appear to use several types of information from the speech signal and the context in which it occurs. The relative, as opposed to the absolute, frequencies of the formants, plus their relationship to the characteristic pitch (fundamental frequency) of the speaker's voice, are crucial variables. We seem to normalize the frequencies of the formants in accordance with the pitch of the voice (R. Miller, 1953; Ladefoged and Broadbent, 1957). Formants of a particular frequency will be perceived as different vowels depending on the consonantal context in which they are placed, so we must also employ information about how the vowel sounds are influenced by the surrounding consonants. Finally, we tend to perceive what we expect to hear, so in some situations we will even fill in blanks in the speech signal with the vowel or consonant that ought to be there given the rest of the linguistic context (Liberman et al., 1967a).

Stop Consonants

Voiced stop consonants that differ in place of articulation ([b], [d], and [g]) are primarily distinguished by the direction and length of the sound transition into the second formant. In the spectrograms in Figure 1 the sound transition corresponding to the [g] in [gɑ] is the dark band of sound swinging down to the second formant in the first panel. This transition is absent for the [b] in [bɑ].

The consonants [b] and [p] are articulated in the same place and mode, but they differ in the presence or absence of voicing. In the spectrograms of Figure 1 this crucial sound feature corresponds to the difference in time of onset of the voiced formants. For the voiced consonant [b] the voicing begins at the beginning of the syllable [bɑ]; for the voiceless [p] there is a lag before the voiced formants begin. This lag is called *voice onset time* (VOT) and corresponds to the pause between release of the air stream when the lips are opened to produce the consonant and the vibration of the vocal cords. For most adult speakers of English the VOT for [bɑ] is 0 msec; the vocal cords are vibrated at the same moment as the lips open. For the syllable [pɑ] the VOT is around +40 msec; voicing begins 40 msec after the beginning of the consonant.

Recent technical advances have enabled researchers to synthesize sounds that mimic the acoustic features of natural speech sounds. In this way a particular acoustic feature such as VOT or the transition to the second formant can be systematically varied in order to study the importance of that feature in distinguishing one speech sound from another. As in the case of vowels, research on the role of formant transitions in our perception of stop consonants has revealed that there is no simple correspondence between the acoustic cues and our identification of the consonants. The synthesized sounds whose spectrograms are shown in Figure 2 are perceived as the indicated sequence of vowels preceded by the consonants [b], [d], and [g] (Delattre, Liberman, and Cooper, 1955). For each vowel, the transitions to the second formant determine which stop consonant will be heard, but these transitions vary across the different vowels for the same consonant. The case of the syllables beginning with [d] is particularly instructive. The length and even the direction of the transition

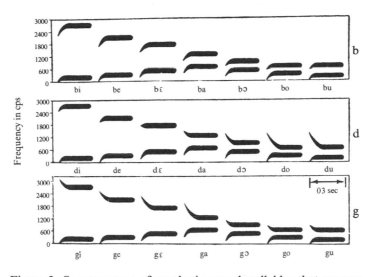

Figure 2. Spectrograms of synthetic speech syllables that are perceived as the indicated sequence of vowels preceded by the consonants [b], [d], and [g]. From Delattre, Liberman, and Cooper, 1955.

changes for each vowel, yet in each case the consonant is heard as a [d]. Indeed, the second formant transition for [du] is much more like that for [ga] than it is like that for [di]; yet the consonants of [du] and [ga] are never confused, and those of [du] and [di] are indistinguishable to us.

The perception of speech is therefore a particularly complex process that must incorporate linguistic and acoustic information. We sometimes perceive identical acoustic cues as different speech sounds, or very different cues as the same speech sound, depending on the linguistic context in which they are placed. Current models of speech perception posit specific neural detectors for the acoustic features associated with sound transitions or VOT (Eimas and Corbit, 1973), but passive detection would be inadequate; the process must be an active one that interprets the acoustic message in the light of information about the sound system of the language and its patterns of articulation (Stevens, 1972; Studdert-Kennedy, 1974).

Segmentation

Finally, we perceive words as made up of separate speech sounds, although the acoustic pattern is continuous. There is in fact no time slice of the stream of speech that can be heard as one of the stop consonants alone. If we take a tape of a syllable like [ba] and start cutting off portions of sound from the consonant end we eventually get a portion where just the vowel [a] is heard, in keeping with our intuition that the syllable is made up of two phones. But if we cut the tape from the vowel end we never get to a point at which just the [b] is heard. The syllable gets shorter and shorter until it suddenly changes into a chirp that does not even sound like speech, let alone a [b]! The acoustic information leading to the perception of the consonant must therefore overlap with that for the vowel, yet we hear two separate speech sounds.

This discussion of acoustic phonetics illustrates the complexity of the task that confronts the child as he begins to decipher the sound system of his language. The study of the development and possible innate bases of speech perception in children is still very much in its infancy, but the use of spectrographic analysis and artificially produced sounds has led to exciting advances in our knowledge. We shall return to the puzzles of speech perception when we discuss the developmental research later in this chapter.

PHONEMES—THE FUNCTIONAL SOUNDS OF A LANGUAGE

The production and discrimination of the speech sounds of a language is a complicated business, but just being able to produce and discern all the sounds is not enough. All languages group particular variations of sound into speech units, or *phonemes*. Phonemes are those categories of sound that function to signal differences in the words in the language. They are best defined in terms of contrasting minimal pairs of words—words that differ by only one sound but have different meanings. The words *pin, bin, gin, din, sin, shin, kin, chin, thin, fin, win,* and *tin* differ only in their initial sound, indicating that at least /p/, /b/, /ǰ/, /d/, /s/, /š/, /k/, /č/, /θ/, /f/, /w/, and /t/ function as different phonemes in English.

What kinds of sound variation are ignored in the phonemic categories of English? First is free variation in the pronunciation of a speech sound in a particular phonetic context. If you say *hot* several times, the pronunciation of the /t/ will vary slightly each time. Sometimes it will be strongly aspirated (breathy), sometimes less so. Sometimes it will be released by separating the tongue from the point of articulation; but at the end of a phrase or utterance it may be unreleased, with the speech organs being kept in contact. This variation does not change the meaning of the word, so we ignore it. The second type of ignored sound variation within a phoneme category results from the different phonetic contexts in which the phoneme occurs. The /k/ sounds in *keel* and *cool* are produced at different locations in the mouth because of the place of articulation of the vowels following them. The /k/ in *keel* is followed by a front vowel, so it tends to be produced nearer the front of the mouth than the /k/ in *cool,* which is followed by a back vowel. However, in English this difference in the /k/ sounds never occurs in the same phonetic context, as in a minimal pair of words where it could signal differences in meaning, so these sounds are said to be in complementary distribution. Similarly, when voiceless stop consonants (/p/, /t/, and /k/) begin words, they are produced with an accompanying puff of air (aspiration); when they follow an initial /s/ the aspiration is absent. The reader can demonstrate this for himself by saying the word pairs *pan/span, tone/stone* and *kin/skin* up against the back of the hand—only when the stop consonant is in initial position will the puff of air be felt. But again, differences in aspiration do not contrast meaning in English, so this difference in sounds is not even noticed by the native English-speaker.

Not all speech sounds in complementary distribution in the language are considered varying forms (*allophones*) of the same phoneme, however. All of the sounds within a phoneme class must also be phonetically similar. The aspirated and nonaspirated /p/ sounds are articulated in a very similar fashion and are never contrasted with each other in English, so they are classified as allophones of the phoneme /p/ for that language. The consonants /ŋ/ and /ð/ are also in complementary distribution in English, but since phonetically they have little in common besides both being voiced, they are separate phonemes.

Although none of the preceding phonetic variations signal a change in meaning in English, they do in many other languages. The difference between the initial /k/ sounds of *keel* and *cool* is important for meaning in Arabic, so they function as separate phonemes in that language. Arabic also contrasts aspirated and unaspirated /p/ sounds. Several phonemes in Zulu are distinguished by their degree of aspiration. The /t/ in *tusa* ("to praise") is contrasted with the more fully aspirated /t^h/ in *t^{h}usa* ("to frighten"), and each of the three click sounds that appear in the language have an aspirated version. For example, the dental click represented by the letter "c" is made by pressing the tip of the tongue against the upper front teeth and gum, depressing the center of the tongue to form a vacuum, and then sharply withdrawing the tip. This is the click sound sometimes made in English to express exasperation, usually written as "tsk!tsk!" In the minimal pair *cela* ("to request") and *c^{h}ela* ("to sprinkle"), the strong aspiration of the initial click in the second word indicates a difference in meaning.

On the other hand, some of the phonemic distinctions in English are not functional in other languages. Spanish uses /s/ and /z/ as allophones of the same phoneme. Japanese native-speakers produce sounds that approximate both our /r/ and /l/, but there is no distinction between phonemes in that range of speech sounds.

The child acquiring English comes to ignore certain variations in speech sounds that are nonfunctional within the language, but attends to others that mark changes in meaning. In fact we learn so well to ignore nonphonemic differences like those of aspiration that adult native English-speakers report great difficulty in learning to produce and hear the different /k/ and /p/ phonemes of Arabic. Similarly, the difficulties of Japanese adults with the English /l/ and /r/ are legendary.

DISTINCTIVE FEATURES

Several linguists, the best known of them being Roman Jakobson, have proposed that phonemes in any language can be uniquely characterized by a fairly small set of distinctive features that are specified in terms of articulatory patterns and in terms of acoustic properties. Each phoneme appears as a bundle of binary features, with the presence (+) or absence (−) of each feature being specified. Thus phonemes can be [± high], [± low], [± back], and [± anterior], depending on the position of the tongue and where in the mouth they are articulated. All vowels and consonants like /b/, /d/, /g/, /v/, and /z/, that are accompanied by voicing, are [+ voice]; voiceless consonants are [− voice]. Acoustic considerations and general mode of articulation add other features like [± strident], which refers to the degree of friction or turbulence generated in the air stream during articulation; and [± continuant], which refers to whether or not there is a continual flow of air through the oral cavity. All sibilants are therefore [+ continuant] and [+ strident]; all nasals are [− continuant] and [− strident]. Some dozen or so features are commonly used to characterize the phonemes of English.

Much research in linguistics has been directed towards identifying the minimum universal set of phonetic features that would include all of the distinctive features (those that distinguish functional categories) in any language. Jakobson claimed that each language uses some subset of these features to distinguish between phonemes, but that some features are used universally in all languages. For example, all languages distinguish between vowels and consonants, the features that characterize that difference being marked as [± vocalic] and [± consonantal]. These features refer to the interruption or lack of interruption of the air stream in the phonemes' pronunciation, and the types of combinations and word positions in which they can occur. Jakobson argued that children acquire phonemic distinctions marked by universal features before those that are more language specific, a hypothesis that we will evaluate later in the chapter.

Evidence for the psychological reality of at least some distinctive features as units in our perception and production of phonemes comes from two sources: variations in the ease with which we distinguish between consonant phonemes (Miller and Nicely, 1955) and slips of the tongue (Fromkin, 1973). Miller and Nicely investigated adults' perception of consonants in noisy conditions. Phonemes like /b/ and /p/, which differ by only one distinctive feature (voicing), were more likely to be confused than those that differ by two features, which were in turn more likely to be confused than those that differ by three, and so on. The easiest consonants to distinguish were those, like /f/ and /n/, that differ by several distinctive features. The individual features like voicing, nasality, stridency, and continuancy were themselves ordered according to how easily they could be discriminated. The confusion errors that we make in our memory for consonants are also in keeping with an analysis in terms of distinctive features (Wickelgren, 1966).

Fromkin collected several thousand slips of the tongue by English-speaking adults. These speech errors are not only highly entertaining— for example, Dr. Spooner's legendary "You have *h*issed all my *m*ystery lectures" (said in chiding a student)—but they also reflect the phonological and grammatical system of the language. A large number of them involve substitutions or permutations of various speech units. Frequently entire words or phonemes are exchanged, as in Spooner's "*Work* is the curse of the *drinking* classes," or in "*s*ack's *j*ute" for "*J*ack's *s*uit." But sometimes only single phonetic features are interchanged. In the slip "*g*lear *p*lue sky" for "*c*lear *b*lue sky" only the voicing feature of the initial phonemes of "clear" and "blue" has been exchanged. Fromkin's findings suggest that our speech production is organized at several levels, with the smallest units being distinctive features, but with phonemes and words also operating as higher level units. The migration of features, phonemes, or words to points earlier in the utterance also demonstrates that we plan quite well ahead when we speak—but the execution of that planning sometimes goes awry.

PHONOLOGICAL RULES

Generative Phonology

We have confined our discussion so far to structural analyses of the functional sound segments of language and how they are pronounced and perceived. But a more recent approach to phonology has noted that there are regular patterns in the way in which those segments combine with each other and the way they are pronounced in different phonetic contexts. The linguist attempts to capture those regularities in a system of general phonological rules that specify the different ways a phonemic segment is pronounced in a given language. Modern generative phonology (for example, Chomsky and Halle, 1968) postulates two levels of description of the sound segments—an underlying phonemic classification, and the surface phonetic realization of those segments in speech. Word sequences are still represented at a phonemic level in terms of distinctive features, but these features are now thought of as abstract classificatory devices and are not assumed to represent particular articulatory-acoustic properties. At the phonetic level, however, the distinctive features do correspond to articulatory-acoustic attributes and can be multivalued, not just binary. A full phonetic analysis will specify the degree of stridency, for example, and not just its presence or absence. Phonological rules relate the underlying phonemic representation to its actual phonetic realization in speech.

What is meant by an abstract level of phonemic representation? An example will elucidate this concept. For English, the phonemes /r/ and /l/ are each analyzed as both a consonant *and* a vowel for several linguistic reasons. They appear in consonantal positions in syllables—before, after, and between vowels—and unlike vowels they can form syllables when combined with a single vowel. On the other hand, /r/ and /l/ can also follow two consonants (as in *stray* and *splash*) and precede three consonants (as in *thirsts*), which is true of vowels and semivowels, but not of any other consonant. Finally, at the end of some words, such as *burgle* and *hinder,* /r/ and /l/ can be syllabic, another property of vowels (Chomsky and Halle, 1968). At the phonemic level they are therefore classified as both [+ consonantal] and [+ vocalic] (Fodor, Bever, and Garrett, 1974). Yet this combination of features would clearly be physically impossible to articulate—for consonants the air stream is interrupted or impeded, but for vowels it is not. The contradiction is resolved if the features at the phonemic level are conceived of as abstract means of classification. They provide the input to phonological rules that specify how words will be realized as articulatory and acoustic patterns. The assumption of an abstract level of representation enables the linguist to write a more parsimonious set of phonological rules to describe the language he is studying and to capture in those rules several general phonological processes.

Plural Formation

Take formation of plurals in English, for example. The regular plural ending is pronounced in three different ways, depending on the noun stem. Sometimes /s/ is added, but in other phonetic contexts /z/ or /ɨz/ are appended to the stem. Compare *pats, pans,* and *passes.* The formalization of these rules in generative phonology suggests that at the phonemic level the regular plural is formed by adding a consonant phoneme *S* having the complex of distinctive features: [+ anterior], [+ coronal],[2] [+ strident], [+ continuant], and [− nasal]. This plural marker does not represent any particular speech sound, since neither the presence nor absence of voicing is specified; instead it is regarded as a formal representative of a class of sounds sharing the features common to just /s/ and /z/. This solution captures the unitary grammatical and semantic functions of the plural despite its phonetic diversity.

Two other phonological rules operate: the first appends /ɨ/ before pluralization in contexts where the noun stem ends in a phoneme that is [+ coronal] and [+ strident] (which includes /š/, /ž/, /č/, /ǰ/, /s/ and /z/); the

---

[2] The feature [+ coronal] applies to those sounds produced with the blade of the tongue raised from its neutral position (Chomsky and Halle, 1968).

second assimilates the voicing of the S phoneme to that of the phonological segment that immediately precedes it.

To summarize the rules:

1. If a word ends in a phoneme that is [+ coronal] and [+ strident], add /ɨ/.
2. Add S to the word.
3. Assimilate the voicing of S to be the same as that of the immediately preceding segment.

By ordering the rules in this way all regular plurals are derived by application of the same set of phonological rules. In addition, Rule 3, which assimilates the voicing of the consonants, reflects a particularly general phonological rule of English that applies to the third person, possessive, and regular past tense inflections, as well as to most consonant clusters.

Generative phonology has only recently had any impact on the study of child language. Within the past few years several linguists (for example, Smith, 1973; Ingram, 1974) have tried to capture the regularities and changes in young children's speech, including their errors and substitutions, by writing systems of phonological rules, often based on distinctive features. We shall consider this approach at a later point in the chapter.

Rules for Consonant Clusters

Phonemes do not occur in isolation but are combined to form meaningful units—morphemes or words. Each language has a set of sequential structure rules that govern the combinations of phonemes that are acceptable in that language. For English the set of rules in Table 2 summarize which consonant combinations can begin a word. A similar set of rules can be written for acceptable consonant combinations at the end of words. English uses very few three-consonant clusters to begin words, and all of them begin with /s/. This fact will be all too familiar to the reader who plays Scrabble and has been faced with the problem of forming a word out of six consonants and a single vowel. It is also captured in this delightful poem by Ogden Nash.

The Lama

The one-l lama,
He's a priest.
The two-l llama,
He's a beast.
And I will bet
A silk pajama
There isn't any
Three-l lllama.

Table 2. Permissible consonant onsets for English words. From Brown, 1965 (based on Whorf, 1956; Hockett, 1958; and Strang, 1963).

$$\text{word} \rightarrow \begin{Bmatrix} C_1 & & \\ C_2 & + & r \\ C_3 & + & l \\ C_4 & + & w \\ C_5 & + & y\,w \\ s & + & C_6 \\ \check{s} & + & C_7 \\ sp & + & C_8 \\ sk & + & C_9 \\ str & & \end{Bmatrix} + \text{vowel} + \ldots$$

yields: *do, brew, bland, dwarf,* C_1 all consonants except ŋ and ž
        (pueblo), few, (dupe), skill, C_2 *b, d, f, g, k, p, š, t, θ*
        (svelte), shmoo, spring, scram, C_3 *b, f, g, k, p, s*
        string C_4 *d, g, h, k, s, t, (p, θ, b, š)*
                                           C_5 *b, f, g, h, k, m, p, v, θ*
also: *loo, frew, fland, dwill, bule,*   *(d, l, n, r, s, t)*
        smig, shloo, splob, sklit, strab C_6 *k, m, n, p, t, w, (θ, v)*
                                           C_7 *l, m, n*
not: *žay, vrew, tland, fwog, wule,* C_8 *r, l, y*
        shap, shpoon, spkay, skbob C_9 *r, l, w, y*

   ( ) Indicates possibilities that exist for some speakers of English but not for all.

The rules in Table 2 not only characterize words that do occur in English (for example, *trill*) and prohibit many words that do not occur (for example, *mrill*), but they also allow for words that do not in fact occur but would be acceptable if they did (for example, *trimp*). Acceptable consonant clusters are actually easier for the adult English-speaker to produce and hear. Brown and Hildum (1956) presented adult subjects with "acceptable" and "nonacceptable" words that do not occur in English (*throop* versus *dwroop*). When the words were presented against a background of noise that made them difficult to hear, the subjects were much more accurate at identifying the "acceptable" combinations of phonemes.

Clearly, one of the reasons for the absence of certain phoneme combinations is ease of articulation. Try pronouncing a word like *bgtal*. But languages vary considerably in the range of consonant combinations that they allow. Most Polynesian languages have no initial consonant clusters at all, while many African and Eastern European languages use combinations that seem impossibly tongue-twisting to us. One of the present authors was raised in South Africa amid the charmingly named villages of *Mbubane, Mmadikoti, Nkwalini,* and *Hluhluwe,* to name but a few. The child must acquire the sequential structure rules appropriate to his native tongue.

PROSODICS

Thus far we have been concerned with the segments of sound that make up the sounds of a language and the rules by which those segments are combined. But there are also important patterns of sound superimposed on the ongoing stream of speech that signal differences in the meanings of words or sentences. These are the *prosodic* features of speech—stress, tone, and intonation.

Stress

Words are typically pronounced with some syllables stressed and others unstressed. In general, stress means that one or more syllables are slightly louder than the others. For English words ending in *-tion* we expect to hear the major stress on the syllable immediately before the suffix, whether it was there before the addition of *-tion* or not. *Define* becomes *definítion, demólish* becomes *demolítion,* and *élevate* becomes *elevátion.* However, English does not have a uniform pattern of stress for all multi-syllabic words, so the English-speaking child has to learn several stress patterns or rules (Chomsky and Halle, 1968). By contrast, the stress consistently falls on the final syllable in French and on the first syllable in German words. Systematically pronouncing German words with the stress on the final syllable produces a passable imitation of a Frenchman speaking German.

Tone

Tone refers to the basic pitch of a word during its pronunciation. While this does not affect the meaning of any English words, it does determine the meaning of words in many Far Eastern and African languages. For example, the one word [sœŋ] in Cantonese has several distinct meanings depending on the pitch pattern in its pronunciation. Produced with a high level pitch, it means "prime minister"; said with the pitch rising from a low to an intermediate level, it means, among other things, "a pair of drawers." We will leave the reader to contemplate the consequences for a foreign diplomat who confused these two pitch patterns on a formal occasion.

Intonation

The pattern of rhythmic stress and pitch across an utterance together determine its intonation pattern. That is, certain words will be stressed and the basic pitch (or fundamental frequency) of the voice will rise or fall as the person speaks. One such intonation pattern will run over a limited stretch of speech, sometimes over the whole sentence and sometimes over phrases or clauses. In English, a falling pitch at the end of a sentence usually marks a complete statement or declaration, and a high rising pitch at the end often marks a query or invites a reply. But not all questions are marked by rising pitch, and rising pitch does not always mark a question. *Yes-no* questions usually take rising pitch, but *wh*-questions do not, unless for rare special effects. Try saying "When are you going home?" with the intonation of "Are you going home?" It will sound very strange.

The rising and falling patterns are only a part of the range of intonation patterns in English statements and questions. Intonation is an important means of communicating the emotions or attitudes underlying our utterances—uncertainty, resignation, dissapproval, delight, or boredom—as well as for distinguishing between statements, requests, and queries. Mastery of intonation patterns is therefore as important to the child as learning the meaning of words and the grammar of language if he is to fully understand and communicate with others.

THE DEVELOPMENT OF SPEECH PERCEPTION

The Special Nature of Speech Stimuli in Infancy

From a remarkably early age, perhaps from birth, the child distinguishes speech sounds from other sounds and responds to them differently. Neonates, infants less than ten days old, are particularly sensitive and responsive to sound frequencies in the same range as adult speech (Hutt et al., 1968). In fact, less than three days after birth they apparently find the sound of speech very rewarding. At this tender age infants will readily suck on a nipple, but if no milk is forthcoming they will stop sucking. However, if the infant is played a brief segment of speech whenever he sucks the nipple with sufficient strength, the rate of sucking will increase substantially. Babies will suck away quite gaily in order to hear voices or songs (Butterfield and Siperstein, 1974). It is not just the rhythm of the music that the infant finds so rewarding; sucking is not increased nearly as much by instrumental music without voices. Speech sounds therefore seem to engage the child's attention from the very start of life.

A still more exotic demonstration of the special nature of speech stimuli within a few days of birth comes from a study by Condon and Sander (1974). Condon and Ogston (1966, 1967) had earlier shown that the brief muscular movements made by adults when speaking or listening to speech tend to occur in synchrony with the speech segments. Changes in the direction of movements occur when there is a break in the ongoing speech, between either phonemes, syllables, or words. Condon and Sander (1974) filmed the behavior of wide-awake neonates listening to an adult speaking to them. By analyzing the film frame-by-frame, they discovered that infants also synchronize the minutest of their movements with breaks in the speech. Further experiments showed that American infants synchronized movements with both American English and Chinese speech, but not with rhythmic tapping or with isolated vowel sounds. This synchronization occurred even though the speech was presented by a tape recorder, so it could not have been the result of the adult synchronizing his speech with the child's movements, nor could it have been related to eye contact between the child and adult. Furthermore, the infants synchronized their movements with both English and Chinese although they had never heard the latter language before, so the phenomenon is not limited to the language the child has heard around him.

This study has potentially important implications, since Condon has shown that adults with aphasic or schizophrenic disorders reveal marked asynchronies between their movements and the speech addressed to them. Further studies of aphasic and autistic children and of infants might provide early indications of children with a high risk of these disorders.

Categorical Perception of Stop Consonants

Adults perceive stop consonants (/p/, /b/, /t/, /d/, /k/, and /g/) in terms of their phoneme categories. This means that they cannot discriminate between two sounds that fall into the same phoneme category, but they can easily tell two sounds apart if they fall into different categories. This was first demonstrated by an elegant series of experiments performed at the Haskins Laboratories. As we mentioned earlier, advances in spectrographic technology have enabled the artificial synthesis of speech sounds that share critical acoustic features with natural speech. It is as if simplified spectrograms (see Figure 1) were played back to the listener. In one of the experiments at the Haskins Laboratories (Liberman et al., 1967b) adult English-speakers were played the spectrographic patterns in Figure 3 in a random sequence. Each of these patterns is heard as a single syllable. Each contains the first and second formants for the vowel /a/, but the transition to the second formant (the rising or falling sweep of sound energy that in large part identifies the initial consonant) varies from what is clearly a /b/ (pattern *1*) to what is clearly a /g/ (pattern *14*) in equal steps. Subjects were asked after each presentation to identify the syllable that they had heard. The frequency with which subjects identified each pattern as /ba/, /da/, or /ga/ is shown in Figure 4.

Patterns *1–3* were perceived as /ba/, *5–8* as /da/, and *11–14* as /ga/. The subjects were then given a discrimination problem. For example, they were presented with two instances of pattern *5* and one of pattern *8*, or two of pattern *2* and one of *5*, and asked which syllable was the odd one out. Ease of discrimination was accurately predicted by the identification functions of Figure 4. Where two sounds were identified as instances of

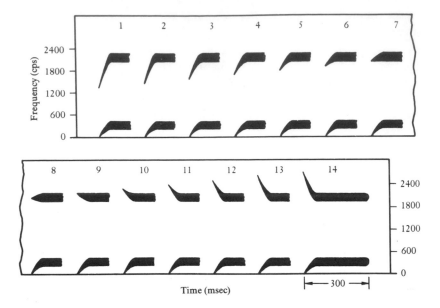

Figure 3. Illustrations of the spectrographic patterns from which the stimuli of the Haskins experiment were produced. From Brown, 1965.

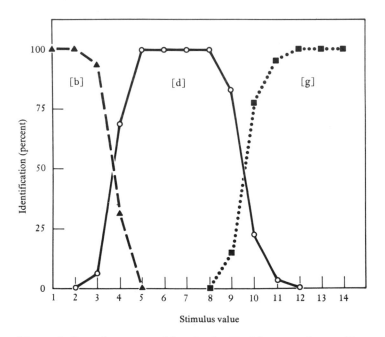

Figure 4. Data from one subject in the Haskins experiment. From Brown, 1965.

the same phoneme category (for example, patterns 5 and 8), they could not be distinguished; where they fell into different categories (patterns 2 and 5), they could be easily distinguished, although the physical difference between patterns 2 and 5 is the same size as that between 5 and 8.

When we look at sounds that differ along the dimension of voice onset time (VOT), like /b/ versus /p/, /d/ versus /t/, and /g/ versus /k/, we find a similar phenomenon. A /ba/ in English is typically produced with a VOT of 0 msec (the first formant begins at the same time as the second); a /pa/ is produced with a VOT of +40 msec (the first formant begins 40 msec after the second). If artificially produced syllables are presented to a listener and the time between onset of the first and second formants is systematically varied from −40 msec (where the second formant begins 40 msec before the first) to +40 msec, there is a sharp boundary between sounds heard as /b/ and sounds heard as /p/. This boundary occurs at about +25 msec. Native speakers of English cannot distinguish between sounds with VOTs of −40 msec and 0 msec (both identified as /ba/), but can distinguish between sounds with VOTs of 0 msec and +40 msec VOT (the first identified as /ba/, the other as /pa/).

This categorical perception of stop consonants is unlike our perception of other sounds or our visual perception, where we can make many more discriminations than the number of categories we use. For example, most of us can discriminate several sounds that fall between the musical notes identified as F and F♯. Thus, we can readily tell that a piano or guitar is out of tune without the sound falling into a different musical category. Similarly, we have a limited range of labels for colors, but we can discriminate between many more shades of red or blue than those for which we have names.

Why might categorical perception be important in our understanding of speech? As we suggested earlier, we have to ignore a great deal of variation within the functional categories of sound or phonemes of our language. For example, a /b/ differs slightly each time it is pronounced by a given individual, even if it is followed by the same vowel. It may vary in the intensity of the explosive puff of air that follows release of the lips, in the delay between release of the lips and the vibration of the vocal cords (VOT), or in overall loudness. It will vary still more when followed by different vowels or when produced by different speakers. In part because of the size and shape of the mouth cavity, the basic pitch of the speech of adult men and women and of children differs. Yet we have to hear it as a /b/ across all the variations in speaker and phonetic context. The work on categorical perception suggests that we simply *cannot* discriminate much of the variation in sound within a phoneme category, at least for stop consonants.

The question then becomes one of the role of learning. Are we so conditioned by our use of the phoneme categories in producing and understanding speech that we come to perceive speech sounds only in terms of those categories? Or is a child born with an auditory system that innately makes the groupings of sound that language will use as phoneme categories?

Infant Categorical Perception

Infants have categorical perception of stop consonants at a remarkably early age, as has been demonstrated in research done chiefly by Peter Eimas and his co-workers at Brown University (Eimas, 1974; 1975). The logic of the experiments is quite simple. Every time the infant sucks on a nipple with sufficient force, he is played an artificially produced syllable /ba/. As we mentioned earlier, babies suck away quite happily in order to hear this speech sound. But after a few minutes of sucking, the sound is no longer novel and the infant seems to get bored with it. The rate of sucking then decreases (habituates) rapidly. At this point the experimenter does one of three things: (1) he changes the VOT of the syllable so that an adult would say the sound was now a /pa/; (2) he changes the VOT of the syllable, but the new sound is still identified as a /ba/ by adults; or (3) he continues to play the baby exactly the same sound. If the child can tell the difference between the old and new sounds, his interest should be renewed and the rate of sucking to hear the sound should increase. But if he cannot tell the difference between the sounds, it will be just like hearing the same old sound again and the rate of sucking should not increase.

Eimas et al. (1971) used this method to study infants' discrimination between VOTs of 0 and + 20 msec (both heard as /ba/ by adults) and between + 20 and + 40 msec (/ba/ versus /pa/ for adults). A third control group of children received a + 20 msec VOT sound all the time. A comparison of the first two minutes of sucking for the changed sound with the last two minutes of sucking for the old sound reveals a significant increase in the rate of sucking for the group of babies that heard + 20 versus + 40 msec VOT (across the phoneme category boundary), but not for the group that heard 0 versus + 20 msec (within the /b/ category). The effect was strongest for four-month-old infants, but even one-month-olds showed categorical perception—discrimination between phoneme categories but not within categories (see Figure 5). Using the same procedure, Eimas (1974, 1975) has found that two-month-old babies also have categorical perception of the adult phonemes /d/ versus /t/, where the distinction is based on VOT, and of the adult phonemes /b/ versus /d/ versus /g/, where the distinction is based on place of articulation.

Research into the perception of phonemes by infants raises several important questions about the interpretation of Eimas's results. First, exactly which features of the sound is the child using to distinguish between /ba/ and /pa/? Other acoustic features besides VOT differ across the boundary between /b/ and /p/, and it is by no means certain which features

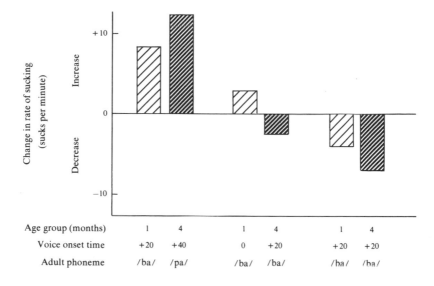

Age group (months)	1	4	1	4	1	4
Voice onset time	+20	+40	0	+20	+20	+20
Adult phoneme	/ba/	/pa/	/ba/	/ba/	/ba/	/ba/

Figure 5. Mean increase in sucking rate for synthetic speech syllables after a change in voice onset time and in the control condition.
From Eimas et al., 1971.

adults use to discriminate the sounds, let alone whether infants use the
same features as adults (Butterfield and Cairns, 1974).

Second, how much experience with language is necessary before the
child will show categorical perception of /b/ and /p/? Eimas's subjects
were one or two months old, but Butterfield and Cairns (1974) have studied neonates younger than 48 hours old. They suggest that some experience with the voiced sound /ba/ is necessary before the infants can discriminate it from /pa/.

Finally, an important question concerns the range of phoneme
boundaries across which an infant can discriminate. All languages that
have been extensively studied use VOT to distinguish between different
phoneme categories, but they do not all put the boundary at the same
point along the dimension. The boundary between /b/ and /p/ in English is
at roughly +25 msec VOT, but in Spanish it is near 0 msec (Williams,
1974). Thai divides the VOT dimension into three phoneme categories, a
/b/ and /p/ similar to those in English with the boundary between them at
+25 msec, and a prevoiced phoneme /$_m$b/ with a boundary near −50
msec. For the prevoiced phoneme the buzz of the vocal chords precedes
the opening of the lips. If the infant comes with an auditory system
already tuned to the phonemic distinctions to be made in speech, he
would have to have the ability to discriminate across the phoneme boundaries of any language. Any innate ability must apply to all languages, since
the child could be born into any language community in the world and

learn that language. However, Eimas and other researchers have not been able to demonstrate that infants can discriminate between synthetic speech sounds across the Thai or Spanish phoneme boundaries.

What are we then to make of the infant's categorical perception of phonemes across the +25 msec VOT boundary? Two explanations suggest themselves. First, it is possible that some experience with the language is necessary before the child can discriminate across a phoneme boundary. Second, the ear may be particularly sensitive to changes in sound at some points along the VOT continuum and not at others. Of course, it is also possible that both of these factors contribute to the development of phoneme perception.

Surprisingly, at least a partial answer comes from studies of chinchillas. These little animals are known and exploited mainly because their pelts make attractive fur coats, but they are also important for research into auditory processes. Through an evolutionary path that is not yet understood, nature has endowed the chinchilla with an inner ear that responds to sounds much like ours does. In an ingenious experiment, Kuhl and Miller (1975) demonstrated that chinchillas have categorical perception of /d/ versus /t/ even though they obviously do not have a language like ours. The chinchilla classes all the /d/ sounds together even when the sounds vary in loudness, whether they are produced by a man or woman, and regardless of the vowel that follows them. In the same way it classes all /t/ sounds together into one category of sound. Chinchillas therefore ignore the same variations in sound within the phoneme categories as we do. Finally, the boundary between /d/ and /t/ falls at the same VOT value for the chinchilla as it does for humans. These results suggest that the categorical perception of some speech sounds is due to innate properties of the auditory system that we apparently share with the chinchilla.

It therefore seems likely that the child comes into the world with an auditory system that is particularly sensitive to sound differences at a particular point along the continuum of VOT but not at other points. It is not known why either our auditory system or that of the chinchilla should have evolved in just this way, but most languages in the world take advantage of this property of the ear and place the boundary between several functional speech units at this point. Where a phoneme boundary falls at some other VOT, the child needs more experience with those phonemes before he can discriminate between them.

Lateralization of Speech Functions

Another major reason for believing that we are innately predisposed to perceive speech differently from other sounds lies in the wealth of evidence that speech sounds are perceived and interpreted in the left half (or hemisphere) of the cortex of our brain. The evidence comes from four main sources:

(1) *Split-brain studies*. In the early 1960s, several surgical operations were performed in the United States to alleviate patients' epilepsy by severing most of the connections between the two halves of the cortex. These "split-brain" patients can readily interpret and respond to verbal input that reaches the left half of the brain, but they are severely limited in their ability to understand verbal input that reaches the right hemisphere. Furthermore, they can only talk about information that is available to the left hemisphere. For example, neural pathways carrying tactile information from the left hand go to the right hemisphere of the cortex. Split-brain patients cannot *verbally* identify familiar objects placed in their left hand when it is out of sight, although they can do so if the object is transferred to the right hand. It is not a problem with the tactile sense, since the patient can identify the felt object from an array of pictures. The tactile information from the left hand is simply not available to the left side of the brain which controls speech (Gazzaniga, 1967).

(2) *Aphasia*. Damage to the left hemisphere of the cortex from head injuries or strokes frequently causes severe deficiencies in production and understanding of speech (aphasia) in adults. If the damage is localized in the right hemisphere, however, such language impairment rarely results (Geschwind, 1972).

(3) *Dichotic listening*. In the typical dichotic-listening experiment, two different digits are played simultaneously to the subject, one to each ear, and he is asked to report what he heard. Subjects are far more likely to report the digit played to the right ear than that played to the left (Kimura, 1961). Since the primary neural pathways from the right ear go to the left cerebral hemisphere, and those from the left ear go to the right hemisphere, this suggests that the left hemisphere of the brain dominates over the right in the understanding of speech.

(4) *Evoked potential*. The electrical activity of nerve cells in the cortex can be recorded by electrodes placed on the scalp. The magnitude of the nerve cell activity evoked by a sound (the auditory evoked potential) is greatest in the left hemisphere for speech sounds, but not for other sounds (Lenneberg, 1967).

All of these findings indicate the functional dominance of the left hemisphere of the cortex for the perception, interpretation, and production of speech sounds. In fact, the region of the left hemisphere concerned with the understanding of speech differs anatomically from the corresponding region of the right hemisphere, being somewhat larger (Geschwind and Levitsky, 1968).

Lateralization in Children

When do children show a similar localization of language functions in the left half of the brain? Up to a few years ago it was thought that this was a gradual process, and that the left hemisphere was not dominant in speech perception until the age of about five years. On standard dichotic listening tasks it is at about that age that children begin to report the digit presented in the right ear significantly more frequently than that in the left (Kimura, 1963). But more recent research indicates that the child's left hemisphere is specialized for perceiving speech much earlier than that, perhaps even at birth. Postmortem research by Witelson and Pallie (1973) demonstrated that the anatomical difference between the left hemisphere speech areas and the corresponding regions of the right hemisphere is present at birth. Molfese (1972, 1973) recorded the electrical activity of each hemisphere of the brain following different types of sounds; speech sounds like /ba/, /da/, *boy,* or *dog,* and other sounds, like a C-major chord or a burst of complex noise. For infants between one week and ten months old, as well as for adults, the evoked electrical activity was greater over the left side of the brain for speech, but greater over the right side for the musical tone or other noises.

An experiment by Ann Entus (1975) at McGill University demonstrates that, from very soon after birth, babies are best able to discriminate between speech sounds in the left hemisphere, but best able to discriminate musical sounds in the right.[3] Entus used the dishabituation of sucking procedure pioneered by Eimas. Her full experimental procedure is pictured in Figure 6. The infants wore tiny stereo earphones. As they sat in a special baby chair, looking for all the world like miniature astronauts, they were rewarded for sucking on a nipple with two different sounds presented simultaneously, one to each ear. When the children became bored with those sounds and the rate of sucking declined, one of the sounds was changed, either in the left or in the right ear. Any increase in the rate of sucking (dishabituation) was measured. Following another period of habituation to the new combination of sounds, one of them was again changed, this time the sound in the opposite ear from the first change. In the speech sound condition, the three pairs of sounds were the syllables /ba/ and /ma/, /ba/ and /da/, and /ga/ and /da/. For some children the change from /ma/ to /da/ (a difference in place of articulation) took place in the left ear, for others it took place in the right ear. In the music condition, the pairs of sounds contained the same note A played on a piano and cello, on a piano and bassoon, and on a viola and bassoon.

---

[3] In a paper presented to the Society for Research on Child Development in April 1977, Khadem and Corballis reported from the same laboratory at McGill University that, using a better-controlled procedure than Entus, they were unable to reproduce her results, despite using the same stimulus materials. This raises some uncertainty about the findings of early hemispheric asymmetry in speech discrimination in infants.

SPEECH   MUSIC

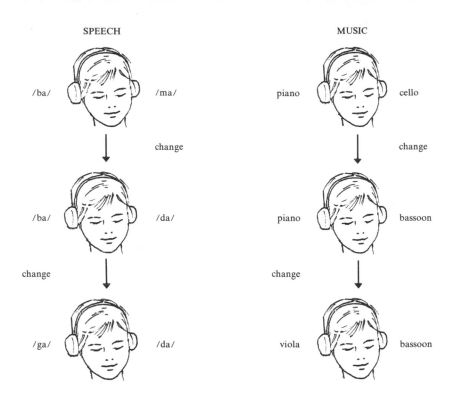

/ba/   /ma/   piano   cello

              change   change

/ba/   /da/   piano   bassoon

change   change

/ga/   /da/   viola   bassoon

Figure 6. Procedure used in the Entus experiment.

Once again, the ear in which each change in musical instrument took place varied among children. The infants' rate of sucking increased most after the change in speech sounds if the sound change was in the right ear; for the change in musical instrument recovery was greatest when the sound change was in the left ear.

What can we conclude from these results? Each hemisphere could discriminate changes in both the speech and the musical sounds since there was a significant increase in sucking following a sound change in either ear. But the differences in the size of the increase in sucking suggests that the left hemisphere (right ear) was more proficient at discriminating between the speech sounds than the right hemisphere. On the other hand, the right hemisphere (left ear) was better at discriminating differences in musical sounds.

Taken together, the preceding studies show that the infant, at a remarkably early age, long before he shows signs of understanding or producing any speech, has the ability to distinguish at least some speech sounds from nonspeech sounds, and can make important fine distinctions between different speech sounds. These fine distinctions are used by most languages to separate different phonemic categories. Furthermore, the infant's brain already reveals an asymmetry between the two hemispheres of the cortex in the perception of different types of sounds—speech in the left, and music in the right.

Perception of Phonemes

Before we go on to talk about the way in which the child develops the ability to *produce* the sounds of his language, we must mention one caveat about the data on his developing ability to discriminate and perceive those sounds. Although the infant can apparently discriminate acoustic differences between stop consonants that differ in VOT or place of articulation, it takes some time before he can use those same differences in sound to distinguish between words that label different objects, that is, use them in a linguistically relevant manner.

For example, Garnica (1973) and Edwards (1974) traced the development of distinctions between phonemes in words by means of an object-labeling task. Children aged one to three years played with two funny objects made up to look like toy people. Each object was given a nonsense syllable name, for example, *bok* and *pok*, chosen so that they differed by only a single sound feature. In the *bok* versus *pok* example, the only difference between the words is in the voicing of the initial consonants: /b/ is voiced, that is, accompanied by vibration of the vocal chords; /p/ is not. The children were asked to do things with one of the two objects, such as "put the hat on *bok*" or "give *pok* a ride in the wagon." If a child chose the correct object on seven or more of ten such trials he was considered to have mastered the distinction between the phonemes /b/ and /p/.

Both Garnica and Edwards found that children did not master the distinction between voiced (/b/, /d/, /g/, /z/, /v/) and voiceless (/p/, /t/, /k/, /s/, /f/) phonemes until they were about two years of age. Younger children were only able to choose the correct object when there were grosser differences between the two nonsense syllables, for example, *bok* versus *lok*. Thus, they were able to associate names with objects and perform the required actions, but they could not do so when the only difference between the two syllables was the presence or absence of voicing of the initial consonant. Yet this is the difference that holds between the /ba/ and /pa/ syllables employed by Eimas in his studies of infant speech perception. We are left with the paradox that the one- to four-month-old infants in the Eimas study could successfully discriminate between voiced and voiceless stop consonants, but at over twelve months of age the children in Garnica's and Edwards' studies could not use that distinction in an object-naming task.

The puzzle is more apparent than real, however. Making a *phonemic* distinction is more than just discrimination. What the child has to understand is that among the many discriminable sounds some variations are used to mark differences in meaning or reference whereas others are accidental or expressive. Even in adults, which discriminable speech distinctions will be thought to distinguish referents depends on the person's phonemic system (see appendix in Bruner, Goodnow and Austin, 1956). The young child must acquire the phonemic contrasts of his language in order to use those speech sound differences in a linguistically relevant manner, and that development takes a few years.

In summary, infants are differentially sensitive to speech at a remarkably early age. This special responsiveness may activate analyzers for the extraction of structure from speech, segmenting it into speech sounds, words, and even larger units; or it may simply enhance this process. Infants are also predisposed to distinguish between certain important speech sounds, apparently because language capitalizes on innate regions of auditory sensitivity. However, it takes considerable exposure to the language before the child comes to learn which of the discriminable speech distinctions actually function to signal differences of reference.

THE PRODUCTION OF SPEECH SOUNDS

Babbling

Speech copious without order, and energetic without rule.

Samuel Johnson

At about three or four months of age children begin producing sounds that approximate speech. The frequency of these babbled sounds increases until it reaches a peak between nine and twelve months of age. While the babbled noises sound like speech and often seem to occur in sentence-like sequences with rising and falling intonation, at this stage none of it seems interpretable. Parents often feel as if the child is speaking his own foreign language, and if only they could crack the code, it would all make sense. But if our children do have interesting things to say to us at this age, generation after generation of parents has failed to understand them. Between ten and fifteen months of age most children start producing their first clearly interpretable words, usually with many false starts and invariably as single words. Often they are reduplicated syllables like *dada, baba, mama,* or single syllables like *da* for *dog* or *ba* for *baby.* The frequency of babbling declines as interpretable words take over the child's verbal repertoire, and for a few children there may even be a short period of near silence intervening between babbling and the emergence of the first clear words. But usually elaborate babbled sentences continue to be produced even while the child is communicating with his parents by means of several single words.

There are also occasions when the child seems to know that much more is required than one word. In the summer of 1973 we spent a very pleasant two weeks in Toronto, Canada, as consultants, writers, and actors for a film on first-language acquisition produced by the Canadian

Broadcasting Corporation. One of many amusing incidents for us in the filming of the program involved a delightful eighteen-month-old in the one-word stage of speech. Katie had just given us some lovely examples of single-word utterances. Looking at a large picture-book with her mother, she had produced, with great precision and apparent effort, "book"; and a few moments later, "look." Then she found her own little book and opening it up began a marvelous imitation of an adult reading, with long "sentences" of utter nonsense complete with elaborate intonation patterns, and with the book clearly upside down.

The relationship between babbling and the emergence of understandable speech is still not clearly understood. One early theory maintained that in babbling the child produced the sounds from all of the languages that man speaks and his parents selectively rewarded, by attention or approval, those sounds that were used in their own language. But while the range of sounds produced in babbling is remarkably wide, the child by no means babbles all of the speech sounds of English, let alone those of all human languages.

A rather more complex theory (Mowrer, 1954; Winitz, 1969) holds that the speech of the parents or other adults who care for the child comes to be associated by the child with primary rewards like close physical contact, warmth, or food—for example, when the mother speaks to the child while feeding him. In this way the parents' vocalizations themselves become rewarding to the child. By a similar process, any of the child's vocalizations that approximate the adult sounds are rewarded either directly by the attention or responsive vocalization of the parents, or indirectly by sounding like the parents' speech previously associated with rewards. Thus the child's own speech sounds will gradually approach those of the parents and the sounds that the parents do not produce or reward will drop out of the child's repertoire.

There are several weaknesses in this theory, however. First, some sounds that are relatively frequent in early babbling, in particular consonants produced at the back of the mouth (like [g], [k], and initial [h] sounds), are quite infrequent in later babbling and in children's early words (Leopold, 1953; Winitz and Irwin, 1958). It is not at all clear from the above theory of speech development why the appropriate back consonants should get less frequent. Second, while imitation of adult sounds may well be an important process in the learning of first words, this theory has nothing to say about any consistent order in which children might acquire the different sounds of the language. In general, while several experiments have shown that rewarding the child by social attention and vocalization increases the frequency of babbling, none has shown that such a process can change the types of speech sounds that the child produces (Rheingold, Gurwitz, and Ross, 1959; Weisberg, 1963; Todd and Palmer, 1968; Dodd, 1972). Most of these studies looked at very young infants,

approximately three months old, somewhat before the age at which babbling reaches its peak in frequency and complexity. Only Dodd (1972)
studied nine- to twelve-month-olds, when both babbling and imitative
behavior are frequent. She found that both the number and length of utterances containing consonants that were babbled by the infants increased
following periods of social and vocal stimulation by an adult. But the
range of consonant types produced by the children remained unchanged
and did not increase to match the wider range of consonants used by the
adult. However, in Dodd's study the adult's vocalizations always preceded those of the children, so the child was not rewarded for imitating.
Thus, the precise role of selective social or vocal reward and imitation in
shaping the vocalizations of the child remains uncertain.

What other role could babbling play in the child's mastery of the
speech sounds of his native language? Some fifty years ago a famous
linguist, Otto Jesperson, drew a distinction between babbling, as free play
with sounds, and a child's first words, as controlled, planned speech. In
babbling it does not matter which sound the child produces as there seems
to be no meassage that must be communicated, but in meaningful words a
particular sound must be produced on command, followed by other particular sounds, if the message is to be understood. The babbling child
therefore seems at least in part to be playing with speech production, ex-
ercising his articulatory organs and gaining control over their movement.
In fact, many children babble more when they are on their own than when
other people are present (Nakazima, 1975), although at a later stage babbling may serve to attract the attention of the parent and communicate the
child's emotional state (Nakazima, 1970).

Biological maturation, rather than the acquired rewarding value of
the child's own vocalizations, probably determines the onset of babbling.
Children babble even if they themselves are deaf and cannot hear their
own sounds, or if their parents are deaf and cannot hear them (Lenneberg,
Rebelsky, and Nichols, 1965). The onset of babbling occurs at about the
same age in deaf children as in hearing children, and is similar in form,
though perhaps a little more monotonous. But the later continuation and
frequency of babbling depends upon the child's hearing himself and
perhaps on vocal and social stimulation. Deaf children stop babbling earlier than hearing children and then have difficulty learning to speak. Infants in orphanages, where there is less stimulation and attention, vocal-
ize somewhat less than children reared at home. On the other hand, few
orphanage studies control for other factors, such as nutrition, and biological maturation in general seems to lag in orphanage children.

These two factors then—the progressive maturation of the child, allowing increased control over the vocal apparatus, and the reaction to his
vocalizations by the adults around him—combine to determine the course
of early development. Several studies have concerned themselves with

determining the course of phonetic development in babbling—how the child begins to approximate the sounds of his language. The most frequent consonant sounds in early babbling (around three to six months of age) are those at the back of the mouth, and front consonants are rare; but by the time the first words appear back consonants are relatively less frequent and the most frequent consonants are those produced in the front of the mouth (like [b] and [d]) (Winitz and Irwin, 1958). There is a similar progressive expansion of the range of vowel sounds produced in babbling. At three months, most vowel sounds are produced in the low front and mid-center regions of the mouth (corresponding roughly to [æ] as in *pat* and [ə] as in *poses*). From there, the range of vowel sounds moves up and back in the mouth until at twelve months virtually the whole range of English vowels is produced (Pierce, 1974). The range of speech sounds produced by the child is therefore somewhat restricted initially and gradually expands to incorporate, by twelve months of age, most, though still not all, of the sounds of the language.

The Phonology of the First Words

Late in the babbling period the child begins to use consistent patterns of sound to refer to actions, objects, or whole situations, or to achieve pragmatic goals. Some of these early *vocables* (Ferguson, 1977a) seem to be the child's approximations for adult words, but many of them are taken from animal or other sounds in the environment. For example, the son of the German linguist Lindner (1898) used a long *m* sound at the age of twelve months to mean something like "Here comes a wagon" or "I hear a wagon coming" (Ferguson, 1977a). A few vocables are sounds that the child has babbled in a particular situation and uses when that situation recurs or in order to allude to it. Between ten and fourteen months the child may have a productive "vocabulary" of about a dozen vocables, only one or two or them based on adult words. This stage provides a link between babbling and the first intelligible words, as the child now appears to be aware that speech sound patterns have consistent meanings or conditions of use and therefore begins to construct his own "words" from his babbles or other sounds (Ferguson, 1977a).

The first clear words that seem to be based on adult models appear around ten to thirteen months for most children. In most cases they consist of consonant-vowel (CV) or reduplicated CVCV combinations, and the consonants are usually stops or nasals produced at the front of the mouth (like /b/, /p/, /d/ or /m/) (Lewis, 1936).

Jakobson's Theory of Phonological Development

One of the most influential theories of phonological development in the early words is that of Roman Jakobson (1968), based on his distinctive-feature analysis of the sound systems of many different languages. Jakobson made the following claims about phonological development: (1) Babbling is essentially unrestricted and bears no relation to the child's later acquisition of adult phonology. (2) Phonological development is best described in terms of the mastery of distinctive features. (3) The child does not just approximate the adult's phonemes one by one, but he develops his own system of phonemic contrasts, not always using the same features as adults to distinguish between words. For example, the child might use the length of vowels to distinguish words, a feature not used in adult English. (4) Finally, the pattern of phonological development in all children is systematic and universal. It is best described as a progression of oppositions between sounds based on finer and finer differentiation between distinctive features. All children first make the gross and universal distinction between vowels and consonants—that is, between speech sounds produced with the vocal tract open and those produced by closing off or impeding the air stream. Thereafter, they acquire progressively finer and less universally used distinctions: first, between oral stop and nasal consonants (as in *papa* versus *mama*), then between labial and apical stops (*papa* versus *tata*), and thereafter between low and high vowels (/a/ versus /i/).

Jakobson's theory has proved difficult to test in studies of phoneme development. Part of the problem lies in the difficulty of determining which sound distinctions function to signal differences in meaning in the child's speech. Children simply do not produce enough minimal pairs, for example, *pin* versus *bin*, words that differ only in one phoneme yet have different meanings. The linguist therefore has to work a little like a detective, looking for clues that the child distinguishes between different phonemes. Braine (1971) provides an example of how these clues are employed. Very often words beginning with /d/, /t/, /ð/, and /θ/ are all produced with a [d] by the child. At the same time, words beginning with /g/ or /k/ might be produced with [d] about 70 percent of the time and with [g] about 30 percent of the time. Braine argues that in this case, even though *cat* and *that* are frequently both produced as [dæt], the child knows that they begin with different sounds. *That* is always [dæt], but *cat* is sometimes [dæt] and sometimes [gæt]; thus, the child does distinguish between the initial sounds but has difficulty in producing them accurately.

The data that do exist (mostly from diary studies of individual children) provide very little support for Jakobson's claim about the specific order of acquisition of phoneme contrasts. Velten (1943) studied the language development of his own daughter, Joan, and found some support for Jakobson's ordering, but Braine (1971) pointed out several counterexamples from the phonological development of his son. Jakobson's theory implies that glides, /w/ and /h/, are acquired late in speech development, but Leopold's (1947) study of his daughter showed that she mastered them quite early. Ferguson and Garnica (1975) note several other counter-instances to Jakobson's predicted order of acquisition.

Studies of the developing perception of phonemes are also equivocal with respect to Jakobson's theory. Svachkin's (1973) study of Russian children supported Jakobson's progression of stages, but Garnica (1973) failed to replicate that ordering in a similar study of English which incorporated stricter experimental controls. Garnica found that the order of difficulty of the distinctive features varied much more among individual children than would be predicted by Jakobson.

In addition, several linguists have argued that, in the first fifty words or so, the units of phonological opposition for the child are not phonemes but syllables (A. Moskowitz, 1973) or even whole words (Ferguson, 1977a). Early on, words may vary greatly in the stability of their pronunciation. Some will remain fairly constant while others will fluctuate widely. Ferguson and Farwell (1975) report cases in which the child seemed to perceive the various phonetic characteristics of the sound segments in a word, such as the features bilabial closure, voicelessness, alveolar closure, and nasality in the word *pen,* but he then mislocated them or spread them over the entire word. Within a half-hour, one of the children produced *pen* ten different ways, each time with a different combination of the phonetic features.

Another curiosity of early phonological development is that certain words may be pronounced in a precise adult way long before other words are. For example, Leopold's daughter Hildegard pronounced the word *pretty* with remarkable exactness between ten and sixteen months of age. As the child develops a system of phonological rules or strategies, these "progressive idioms" (A. Moskowitz, 1973) are often brought in line with the rest of the child's pronunciation. So Hildegard's [*prɪti*] became [*bɪdi*] at around eighteen months of age and remained like that for several months.

All of these findings make it impossible to regard the early stages of phonological development in terms of phoneme contrasts. They suggest that the child has to build up a fairly sizable productive vocabulary before developing any consistent phonological system that relates the words to each other or to the adult models (Glucksberg and Danks, 1975). Ingram (1976) has suggested that the development of such a system awaits the onset of symbolic representation in the late sensorimotor period of intellectual development (Piaget, 1970).

Two other phonological aspects of the child's early words are worth noting. First, children seem to actively avoid producing words containing certain speech sounds and prefer words with other sounds that they have mastered (Ferguson and Farwell, 1975; Menn, 1976; Vihman, 1976; Ferguson, 1977a). A child might understand several adult words with nasals, but attempt to produce very few or none of them (Vihman, 1976).

Other children might produce many words with bilabial stops or nasals and avoid fricatives or velars (Leopold, 1947). In each case the child seems to perceive the words appropriately in comprehension, but does not try and produce them.

A second basis for selective production seems to be word shape. Some children will almost exclusively attempt CVCV words like *doggie, mommy, pretty,* or *baby;* others will only attempt CV(C) words. Children also frequently impose a specific word shape on their early words regardless of adult models, normalizing all words to CVCV or CV forms. The adult "baby talk" of most language communities typically provides similar phonologically simplified models for the child (Ferguson, 1964; 1977b).

The Acquisition of Distinctive Features

In phonological development after the age of two, there is some evidence supporting Jacobson's claims about the reality of distinctive features. Once they have mastered a distinctive feature contrast between two phonemes, for example, the voicing contrast between /p/ and /b/, some children quickly extend it to all the phonemes distinguished by that feature (Burling, 1960; Smith, 1973). On the other hand, Olmsted (1971, 1974) found accuracy of production of distinctive features varied across phonemes for longer periods of time. Voicing was used to distinguish between one pair of phonemes well before it was used to distinguish others.

Stronger support for a distinctive-feature approach comes from a study by Menyuk (1968). She analyzed the speech of English (two-and-a-half to five years old) and Japanese (one to three years old) children in terms of the correct use of distinctive features in their words or syllables. For example, if a child attempted to pronounce the word *dog,* both the /d/ and the /g/ should be voiced. Menyuk determined the presence or absence of voicing and several other features in a child's speech and calculated the percentage of occasions on which each was correctly supplied. The order in which the child mastered the production of six distinctive features was the same for Japanese and English children. Furthermore, the order of acquisition differed from the relative frequency of those sound features in English. These results suggest that the order of acquisition of distinctive features may have more to do with the maturing control of the child over articulation (or the ease of articulation of the features although this is difficult to measure independently of acquisition) than their frequency in the speech to the child.

We conclude, therefore, that there appears to be a regular development of correct production of distinctive features, as Jacobson claimed, but his specific predictions about the order of acquisition of phoneme contrasts are difficult to apply to the child's early words and seem to be incorrect in many instances. There is also a great deal of individual variation among children in their early phonological development. Finally, we shall see later in the chapter that Jakobson's arguments for the strict discontinuity between babbling and speech, and his claim that there is no general order of development in the babbling period, are false. Jakobson's contribution to the study of child phonology was his stress on the orderliness of the child's development and his concentration on the child's own phonological system.

Phonological Processes in Child Speech

We have so far considered two very different approaches to the development of speech sounds. One looks at the successive approximations of the child to the adult speech sounds (phones) and measures accuracy and frequency of production of the various vowels and consonants. The other examines the acquisition of phonemic contrasts and distinctive features. This second approach attempts a phonemic analysis of child speech and measures the accuracy and frequency of production of distinctive features.

But there is a third approach that supplies us with information about regularities in the child's phonological development that is not captured by the other two. Neither of the other approaches concerns itself with consistent errors or regular substitutions for adult sounds that children typically make. The third approach attempts to characterize the child's development in terms of regular stages in his own speech sound system, to say why he consistently substitutes certain sounds for the adult sounds, and to characterize systematic strategies that he adopts to simplify his pronunciation of adult words. This is done by writing a set of phonological rules, rules for the combination of distinctive features or phonemes into words, for each stage of development. These rules relate what the child actually produces to what he is aiming at. Some linguists (for example, Smith, 1973) maintain that the child represents the adult word (his target) exactly. This assumes that the child *hears* the adult word correctly, but just cannot *produce* it. But the Garnica (1973) and Edwards (1974) studies of the developing perception of distinctive features demonstrate that the child's perception of the adult form of a word may often be inaccurate. The child is developing the ability to perceive the adult sounds at the same time as he is learning to produce them. Nevertheless, the phonological rules are usually written relating the adult form to the child's form of the word since it is extremely difficult to establish for each child his perception of the adult word at each stage of development.

Why is it useful to describe phonological development in terms of changing rule systems? Why not just say that the child mishears the adult word and accurately produces a match to what he hears? Substantial evidence indicates that a child's perception of speech is in advance of his production of the same forms (Edwards, 1974). For example, Smith (1973) tells of his son Amahl being easily able to tell the difference between *s* and *th* as in *mouse* versus *mouth*. Given a choice between pictures of several objects, he could pick out the object appropriate to the word. Yet he couldn't produce *th*, so both were pronounced as [maus]. So the child does not just reproduce what he hears.

Why is it not enough to say that the child simply cannot produce certain adult speech sounds correctly when they follow other sounds? Again Smith provides an instructive example. Amahl went through a stage of saying *puggle* for *puddle*. Smith thought at first that Amahl just could not get his tongue around a /d/ in that phonetic context, but at the same stage, when Amahl attempted to say *puzzle,* he said *puddle!* Another amusing example from Amahl concerns his pronunciation of the words *sick* and *thick*. Although he did not confuse *sick* with *thick* when he heard them, at one stage in his phonological development Amahl consistently replaced *s* by *th* in initial position. Thus *sick* was pronounced as *thick*. But at the same stage, he consistently produced *f* for *th*. Thus *thick* became *fick!* We are left with the puddling observation that Amahl could say *thick* perfectly well, but on the wrong occasions. The important determinant of what the child produces is therefore what he is aiming at.

Linguists studying phonological development attempt to characterize the processes by which the child simplifies his pronunciation of adult words, leading to the consistent use of certain forms at each stage of development. The sets of phonological rules that they write represent a summary description of these processes. In particular, linguists are interested in any general or universal phonological processes that may occur in children learning many different languages. These would indicate constraints on the course of language acquisition that may be set by biological maturation as opposed to cultural or language differences.

In the detailed studies of phonological development that have been carried out using this approach, many individual differences have been found among children. But the following processes are extremely general, if not universal [4]:

(1) *Deletion processes*

(a) *Cluster reduction.* Earlier in this chapter we described the rules for the formation of acceptable consonant clusters in English. However, children in the early stages of language development typically reduce the consonant clusters that begin words, (for example, *tring* for *string,* or *top* for *stop*). Consonant clusters are one of the last phonetic aspects of speech to be mastered, some children continuing to have problems with them until their fourth year or so. On the perceptual side, Messer (1967)

---

[4] For a more detailed set of proposed phonological processes, see Ingram (1976).

demonstrated that three-year-olds are well aware of the restrictions on consonant combinations in English. Given nonsense syllables containing acceptable and unacceptable consonant clusters, the children could correctly say which could possibly be words in English. Thus again, perception precedes production of the phoneme combinations.

(b) *Deletion of final consonants*. In his first words, the child often leaves off a consonant at the end of the word, but almost never omits a single consonant at the beginning. Thus *dog* becomes [da], not [og]. In fact, it is a very common finding that consonants are correctly pronounced in the initial position of a word before they are correctly produced in the final position.

(2) *Substitution processes*

(a) *Voicing and devoicing*. This is another process tied to the position of the consonants in the word. Many children go through a stage in which they voice all initial consonants and devoice all final ones. For example, Joan Velten at twenty-one months of age (Velten, 1943) produced *bie* for *pie* and *doe* for *tow,* but at the same time produced *knop* for *knob* and *hos* for *hose*.

(b) *Substitution of stops for fricatives and vice versa*. Jakobson (1968) reported for numerous languages that children tend to substitute stop consonants for fricatives when they are in initial position. On the other hand, they substitute fricatives for stops in final position (Olmsted, 1971; Ferguson, 1973).

(c) *Fronting*. Jakobson (1968) and Ingram (1974) cite several examples from many different languages showing that children much prefer front over back consonants in early speech. Front consonants, produced with the lips and teeth—for example, /b/, /p/, /d/, and /t/—are much more frequent in early words and are often substituted for back consonants like /g/ and /k/.

(d) *Substitution of glides for liquids*. Several investigators (Jakobson, 1968; Smith, 1973; Ingram, 1971; Edwards, 1971) have reported the consistent substitution of glides (/w/ and /y/) for liquids (/l/ and /r/) when they precede vowels.

(3) *Phonological assimilation*

Some of the above substitutions may be due to a more general underlying process of phonological assimilation, the tendency to maintain the same place of articulation for all of the vowels or consonants in a word. This process can work in both directions, the initial consonant being produced in the place of articulation appropriate for the final consonant or vice versa. Thus, *doggy* might for a time be produced as *goggy* or as *doddy*. Similarly, later vowels can be harmonized to the same place of articulation as earlier ones.

This is a very widespread process in adult speech as well, and we mentioned cases of its occurrence earlier; for example, the [k]'s in *cool* and *keel* are different because of the place of articulation of the following vowel. Vowel harmony is in fact a phonological rule in some languages. Vowels in Turkish words must either be all front or all back vowels. For example, there are two plural affixes in Turkish, *lar* and *ler*. *Adam* (''man'') becomes *adamlar* in the plural (all back vowels), whereas *ev* (''house'') becomes *evler* (all front). This is a case where a language makes use of what may be a universal phonological tendency in acquisition. It has been found in children learning languages as different as English, Chinese, French, and Hebrew.

To summarize, the errors that children make in phonological development are not random. Children develop consistent phonological systems that seem to follow several very general processes, regardless of what language they are learning. To be sure, individual children demonstrate these processes in varying degrees, but all children show evidence of some of them. Ingram (1976) has recently noted several questions about these phonological processes that future research must answer:

(1) How universal are they among children learning English or other languages? Several linguists have recently stressed the prevalence of individual differences in phonological development (Ferguson, 1977a).

(2) When do they first appear? Ingram suggested that they are only characteristic after the child's first fifty words, but some of them may appear earlier than that (Ferguson, 1977a).

(3) How long do they generally last? Are some more persistent than others?

(4) How quickly are they eliminated or replaced by others?

(5) Does the existence of one process in a child's phonology imply the use of any of the others?

To these we might add: How, if at all, do they relate to the specific language that the child is learning? And how does experience or linguistic input modify their use by the child?

These processes plus the avoidance of sounds in the early words suggest that the child is an active contributor to the process of phonological acquisition, adopting simplifying strategies as well as being influenced by the language that he hears.

Babbling and Phonological Processes

The sharp distinction made by some linguists between babbling and early words may be unwarranted. The systematic substitutions and deletions children make in their early words may arise from phonetic preferences developed in the later stages of babbling as the children progressively gain control over their articulation. In a detailed study of the babbling of three children aged six to eight months and five aged twelve to thirteen months, Oller et al. (1976) showed that the general phonological processes summarized above reflected the frequency of the sounds produced in later babbling. For example, almost 90 percent of all consonants babbled occurred on their own, less than 10 percent in clusters (see process 1a). Initial consonants outnumbered final consonants two to one, and final consonants were almost all unvoiced (see 1b and 2a). Initial stop consonants outnumbered initial fricatives ten to one, but final fricatives were much more frequent than final stops (2b and 2c). Before vowels, glides ([w] and [y] outnumbered liquids ([l] and [r]) nearly seven to one (see 2d). Finally, for the youngest children back consonants were more frequent than front consonants, but for the twelve- to thirteen-month-olds, front consonants were seven times more frequent than back (2c). Later babbling therefore seems to be governed by the same general restrictions as phonological development in the early words. These constraints reflect the maturing control of the child over his speech apparatus and may determine the types of pronunciation errors and substitutions that the child makes in his first interpretable words.

It remains to be shown whether individual preferences for sounds in babbling can account for any later avoidance of sounds or for differences in the degree to which children employ the general phonological processes just described. To determine that, longitudinal studies of children beginning during the babbling period are essential, but most available longitudinal research has begun at the first words.

The Mastery of Adult Phonological Rules

Most of the research discussed so far concentrates on the first two or three years of life. But phonological development is far from complete at this point. Pronunciation of some speech sounds, particularly fricatives like [θ] and [š] and liquids like [r], continues to trouble the child until the early school years. He is also still acquiring several adult phonological rules, such as those for the various inflectional endings of nouns and verbs.

Several studies have explored children's productive control of the different phonological forms of the plural, possessive, third person singular, and other inflections. Berko (1958) investigated the ability of preschool and first grade children to append the appropriate forms of these inflections to nonsense syllables with differing terminal phonemes. The children performed best on those inflectional forms that were determined by the general phonological rule of voicing assimilation, which applies to all four inflections as well as in other areas of English phonology (Brown, 1973). They did worst on those forms that involved appending /i/ after certain phonemes before adding the inflectional ending. This rule differs for the $-s$ and the past tense inflections. The child first masters the rule that applies throughout the English phonological system, and only later acquires the more specific rules. (For other adult phonological rules that are only acquired around six to eight years of age, see B. Moskowitz, 1973.)

INTONATION

We have described in some detail what is known about the acquisition of the sound segments of speech, but what about the suprasegmental aspects, such as intonation? One of the factors that leads parents to believe that the infant's babbles are speech is the variation in intonation patterns. Up to the age of six or seven months most babbles are produced with a falling, declarative intonation, but then the child begins producing both the falling and the rising, questioning intonation pattern (Tonkova-Yompol'skaya, 1969). At about the same age the child begins to imitate the intonation of the adults talking to him (Nakazima, 1962). Lieberman (1967) showed that the basic pitch of the babbling of two children at ten and thirteen months of age shifted towards the pitch of the voice of the adult speaking to them. When the father was playing with the child, the pitch of the babbling was lowered to nearer that of father; when the mother spoke to the child, the babbling occurred at a somewhat higher pitch, in keeping with the higher voice of the mother. The child is an accomplished mimic of the intonation and pitch of the adult voices around him.

With respect to the perception of different adult intonation patterns, by the age of eight months children can discriminate between a syllable pronounced with a rising intonation and the same syllable said with a falling intonation (Morse, 1974). At around the same age children show the ability to discriminate question intonation from statement intonation (Kaplan, 1969).

These observations and anecdotal accounts have led some linguists to claim that the child masters the intonation patterns of his language in essentially the adult form before he has learned any recognizable words at all (Dale, 1973; Bever, Fodor, and Weksel, 1965). But this conclusion is rather premature. The full English intonation system is by no means fully developed in the speech of young children. As we mentioned earlier in the chapter, intonation patterns of English are considerably more complex than the simple falling or rising pitch at the end of an utterance. Furthermore, full mastery of even the contrast between rising and falling intonation may be achieved later in some children than in others, and some children develop very idiosyncratic uses of intonation (Bloom, 1973). Two of the young children studied by Miller and Ervin (1964) used features of intonation in their early speech that had no analog in adult English, and their rising and falling intonation patterns did not always correspond to the distinction between questions and statements in their speech.

The point at which children can produce and discriminate rising and falling intonation is of considerable interest in itself. Nevertheless, the crucial question for linguistic analysis is not whether children can tell those two acoustic patterns apart, but whether they can appropriately produce and respond to questions versus statements, as signaled by these patterns. This question can best be argued for children producing intelligible words with apparent communicative intent. Then the situation in which the word is produced and the intonation contour that accompanies it become important factors in determining whether the child's utterance is interpreted as a query or an assertion.

MEANING IN THE SINGLE-WORD STAGE

Let us turn now to the period when most of the child's utterances consist of only a single word and consider not the pronunciation of those words, but their meaning. The distinguishing characteristics of the first words seem to be twofold: a recognizable phonetic approximation to some adult word and a fairly consistent use of a particular word in the presence of a particular object or situation. In practice the second criterion seems to be more important than the first. Parents will often say, "Oh, that's Fred's word for _____," based on consistent use of a speech-like phonetic sequence in a given context.

What do these first words mean? Most parents believe, with good reason, that their offspring mean more than they say when they utter a single word. Many of the early single-word utterances do not seem to serve just a labeling or referential function. The actual meaning of the single words of children has been a question of considerable controversy for some time. Dore (1975) points out that as long ago as 1893 an authoritative linguist claimed that "though an infant's first words are commonly such as are used by us in nominal relations, yet in the infant's speech these words are not nouns, but equivalent to whole sentences. When a very young child says 'water,' he is not using the word merely as the name of the object so designated by us, but with the value of an assertion like 'I want water' or 'Here is water,' the distinction in meaning being shown by the child's tone of utterance." This claim that the child's single words represent whole sentences or complex thoughts and propositions has been made often over the years. The term *holophrase*—one-word sentence—thus came to be applied to the child's single-word utterances.

On the other hand, several linguists have strongly criticized this view. In 1922 Jesperson wrote, "When we say that such a word means what we should express by a whole sentence, this does not amount to saying that the child's 'up' *is* a sentence, or a sentence-word . . . We might just as well assert that clapping our hands is a sentence, because it expresses the same idea (or the same frame of mind) that is otherwise expressed by the whole sentence 'This is splendid.' The word *sentence* presupposes a certain grammatical structure, which is lacking in the child's utterance.''

This, then, is the central question for research on the child's first words and their meaning: Where should we draw the line between the child's nonlinguistic and linguistic knowledge? Several investigators have maintained that the child has implicit knowledge of fuller forms at this stage, but that they do not get expressed in speech because of some production limit. The child conceives of something akin to whole sentences but is limited to speaking one word at a time. The evidence on which this proposal is based comes from four distinct sources, stressed to varying degrees by different researchers:

(1) *Comprehension.* It is clear that the child who only says single words comprehends a good deal more than that in the speech of others. The claim is that he understands sentences but cannot produce them because of a constraint on speaking.

(2) *Intonation.* It has been reported that children in the one-word stage impose consistently different intonation on their single words to signal the difference between questions and statements, emphatics and imperatives, thereby communicating more than labels.

(3) *Word selection.* Greenfield and Smith (1976) report a change throughout the holophrastic period in what children select to say. Given identical contexts, the child apparently expresses a different portion of the proposition at different stages. For example, suppose the child picks up a hammer, bangs on a peg and says ''hit.'' He is then selecting to label the action. On another identical occasion he might say ''peg,'' that is, the object of the action, another time ''hammer,'' that is, the instrument. This selection is apparently not arbitrary but quite orderly over time; in other words, there is a progression in the concepts the child labels or encodes in language. This suggests that the child has in mind the whole proposition but can only express one aspect at a time, and so he relies on the context to convey the remainder.

(4) *Replacement sequences.* Towards the end of the holophrastic period children are observed to say several single words in a row concerning the same situation, for example, ''daddy—car—ride.'' It is argued that this illustrates how complete a conception the child has of the situation.

It is important to evaluate the evidence that the child has substantially more *linguistic* knowledge than his speech would indicate. There are counterarguments to each of the above types of evidence:

(1) *Comprehension is not linguistic.* The child's language comprehension in a controlled test is in fact not that far in advance of his speech. If all cues from eye contact, direction of gaze, pointing, gesturing, and particularly familiar contexts are eliminated, his comprehension undergoes a substantial drop! The one-year-old child is quite sophisticated in personal interaction and of course understands more than a single word

in context, but his knowledge is not primarily based on linguistic information at this stage (Shipley, Smith, and Gleitman, 1969).

(2) *Intonation*. The best data in support of consistent intonation come from Menyuk and Bernholtz (1969), who studied a single child between the ages of eighteen and twenty months. Three versions of each of five words in the child's speech were judged, in context, to convey each of three different intentions: statement, question, and emphasis. The fifteen versions were tape-recorded and it was found that adults could classify the recordings with more than 80 percent agreement. When the sounds were displayed on a spectrograph, distinct patterns were found to correspond to the utterance types. However, as mentioned earlier, Bloom (1973) and Miller and Ervin (1964) found no apparent consistency in the use of intonation with single words in the children they studied. Halliday (1975) did notice distinct intonations that emerged quite late in the holophrastic period for one child and signaled different utterance types, but they were not isomorphic with adult intonation patterns. Although this area is a potentially rich one for future research, the evidence so far is unconvincing.

(3) *Word selection*. Greenfield and Smith (1976) proposed a development within the one-word stage in what children choose to label. The difficulty lies in controlling for the vocabulary that the child has at his disposal at these various points. In assessing the claim that the child selected a word, it is critical to know the extent of his choice. The word he produced was perhaps the only word he knew in that situation.

(4) *Replacement sequences*. Bloom (1973) has pointed out that the strings of single words cannot strictly be called sentences or whole propositions, as they are neither spoken within the same intonation grouping nor are they ordered as they would be in real sentences. The child pauses between words and does not carry over the intonation, and the word order varies freely. Thus, neither of the linguistic characteristics of sentences are present. However, Branigan (1976a, b) has recently presented an illuminating spectrographic analysis of the speech of two children in the successive single-word stage. He describes several acoustic consequences of words being spoken as part of sentences rather than singly: the pause between them decreases, the fundamental frequency contour does not fall to terminal position until the end of the last word, and the duration of each word is affected by the other words in the sentence. To take an oversimplified example, in (*1*) the two words spoken in isolation from each other are separated by a pause, are equal in duration, and each has a terminal contour.

(1) k i c k   t h a t

(2) kick t h a t

In (2), with the same words in a sentence, the pause is shortened, the first word is compressed in duration relative to its duration in (1), and the fundamental frequency does not fall as completely at the end of the first word.

Branigan contrasted the duration of words spoken singly with that of words in the initial position of successive single word utterances, defined by the existence of a pause of between .4 and 1.1 seconds. He found evidence that the two words of a successive single word utterance were embraced by a single frequency contour, as in (2), and the duration of the initial word was compressed compared to the words spoken in isolation. Thus, the only articulatory aspect of simple sentence planning that was not controlled was the duration of the pause between words.

At this stage of development it seems that children plan to say more than the single word they utter, and are acquiring mastery over the integration of words into a single organizational schema. We must await confirmation of this finding in a larger sample of children, for it may be the case that individual children acquire control of these aspects in different ways. For example, it is not obvious that duration of the pause must be mastered later than relative word duration or frequency contour, so children might proceed by different routes.

In discussing the relationship between comprehension and production, Bloom (1974) has put forward a simple model that enlightens the distinction between the child's knowledge of language and his knowledge of the world. First, we note that there are two sources of information available to a child; the events he witnesses, and the speech he hears. We can assume that the one- or two-year-old child has a fairly sophisticated understanding of events. He no longer confuses people with objects, actions of his own with those of others, or actions with their effects (Piaget, 1970). So the child's perception of the world is rich enough to support his early communication. Let us also allow him some extra information, such as stored memories of what things are likely to happen, who people are, and how to accomplish simple goals. These are the contents of his information store. Finally, the child has a language processor with specifically linguistic knowledge of word meanings, intonation, the meanings conveyed by word order, and so forth. These three components of the child's knowledge are shown in Figure 7.

With the help of this model we can better explain the holophrase controversy. In comprehension, it is clear that the child has much more information available than the speech he hears. He is able to make use of his conception of the events being spoken about, as well as his stored information about what is likely in a situation and what people expect of him. If this contextual information is removed, as in formal testing, the child is thrown back on only his language processor, which is much less adequate on its own.

In production, the child has a rich representation of events but can

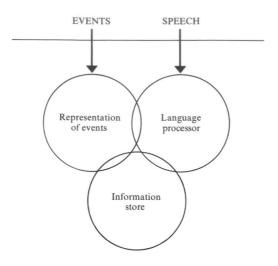

Figure 7. The child's knowledge.

only encode limited aspects in words. The adult listener makes use of *his* conception of the events plus the child's word, and so there is little loss of communication in context. Actually, even if the adult misinterprets the child's meaning, the child learns something. One of our favorite cartoons depicts a small girl waving her hands and saying "wawa!" Her mother happily brings her a drink of water, and the last picture shows the puzzled infant complete with a thought balloon that reads, "Well, now I know not to say 'wawa' when I want milk!" So in fact it is highly adaptive of parents to read a lot into what the child says, whether they are right or not!

It would seem prudent, until further evidence is forthcoming, to conclude that while the child *does* know more than the single words he speaks, this knowledge has no clear linguistic manifestation beyond the word uttered. We do not gain by saying that the single word stands for a whole sentence. However, the child at this stage can use his single words in combination with gestures and possibly intonation to serve a variety of pragmatic goals. In this way he communicates his desire for an object, makes queries or demands, and labels objects and events (Dore, 1974). He need not possess a great deal of linguistic knowledge to be successful in communicating with adults in situations in which the word is highly redundant given the context.

3

Early
Grammar

It may come as a surprise to many people that the two-year-old child learns grammar. For surely most of us remember our first exposure to that never-popular subject in school, where we endlessly divided chalky sentences into subject and predicate for no obvious reason except as preparation for worse to come in Latin. Yet to be skilled speakers of the language, it is necessary to know the rules that make it possible to construct new sentences that can be understood by others. One of the contributions of modern linguistics has been to highlight the creativity of everyday language, for novel sentences are always being spoken. They are understood because they follow the rules of word combination that the speakers of that language have learned, and a child must master those rules to join his linguistic community.

The question we address in this chapter is: how does the child begin to express propositions through multiword sentences? Linguistics attempts to describe which word combinations are permissible in a language and how propositions are conveyed by sentences. In doing so, linguists use evidence gleaned from three aspects of adult speech: intuitions of grammaticality, detections of ambiguity or anomaly, and judgments of which sentences are related to each other. As adults we can reflect on the language that we speak and argue about its rules; as we shall see in Chapter 6, this is a relatively late accomplishment for children. Since children cannot be taught rules explicitly, they must extract them from the speech they hear by making use of regularities in the speech in the context in which it is spoken. The rules a child has extracted at a given stage can be determined by linguistic analysis of a sample of the child's speech. As we shall see, there is a certain amount of indeterminacy in the choice of this description, for several different rules may appear to capture the regularities in the child's sentences and it is difficult to determine which one the child is actually following. The importance of this question will become evident later, when we present the debate between those who see the child's earliest language as an outgrowth of his cognitive development and believe the child is relatively slow to attain adult grammar, and those who believe the child is from the start endowed with a very abstract grammatical knowledge that does not find full expression in speech because of memory or attention limitations. A consequence of the latter position is that language learning is considered to have a substantial innate component.

This debate is intricately related to our view of the adult's grammatical knowledge, for we shall see that how we characterize the end point of language acquisition has important ramifications both for our view of the child's beginning state and for what we consider a satisfactory account of the learning process (see Chapters 7 and 8).

LINGUISTIC CATEGORIES AND GRAMMATICAL RULES

According to all current linguistic models, the child has to learn rules that act upon different linguistic categories, ranging in scope from inflections and words to whole sentences. As a vehicle for introducing these necessary concepts to the reader, we have chosen the following scenario: we have in our charge a foreign student, of fairly remarkable talents, who knows how to make active declarative sentences of the sort:

The man walked the dog.

but he wants to learn how to form passive sentences out of them, like:

The dog was walked by the man.

Adult native speakers of English can do this effortlessly and may regard it as trivially easy to describe the applicable rule. But by making that rule explicit for our foreign student, we hope to illuminate the different categories that must be dealt with in grammar and the problems that confront the child who has to learn them.

Let us begin with a list of simple sentences and their corresponding passives, and consider the easiest rule we might extract:

Fido trampled the daffodil. → The daffodil was trampled by Fido.

The baby shredded the newspaper. → The newspaper was shredded by the baby.

Watergate destroyed Nixon. → Nixon was destroyed
by Watergate.

Evidently, the rule is a simple one of permutation, of moving around certain elements and adding some others. What exactly is it that changes position? *Fido* exchanges with *the daffodil*. *The newspaper* moves to the front, while *the baby* moves to the end, and *Nixon* and *Watergate* switch places. We simply have to tell our foreign student how to recognize the beginning and end words of the sentence, ignoring the article *the* for the present, and simply regarding it as part of the word it precedes. In addition, the middle word has two small words *was* and *by* added to it, one on either side: so *trampled* becomes *was trampled by; destroyed* becomes *was destroyed by* and so forth. Let us formulate the rule as concisely as possible to help the student deal with future sentences:

Rule 1: Identify the words in the sentence, counting *the* or *a* as part of the word each precedes. Exchange the initial and final words. Add *was* between the initial and the middle word, *by* between the middle and final words.

Some examples should reveal the generality of this rule:

The cat chased the dog. → The dog was chased by the cat.

The gardener watered the philodendron. → The philodendron was watered by the gardener.

So far so good. But:

Today Alan hit a homerun. → A homerun was Alan hit by today.

What went wrong? *Today* is not the kind of word you exchange; it should not enter into the rule. It is the wrong part of speech. Parts of speech describe the traditional division into nouns, verbs, adjectives, and so forth; but how can we teach our pupil what that means? A noun is taught to schoolchildren as "the name of a person, place, or thing," which is no definition at all when one speculates on what kinds of things justice, wind, or epistemology might be, though all are certainly nouns. Neither is a verb always an action of any sort. Parts of speech are best defined in terms of their privileges of occurrence, the positions they can occupy in sentences and the roles they play in them. For example, articles such as *a* or *the* precede nouns but not verbs; verbs have tense markers such as *-ing* or *-ed* but nouns do not. What if we then reformulate the rule?

Rule 2: Exchange the initial and final nouns in the sentence. Add *was* and *by* on either side of the verb.

That version looks neater, so let's try it out:

Unfortunately the man broke the bicycle. → Unfortunately the
                                    bicycle was broken by the man.

Until yesterday the girl washed the car. → Until yesterday the car
                                    was washed by the girl.

That is an improvement. But what about:

The man in the Homburg found the dog. → The dog in the Homburg
                                    was found by the man.

The baby who had a cute dimple kissed the politician. →
                                The politician who had a cute dimple
                                    was kissed by the baby.

Something has gone awry again. It was the man who wore the Homburg, not the dog, and the dimple belonged to the baby, not the politician. So the whole string of words should move together, but how can we convey that in a rule? There is an analogy with arithmetic, where the answer can change according to the bracketing. For example:

3 × 4 + 5

gives a different result if it is

(3 × 4) + 5 = 17

or

3 × (4 + 5) = 27

In language also, the way words are grouped together changes the overall picture. We saw a nice example this summer at a country fair in Acton, Maine. A notice read:

Larger rabbit and guinea pig show.

Now was it:

(1) [(larger rabbit) and guinea pig] show?
(2) [larger (rabbit and guinea pig)] show?
(3) larger [(rabbit and guinea pig) show]?

It turned out to be the last, for we saw no gargantuan specimens of either rodent!

When the examples become complex, it is easier to spot the difference if the brackets are spread out into two dimensions so that the groupings hang on the branches of a tree, so this device is frequently used in linguistics:

(1)

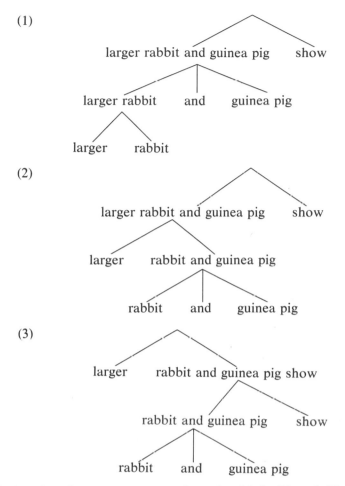

(2)

(3)

Notice that the trees are sometimes lopsided: (*1*) and (*2*) are predominantly left-branching, that is, the branches are more numerous to the left of the topmost node, and (*3*) is mostly right-branching.

To return to our foreign student's problem: sentences are more than just strings of words, instead they have structure, that is, their words fall into natural groups called constituents. Roughly speaking, constituents called noun phrases can be replaced by single nouns, for example:

The baby who had a cute dimple.

occupies the same role and position in a sentence as:

The baby.

or even a pronoun alone:

She.

Verb phrases have the same privileges of occurrence as single verbs. Simple sentences (S) consist of a single noun phrase (NP) and a verb phrase (VP):

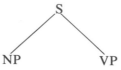

The noun phrase can be very simple, as in this sentence:

John fell.

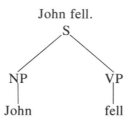

or it can be very complex, as in:

The fact that sentences contain constituents confuses me.

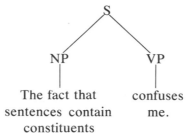

The verb phrase can also be complex, and can include further noun phrases, as in:

He asked whether it was true that sentences contain constituents.

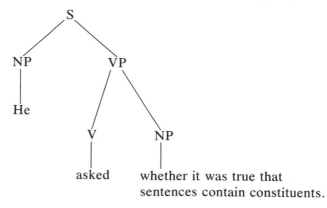

What now is the status of our passive rule? We first changed the rule from one involving words to one operating on parts of speech and now we have introduced the notion of the constituent. So we now have:

Rule 3: Interchange the initial and final noun phrases, adding *was* and *by* on either side of the verb.

Let us try an example:

The woman who came to see us on Saturday called my uncle. → My uncle was called by the woman who came to see us on Saturday.

Now another example:

The goat with the long beard gave the boy a kick. → A kick was given by the boy the goat with the long beard.

The student performed correctly by our rule, as he did move constituents around, but he chose the wrong ones. Something is wrong in our specifying that it must be the initial and final noun phrases that get interchanged. It is the role of the noun phrases that seems to be important. As a first guess, the noun phrase that refers to the agent or doer of the action should interchange with the patient, or thing affected by that action. That is, we should consider the *semantic roles* played by the noun phrases, not just their position. So:

The goat with the long beard gave the boy a kick → The boy was given a kick by the goat with the long beard.

Rule 4: Interchange the noun phrase corresponding to the agent with the noun phrase corresponding to the patient of the action. Add *was* and *by* to either side of the verb.

However, a moment's reflection will reveal cases in which the semantic roles of the noun phrases in the sentence are not those of agent and patient. For example, we would be unable to passivize by Rule 4 either:

Bill received the Ford Edsel.

or

Jane adored strawberry shortcake.

since neither Bill nor Jane acted, and neither the Ford Edsel nor the strawberry shortcake were affected. Perhaps the answer is to make a list of the semantic roles that noun phrases can play, and then to commit to memory those roles that are interchangeable in passive sentences. For example, in a sentence such as:

The crowbar opened the safe.

it is clear that the crowbar is not performing the action, so *the crowbar* is called the instrument of the sentence, *the safe* is the patient, and these can be interchanged to form the passive:

The safe was opened by the crowbar.

In the sentence:

The thief opened the safe.

the thief is an agent, *the safe* is again the patient, and we get:

The safe was opened by the thief.

Notice that in this new scheme, our student must know a great deal more about the meaning of the sentences than he might have needed for the previous rules, for he must decide what the noun phrases and verbs mean and then allocate them to appropriate semantic roles in the sentence as a whole. He must know, for example, what kinds of nouns can serve as agents and what kinds can serve as instruments (which typically do not act alone) and therefore his knowledge of the real world must supplement his linguistic knowledge. To some extent this was necessary for the previous definitions also, but it becomes most evident here.

To return to the examples: the real problems with Rule 4 arise when we confront our pupil with a three-role sentence, such as:

The thief used the crowbar to open the safe.

We have now provided him with two options: interchange agent and patient, or interchange instrument and patient. So in turn we will get either:

The safe was used by the crowbar to open the thief.

or

The thief was used by the safe to open the crowbar.

How can we explain that in this case, neither is right and we must interchange agent and instrument? It appears that for each separate combination of semantic roles we must specify which ones interchange, and our passive rule becomes increasingly unwieldy.

TRANSFORMATIONAL GRAMMAR

The most parsimonious and elegant solution to this problem is provided by a transformational grammar such as the one proposed by Chomsky (1957, 1965).[1] It may not provide much relief for our foreign student, how-

---

[1] There are now many different transformational grammars and we recognize that the weaknesses of one model may not be shared by all. However, the standard version (Chomsky, 1965) is the grammar that child-language researchers, and psycholinguists in general, have referred to and argued about most, and hence it will receive the lion's share of attention here.

ever, for although the passive rule can be stated simply enough it is at the expense of introducing another abstraction, the idea of *deep structure*. Basically, the revolutionary idea was to propose that every sentence of a language has both a deep structure and a surface structure. The deep structure is a configuration that defines the basic grammatical relations such as subject and object in a purely formal way, that is, without taking meaning into account. The subject is the noun phrase (NP$_1$) directly beneath ("dominated by") the S node in the deep structure tree diagram, the object is the noun phrase (NP$_2$) directly beneath the verb phrase node.

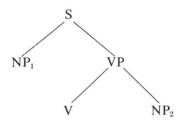

Actives and passives alike share this deep structure, which is a way of accounting for our intuition that they describe the same event. Their deep structure subjects and objects are the same, though their surface arrangement of noun phrases is not. In the passive case, a rule called the passive transformation acts to change the order of NP$_1$ and NP$_2$ to result in the surface structure arrangement of the passive sentence, for example:

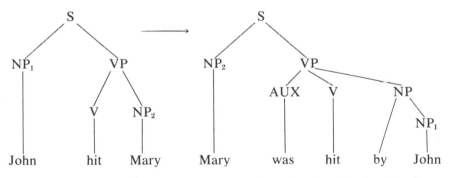

In addition, the morphemes *be* and *by* are introduced and ordered to form the full passive sentence. The passive rule then becomes:

Rule 5: Interchange the deep structure subject and the deep structure object. Add *was* and *by* on either side of the verb.

So the solution to our puzzle is that the categories on which the passive rule operates cannot be defined by superficial aspects of the corresponding active sentence, like words or parts of speech or constituents, or by considering semantic aspects such as agent and the like. It is instead necessary to depict the deep structure to ascertain which are the correct noun phrases to permute.

Ordered Rules

Transformational rules must be applied in a certain order to the deep structure, or the outcome is ungrammatical. We purposely avoided introducing plural nouns into our previous examples because of the issue of number agreement, which illustrates very nicely the necessity for using rules in order. Take a sentence like:

Fido chased cars.

where the subject and object are different in number. In our previous examples of passive sentences we simply added *was* and *by* on either side of the verb, but the form of *be* must agree in tense with the verb and in number with the surface subject. The rule that controls the number agreement must be applied *after* the transformational rule that permutes the noun phrases, or else the result will be ungrammatical, as in:

Rule 1: Add *be* and *by* on either side of the verb:

Fido be chased by cars.

Rule 2: Make *be* agree in number with the surface subject:

Fido was chased by cars.

Rule 3: Interchange deep structure subject and object:

Cars was chased by Fido.

Instead, the rules must be ordered as follows:

Rule 1: Add *be* and *by* on either side of the verb:

Fido be chased by cars.

Rule 2: Interchange deep structure subject and object:

Cars be chased by Fido.

Rule 3: Make *be* agree in number with the surface subject:

Cars were chased by Fido.

Underlying Structure

The relationship between passive sentences and their active counterparts is thus made explicit in the grammar by positing a shared deep structure for both types of sentence. A grammatical analysis that focuses on surface structure regularities fails to account for all kinds of facts about language, not just the relations between actives and passives, or interrogatives and declaratives. Therefore, in transformational grammar *all* sentences are conceived of as having a deep structure, and the three illustrations that follow demonstrate the utility of an underlying level of description in solving certain problems in grammar.

(1) *Ambiguity*. The concept of constituent structure is helpful in disambiguating sentences such as:

Chocolate pies and cakes are fattening.

However it is no help in solving this ambiguous sentence: .

Visiting relatives can be boring.

The constituent structures of the two meanings of the sentence are identical, yet we recognize that one meaning can be paraphrased as:

For someone to visit relatives can be boring.

and another as:

Relatives that are visiting can be boring.

How do we appreciate both possibilities if the sentence has only one possible surface structure? One solution is to allow each meaning to be associated with a distinct deep structure in which the different grammatical roles played by *relatives* and *visiting* are represented.

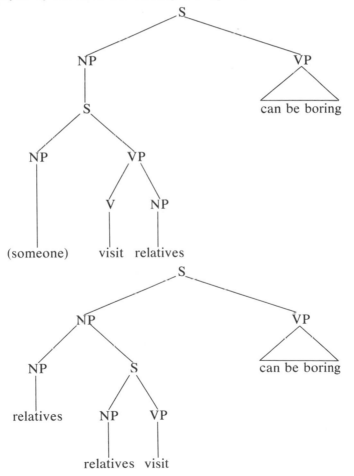

The two different deep structures converge on the same surface structure, and we retrieve them to appreciate the ambiguity of the sentence.

(2) *Similar surface structures mean different things*. The classic example (Chomsky, 1957) of similar surface structures being quite distinct in meaning is provided by the following pair:

John is easy to please.
John is eager to please.

That they are distinct can be shown by their paraphrases:

It is easy to please John.

but not

It is eager to please John.

rather

John is eager to please someone.

Again, this difference is not appreciated by examining their surface structure; the deep structure of each sentence contains the information that reveals that *John* is the deep object of *please* in the first sentence, but the deep subject of *please* in the second sentence.

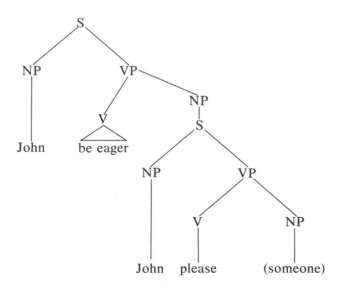

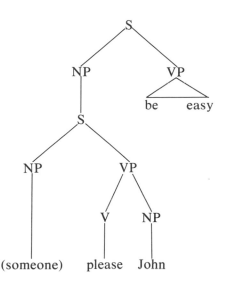

(3) *Some surface structures have missing information.* Coordinated sentences such as:

The albatross hovered and swooped.
The bishop and the cardinal retired.
Jane is tired and I am too.

are understood as containing two propositions, yet they are not explicit in the surface form. For example, the first sentence is understood as meaning:

The albatross hovered and the albatross swooped.

The information that is not explicit, namely that *the albatross* is also the subject of swooped, is contained in the deep structure of the sentence.

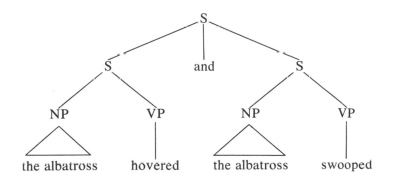

Thus the fact that there are two propositions is explained by including them in the deep structure. The deep structure is then related to the surface structure by a deletion transformation that deletes the redundant information.

Basically, then, every sentence is conceived as having an abstract deep structure that defines the basic grammatical relations, and this, together with information about word meaning, determines the meaning of the sentence. Transformational rules operate on this deep structure to permute and delete elements to arrive at the surface structure of the sentence. Phonological rules act on the surface structure to relate it to the phonetic string that is the spoken sentence.

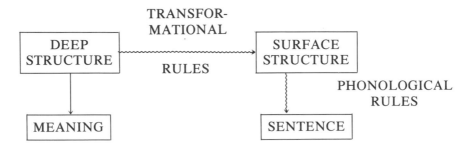

It can be seen from the above examples what a powerful notion deep structure really is, for, through it, the rules of grammar become both enormously simplified and much more general. Instead of being restricted to a description of sentences as they are spoken, the linguist can incorporate a wide variety of phenomena and relationships among sentences into a more abstract description of a sentence, namely its underlying deep structure. The same solution, of deep structure plus transformational rules, accounts for diverse phenomena and illuminates the general form of rules such as passivization, which eluded our stumbling attempts at description.

Psychological Reality

The rules and categories of transformational grammar are meant to represent as simply and as elegantly as possible what adult speakers know about their language. We can recognize ambiguity, spot differences in meaning, react to ungrammatical strings, paraphrase sentences, and so forth. The linguist tries to capture these phenomena in his description of language. But what is the relationship between the most elegant description of a language and what speakers know? We cannot give a satisfactory answer at this point, for there are many different versions of transformational grammar competing as models of linguistic knowledge, and existing tests of their psychological reality are far from adequate. As we shall see in Chapter 4, it is tempting indeed to borrow the descriptive model given above as a model of actual language processing: in production we start with the meaning and the deep structure, apply transformational rules to obtain the surface structure, then use rules of phonology to produce the phonetic string we actually speak. In comprehension, we retrieve the deep structure to arrive at the meaning. The problem is, how do we get started? How does the child, or our foreign student, successfully represent the deep structure of sentences, when by definition it is not equated with the surface form, nor can it be identified with the meaning? Our futile attempts to describe the way to convert actives into passives were misguided and faulty, but we tried to make the rules learnable. It is a serious dilemma if the most powerful and successful descriptive system provided by linguistics is one that cannot be learned! This issue will be taken up at length in Chapter 7.

Meanwhile, the present chapter has a more modest goal, namely, to examine children's early sentences for evidence of syntactic rules and to determine how complex they are. Can children's utterances be described in terms of rules of *word* combination, or do they, from the start, show knowledge of constituents, or semantic roles, or deep structures? In tracing the arguments, it will be prudent to keep in mind the two horns of the dilemma:

(1) Any set of sentences, no matter how simple, can be given a very abstract description; however, we must ask whether child language warrants such complexity to the same extent that adult language does. It may be that children's rules are much simpler and more easily learned than the adult rules we have been discussing.

(2) If we can give a simpler description of children's rules, are they enough for describing adult language also, or must we revise our description as the child approaches adulthood? If so, when does such revision become necessary?

EARLY GRAMMATICAL DEVELOPMENT

We shall turn now to descriptions of the child's acquisition of grammar at the point where he begins to combine words into simple sentences. The descriptions vary widely, even for the restricted domain of two-word sentences, and we shall examine several alternative accounts.

The Length of Utterances

Most children begin with single words, and the length of their sentences increases gradually as they get older. Utterance length therefore provides a simple measure of development. Researchers have chosen the *morpheme*, rather than words or syllables or phrases, as the measure of length. Morphemes are the minimal meaningful units in speech. Single words can be morphemes, but in some cases a word consists of more than one morpheme, for example, *trustworthy, steeplejack*. Some words contain bound morphemes that cannot exist alone, such as the *-ed* in *opened*, which distinguishes it from *open*. Thus *opened* consists of two morphemes. So do the words *cats, driver* and *unhappy*. Once the unit of analysis has been decided, it is a simple matter to compare one speech sample with another in terms of the average or *mean length of utterance* (MLU for short) measured in morphemes. Suppose a child produced the following sample of speech:

Mommy drink	2	Pick that up	3
Hit trucks	3	It dropped	3
Yeah	1	I running	3
Hi man	2		

Total = 17 morphemes
MLU = 17/7 = 2.43

The researcher tallies the number of morphemes in each utterance, then simply averages as shown to get the mean length of utterance. Irregular verb forms, such as the past tense *fell*, are considered as single morphemes, as are routines like *choo-choo train* or *all gone* if there is no evidence that the child thinks of them as anything more than a long word, for example, if the child never says *fall, train* or *all* alone. Researchers sometimes recalculate MLU without the *yes* and *no* replies of the child, since these usually follow yes/no questions asked by the interactor. Their frequency therefore varies with the interaction and the shyness of the child and may deflate the MLU as a measure of linguistic development. It is often important in a study to know whether a particular phenomenon is related to the child's age or linguistic maturity. MLU provides a quick and easy index of the latter. Other studies have been concerned with individual differences; for example, do the variations in MLU at a particular age relate to other aspects of the child's upbringing, such as the number of hours of television he watches, or the age of his nearest sibling?

As the questions posed become more sophisticated, the MLU will undoubtedly prove inadequate to the task of either classifying children as similar or distinguishing between them. However, since many studies make reference to MLU, it is a useful item to have under one's belt. Our present concern is more with similarities in language development than with individual differences. Having said that the MLU of most children increases as they grow older, is that where the uniformity ends? Fortunately it is not, and we will describe several attempts to capture the regularities in early child speech.

Telegraphic Speech

The first generalization that seems to be true, not just for children learning English but for all other languages that have been studied, is that children's speech is *telegraphic*. That is, some words are more likely than others to appear in the child's first sentences. These are the content words, primarily the nouns and verbs necessary in the situation. Words that have grammatical functions, but do not themselves make reference, such as articles, prepositions, and auxiliary verbs, do not occur as often. If we look at transcripts of parent and child speech at this stage, it seems as if the parent does not hear anything impoverished about the child's sentences. The discourse continues with little apparent loss in communication:

> Child: Get truck.
> Parent: O. K., I'll get your truck.
> Child: It drop.
> Parent: Oh, it dropped, did it?
> Child: Me sit truck.
> Parent: I can see you're sitting on it.

"Telegraphic" is an apt adjective because adults produce similar sentences under conditions where words cost money, in a telegram or a classified advertisement:

> Lost dog. Reward. Name Rover.
> Nice house, Overlook Thames. Own wharf.
> Meet 10 Saturday. Bring cash.

The omitted words tend to contain little extra information, in that they are a fairly small, closed set (When did you last hear a new preposition?) and are predictable or redundant in context. In contrast, content words are a potentially infinite set, they make clear reference and are less predictable from the context. Compare:

> The boy jumped out of the _____

with

> She put the mixture _____ the oven to bake.

There seem to be many more possibilities for the missing item in the former case than in the latter.

This suggests that the child's telegraphic utterances are a more successful economy than just choosing any two words from an equivalent adult sentence. The assumption is that the child is taxed, in some other way than financially, for producing more than two or three words at a time. But how does the child know to produce content words rather than function words? The very properties that make content words more necessary in speech also make them more salient for the child to learn: they have clear meanings. In addition, nouns and verbs receive heavier stress in speech than function words, enabling the child to hear and imitate them more readily (Brown, 1973).

It is worth noting that one could write a rule that would accurately describe the child's speech at this stage: "Omit function words," yet this rule would be a very poor description or what the child knows. We have no evidence that the child knows the meanings signaled by the function words and decides that they are not as important to his listener as the content words. The child exercises no choice; the selection is a consequence of the properties of speech and of the child's limited knowledge and memory.

As always, there are qualifications to be added to the claim that the child's speech is telegraphic at first. It is not the case that *no* function words appear, as Park noted in his 1970 study of the acquisition of German. The function words that do appear have some semantic content, for instance, *my* and *your* (important contrasts for a two-year-old!), *this* and *that*, and *off, on,* and *up,* which seem to be used as verbs in the beginning in commands such as *coat off* and *up.*

Pivot Grammar

The first intimations that the child may be doing more than producing reduced adult sentences came from Braine (1963a). He suggested that the child had a set of rules of his own, called a *pivot grammar*. The rules were unlike anything in adult grammar and could generate a large number of simple sentences. Braine discovered these rules by doing what is called a *distributional analysis* of a sample of speech from three children in the first stages of language development. A distributional analysis examines the constructions or words that combine with each other and searches for regularities in these combinations. Linguists often use such a procedure to begin an analysis of an exotic unknown language. Let us invent a sample of child sentences and imagine we are dealing with an unknown language.

Hi doggy	That fell	More soup
Hi Mommy	Doggy fell	More swing
Hi truck	Teddy fell	More milk
Hi dolly	Bottle fell	More jump
Hi horse	Me fell	More bottle

The sample has been organized to show clearly that there are three highly frequent words—*hi, fell,* and *more*—that occur in fixed positions in the sentences. There are other words that are not so frequent and change position: *bottle, doggy*. Braine's conclusion, drawn from data not so artificially neat as these, was that the high-frequency, fixed-position words are *pivots* that can combine with the *open* words, which can vary position and comprise the rest of the child's expanding vocabulary. The child's vocabulary is divided into the three types of words: first- and second-position pivots, and open words. To state the rules explicitly, the following can occur:

pivot$_1$ + open

open + pivot$_2$

open + open

open

We can now predict new utterances on the model of the old: for example, we might expect the child on future occasions to say:

Truck fell

Hi Teddy

More dolly

and so forth. According to this description, a child learns certain words in particular positions, and structures his sentences around them. *Hi* always goes first, *fell* always last, and so on. Braine did more than just show that the rules adequately described children's sentences. He demonstrated that preschool children could remember the position of words in an artificial language and the rules for their combination (Braine, 1963b). Thus, the rules of pivot grammar may be psychologically plausible as well as descriptively adequate.

Pivot grammar was an attempt to describe the rules a child might use to produce a variety of sentences. The ideas were enthusiastically received, and other investigators reported similar constructions in early child speech (Brown and Bellugi, 1964; Miller and Ervin, 1964). McNeill (1970a) acclaimed pivot grammar as a universal first step in language learning, and tried to demonstrate how the child might proceed from these simple rules to the full adult grammar.

Therein lay the problem. It is very difficult to see how a child following this road could develop as an adult the structural knowledge proposed in the introduction to this chapter. To take a simple example, suppose the child had the words *Mommy* and *Daddy* both as first position pivots, and could construct sentences like *Mommy wash, Daddy run, Mommy eat, Daddy shoe,* and so forth. What would happen if he wanted to express the proposition *Daddy see Mommy?* Because his words occupy fixed positions, he would be unable to describe that event appropriately. Braine himself suggested the pivot-open stage was only transitory and was soon replaced by structures with more potential for generalization. As Brown (1973) so aptly puts it, "But does nature build a universal cul-de-sac?"

Meanwhile, evidence was accruing that pivot grammar was not as accurate nor as universal as had been hoped. There are two general ways in which a set of linguistic rules can fail: (1) sentences can occur that violate the rules; (2) the rules can underrepresent the facts, that is, they can be inadequate to specify which sentences are allowed and which can never occur. For example, as we saw above, it is inadequate to say a child says *any* two words out of a possible adult sentence.

Both Bloom (1970) and Bowerman (1973a) found the pivot rule violated in the first way by the children they studied. They not only found pivot words occurring alone, but also high-frequency words that varied sentence position. Under these conditions there is no basis for distinguishing pivots from open words, and Brown (1973) points out that the rules reduce to:

sentence = word + (word)

where the brackets indicate that the second word is optional. There is no inherent structure to this characterization: it is even worse than telegraphic speech because it says nothing about the type of words occurring in either position.

Bloom's criticism of pivot grammar went further than showing it was not universally true. For she pointed out that even in cases where it fitted the data, it would underrepresent the child's knowledge. In Chapter 2 we discussed at length the problem of the holophrase: that we have no clear evidence that the child intends more than he can express at the one-word stage, however various the contexts in which he says his one word. At the two-word stage we have additional evidence: the child's use of word order. If the child were merely labeling aspects of his environment one at a time, the order of words ought to be quite free. He should say *shoe Daddy* as often as *Daddy shoe, eat Mommy* as often as *Mommy eat!* Investigators have long been aware that this is not the way a child proceeds. Instead, the English-speaking child produces only a small set of the possible word orders, even at the start. This suggests he is using word order as an expressive device, as a way of encoding contrasting meanings. For example, suppose we showed a child at this stage a picture of a bear carrying a monkey. He might produce *bear carry, carry monkey, bear monkey,* but not *carry bear, monkey carry,* or *monkey bear.* Asked to act out simple sentences in which the only cue to meaning is the word order, such as:

The cat kissed the dog.

children who are only just combining words in their own speech can use word order to comprehend the sentences correctly most of the time (de Villiers and de Villiers, 1973a).

Semantic Relations

The majority of children in the two-word stage produce just the word order that an adult would use to convey that particular semantic relation in English. In the above example, an adult would say the agent first and the patient of the action last, and so does the child. Talking about possessions, an adult would use the order possessor-possessed as in *Jane's car,* and the child does too. So both the adult and the child know more than the meaning of the two words in isolation: they also know the relation that holds between them and is conveyed in part by word order.

The issue centers on the generality of the rules we think the child possesses in forming his simple sentences. He might, as a pivot grammar would have him do, simply learn the positions of many single words, for example, that *Daddy, Mommy, Teddy, Granny* all come first in sentences. But this would not be any help when he learned a new word, such as *Auntie.* He would have to learn a new rule to order the words in sentences involving her. It seems more probable that the child does not, after a certain point, learn the positions of all new words individually, but rather has a concept like agent that embraces all new instances that fit a particular mold. We can tell this by the fact that the child's word order is surprisingly invariant and extends to new instances he has not heard or spoken previously in sentences. In contrast to pivot grammar, on this account children do not learn the order of particular words but rather how to arrange particular semantic roles such as agent or patient (Fillmore, 1968). Any particular word may occupy several positions depending on its role in the sentence.

The major impact of this alternative description has come from suggestions that children speaking many different languages seem preoccupied with the expression of the same relational meanings. Brown (1973) agrees with Bloom that the child's use of word order to signal contrastive meanings is justification for such a rich interpretation of the child's speech: it is evidence that the child intends the relation signaled by the order of words and disambiguated by the adult's knowledge of the context. Brown surveyed all the most fully reported studies on very early child speech, which include languages as remotely related as French, Samoan, Luo (spoken in Kenya), German, Finnish, and Cakchiquel (a Mayan language spoken in Guatemala). In some of these languages, word order is not the means by which adults express contrasts in meaning. Some languages have relatively free order and contrasts in meaning are expressed by suffixes or prefixes on the words. Where in English we signal the difference between:

The boy chased the girl.

and

The girl chased the boy.

by word order, in other languages (such as Japanese or Russian) there might be a suffix attached to the agent of the action to distinguish it from the object—say the suffix "nog." Then we could say:

The girlnog chased the boy.

or

The boy chased the girlnog.

or

The boy the girlnog chased.

and they would all mean the same thing.

Needless to say, children learning languages of this latter sort do not seem to use order to signal contrasts in meaning in their own speech. This is not surprising, as they hear no consistent order. Some children latch on to one of the adult orders, others seem to produce all possible orders. There may be general strategies that have not yet been revealed, as only a small number of children speaking such languages have been studied extensively.

Brown found strong evidence that children learning these distinct languages express a narrow range of all the possible adult meanings. A small set of semantic relations accounts for the majority of the children's utterances during Stage I, when the MLU is 1.0 to 2.0. It is a fair generalization to say that children the world over express such meanings as possessor-possessed (for example, *Daddy chair*), agent-action (*Mommy eat*), and entity-attribute (*big kitty*). Brown found this list accounted for some 70 percent of the child's utterances in Stage I:

    agent and action (boy kick)
    action and object (pull train)
    agent and object (Daddy ball)
    action and locative (sit chair)
    entity and locative (cup shelf)
    possessor and possession (Mommy scarf)
    entity and attribute (ball red)
    demonstrative and entity (there car)

Pivot grammar provides no way for the child to proceed, but the semantic relations hypothesis can account for the next steps the child takes. Brown discovered that progress from Stage I occurs in one of two ways: in one, the child strings together two relations and omits the common word, as in:

(agent + action) + (action + object) → agent + action + object,

or, as an example:

Daddy throw. Throw ball. → Daddy throw ball.

Alternatively, the child expands one element of a relation into a relation itself; for example, he might further specify an object as follows:

(action + object) → action + possessor + possessed

(possessor + possessed)

An example:

Bring shoe. My shoe. → Bring my shoe.

The relations have enormous combinatorial potential and can thereby express a wide variety of fairly complex meanings.

Prerequisites for Language

We have come very far from saying that the Stage I child just knows how to produce:

word + (word)

Are we perhaps ascribing too much knowledge and sophistication to the two-year-old child? Piaget has spent many years in research into the conceptual development of the child. He too would allow that the eighteen-month-old infant can distinguish agents from objects of action and can recognize recurrence and identity and location. Piaget regards these concepts and distinctions as the culmination of the sensorimotor period of intelligence, which ends at around eighteen months of age. The child in the first year of life is preoccupied with objects, the results of his actions, and the stability of objects over time and place. Similarly, the earliest meanings expressed in speech are conceptual relationships between people and objects that the child has mastered nonlinguistically just prior to the beginnings of grammar (Sinclair, 1971; Brown, 1973).

Carving into Categories

The semantic-relations hypothesis has several advantages over the pivot-grammar approach: it takes into account the meanings the child intends, it gives evidence of universality in the early stages, and it provides continuity with later linguistic developments on the one hand and with earlier cognitive development on the other.

Nevertheless, controversy abounds here also. The major problem is a methodological one: how does one decide how broad or narrow the semantic categories should be? Take an utterance like *Mommy hit ball.* What makes one set of categories—agent, action, patient—superior as a description over another set—animate being, movement, thing moved; or female human, propellant movement, thing propelled? Or even, *Mommy, hit, ball?* The most general description would cover more instances, but does it reflect what the child knows, or does the child in contrast know a larger number of rather specific rules? The naturalistic observations so far collected are often inadequate to the task of deciding which categories the child employs. Of critical importance for this task is establishing how the child would generalize to describe an event he has never heard described before but for which he knows the vocabulary. We do not have sufficient data from the children studied to date to know how this is done.

Rather than relying on our adult categories and perceptions, Braine (1976) applied stringent criteria to decide the appropriate level of description for the child's linguistic knowledge at the two-word stage. The first step was an obvious preliminary: he classed separately those expressions that he judged semantically unrelated, for example, expressions of negation and expressions of location. Then he searched the records for distributional evidence to subdivide the classes even further. For instance, a child may have in his speech several expressions that we might class together as involving an attribute and entity, but in some expressions the attribute may precede the thing described, in others it may follow it. Suppose the child produced: *big kitty, little one, big truck, ball red, truck green, sock brown*. Braine would not categorize all of these as expressions of attribute and entity having variable order; he would slice the categories more finely, perhaps into size + entity and entity + color. As still further evidence, he looked for creative extensions of the order rules to new expressions, since this generalization provides the best basis for identifying the categories and their limits.

Braine used syntactic evidence, predominantly positional in nature, to decide upon the appropriate level of description of the semantics of these early sentences. He found evidence for what he called "limited-scope formulae"—patterns dealing with the expression of quite narrow semantic content. Some examples are: possession, plurality or iteration, recurrence or alternative, and actor-action. He found large differences in the various speech samples that he studied in the particular patterns governing the earliest sentences, not so much in the semantic scope of the formulas but in their order of emergence. This led him to conclude that children start out by selecting from among a limited set of formulas like the above, and from these very distinct bases they converge on a similar form of simplified English as they add formulas.

Braine's finding contrasts sharply with the work of Bloom, Lightbown and Hood (1975), Wells (1974), Ramer (1974), and Leonard (1976), all of whom claim a fairly stable order of emergence of the basic semantic categories of Stage I. Leonard's (1976) position is illustrative. He found the operations of reference (nomination, notice, recurrence, and negation) emerge as a group earlier than relations involving actor, action, and object, which in turn precede expressions involving attribution, location, and possession. Finally, experience, experiencer, and instrument are only marginally present in Stage I speech.

Bowerman (1976) surveyed much of this work and suggested that some of the discrepancies among the studies could be due to the shifting size of the categories of description. For example, Wells (1974) found that verbs that encode functions of people, like *play, eat,* and *sing,* come in much earlier than verbs describing changes of state, such as *break, cut,* and *open.* Bloom et al. (1975) classed them all together as the category of action, which, they found, emerged early. When Leonard (1976) re-analyzed Braine's data in his own terms, he found it concordant with the other research; but in so doing he discarded the positional evidence on which Braine's semantic characterization was partially based! For a comprehensive view of the alternative approaches to the analysis of semantic relations in Stage I speech, see Leonard (1976, Appendix B).

It is unfortunate that there is not more consistency in the methodology used to study Stage I speech, for it is very difficult to determine whether the discrepancies are due to differences in methodology or real differences in children's linguistic knowledge. Is there a stable order of emergence of the semantic categories or are individual differences the more striking aspect of development? Would the claimed consistency in acquisition still be found if the more stringent criteria of Braine were applied to the analyses of all of the existing data? Although a plausible argument can be made for analyzing child speech at a level of description that reveals orderliness, there is no a priori reason to believe that such orderliness exists, and the argument must be buttressed by better evidence for the child's knowledge and use of these semantic categories.

The ramifications of this problem extend into other areas of cognitive development. We have already mentioned the argument that the child's early linguistic achievements build on his cognitive achievements during the sensorimotor period. Yet, in considering the nonlinguistic data, the problem of the best level of description arises again. Piaget describes how an infant at one stage will uncover a doll at location A, watch it being hidden at location B, but search immediately for it at A again. This is cited as an example of the infant's failure to distinguish objects as entities separate from his own action toward them. At a later stage, towards the end of the sensorimotor period and just prior to language, the infant will show no hesitation in searching for the doll where it was hidden rather than where it was last found. Similarly, a baby may initially only shake a particular rattle, but later may perform a variety of actions on it: banging, throwing, chewing, and so forth. These accomplishments are seen as evidence that the baby now distinguishes object from action. However, it may be that for a while he only distinguishes doll from the act of searching, rattle from the act of shaking, and so forth: he may not distinguish *all* objects from *all* actions for some time. It should be possible to determine what generalizations the child can make from his initial discovery, but this has not been done. Yet, until the same criteria are applied to the description of both linguistic and nonlinguistic achievements, it will require an act of faith to believe that the linguistic categories sit so readily upon a cognitive framework that provides just the right groupings and distinctions (see Chapter 8).

Underlying Structure

Given this methodological uncertainty, it is worth examining a somewhat different approach (Bloom, 1970). On Bloom's account, the child's early sentences are best represented as having complex deep structures in which grammatical relations are depicted in abstract configurations, the way these relations are depicted in transformational grammars for adults. She began, as did Brown, with the observation that children encode meanings by word order. In particular, she considered the child who says the same thing in two different contexts, when the word order is appropriate for both contexts. Kathryn, one of the children studied by Bloom, said *Mommy sock* on two occasions: once when Kathryn's mother was putting Kathryn's sock on Kathryn, and once when Kathryn found her mother's stocking. The speech contexts suggested quite different interpretations of the superficially identical utterances.

Another example from Kathryn illustrates the problem: on one occasion Kathryn was searching for a pocket in her mother's apron; she failed to find one and said:

No pocket

On another occasion she was pushing away a piece of worn soap in the bathtub, determined to be washed instead with a new pink bar, and she said:

No dirty soap

In each case the meaning was clear to the listener. In the first case, *no* denied the existence of *pocket,* but Kathryn was certainly not denying the existence of the soap in the second case. Instead, she was *rejecting* it, and the relationship of *no* to *dirty soap* therefore seems to be of a fundamentally different kind. Various kinds of ambiguity can occur in speech, and a grammar must represent all of the alternative meanings. It is obvious that pivot grammar fails in this respect, as it would describe both utterances the same way, with *no* as a first-position pivot:

$pivot_1$ + open

Bloom proposes instead that the utterances should be described as having

two distinct deep structures that formally define the underlying relationships, a solution similar to that used for:

Visiting relatives can be boring.

Remember that the deep structure contains information that is not explicit
in the surface structure. Transformations change the order and delete elements to arrive at the surface form. To explain the surface form of the
child's utterances, Bloom suggests a deletion transformation that
operates on the deep structure to delete all but two major constituents.
For example, a child may be incapable of producing *Daddy pat dog,* but
might produce in sequence:

Daddy pat
Pat dog
Daddy dog

These so-called "replacement sequences," noticed by both Braine
(1963a) and Bloom (1970), seem convincing evidence that some kind of
"length constraint" is preventing the child from saying all that he knows
at one time.

Bloom's approach introduces another level of representation, and
this has some advantages over the pivot-grammar account, for the pivot
approach would fail to represent the alternative readings of the sentences.
On the other hand, Braine demonstrated that the rules of pivot grammar
were within the learning capabilities of the young child, whereas deletion
transformations present a dilemma in this respect. The transformations
provide a useful way to describe formally the relation between the deep
structure and the surface structure of superficially identical sentences.
However, if they are taken literally as psychologically real rules for the
child, one is left with the rather absurd picture of development consisting
of the deletion of deletion rules! Students of development are not comfort-
able with the idea of the child losing knowledge as he grows older!

Other arguments have been raised against attributing knowledge of
grammatical roles such as subject and object to the young child. Subjects
are not synonymous with particular semantic roles. For example, the first
noun in each of the following sentences is the subject, though the semantic role varies considerably as shown in the parentheses:

John opened the door.   (agent)
The door opened.   (object involved)
The key opened the door   (instrument)
John wants milk.   (person affected)

The linguistic definition of subject derives from the deep structure: the
subject is the noun phrase at the same level in the tree configuration as the
whole verb phrase, directly under the sentence node.

Many linguists argue that we need the concept of subject because certain grammatical rules operate on formal relations rather than semantic ones; the passive transformation is one such case. The passive involves changing the order of underlying subject and object, not of agent or instrument or the like. Just as we see a certain economy in the child's learning to group disparate entities together to form a class of agent for his simple rules of word order, there is a similar saving in grouping together distinct semantic concepts into a formal role like subject for the purposes of certain higher-order rules.

It has been proposed that the child has notions like subject from the start, perhaps as part of the conceptual apparatus he brings to the language acquisition process (McNeill, 1970a, see also Chapter 7). If so, it is not necessary to account for his learning them. Alternatively, the acquisition of grammatical roles is seen as a relatively late achievement, if it occurs at all, with the roles arising from initially semantic concepts (Bowerman, 1973b; Schlesinger, 1974). There is every reason to suppose that young children begin with a restricted notion of agent, perhaps a concept similar to "animate," since sentences with inanimate agents like *cup hit* or *tractor go* are very rare (Bowerman, 1973b). This same observation renders it unlikely that the child at an early stage has the relatively abstract grammatical notion of subject. An illustration may help demonstrate how children could learn rules that operate on a category narrower than the one adults use.

Bowerman (1973b) gives an example from Russian, a language that relies extensively on inflections rather than word order to identify grammatical roles of subject and object. A child initially used no inflections at all to mark the accusative (direct object) case; then he began to use the correct inflection only on direct objects of verbs of movement, like *bring* and *throw*. It was some time before he extended his use of the inflection to the direct objects of verbs like *read* or *draw*. So he had a much more restricted semantic notion of direct object, much as English-speaking children seem to have a narrower idea of subject at first. Observations like these are rare in the literature, possibly because investigators up until a few years ago had a more formal view of grammar, and were thus not motivated to search their records for evidence that later rules like passives or negation might initially apply in a restricted semantic domain (but see Maratsos, 1977).

We agree with Bowerman that much of the crucial evidence in favor of the grammatical roles of subject and object is missing in early child speech. Children do not typically produce passives, for example, until later in development; nor do they understand them until age four or five, and even then their comprehension may not be free of semantic considerations (Maratsos, 1977). It is therefore not terribly convincing to claim that the grammar of a two- or three-year-old child can be more economically described in formal terms.

Nevertheless, the most widely accepted current view in linguistics requires abstract grammatical relations for adult rules. If we do not allow that the young child has them from the beginning of speech, we have to specify how and when he makes the transition from a simpler grammar. If, on the other hand, we credit the young child with this knowledge, we are presented with a problem of unsuspected proportions in accounting for how he discovers abstract deep structures in the first place. Some theorists have therefore concluded that such knowledge must be innate (see Chapter 7).

The Pattern of Development

What can we then conclude about the child's early sentences? One possible view of grammatical development is that it proceeds along the same general lines as our attempts to formulate the rules for forming passive sentences. The child might begin with rules based on how to combine and order individual words. After a certain point the sheer number of such rules becomes burdensome and they fail to provide him with the apparatus to express all that he wants to say. Perhaps then the rules are reorganized to operate at the level of the semantic roles that the words play, and the child can now generate new sentences on this basis. Such a semantically-based grammar would become cumbersome only later, when the child is using rules like those involved in making passive sentences, whose formulation typically requires more abstract structural knowledge. At this stage the new system might have to be abandoned in favor of a standard transformational grammar (see Chapter 4).

Another possibility is that there are marked individual differences in this early period of language acquisition. All children may not begin with very specific formulas for generating sentences and proceed to increasingly abstract rules. Some may enter at a point further along the continuum, with combination rules based on semantic or grammatical relations.

Bloom, Lightbown, and Hood (1975) claim that of the four children they studied, two showed what they called a pivotal approach to sentence construction, the other two a categorical approach. The pivotal approach coincides with the beginning of our continuum; the children began with certain words in fixed sentence position (for example, *more X, see X*) so that their rules operated at the level of individual lexical items with fixed meaning. In the categorical approach, on the other hand, the children formed rules for expressing certain semantic relations that were independent of particular words. For example, *Mommy* might be an agent on one occasion, patient on another, possessor on yet a third, and the word would be positioned in the sentence according to its semantic role.

What we presently lack is any evidence as to whether these strategies relate to the child's level of cognitive development at the beginning of sentence-making,, or to the quality of the language he has heard, or any other potential influences. However, the alternative strategies observed by Bloom et al. had implications for later aspects of the children's speech, most notably the relative predominance of nouns and pronouns. The two subjects who followed the pivotal strategy tended to use more pronouns, while the categorical strategists used very few pronouns and a wider variety of nouns. Since later work has cast doubt on the generality of this latter finding (Bowerman, 1976), it remains uncertain whether early sentence construction strategies are important for the language learning process as a whole.

SHADES OF MEANING

It is difficult to discover what motivation there is for the next step the child takes in language learning. If he can express the major relational meanings with the use of two words and word order, and they have the potential for combining into more complex meaning, what more does the child need? We are in fact asking: What more does a human language require? What is presently missing are all the modulations of meaning, the fine tunings, which add immensely to the subtlety of what we can express.

Consider the shades of meaning in the following sentences:

> He played.
> He's playing.
> He was playing.
> He has played.
> He had played.
> He will play.
> He will have played.

It is important not to become too ethnocentric, however, for not all languages make these distinctions explicitly, and some languages make distinctions that English does not. One example is the future tense in Russian, where there are different inflections for habitual versus single actions. In the English present tense, we can make that distinction explicit—for example, *he sings in the bath* versus *he is singing in the bath*—but in the future we have only one form: *he will sing in the bath*. There are numerous examples of different languages splitting up reality in different ways, which led to the famous hypothesis by Benjamin Whorf (1956) that the form of one's language must affect the way one sees the world. So if a language has no mechanism for expressing the past tense, Whorf argued, the speaker's thought will be different from what it would be in a language with a past tense. This hypothesis is not so popular now, for it is recognized that people can express meanings in different ways than by inflections: they can set up a prior context, use content words with different connotations, or use elaborate qualifying clauses. In addition, it is clear that we are capable of making thousands of subtle distinctions that never find expression in our particular language, but we can nevertheless appreciate them in languages that make them explicit:

> When we observe an object of the type that we call a "stone" moving through space towards the earth, we involuntarily analyse the phenomenon into two concrete notions, that of a stone and that of an act of falling, and, relating these two notions to each other by certain formal methods proper to English, we declare that "the stone falls." We assume, naively enough, that this is about the only analysis that can be properly made. [However], in German and in French we are compelled to assign "stone" to a gender category . . . in Chippewa we cannot express ourselves without bringing in the apparently irrelevant fact that a stone is an inanimate object. If we find gender beside the point, the Russians may wonder why we consider it necessary to specify in every case whether a stone, or any other object for that matter, is conceived in a definite or an indefinite manner, why the difference between "the stone" and "a stone" matters. "Stone falls" is good enough for Lenin, as it was good enough for Cicero. And if we find barbarous the neglect of the distinction as to definiteness, the Kwakiutl Indian of British Columbia may sympathize with us but wonder why we do not go a step further and indicate in some way whether the stone is visible or invisible to the speaker at the moment of speaking, and whether it is nearest to the speaker, the person addressed, or some third party. "That would no doubt sound fine in Kwakiutl, but we are too busy!" . . . The Chinese get on with a minimum of explicit formal statement and content themselves with a frugal "stone fall." (Sapir, 1949, p. 157)

In discussing the child's acquisition of meaning modulation, then, it stands to reason that we shall be more concerned with English than with universals, because different languages encode these meanings in such disparate ways.

Splitting up the Stream of Speech

Before the child can learn to produce correctly the grammatical morphemes such as tenses and noun inflections, he must be able to distinguish them in the speech of others. We have mentioned that the elements having grammatical functions are normally unstressed in speech, and are not singled out for emphatic stress the way content words are. For example, content words can be said in reply to the following questions, usually called *wh*-questions:

Who did you say came?	The milkman
Which will you have, white or black?	Black
Where were you going?	Outside

When do you leave?   Saturday
What has he done?   Fallen

Few questions can be appropriately answered by grammatical elements such as *the, in,* or *to.* And these are at least words. There is no question in English that calls for an isolated inflection in reply: *-ed, -ing, -er, -s.* This presents something of a problem for the child: how does he learn to distinguish the inflections from the words attached to them? He must do this if he is to apply the inflections productively to new words he has never heard inflected. The problem is one of segmentation, and it affects content words too, a fact that was exploited in the old song "Doeseatoats and Mareseatoats." Contrary to popular opinion, there are no silences between spoken words: speech is a continuous stream. The child's dilemma is more complex than that a reader faces in trying to solve a word puzzle containing "buried" words to spot, for in that case the patterns are already familiar and it is only necessary to distinguish them from the background noise. How does the child learn the familiar patterns in the first place? Fortunately, he is not surrounded by adults speaking in long, continuous monologues, since adults speak to children simply and repetively (see Chapter 7). In addition, when adults introduce a new word, they often embed it in a sequence with only slight changes in the accompanying words. The variety of forms of English sentences perhaps serves at first as a shifting background against which the important word is displayed. We have many transcripts of adults speaking to children in the following way:

Look at that *dog.*
What a nice *dog!*
See the *dog's* eyes?
Is the *dog* looking at you?

Exposed to several hundred examples, probably considerably fewer, the child will now recognize *dog* in almost any verbal context. Although the acoustic form is not identical, the many instances form a familiar pattern when cued by the real-world referent. In the absence of the referent, pattern recognition would take much longer, for the child would not know which changes in stress or acoustic pattern were incidental and which signaled a change in meaning. Presumably, when the child knows the meaning of the rest of the sentence, a new word can be learned on a single hearing because it can be distinguished from the familiar background.

Brown, Cazden, and Bellugi (1969) present an invented set of expressions a child might hear:

mybook, yourbook
mybath, yourbath
myballoon, yourballoon

Having heard only these expressions, the child would be justified in segmenting them as follows:

myb, yourb, ook
myb, yourb, ath
myb, yourb, alloon.

He might then, on the basis of this evidence, produce *myb desk* or *yourb cup* or *her alloon*. Luckily, a child would be unlikely to hear such a restricted subset of possibilities; he would soon hear disconfirming cases such as *my coat* or *your apple*.

Segmentation errors do occur in child speech, and it is not clear how they become established and when they are given up. Adam, one of the children studied by Brown, sounded very correct when he said, "it's going," "it's playing," "it's gone," "it's blue." He gave himself away, however, when he produced, "it's went," "it's played," and "it's was going"! Adam simply used *it's* instead of *it* in initial sentence position. The error persisted for several months, probably because it was accidentally right so much of the time and confirmed in much of the speech Adam heard.

One theory about autistic children is that they never segment speech into its component units, and thus they have no basis for making novel constructions. (see Chapter 9). It is almost incomprehensible to imagine a world in which each utterance sounds like an impossibly long new word: there would be no patterns to be connected with real-world events. Is it any wonder autistic children latch onto advertising jingles as the one predictable sound in their world?

One error that always captures the attention of parents and teachers is the error of overgeneralization: a rule is learned, then overgeneralized to new instances where it is inappropriate. Thus a new form is made regular or rule-governed when it should not be. Common errors are extension of the plural *s* to irregular nouns, as in *foots* or *sheeps,* or extension of the regular past tense to irregular verbs, as in *comed, bringed, falled,* or even *falleded!* A colleague's child was ploughing valiantly through a huge dish of oatmeal and said victoriously, "It's getting middle-sizeder"! This is the opposite of the segmentation error: in overgeneralizations the morpheme has been correctly segmented but erroneously extended to irregular cases. Two requirements must be met in the learning of morphemes: they must be discriminated as units with the power of combination with new elements, and the child must learn idiosyncratic exceptions to those rules of combination.

A Study of Morpheme Acquisition

In the second half of his important book on the first stages of language development, Brown (1973) reports the findings of a comprehensive study of the English-speaking child's acquisition of grammatical morphemes. Many people had reported partial findings before, but the mosaic was fractured and incomplete, of little interest to developmental psychology as a whole. Brown's in-depth study revealed substantial uniformity among three children in the learning of these fine details of language. He concluded that children do not randomly add bits and pieces of tenses, noun endings, and articles, eventually piecing together the whole pattern of adult English; instead, they acquire these morphemes in a relatively fixed order.

In the early 1960s Brown and his research group had undertaken a longitudinal study of three children with the pseudonyms Adam, Eve, and Sarah. The study extended over a period of years from the time the children were about two years old. Every two weeks or less, a two-hour transcript was prepared from tapes of the children's interactions with their mothers. Brown selected for study fourteen of the grammatical morphemes that occur frequently in the speech of older children but are absent from the speech of young children. These fourteen morphemes also share another property: obligatory contexts can be identified, where the morphemes would be required in adult speech, as in the following:

> Bring me two shoe. (plural "s" missing)
> Yesterday he play with me. (past tense missing)
> Put clothes washing machine. ("in" missing)

Of course, since it is so easy in many circumstances to fill in the missing element, it is hard to argue that the child is more successful in communicating with the morphemes than without: if he is not misunderstood to begin with, why does he progress? This complex issue will be addressed in Chapter 8.

The Fourteen Morphemes

The fourteen morphemes Brown selected to study were as follows:

In and on. The prepositions *in* and *on* occur early in child speech, are fairly clear in meaning, and provide a nice contrast to each other: *in* is used with containers and *on* with flat surfaces. In their play with blocks and trucks and boxes, young children have rich occasions to use these words.

Possessive s.   The possessive ending *s*, as in *Daddy's chair*. Again, possession seems to be very important to the young child, possibly as an extension of understanding his own body and its properties and limits. Children at this age delight in pointing out the ears and eyes and noses on other people and toys. In English there is no distinction linguistically between alienable and inalienable possession, for example, between *my book* and *my nose,* though clearly one can be parted more easily from one's book. A friend of ours with a communal philosophy was most upset by his two-year-old daughter's possessiveness toward objects, and he was trying with diminishing patience to distinguish the two uses: *my* in the sense of inalienable, attached to me, and *my* in the sense of "the one I happen to be using." She would listen carefully as he explained, "That's *your* nose, but this is not *your* scarf; it's just thé one you happen to be wearing." We personally tend to think the roots of possessiveness go deeper than the lack of a linguistic distinction, and we were thus delighted when at a meal together, the possessive daughter hid the "cider she happened to be drinking" in the sideboard to avoid sharing it!

Plural s. The plural-*s* ending is very frequent in English and the child seems to mark the distinction between one and many quite early.

A and the. The articles *a* and *the* are treated together by Brown, and Maratsos (1976) provides a fascinating analysis of the complexities of their use in English, especially as it relates to egocentrism. Piaget characterized the young child as egocentric, that is, unable to take the other's point of view. Yet use of the articles requires awareness of the listener's state of knowledge. Imagine someone asking you out of the blue, "Have you seen the film?" You would be justified in retorting "*which* film?" unless it had been otherwise specified. *The* is used in circumstances where both listener and speaker know the referent, as when one person asks another, at home, "Will you walk the dog?" (It would be peculiar indeed to ask, "Will you walk a dog?") *A*, in contrast, is used when the speaker but not the listener knows the referent, as in: "Did you see a blue Volkswagen go past?" or in circumstances where the referent is unspecified, for example: "Pass me a pencil" (out of a bunch of pencils). Clearly, then, the child who gains mastery over the English article system is fairly sophisticated in his appreciation of his listener's needs. And articles are mastered surprisingly early.

Past tense (regular and irregular). The past tense marking -*ed* has already been mentioned in connection with overgeneralization to words such as *breaked.* Brown traces its development as well as that of irregular past tenses such as *broke, fell,* and *threw.* Use of the simple past tense precedes by several years the occurrence of more complex past tenses, as in:

I have been traveling.
I have eaten.

and there is evidence from Cromer (1974a) that the delay is due not so much to the grammatical complexity of these forms as to the complexity of the ideas being expressed, since such tenses presuppose a sophisticated awareness of time and the completion of activity.

Third person regular and irregular. Unlike French, which has only one present tense, English has two: the present progressive (see next section) and the present that refers to habitual activity, as in: *he works, I play golf, they often swim.* Notice that in English the verb is uninflected except for the third person singular, which requires an *s* on the verb. Probably because the inflected form is the exception, we have not heard many errors of overgeneralization to *I goes* or *they likes,* for example. The inflection is only required for regular verbs: in the case of irregular verbs, such as *have* and *do,* the third person verb form is, for example, *has* and *does.* We have heard *doos* from children on occasion, but *haves* is hard to pronounce. Thus, the set of rules for the present habitual is complex and learning it is quite an accomplishment.

Present progressive. The progressive tense is that used for the immediate present: *I am driving, they are watching.* Most of the child's activity is of this type. At first the child does not use the auxiliary verb, but produces sentences like *I baking, he riding.*

Be auxiliary (contractible and uncontractible). To complete the analysis of the progressive tense in English, Brown studied the acquisition of the auxiliary *be,* which is obligatory with the *-ing* ending. The form of *be* varies with the case and number of the subject as well as with tense. Note the variations: I *am* swimming, you *are* swimming, he *is* swimming, they *are* swimming, I *was* swimming, and so forth. Brown distinguished the contractible forms, for example:

I am cooking → I'm cooking

He is drinking → He's drinking

from the uncontractible forms, which are always syllabic:

The horse is winning.
They were cheering.

Be copula (contractible and uncontractible). The last of the fourteen grammatical morphemes is *be* used as a main verb called the *copula,* instead of as part of another verb. Some examples are:

This is hot.
He's a clown.
She was happy.

Again, Brown considered contractible and uncontractible forms.

Parts of speech

To use the grammatical morphemes properly and productively, that is, to use them with new words, the child must distinguish nouns and verbs. It is not clear that the very young child respects the distinction between nouns and verbs because they occur in many of the same contexts: *more swim, more lunch,* etc. In adding grammatical morphemes though, the child cannot inflect nouns for past tense, or place articles before verbs, so there are grounds for saying he knows the distinction between the major parts of speech.

There are instances in child speech of a failure to recognize the distinction between mass nouns, like *snow,* that cannot take an indefinite article or a cardinal number, and count nouns, such as *chair.* For example, children will occasionally say *a water* or *a spaghetti.* However, the children Brown studied showed an awareness early of the distinction between process verbs, like *hit, run,* or *read,* and verbs that describe a person's state of mind, such as *want, believe,* or *know.* In English we can use the progressive with process verbs but not with state verbs; we cannot say *I am believing* or *I am knowing.* Although it would seem a likely overgeneralization, the child does not make that error and respects the distinction apparently as soon as he uses the progressive inflection.

In an ingenious experiment with nursery school children, Brown (1957) demonstrated that three-year-olds can guess the meaning of a new word by using information that suggests what part of speech it is. Most verbs the young child encounters are actions (*kick, eat*), most count nouns are objects (*cup, dog*), and most mass nouns are substances of indeterminate form (*rain, soup, porridge*). Brown addressed the question: given a brand new word such as *sib* or *lek* used in a sentence, could a child guess what it means from grammatical cues? He made up pictures with three unknowns: a person using a strange instrument to perform a strange action on a strange substance; for example, a person using a tool to knead a spaghetti-type substance. He then showed the child each picture, saying either:

> Here's a picture of *a sib*. (count noun)

or

> Here's a picture of *sibbing*. (verb)

or

> Here's a picture of *some sib*. (mass noun)

Brown then presented the child with three different pictures, each containing one of the unknowns—the tool, the action, or the substance—and asked the child to point to the picture of *a sib/sibbing/some sib,* depending on the initial sentence. Three- and four-year-olds proved capable of picking out the correct picture on the basis of the grammatical cue alone. Thus, children not only respect the distinction in their own speech but can use the different grammatical contexts to select the probable referents of new words. Of course, not all nouns and verbs can be pointed out— What about *idea* or *liberty* or *believed?*—But abstract words are not often found in the preschool child's speech. How children learn these abstract nouns and verbs is very much unknown.

Order of Acquisition

Brown calculated how frequently children used the fourteen grammatical morphemes in contexts where they were obligatory. In the following sample, the article is produced only 60 percent of the times it is required:

> I see dog.
> See the dog?
> Pick cup up.
> Give me a cup.
> I want the book.

It is not surprising, when one considers the range of circumstances in which the rules have to be applied, that the percentage of correctly used morphemes increases slowly. A morpheme that has been absent from a child's speech is not suddenly supplied wherever it is needed; instead, there are frequently several sentences in a row in which the morpheme waxes and wanes for no clear reason:

> Peter: Which one is that?
> Alex (30 months): Dat's greem. [an orange car]
> Peter: O.K.
> Alex: Dat greem.
> Mother: No, that's orange.
> Alex: Dat's greem.
> Peter: Is it?
> Alex: Dat greem.
> Peter: It is, is it?
> Alex: Dat's greem.
> Peter: I think that's the orange one.
> Mother: It's orange. There's the green one.
> Alex: Dat's greem.
> Mother: Yes.
> Alex: Dat's greem.
> Mother: Green.
> Alex: Dat's greem too.
> Mother: No, that's the blue one.

Eventually, this fluctuation disappears and the child consistently supplies the morpheme. Brown (1973) set the criterion for acquisition of a morpheme at 90 percent correct usage for two successive two-hour transcripts. Once a child reached this degree of mastery there was rarely a regression.

Then came the surprising discovery. The first morpheme Adam acquired was the present progressive; next were the prepositions *in* and *on* and the plural. For Eve, the first morphemes were the present progressive, *in, on,* and the plural. For Sarah, the plural came first, then *in, on,* and the progressive. For all three children, the contractible auxiliary was the last to be acquired. Remember that these were three unacquainted children from different backgrounds. When Brown compared the order of acquisiton of the fourteen morphemes, defined in terms of the time to reach the 90 percent criterion, he found substantial agreement. Agreement was assessed by a correlation coefficient, a mathematical formula that ranges from 0 if there is no agreement to + 1.0 if two orders are identical. Between Adam's and Eve's orders of acquisition of the morphemes the correlation was 0.86; between Adam's and Sarah's it was 0.88; between Sarah's and Eve's it was 0.87. A cross-sectional study of the same morphemes was carried out on twenty-one English-speaking children, and the order of acquisition was confirmed in this wider group of children (de Villiers and de Villiers, 1973b).

Explaining the Order

Why did the children acquire the fourteen morphemes in essentially the same order? Presumably because they found the present progressive easier than the past tense, and so forth. But that has no explanatory value unless we provide independent evidence that the present progressive entails simpler concepts or less complex rules than the past tense.

Brown (1973) provides two independent rankings of complexity for the fourteen morphemes. The first is based on a linguistic treatment by Jacobs and Rosenbaum (1968) and measures the number of transformations required in the derivation of each morpheme. Transformations, remember, are the rules that change the deep structure into the surface structure, and the number of transformations involved for a particular form can be considered an index of how abstract the deep structure is, in other words, how remote it is from the surface structure. If the linguistic description has psychological reality, the child might be expected to have difficulty acquiring a morpheme whose surface structure is distantly related to its deep structure, that is, involves more transformations.

Brown obtained a ranking of the morphemes in terms of the number of transformations they involved, and compared this order with the order of acquisition by the children. There was a very good fit between the two orders: the correlation coefficient was 0.86. However, it is not strictly legitimate to say that a morpheme involving two transformations, say *a* and *b,* is more complex than one that involves only transformation *c. a* and *b* may be very simple rules, and *c* very complex. A better way would be to look at morphemes that share transformations in common: so compare *a* plus *b* with *a* alone. A number of such predictions could be made with the fourteen morphemes, and they were all confirmed in the acquisition order: a morpheme involving two transformations was acquired later than a morpheme requiring only one of the two transformations.

The second index of complexity came from considering the meanings expressed by each morpheme. As noted earlier, to use the copula *be* correctly one must take into account the person of the subject (either *am, are,* or *is*), the number (*is* or *are*), and whether the topic is in the past or present (*is* or *was*). For another morpheme, the past tense ending *-ed* on a verb such as *dropped,* it is irrelevant whether the subject is *you* or *I* or *he,* plural or singular. The form remains the same. The copula and past tense therefore both require a specification of "earlierness," but the correct use of the copula requires more information to be taken into account. This would provide a prediction, based on cumulative semantic complexity, that the past tense should be mastered before the copula. This and all other such predictions were confirmed by the acquisition order.

Syntax or Semantics?

We have here two remarkably good independent predictors of what makes a morpheme difficult for children to learn: the transformational complexity and the complexity of the meaning. Unfortunately, they make overlapping predictions because many of the grammatical aspects are also aspects of meaning: tense and person, for example. The difficulty of a form will be a conglomerate of both meaning variables and grammatical complexity and it is hard to distinguish their relative contributions.

Both the grammatical and the semantic-conceptual accounts attempt to describe the conditions that make a morpheme obligatory in speech, and the child must learn to recognize those contexts. But if the child does not supply a morpheme, does it mean that he does not know the meaning that it carries? We doubt that, for the same reason some people doubt Whorf's hypothesis: it is not necessarily the case that the child does not understand pastness before he expresses it fully. What the child must learn is which of the many possible conceptual distinctions remain implicit, and which are expressed by grammatical forms. Similarly, the child has to learn which sound distinctions function as phonemes in his language, as discussed in the previous chapter.

Bilingual Children

One way of separating the effects of grammatical and semantic complexity is to study children who learn two languages at once, and to identify forms that have the same meaning in the two languages but differing grammatical complexity. Slobin (1973) provides the example of two children who were learning both Hungarian and Serbo-Croatian. Certain meanings carried in English by the prepositions *into, onto,* and *out of* are carried in Hungarian by inflections on the noun. In Serbo-Croatian, they require not only an inflection on the noun but also a preposition, so their form is more complex but their meaning is equivalent. The two children both used the inflections in Hungarian before they used the equivalent forms in Serbo-Croatian, showing that they knew the concepts before the means of expression in the latter language. Unfortunately, such cases of perfect bilingualism are quite rare and it would be impractical to rely on this method alone for answering questions about the psychological complexity of linguistic forms. People who learn English as a second language do not show the same invariant order of morpheme acquisition as children (Hakuta, 1974; Dulay and Burt, 1974). Why they do not is uncertain. There is controversy, for example, about the extent to which one's first language influences the learning of one's second language. Dulay and Burt believe the influence is minimal; Hakuta (1974) and Selinker, Swain and Dumas (1975) report cases in which the first language interfered with the learning of the second. A general possibility is that if the first language makes a distinction that the second does not, it will be relatively easy to learn that grammatical form in the second. An example might be learning that the single present tense in French is used for both the English present tenses. But if the new language makes distinctions that the first language does not, it will be harder to remember to mark them in the new language. In the case of the Russian future, even though we can appreciate the distinction between habitual versus discrete actions, we are not used to making it explicit in the future tense. Uguisu, a child studied by Hakuta (1974, 1975, 1976), until age five knew only Japanese, which does not use plural markings. Her mastery of the plural and of number agreement in English was correspondingly delayed relative to the grammatical morphemes, such as tense, that are expressed in Japanese. Such interference may, however, be a small factor in the initial stages of mastery of the new language, and may depend on the extent of independence of the two languages in use.

SUMMARY

Sentences in adult language have an abstract underlying structure that formally defines the basic grammatical relations. Rules for sentence formation operate at the level of these grammatical relations. Children, however, learn rules of more limited scope that combine semantic relations such as agent, patient, possessor, and locative. The difficulty arises in deciding just how broad these semantic categories are for the child.

Having acquired rules for expressing simple two- or three-term propositions, the child proceeds by adding the subtler shades of meaning signaled by grammatical morphemes. A remarkable degree of invariance exists in the order in which English-speaking children add these elements to their speech. This order cannot be definitively explained, however, because the grammatical and semantic descriptions of the morphemes are far from complete. Nevertheless, the stable ordering of these morphemes in the normal acquisition of English as a first language provides a standard of comparison for determining whether the pattern of acquisition is similar or deviant in people learning English as a second language or in abnormal populations (see Chapter 9).

4

Later
Grammar

PHRASE STRUCTURE

Whereas the two-year-old child uses very simple sentences consisting of single nouns and verbs, the slightly older child expands these constituents. The single noun gives way to noun phrases serving the same grammatical roles but expressing much richer meanings. The two-year-old may talk of *dog,* but the three- or four-year-old will have expanded this to *that big dog* or *Mrs. Brown's dog* or *the dog with the wiggly tail.* In similar fashion, the single verbs become expanded not just by the addition of the inflections discussed in the last chapter, but also by the rapid growth of the auxiliary verb system: from *play* to *played* to *will play* and *will have played.* By this means a much richer variety of ideas can be expressed and the burden of interpretation for the listener is greatly relieved.

Noun Phrases

The simple sentences children produce can be divided into two types: those with a main verb between two nouns and those with a copula between two nouns, for example:

> The dog ate the candy.

versus

> The puppy is a pest.

So the noun phrases children use can serve four distinct roles: as subject or object of the first type of sentence, and as subject or predicate nominative of the second type. Interestingly, for the children studied by Brown and his colleagues, the noun phrases playing these four roles were at first quite distinct. The subject of copular sentences was often the pronoun *it* or *that,* as in:

That a car.

But the object of copular sentences was never a pronoun. The subject of sentences with main verbs was almost always an animate noun, the object an inanimate noun, as in:

Man drive truck.

Furthermore, noun phrases in object position were frequently more elaborate than noun phrases in subject position, as if the children were learning to express complexity at the ends of sentences first. Now this may not seem surprising until one realizes what a restriction it imposes on the meanings that can be expressed. Imagine if, as adults, we could only express a complex referent like "the woman who came to dinner last night" if that phrase happened to be the object of our sentence. Obviously, we can use the same noun phrase in any sentence role, but children apparently cannot, at least at first. With time, the noun phrases in the different sentence roles become increasingly alike and therefore interchangeable (Brown, Cazden, and Bellugi, 1969).

Children at an early age demonstrate their recognition that noun phrases can substitute for pronouns and other items. For example, *wh*-questions replace a sentence constituent with a *wh*-word: *what* and *who* replace noun phrases; *what do* replaces verb phrases; *when, how,* and *where* replace adverbs of time, manner, and location. The child who answers these questions appropriately demonstrates his mastery of sentence constituents. Of course, the very first questions he answers, such as "What's that?", are probably unanalyzed routines to the child, but the answers to later questions reveal his understanding of noun phrases and their roles:

What is that on your head?	My hat.
What are you looking for?	The blue book.
Who is coming on your birthday?	Grandma Jones.

It is frequently noticed, however, that young children have some trouble expressing a complex noun phrase in a spontaneous sentence. At a particular stage they often repeat themselves several times, alternately expressing separate parts of the sentence. It is as if there were a length limit that prohibits them from expressing it all at once:

See dat?
Dat big.
Big red one.
Get dat.

They only gradually incorporate the complex noun phrases into a single utterance.

Verb Phrases

Among the earliest verb expansions learned by the child are the inflections for the third person, simple past tense, and progressive endings. Other expansions that are acquired early include the concatenatives *wanna, gonna,* and *hafta.* The first true auxiliaries to appear are the negative ones, *don't, can't,* and *won't* (a fact that won't surprise any parents), but they seem to be mere variations of the word *not.* For instance, the positive forms *do, can,* and *will* only appear later, and the child at the early stage produces no variants like *doesn't* or *didn't.* The full auxiliary system of English blossoms forth shortly after this period, around age four (or MLU 3.5). There are some aspects of verb modulation that the child takes considerably more time to master, in particular the hypothetical markings, such as *would* and *might,* and the perfective forms with *have.* As mentioned earlier, these seem to await the child's conceptual development rather than his grammar.

Children make surprisingly few errors with verb phrases; for example, they rarely produce imperative sentences with auxiliaries or inflections that are out of place. Adam produced *please read* but not *please reading* or *please will read.* At the same time, Adam's verb system was exclusive in that only one verb marking would appear at one time. He did not produce forms like *he wanna readed* or *I will reading,* but neither did he produce those verb combinations that are permissible in adult grammar, such as *he wanted to eat* or *I was reading* (Brown et al., 1969). Again, it appears as though there is a restriction on the complexity the child can express at any one time.

Some *wh*-questions allow a verb phrase in reply, and discourse provides evidence that the child can isolate that constituent appropriately:

> What are you doing?   Playing the fiddle.
> What must I do?   Read.

These responses are perfectly acceptable in discourse even though they are not whole sentences; they are known as ellipses.

Adverbial Phrases

The earliest type of adverbial constituent to appear in child speech seems to express location, usually in simple prepositional phrases like *on top* or *in here.* Like noun and verb phrases, adverbials can be elaborated indefinitely to specify more exactly:

> On top of the tallest chest of drawers in the back bedroom.

(In Chapter 6 we will discuss how the child learns the needs of his listener in deciding on the degree of specificity of reference required.) Very late developments include the adverbs of time and manner, reflected again in the child's replies to questions. Ervin-Tripp (1970) showed that young children often answer *when, how,* and *why* questions erroneously, though they can deal with *what, who,* or *where* questions comparatively early. There is nothing grammatically more difficult about them, so one must assume that the underlying concepts take time and experience to develop.

There are also subtle differences within adverbial phrases of manner. One was drawn to our attention when we were playing with a two-and-a-half-year-old girl who had made a "meal" from Playdo. One of us was valiantly trying to steer the child to ask for an eating implement such as a spoon, which is relatively easy to make from Playdo compared with some things we are instructed to produce. The dialogue went as follows:

> Terry (2½): Look, a meal.
> Jill: Oh, but what are you going to eat it with?
> Terry: With my bib on.

On another occasion, a child had made Playdo spaghetti that cried out for Playdo meatballs, so we asked him:

> Jill: Oh, but what are you going to eat with it?
> Alec: A fork.

Routines

Linguists have two other sources of information about the constituent structure of adult sentences. First, they can ask adults to judge the "belongingness" of certain groups of words, to discover the natural breaks in sentences. For example, which is a more natural break:

> The thought that King Kong might appear on my balcony/terrifies me.
> The thought that King Kong might appear/ on my balcony terrifies me.

Second, if two constituent structures are possible for a single sentence, an adult will find it ambiguous, as in:

> The old men and women stay home.

Unfortunately for the child-language researcher, intuition is a rare commodity in the pre-school years, and only around third grade can children perceive phrase structure ambiguities. The child's rules must instead be discovered by analyzing transcripts of speech, but it is important that these be sufficiently long for the researcher to gain an accurate impression of the child's rules. In the early stages, children may rely heavily on other strategies for generating longer sentences, as illustrated by R. Clark (1974). Her son produced many sentences by copying whole segments from his preceding utterance, as in:

Baby Ivan have a bath, let's go see *Baby Ivan have a bath*.

or from his parents' sentences:

We're all very mucky.
I *all very mucky* too.

A child we tested had a peculiar way of answering questions addressed him by his mother, particularly when he was preoccupied with toys. Some examples:

Adult: What color's the car?
Child: It's colors a car.
Adult: What kind of car do you think that is?
Child: It's a think that is.

Though we have no direct evidence, we suspect this inappropriate strategy arose initially in answering "test" questions posed by his mother. Many parents ask children questions that are not true questions, in that the parent does not lack information but wishes to display the child's knowledge (Holzman, 1973). A common example is demanding names by asking *What's that?*, *What's this?*, *You know this one, it's a?*, *Is it a bunny rabbit?*, and so forth. The child we tested who borrowed heavily from his mother's question in answering may have been trying to get off the hook with the minimum of effort. On occasions, the response is sufficient to stop the questioning:

Adult: Is it upside-down, hm?
Child: It upaside-down.
Adult: What kind of truck is it, Billy?
Child: It's a kind of truck.

The prevalence of such phenomena has not been documented, but these examples suggest that at least some children may proceed to longer sentences by another route, and only subsequently learn the more orthodox phrase structure rules that describe adult speech.

TRANSFORMATIONS AND DEEP STRUCTURE

Linguists studying adult language have found it necessary to distinguish between the surface structure and the deep structure of sentences. Bloom

(1970) has claimed that young children's sentences also have a deep structure richer than their surface form. If the linguistic description is also correct as a psychological account, then the child must learn the transformational rules that relate deep and surface structure.

This section will more critically address the issue of the psychological reality of transformational rules in child speech. To do this we must first acquaint the reader with the history of attempts to determine the reality of transformations in adult speech, or more usually, in adult comprehension of speech.

Adult Comprehension

Psychologists in the early 1960s enthusiastically took up the model of transformational grammar proposed by Chomsky in 1957. They reasoned as follows: if to describe fully the meaning of a sentence it is important to take into account its deep structure, surely it is also necessary for a listener to get to the deep structure of a sentence he hears. Might not the steps in the linguistic derivation of the surface structure from the deep structure, namely the transformations, correspond to the mental operations the listener performs in understanding a sentence? It would mean the listener would "unpack" the transformations to arrive at the deep structure. This was an exciting step forward towards a model of psychological processes in sentence comprehension. Up until this point there had only been rather barren attempts to measure sentence complexity using variables such as length in words or the probability of certain word sequences.

Several clever experiments were performed to test the so-called derivational theory of complexity. The experimenters needed an indication of the complexity of a sentence for an adult, but since adults make rather few errors in understanding, more subtle measures had to be devised. One candidate was the time taken in transforming sentences of one type into another, for example, making questions out of statements compared with making negative questions out of statements. Another idea was to measure the space taken up in immediate memory by various sentence types (Savin and Perchonok, 1965). The hypothesis went as follows: In remembering a sentence, say:

The dog was not caught by the bear.

adults would decode it into its deep structure plus a set of transformations to derive the surface form, in this case, the passive and negative transformations. The more transformations involved in this derivation, the more transformations would have to be stored in memory, leaving less space for other items. They asked subjects to remember sentences and also a list of random words. The prediction was that the more transformations involved in the sentence, the fewer random words the subjects would have room to store and therefore recall. The sentence types they looked at included simple active affirmative declaratives:

The bear caught the dog.

negatives:

The bear didn't catch the dog.

passives:

The dog was caught by the bear.

questions:

Did the bear catch the dog?

and combinations of these, like passive questions:

Did the dog get caught by the bear?

They also looked at passive negatives and negative questions, as well as passive negative questions involving all three transformations:

Didn't the dog get caught by the bear?

Almost exactly according to the predictions, subjects remembered fewer random words in conjunction with the more transformationally complex sentences. Even more interesting, it looked as if a given transformation, say the question, always added the same increment to storage needs; that is, the *passive question* took up as much extra space compared with the *passive* as the *negative question* took up compared with the *negative*. Here surely was very strong evidence that transformational rules corresponded in some constant way to mental operations.

Unfortunately, when later experiments tried to extend the findings beyond the small set of sentences explored, the results did not turn out so well. All the sentences initially examined differed in meaning as well as transformations, so later research focused on pairs that shared the same meaning. For example, sentences involving a separation of the verb from its particle:

John called the girl up.

supposedly involve more transformations than the unseparated alternative:

John called up the girl.

When meaning and length were controlled, transformational complexity failed to predict the relative difficulty of the sentences.

Furthermore, there was a fundamental change in linguistics in 1965 that made the early experimental findings out of line with the new grammar! In Chomsky's 1957 grammar, passives, negatives, questions, and the other favorites of experimenters were derived from a common deep structure. This common deep structure was permuted by applying as options either the passive transformtion or the negative or both. The forms were therefore related. But in Chomsky's 1965 grammar, all this changed. Negatives now had a different deep structure from passives and from questions, not just a different set of transformations. There was a good reason for this change within formal linguistics—it did not stem from any psychological considerations—but it meant that the model so fervently adopted by psychologists was no longer acceptable in linguistics! The derivational theory of complexity thus fell into disrepute.

Child Speech

Why, then, in studying child speech, do we even consider the derivational theory of complexity? Brown argued that different assumptions are used in applying the theory to child language (Brown and Herrnstein, 1975). The preceding experiments were testing the hypothesis that transformations correspond in some direct way to the mental operations we perform in decoding a sentence for its meaning, that is, in processing speech once we have acquired language. Brown believes it is a different matter to propose that transformational grammar provides a sensible description of the knowledge children have to acquire in learning language. It is possible that children learn by acquiring the kinds of structures and rules proposed by the grammar, and then adults develop short cuts and alternatives for actually using and listening to speech, which complicated the testing of derivational theory in adults.

Some examples of child speech show how revealing transformational grammar has proved to be. It would be particularly nice for the theory if the child first produced sentences rather like the proposed deep structure, then acquired the transformations to produce a closer and closer approximation to the surface form that adults use. (Of course the deep structures proposed by linguists are not utterances; sentences are not given phonological form until the very last step in the derivation.) It has been claimed that one structure in child speech—the negative sentence—emerges in just this way.

Negation

Ursula Bellugi (1967) wrote her doctoral thesis on the acquisition of negation by the children Adam, Eve, and Sarah. It is hard to believe that Adam did not know her interest was in negation when one reads this delightful dialogue in the preface to her thesis:

(Adam had just claimed he had a watch, but he has never in fact had one and can't tell time.)
Ursula: I thought you said you had a watch.
Adam: I *do* have one (with offended dignity). What do you think I am, [a no boy] with no watch?
Ursula: A what boy?
Adam (very clearly): *A no boy with no watch.*

At that time the model of negation in transformational grammar proposed that negatives had a separate deep structure that included a negative "marker." At a certain point in the derivation of the surface form, this marker triggered certain transformational rules that inserted a negative morpheme adjacent to the verb. This morpheme then had consequences for the morphology and phonology of the verb at the final step in the process, for example, *do* plus *not* became *don't.*

The speech of Adam, Eve, and Sarah, tended to mirror these steps in the linguistic derivation. Many of the earliest sentences they produced consisted of a simple proposition preceded or followed by a negative morpheme such as *no* or *not:*

No money.
No sit there.
No Mom sharpen it.
No Fraser drink all tea.

This form, *no + proposition,* parallels the deep structure form proposed in the grammar.

The next step in the derivation of a negative involves placing the negative marker adjacent to the verb stem to be modified; and in the next period of development Bellugi found sentences like the following:

I no want envelope.
I no taste them.
Don't leave me.
I can't catch you.

Bellugi argues convincingly that the forms *don't* and *can't* were not true negative auxiliaries, since the positive forms *do* and *can* only appeared later. Instead she maintains that at this point the children had four forms of negative marking: *no, not, can't,* and *don't,* inserted in appropriate places in the sentences.

In what Bellugi calls "period C," MLU in the range 3.4 to 3.9, many different auxiliaries, both positive and negative, began to appear. At this point the rules for negation of the full verb system seem to have been mastered:

Paul can't have one.

You didn't eat supper with us.
No, I don't have a book.
I gave him some so he won't cry.

Of course, true mastery of all features of negation takes much longer, especially when indefinite forms are included. Children characteristically make errors on indefinites for many years, which is not at all surprising given the complexity of the rules for their combination. Some typical errors are:

I'm not scared of nothing.
Why can't we have no milk?
He's not doing nothing but standing still.
I don't got no brothers and sisters.

It appeared from Bellugi's observations that the stages children go through in acquiring the negative system of English run parallel to the stages of the derivation of negative sentences in transformational grammar. This was held to be strong evidence for the psychological reality of the linguistic description.

Let us examine what this claim amounts to. It is rather hard to see an alternative path the child could take; for example, it is unlikely he would master the auxiliary system before he attempted to produce negatives. Less predictable is the placement of the negative marker outside the proposition. Obviously we must exclude those utterances that are only two words long, as these confirm the hypothesis in a trivial way. More interesting would be instances in which the negative marker preceded the subject of the sentence rather than occurring between the subject and the verb. Bloom (1970) observed sentences beginning with *no,* but at first only in sentences *without* subjects. These could be interpreted as *no + proposition;* however, Bloom interpreted them instead as *subject + no + predicate,* but with the subject deleted. In sentences without subjects, then, the finding of an initial negative element is ambiguous in interpretation.

At a slightly later stage Bloom found negative utterances that included sentence subjects, and some of these had the negative marker placed initially. However, in all these instances the negative element was negating something other than the proposition to which it was attached, a form known as *anaphoric* negation. For example, the child who said:

No dirty soap.

was *not* denying that the soap was dirty, nor that it was soap. She was resisting being washed by it, in other words:

No [not that one, that's] dirty soap.

Bloom found no evidence of sentences such as:

No the sun shining.
No I see truck. (Bellugi, 1967.)

in which *no* negated a following utterance with expressed subject. If the early *no*-external sentences are generally anaphoric, then it is a mistake to say they are the forerunners of the sentences of the next stage, when the negative marker has migrated next to the verb. The *no*-external sentences could not be the prior versions of the later forms, as the two mean different things. For instance, a child in the first stage might say:

No mommy do it.

and mean

No, don't *you* do it, *mommy* do it.

This early form would not be the developmentally prior version of:

Mommy don't do it.

as it means something quite different. It is thus doubtful whether the data on negation are relevant as a test of the transformational model.

Wh-questions

In a study of *wh*-questions, Brown (1968) also held that a child's grammatical development proceeds through the acquisition of transformations. The claim was not that the child began with a form akin to the deep structure but that an intermediate step in the derivation made its appearance in child speech. The detailed studies of Adam, Eve, and Sarah reveal interesting stages in mastery of the inversion rule in questions. In forming a *yes-no* question, there is a transformational rule that permutes or inverts the order of the subject and auxiliary:

He is coming home. → Is he coming home?

However, in forming the *wh*-question, there are two steps to the process, according to transformational grammar. The *wh*-word begins in the position in the sentence that the missing constituent would occupy, for example:

Who is singing?
He is doing what?
She is going where?
They are leaving when?

These forms are known in English as *occasional* questions and are frequently used by mothers (see Chapter 7). The first transformation moves the *wh*-word to the front of the sentence:

When they are leaving?
Where she is going?

then the second transformation inverts the order of subject and auxiliary:

When are they leaving?
Where is she going?

At the same time as Adam had apparently mastered inversion in *yes-no* questions:

Are they leaving?
Is she going?

he produced uninverted *wh*-questions:

When they are leaving?
Where she is going?

yet these forms do not appear in adult speech, so he could not have been imitating them. The claim was that, although Adam knew the inversion transformation, he could not use it together with the *wh*-fronting transformation to produce correct *wh*-questions, that is, he could only apply one transformation at a time. Brown argued that the uninverted *wh*-questions reveal that Adam was learning steps that coincide with steps in the linguistic derivation of *wh*-questions from deep structure.

There are several problems with this conclusion. First, one would be most likely to hear children making "errors" of the sort:

He is going where?

at an earlier point, since these are even closer to the deep structure than the uninverted forms, and adults use them a lot when speaking to children. Yet most unobligingly for the hypothesis, children do not produce them in noticeable quantity.

Brown's argument has been weakened on two more counts. It is certainly true that many children produce *wh*-questions without inversions, often for a long period. But it is not true that adults never produce them. These forms occur all the time but they are embedded in other sentences:

Do you know *where I put it?*
Have you found out *where you can catch the bus?*
Did I tell you *what he was singing?*

It is therefore not so surprising that children hit on the idea that inversion is not required in *wh*-questions. Nevertheless, it remains to be explained why the embedded forms influence the form of the questions rather than vice versa. (But, see Hakuta [1975], for a reverse case in second-language learning.)

Furthermore, there is now evidence that conflicts with the claim that inversion in *yes-no* questions precedes inversion in *wh*-questions. First Ingram (1973) and then two students of ours, Hecht and Morse (1974), tallied the rate of inversion in the two question types in a large group of young children and found essentially no difference. The current evidence is therefore considerably less compelling than it was in 1970, when Mc-Neill concluded that children begin by speaking the underlying structure of sentences directly and their later grammatical development consists of learning transformations that coincide with the steps in the derivation.

There is, however, a different approach that makes a more plausible claim, namely, that derivationally complex forms should appear later in child speech than simpler forms. This claim is based on the appearance of fully derived constructions of more or less complexity, and does not necessarily predict that incompletely derived forms should precede the correct form. We saw in the last chapter how well this claim was borne out in predicting the order of acquisition of fourteen grammatical morphemes. It turns out to be equally good at predicting the order of appearance of certain larger constructions.

Tag Questions

Tag questions are the little requests for confirmation that British speakers in particular "tag" onto the end of declarative sentences:

> It is Saturday, isn't it?
> You're good at tennis, aren't you?
> It should arrive on time, shouldn't it?

They are particularly fascinating because they require so much grammatical sophistication. To produce a tag, the speaker has to:

1. Match the pronoun to the subject:

> *The girl* is getting wet, *isn't she?* (not: isn't he?)

2. Shorten the verb phrase to the auxiliary or the dummy form *do:*

> He *likes* apples, *doesn't* he? (not: liken't he?)

3. Negate the positive or affirm the negative:

> They *don't* like snow, *do* they? (not: don't they?)

4. Invert the auxiliary and subject:

> She can talk, *can't she?* (not: she can't?)

These steps are all necessary, though their order is not specified. But all this can be avoided easily, with little loss in communication, by using another form:

It's raining, right?

Tags can become an obsession, and Adam is not the only child to have catered to his listener's eccentric interests. Two summers ago, in early morning, we were riding in a car to Heathrow airport to return to Harvard after visiting our family in England. One of us is not known for her friendliness at predawn hours, and she was listening to a discussion between her four-year-old niece Elizabeth and her mother, Elizabeth's doting grandmother. They had just seen the sun come up as a huge red disk over the horizon, and the following dialogue ensued:

> Gran to Elizabeth: Ooh! Look at the sun peeping out through the trees! Look at his big red shiny face. Here he comes again!
> Jill: For goodness sake, no wonder children have animistic ideas about the world. Just listen to the grown-ups!
> Gran (ignoring interruption): Can you see him, Elizabeth?
> Jill: Look, at *least* don't call it a *he,* otherwise you can say anything you like.
> Elizabeth: No . . . oh! *You can't say "he's horrid, isn't it?"*

To return to our analysis of these peculiar appendages: Brown and Hanlon (1970) noticed that to form a correct tag question a series of quite explicit transformations must be made of the declarative sentence. Each of the component transformations is needed for other forms in English.

Shortening the verb phrase, called *truncation* (Tr), is required in ellipsis:

> They are playing.   Yes they are.
> I didn't know he was coming.   I told you he was.

Negation (N) is obviously used elsewhere:

> They are playing. → They aren't playing.

Inversion (Q) has also been discussed earlier:

> They are playing. → Are they playing?

Paralleling the argument made for morpheme acquisition, Brown and Hanlon maintained that tag questions should appear in child speech later than constructions involving only one or two of the component transformations. The simple active affirmative declaratives (SAAD) should come first, then forms involving only one of the transformations:

Even later should be constructions that require two of the transformations, like negative questions (NQ):

Aren't they playing?

truncated negatives (TrN):

They aren't.

and truncated questions (TrQ):

Are they?

Finally, tags (TrNQ) should appear last, as they require all three transformations:

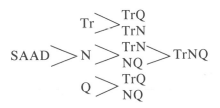

Notice that the predictions only hold for constructions that share a transformation; for instance, we cannot order N relative to TrQ, or Tr relative to NQ.

Brown and Hanlon then counted the number of times each construction appeared in the various samples of speech from Adam, Eve, and Sarah. The point of appearance was set as six occurrences of the fully formed construction in one transcript, as this was the minimum frequency in the parental speech to the children.

Their results substantially confirmed the notion that the ordering in terms of derivational complexity would predict the order of appearance. Tags were late-appearing; in fact they seemed to flourish suddenly in Adam's speech in a single session when he was four years old. In contrast, simple negatives and questions were mastered much earlier. The scheme made fifty-seven predictions for the three children, of which forty-seven were confirmed, six were not settled either way, and only four were disconfirmed by the data. This is a very robust effect and seems to be one case where the derivational complexity argument finds support.

Nevertheless, there is a caveat. Brown and Hanlon themselves discuss the possibility that frequency in parent-to-child speech is the true determinant of the acquisition order, since it makes predictions that are virtually identical to those made on the basis of derivational complexity. It proved impossible to unravel the relative contributions of parent-to-child frequency and derivational complexity for these constructions. To settle this issue will require further predictions based on derivational complexity that are in conflict with those based on frequency.

Also, it is not clear that the results discriminate between the derivational theory of complexity and an alternative model that uses a more general characterization of language knowledge. Whatever it is a child has to know to produce negative questions, whether that knowledge involves syntax, semantics, or rules of discourse, he has to know how to make questions and then something more. The problem is that the constructions vary along too many dimensions for us to be confident that the derivational theory of complexity is the only one that could capture, for example, the way the child's knowledge of negative questions builds on his previous knowledge of questions. With the possible exception of truncation, the constructions also differ in meaning or function in conversation, as well as in derivational complexity.

The ideal approach would be to investigate pairs of sentences that share a common deep structure and meaning, but in which one type is considered more derived, involving more transformations, than the second type. The less derived form should make its appearance earlier in child speech than the more derived form, according to the hypothesis. One example is provided by sentence coordination.

Coordination

In English, sentences formed with the conjunction *and* have been analyzed by transformational grammar. Sentences like:

John and Mary went to school.

or

I ate apples and bananas.

are supposed to be derived from the conjunction of two distinct propositions; in other words, the deep structure contains information that is deleted in the surface form. In the first example, the two propositions are:

John went to school and Mary went to school.

One of the two identical portions is omitted to form:

John and Mary went to school.

Likewise with:

I ate apples and I ate bananas.

The redundant elements are removed by deletion transformations. It has been claimed that these reduced coordinations appear later in children's speech than complete sentences conjoined by *and*. Some of the evidence comes from spontaneous speech (Menyuk, 1969; Limber, 1973), but the strongest evidence is from elicited imitation, in which the child apparently produces the derivationally simpler form (Slobin and Welsh, 1973):

Adult: Say "the red beads and brown beads are here."
Child: Brown beads here an' a red beads here.

But spontaneous speech data from Adam, Eve, and Sarah do not offer any evidence to suggest that full sentences precede the deleted forms. In fact, the deleted forms come into the children's speech some months before any full sentential forms. It looks as if, in this case, the data are not even in keeping with the predictions (de Villiers, Tager-Flusberg and Hakuta, 1976).

Other Constructions

Maratsos (1977) provides four more examples of sentence pairs that provide a strict test of the theory of derivational complexity.

(1) *Adjectives.* An adjectival phase such as:

the blue car

is derived in the grammar from a predicate:

The car is blue.

One would therefore expect simple sentences like:

The car is blue.
John is happy.
It is pretty.

to precede the use of adjectives as noun modifiers:

Bring the blue car.
See the happy clown.
I want the pretty block.

since the former are closer to the deep structure forms. In fact, both types occur from the beginning in child speech with no clear preference for the predicate forms at all.

(2) *Subjectless complements.* A sentence like:

John wants to go.

is supposedly derived from a form in which the subject of the complement is spelled out:

John wants John to go.

making this form parallel to similar cases where the subject is different:

John wants Bill to go.

According to the theory of derivational complexity, children should produce the full forms before the deleted forms; but in fact, the opposite is the case: the subjectless forms occur several *years* before those with specified subjects, so it is highly unlikely that they represent deleted versions. At the time children learn the forms with distinct subjects such as:

Bill asked Mary to leave.

there is no evidence that children make errors of the sort:

Bill asked Bill to leave.

in forming same-subject complements. The rule does not seem to describe development realistically.

(3) *Truncated passives*. Passives of the type:

John was pushed.

are treated in the grammar as deleted forms of the full passives:

John was pushed by someone.

Again, the deleted form appears years before the full form, so it is developmentally prior although it is derivationally more complex.

(4) *Datives*. There are two forms of the dative in English:

(a) John gave Mary a present
(b) John gave a present to Mary.

(*a*) is derived from (*b*) in transformational rules, yet children are observed to produce datives like (*a*) before they produce (*b*). Once again, the derivational complexity order is the opposite of the order of appearance in child speech.

The What? Game

A different application of the derivational theory of complexity arises in a study by Valian, Caplan, and de Sciora (1976) with children aged six to ten years. The study compared pairs of sentences that in most cases share a common deep structure but differ in derivational complexity. The construction types are shown in Table 3, where ''clear version'' refers to a form supposedly less derived than the ''distorted version.'' The source of data was not spontaneous speech, however, but children's responses to a request for clarification. The children were tested individually, and at the start of the session they received the following instructions:

> We want to play a game with you called the What? game. I'll explain it to you. You know, it happens sometimes that you'll say something to your mother or father and they'll say What? because they didn't hear and understand you. Then you'll have to say what you said all over again. Sometimes you say it the same way and sometimes you say it a different way. In the What? game we pretend that somebody doesn't hear and understand what we say. E_2 [the other experimenter] and I will show you how we play the game. E_2 is going to put on those earphones so it really will be harder for her to hear what you say.

Table 3. Examples of clear and distorted sentence versions for each linguistic construction. From Valian, Caplan and de Sciora, 1976.

Construction	Clear version	Distorted version
1. Subject relative	The games that he bought were fun.	The games he bought were fun.
2. Relative with progressive	The children who were chewing gum made a lot of noise.	The children chewing gum made a lot of noise.
3. Object NP complement	The doctor said that I had the measles.	The doctor said I had the measles.
4. Subject NP complement, transitive verb	It surprised them that Linda was late.	It surprised them Linda was late.
5. Subject NP complement, intransitive verb	It seemed that the dog was lost last night.	It seemed the dog was lost last night.
6. Tag (*yes-no*) questions	Mary's parents are mad at her, aren't they?	Aren't Mary's parents mad at her?
7. Manner adverbials	Superman quickly attacked the robbers.	Superman attacked the robbers quickly.
8. Deleted noun phrase–verb questions	Why don't you finish your homework now?	Why not finish your homework now?
9. Permuted relatives	Everyone who went to the party had fun.	Everyone had fun who went to the party.
10. Verb + particle	Bobby put on his shirt.	Bobby put his shirt on.
11. *To*-dative	I gave a nickel to my friend.	I gave my friend a nickel.
12. Passive	Her brother called Carol a little brat.	Carol was called a little brat by her brother.

113

After a model sentence and some practice trials, the children were presented with the construction types in Table 3, each child receiving
thirty-six sentences to repeat, half of them clear versions and half distorted versions. No child received both versions of the same sentence.
When the child repeated a sentence read to him by the first experimenter,
the second experimenter said in a natural, questioning intonation,
"What?" The child's task was to repeat what he said, either exactly the
same way or by modifying it to more easily get his message across.

The rationale behind the study was as follows: the child (or adult) has
available to him both versions of a particular sentence and knows the relation between them. Further, he has a theory about the listener that coincides with the derivational theory of complexity, that is, he believes that
"clear," less derived versions should be more easily understood than
"distorted," more derived versions. Therefore, when asked for clarification he should have a greater tendency to change distorted to clear versions than vice versa. Notice that this is quite a distinct use of the derivational theory of complexity, in that it has less to do with the acquisition of
the constructions than with the child's use of them once the knowledge is
acquired.

The prediction was confirmed for all age groups from 6 to 10 in Valian
et al.'s study, and for adults in Valian and Wales (1976). Subjects were
more likely to change distorted versions to clear versions than the reverse. There were some trends with age, primarily in the likelihood of
making any change at all. The youngest children apparently found it easier merely to repeat the sentences as given. The oldest children more
often than the younger ones changed clear versions to distorted versions,
and the explanation advanced by Valian et al. was that the older children
had productive control over the distorted versions, hence they could
change to them more readily than the younger children, who merely repeated the clear versions.

However, the prediction held less well for some constructions than
others. For example, for object noun-phrase complements, tag questions,
and manner adverbials the children made more frequent changes in the
wrong direction, that is, from clear to distorted, and to-datives were also a
marginal case. Furthermore, there exist other pairs of sentences in
English that have the same property as the constructions in Table 3,
namely a shared deep structure but different derivational complexity, but
for which we would expect the more derived version to be "clearer" than
the less derived version. Some examples are provided in Table 4.

Until the relevant experiment is done this remains a conjecture, but it
raises the question of the representativeness of the constructions that
proved successful for the theory in Valian et al.'s study.

Table 4. Other examples of constructions having both a less derived and a more derived version.

Construction	Less derived version	More derived version
1. Adjectives	The horse that was brown won the race.	The brown horse won the race.
2. Object Coordination	The boy ate an apple and the boy ate an orange.	The boy ate an apple and an orange.
3. Subject Coordination	The boy went to school and the girl went to school.	The boy and the girl went to school.
4. Extraposition	That he smoked bothered me.	It bothered me that he smoked.
5. Tough movement	It is easy for me to hit you.	You are easy for me to hit.
6. It-replacement	It seems that you are happy.	You seem to be happy.
7. Nominalization	To paint is fun.	Painting is fun.

The Acquisition of Transformations

In summary, our opinion is that the derivational theory of complexity finds little support in the child-language literature, particularly in predicting the course of acquisition. As things stand, however, it appears that school-age children, like adults, have linguistic knowledge that is best described by a transformational grammar. Ingram (1975) defends the opinion that the major transformations of English only enter children's speech around the early school years, in particular the transformations having to do with embedding one sentence into another. He argues that up to age five or six, children develop a phrase structure grammar together with a set of transformations for the simple sentence, such as auxiliary inversion and negation. From ages six to twelve, children acquire the major transformational component of their grammar, the portion that is concerned with complex sentences.

Ingram's evidence is drawn from many sources but the clearest data come from stories told by children between the ages of two and six years, in a collection by Pitcher and Prelinger (1963). At two or three years of age, there is nothing in the children's speech to suggest that they know how to use sentence-embedding transformations. They tell stories by using short, simple sentences that are not joined, merely juxtaposed. At age three to four, the children begin joining sentences by *and,* and it is only at age five or six that sentence embeddings, such as relative clauses, appear in any quantity. When these first appear, the children do not seem to have productive rules for them, but rather they use stock expressions such as *named* or *with* that masquerade as relative clause constructions, as in:

> Once upon a time there was a cat named Zero.
> Once there was a big scary man with lots of faces.

A major development in this ability to use sentence embeddings takes place between first and seventh grade (O'Donnell, Griffin, and Norris, 1967). Therefore, Ingram contends that prior to the age of 6 years, a transformational grammar is unnecessary to describe children's speech, but thereafter the child acquires productive transformational rules.

Models of Performance

The preceding discussion leaves us at something of an impasse. We are not interested primarily in characterizing the beginning and end points of language development, but rather in the process of acquisition. Yet the derivational theory of complexity is not very revealing of that process: it makes predictions that are contrary to observations of the course of acquisition, and it fails to capture many of the stages children go through and the consistent errors they make. The problem is that transformational grammar is posited as an account of the *knowledge* a native speaker-hearer must possess, but not necessarily (in fact for Chomsky, avowedly *not*) a model of how a person *uses* that information in speaking and understanding. The only way to tap that knowledge is by observing the performance of children when they speak or understand, but it continues to be the case that the grammar's predictions about, for example, the difficulty of certain sentences, frequently fail.

This dilemma has led to an increased interest in trying to build a model of linguistic performance itself. People who speak and understand sentences do so in orderly ways, so psychologists are trying to capture that orderliness, borrowing what they need from the linguist's description but not being limited by it. Most of the current models are computer simulations of the processes of understanding speech rather than of speaking. For example, one model (Wanner, Kaplan and Shiner, 1974) tries to simulate the steps people go through when they are led astray by their initial interpretation of a sentence—aptly called the Garden Path phenomenon. Take the following:

> The horse raced past the barn fell.

or the wonderful *Boston Globe* headline:

> Delays dog deaf mute's murder trial.

These sentences are useful because they are exceptions that highlight the strategies adults use in decoding the meaning of a sentence. A complete account of the strategies may eventually replace transformational grammar as a description of language performance. Alternatively, they may be regarded as adjuncts to grammatical knowledge: tricks and short cuts people learn in dealing with everyday conversations. Whichever turns out to be the case, it is interesting to trace the ontogenesis of these strategies in young children.

Comprehension Strategies

Bever (1970) was the first to draw attention to one guiding principle children use, sometimes erroneously, to understand sentences. If they hear a sequence consisting of a noun followed by a verb followed by another noun (NVN), they assign it the meaning agent-action-object. So if the sequence is *the truck bumped the car,* they, like us, believe the truck crashed into the car. That is the common active declarative word order. However, if children hear a passive sentence such as:

The truck was bumped by the car.

they treat it as having the same meaning as the previous active sentence, that is, *the truck bumped the car.* This is the opposite of the true meaning. Young children are not sensitive to the morphemes signaling the passive, namely *by* and the copula *was,* so they attend only to the order of the content words. We repeated Bever's study and got essentially similar results (de Villiers and de Villiers, 1973a). Young children easily understand a simple active when they are asked to act it out, but perform at random when given a passive sentence, showing they at least perceive it as different. However, at a certain stage when the active word order has become well established, they seem to develop an inflexible strategy and consistently reverse the meaning of a passive like:

The cat is kissed by the rabbit.

by making the cat kiss the rabbit. This strategy persists for some months, presumably because passives are so rare that the children receive little opportunity to disconfirm their hypothesis.

The same strategy gets children into trouble when they hear a sentence like:

The man who saw the deer ate the pie.

They frequently only attend to the last segment:

The deer ate the pie.

and consequently misinterpret the meaning of the whole sentence. The principle here is very similar to that in adult processing: the standard procedure we develop for dealing with sentences occasionally leads us astray. The difference is that adults can stop and rework a sentence until it does make sense; children have to accumulate enough examples to establish the alternatives to their interpretation.

Another principle was discovered by Carol Chomsky (1969) in her work with children between five and ten years—a period when children were thought to have already acquired a full adult grammar. She called it the *minimal distance principle,* or MDP, because it is based on the hypothesis that the noun most closely preceding the verb, particularly in a complement phrase, will be treated as the subject. It is not identical to the NVN strategy, as a few examples should make clear. In the sentence:

John is easy to see.

children aged five or six typically make the error of believing that *John* is the subject of *see* rather than its object, therefore interpreting it as:

John can see easily.

Only by the age of eight or nine can children get sentences of this sort correct.

Children also make errors in understanding sentences of the sort:

Ask Mary what to feed the doll.

They frequently treat *ask* in this instance as if it meant *tell,* and reply "ice cream," instead of asking Mary. The error does not involve the word *ask* itself, as the children do not fail on sentences like:

Ask Mary her name.

In this type of sentence there is no following verb to take Mary as its subject, so the MDP cannot be applied.

Another error occurs in sentences involving the word *promise,* which has a similar property. Children aged five to nine or so believe a sentence like:

John promised Mary to water the garden.

means that *Mary* watered the garden, rather than John, as in:

John told Mary to water the garden.

Once again, they employ the MDP, which overextends the more usual case and applies it to the exception.

A brief survey of complement constructions in English reveals the source of the children's MDP error:

John told Mary to leave.
John persuaded Mary to leave.
John encouraged Mary to leave.
John allowed Mary to leave.
John selected Mary to leave.
John caused Mary to leave.
John asked Mary to leave.
John begged Mary to leave.
John expected Mary to leave.   (from Chomsky, 1969)

It is not at all surprising, then, that children develop a strategy like the MDP for dealing with complex sentences, and thus fail to understand the exceptions until they establish them as such. It is in much the same way that they first overextend the past regular -*ed* ending and only later acquire the individual past tenses for the irregular verbs.

A combination of these two principles, NVN and MDP, accounts nicely for the difficulty children have with various types of relative clause constructions. For example, four- to six-year-olds are quite good at understanding sentences of the sort:

The cat chased the mouse that frightened the girl.

because they correctly assign *cat* as the subject and *mouse* as the object by the NVN strategy, then *mouse* as the subject of *frightened* by the MDP. However, a sentence like:

The cat chased the mouse that the girl frightened.

gives them slightly more trouble as they are not sure which animal the girl frightened: their strategies give them no clues. The hardest of all are sentences like:

The girl that the mouse frightened chased the cat.

Here there are no good NVN sequences to latch onto, and the subject of *chased* is far distant from the verb. As in other types of complex sentence, the simple strategies fail to provide a correct interpretation.

SUMMARY

Any attempt to survey the child's progress toward adult grammar is hampered by inadequate psychological models of adult language. But we do know that for the child to make progress toward adult grammar, certain structural knowledge seems to be an inescapable prerequisite: an adult grammar has to rely on linguistic categories like parts of speech or on constituents like noun and verb phrases, and these structures are mastered early by young children. Furthermore, it seems likely that older children possess the kind of knowledge proposed by transformational grammar, namely the separation of deep structure from surface structure, and an appreciation of interrelationships among sentence types. It is open to dispute whether our mental operations in speaking or understanding sentences are akin to transformational rules, or whether children proceed by acquiring transformations. Neither claim has gained much support.

5

The Development
of Word Meaning

Elizabeth (aged 3½ years): You know what, Mommy? Yesterday
today was tomorrow.

There are several facets to semantic development, or the acquisition of
meaning. Children's early sentences express underlying semantic relations such as agent-action-object, locative, or possessor-possessed. These
semantic categories represent the propositional meanings of sentences, a
verbal encoding of the relationships among objects and interactors in the
world. But from the earliest stages of language development, children also
use their utterances to serve different functions—to query, request, describe, deny, and so forth. These functions represent the pragmatic
meanings of sentences, the roles they play and the purposes they serve in
conversations.

A third aspect of semantics concerns the meanings of the individual
words in sentences. The child has to learn the words for objects, actions,
or the properties of those objects and actions, as well as for the relationships between objects and their positions in space and time. This task requires far more than simply the association of a complex sound uttered by
an adult with a particular object that may be present at the time. The
quote from Elizabeth that begins this chapter not only represents a
remarkable discovery on her part, but also illustrates the complexity of
the meaning of some words. Here the child has to learn that words like
yesterday, today, and *tomorrow* do not have any single day as their referent; instead they relate the days to the time of the utterance. The
understanding of these relational terms is one of the later achievements in
semantic development.

121

The words that the child learns differ in the complexity of their conditions of use:

(1) At the simplest level come *proper names*. Here there is only one referent for each word, though the referent must be recognized through many transformations arising from changes in clothing, distance, angle of regard, and so on. Around the age of six to nine months, children can recognize familiar persons and objects in many different orientations and contexts (Bower, 1974). Hence, the cognitive abilities that are prerequisites for learning proper names are present well before speech. Many of the child's first words are proper names like *Daddy* and *Mommy* or names for favorite toys, and some early common nouns may start out having single referents.

(2) *Common nouns* are somewhat more difficult, since they apply to a whole class of objects with a fairly complex resemblance to one another (see Rosch and Mervis, 1975). The problem for the child is to map the words of adults onto the appropriate classes of objects, for example, *dogs* or *chairs*. In most cases he will have already formed the appropriate categories on the basis of perceptual or functional similarity (Nelson, 1974) prior to the acquisition of the words. But at other times the adult words will subdivide one or more of the child's concepts or encompass a larger category of objects, and in these cases the labels provided by adults may serve to alter the child's classifications of objects.

Simple *verbs* and *adjectives* reveal a similar complexity. Several objects may share a property or be associated with the same activity, so the child has to ignore the particular objects and extract the invariant properties or patterns of activity associated with adults' words.

As noted earlier, this description of nouns, verbs, and adjectives greatly oversimplifies their linguistic characterization. Not all nouns refer to objects (for example, *justice* or *sanity*) nor do all verbs refer to actions or activities that can be seen or heard. Nevertheless, these descriptions are appropriate for the early semantic development of the child. More abstract types of nouns and verbs, defined by formal linguistic criteria, are not acquired until quite late in childhood.

Miller and Johnson-Laird (1976) have pointed out that in the acquisition of words there is a complex interaction between the child's perceptual/conceptual development and his lexical development. Take, for example, the acquisition of color words. On the side of conceptual development several aspects of color must be appreciated. (a) The child must distinguish color from other dimensions of visual experience, such as size, texture, or shape. (b) He must isolate certain focal or primary colors (Heider, 1971; 1972). (c) He must identify other intermediate colors with respect to those focal colors. Told that puce is a color between red and dark purple, we have a good idea what it is like without seeing it ourselves.

On the side of linguistic development, the child must learn three more features of color words. (a) He must learn the use of specific color words in particular contexts; many children learn very early such frames for color words as "Little _____ Riding Hood" or "Mary had a little lamb, its fleece was _____ as snow." (b) He has to learn that color words are a contrasting set of words linked to one another, all being covered by the general term "color" and appropriate as answers to questions like "What color is this?" (c) He has to map each color term onto its appropriate color.

Development can proceed on the conceptual and linguistic sides simultaneously, with the child at the same stage being able to provide color words in response to questions like "What colors are your crayons?" and also being able to match up colors, for example, by coloring the grass green in a drawing. Yet he may not know which words refer to which colors. We will return to the acquisition of English color terms later, but here it serves to illustrate that in semantic development there is an intricate relationship between the child's growing linguistic knowledge and his conceptual knowledge.

(3) Still more complex are the meanings of *relational words,* such as the dimensional adjectives *big* and *little, tall* and *short,* or *thick* and *thin.* Their correct use depends on reference to some standard that varies with the object described and with the context in which it is placed. We compare a "big" elephant to a rather different standard of size than a "big" ant, so a "little" elephant is still substantially larger than most other "big" animals. This standard of comparison for objects can shift depending on the context and does not usually need to be specified. So a child at the zoo might be told, "Look at that big elephant," when in fact the elephant in question would be a rather puny specimen if set among a herd of its kin. Here the other animals at the zoo or perhaps the child himself serves as the implicit standard for size. In order to correctly understand the meanings of these adjectives the child must not only identify the relevant properties of the objects but also perform a comparison to the standard. He must learn that they come in pairs of antonyms (*big* as opposed to *little, tall* as opposed to *short,* and *wide* as opposed to *narrow*), and that they all refer to measurement along spatial dimensions. So again the child's linguistic knowledge must be mapped onto his conceptual knowledge about spatial relationships.

(4) The most complex relational words that we will consider in this chapter are certain *deictic expressions.* Deictic expressions draw the attention of the hearer to a particular object in the situation of the utterance, not by naming it, but by locating it in relation to the speaker. Examples of these are the demonstrative adjectives, *this* and *that,* and the locational adverbs, *here* and *there.* Deictic expressions of time, like *now, yesterday, today,* and *tomorrow,* locate events in time relative to the mo-

ment of utterance. Children have difficulty in learning these terms because the implicit standard of distance that contrasts *this* from *that* or *here* from *there* shifts as the context of the utterance changes. In the context of doing a jigsaw puzzle, asking for "*that* piece" could refer to something within arm's reach. In contrast, a tour guide describing a building, "*This* cathedral represents the best of Gothic architecture," could be standing some fifty yards away from it. In producing speech, the child has to use the words in accordance with these shifting criteria of distance; in comprehending speech his task becomes even more complex, as he must also translate from the speaker's perspective to his own. "*This* building" for the speaker may also be "*this* building" for the hearer, if both persons are in roughly the same location relative to the building; but "*that* statue" for the speaker may be "*this* statue" for the hearer if he is standing next to it while the speaker is some distance away. Many deictic expressions therefore depend on individual viewpoints as well as on implicit standards of distance for their interpretation.

THE FIRST TERMS OF REFERENCE

When one examines the first fifty or so words in a child's vocabulary several things stand out. The early words typically refer to objects familiar to the child or to events in which those objects are in interaction with the child or each other. Important persons like Mommy, Daddy, and Granny; the family pet; foods and drinks; animals (most learned from picture books) and the noises that they make; these are the focus of the child's early activity and are usually the first things labeled by him, at least in English-speaking Western societies (Nelson, 1973). In other cultures the particular objects may vary, and names for animals may even be learned from direct contact with them, but again the earliest words acquired will be labels for the salient things in the child's world.

In a thorough study of the early vocabulary development of eighteen American children, Katherine Nelson (1973) has suggested that important individual differences exist in the types of words first learned by children. At one extreme Nelson identified *referential* children, children who first learn and employ words that name objects. At the other extreme come *expressive* children, children with a majority of words for personal desires or aspects of social interaction in their early vocabulary, for example, *bye bye, want, need, naughty*. By age two years, referential children use a significantly larger vocabulary than expressive children, but are not any more advanced in terms of MLU or other measures of grammatical development. Nelson points out that the referential/expressive classification refers to a continuum rather than a dichotomy, so many children fall somewhere between the two extremes. Nevertheless, Nelson's classification reflects the predominant functions served by language for children at each extreme. Children at the referential end of the continuum seem most concerned with labeling and drawing attention to objects, while expressive children use language to regulate their social interaction with others. To some extent a child's use of language reflects his mother's verbal style. Mothers who use language to point out properties and objects in the world tend to have referential children; mothers who use language primarily to direct the behavior of the child tend to have expressive children, but there are some exceptions. At thirty months of age, the most advanced referential children possess and employ many adjectives with the nouns in their speech, but the expressive children use possessives in place of adjectives. Referential children also use a higher proportion of impersonal to personal pronouns than expressive children. In this way, the referential children still seem to be more concerned with objects and their properties, the expressive children with people and their relationships (Nelson, 1975).

Nouns

At first, a noun may be used by the child almost as a proper name, referring to only a single object, but he soon extends its use to other objects that are similar in some respect, usually in function or perceptual form. Children may also utilize grammatical features of speech at a surprisingly early age to determine whether words are proper or common nouns. Proper nouns are seldom preceded by the articles *the* or *a* in English, but articles must precede most common nouns in the singular form. Katz, Baker, and McNamara (1974) discovered that seventeen-month-old girls paid attention to the presence or absence of articles when new objects were introduced to them, as well as being able to tell whether the object was of the sort appropriate to have its own name. When told "This is zav" on being shown a new doll, they reserved the word for that doll, tending to use only that doll and not a similar one that was also present when asked to dress or feed *zav*. On the other hand, if the doll was introduced to them as "This is *a* zav" and thereafter referred to as *the* zav, the children used either of the two dolls when asked to do something with *a zav*. If the two objects were blocks, the children never regarded the nonsense word as a proper name, even if it were introduced without the article. They were equally inclined to use either object when told to do something with *zav* or *a zav,* suggesting that they could discriminate that dolls but not blocks could be individuated and have their own names. The little boys in the study did not show this ability, even at twenty-four months of age, possibly because of their lack of familiarity with dolls or perhaps due to sex differences in language acquisition. Several studies have reported that vocabulary (and in some cases syntactic) development is faster for girls than for boys (McCarthy, 1954; Maccoby and Jacklin, 1974).

Overextensions

The most striking aspect of vocabulary development to early investigators was the child's overextension of many of his first nouns to objects outside their normal range of application for adults. For example, a child might use *doggie* to refer not only to the family mutt and other dogs, but to horses, cows, sheep, and cats as well. This overextension of a word seldom lasts for longer than a few months and often occurs only briefly. Furthermore, only some of the child's words will be overextended; others seem to approximate adult usage from the start. The period of overextension of common nouns generally lasts from one- to two-and-a-half years of age and typically ends with a sudden burgeoning of the child's productive vocabulary, usually accompanied by frequent questions of the "What's that?" variety.

An influential theory of semantic development first spelled out in detail by Eve Clark (1973) attempts to account for overextensions. Clark's *semantic feature hypothesis* proposes that for adults the meaning of any word is composed of smaller components or features of meaning that serve to distinguish that word from other words of similar meaning (Katz and Fodor, 1963; Bierwisch, 1970). For example, among the semantic features of *boy* are [male], [nonadult], and [human]; among those for *girl* are [female], [nonadult], [human]. *Man* is represented as [male], [adult], [human]. Some of these features serve to distinguish the meanings of many different words. The features [male] and [female] characterize the difference between *bachelor* and *spinster, husband* and *wife, gander* and *goose,* and many others; [adult] and [nonadult] distinguish *goose* from *gosling, cow* from *heifer,* and so on.

With respect to development, the semantic feature hypothesis suggests that when a child first begins to produce identifiable words he does not know their full meaning for adults. Instead, he identifies the meaning of a word with only some subset of the features or components of meaning that adults might associate with it. The child may therefore make errors of reference because he has not yet acquired the combination of features that specify the correct class of objects; he will use only one or two features or properties of the object as criteria for application of the word. For example, if a child extracts from all of the instances of dogs that have been labeled for him as *doggies* only the property four-legged, he might extend *doggie* to all other four-legged creatures.

Clark summarized many of the early diary studies in which linguists kept a record of children's early words and the referents of the words, and showed how overextension could be explained by a child's identifying the meaning of a word with only a subset of its components of meaning. Table 5 gives a sample of these overextensions and the defining features that the children may have been using.

Table 5. Overextensions and defining features.

Study	Word	First referent	Extensions and overextensions in order of occurrence in speech	Possible defining features
Moore, 1896	bird	sparrows	cows, dogs, cats, any animal moving	movement
Chamberlain and Chamberlain, 1904	mooi	moon	cakes, round marks on window, writing on window and in books, round shapes in books, tooling on leather book covers, round postmarks, letter O.	shape
Moore, 1896	fly	fly	specks of dirt, dust, all small insects, his own toes, crumbs of bread, a toad	size
Pavlovitch, 1920	koko	cockerel crowing	tunes played on violin, piano, ac-cordian, phono-graph, all music, merry-go-round	sound
Taine, 1877	cola (chocolat)	chocolate	sugar, tarts, grapes, figs, peaches	taste
Leopold, 1949	wau-wau	dogs	all animals, toy dog, soft slippers, pic-ture of old man dressed in furs.	texture

As the child gains more experience of the world and learns more words, he will have to add the missing features to his word meanings to distinguish them from one another. When a child who overextends the word *doggie* to other animals comes to learn the words *cow* and *kitty*, for example, he will need to specify further the meaning of *doggie* to dif-ferentiate it from the other two words. He might add to [four-legged] as the defining features of *doggie* such properties as [barks] and [wags tail]; further specify *kitty* as [has whiskers], [meows], and [relatively small] (relative to cows and dogs); and specify *cow* as [moos], [has an udder], [has horns], and [relatively large]. The child need not know the names for these properties but just needs to identify them perceptually to determine whether to use the word or not. Note that features like [four-legged], [has horns], [furry] and so on are much more concrete and perceptual than the semantic features [male] or [adult] proposed for adult words. Little is known about the process by which the child shifts to the more abstract adult characterizations (Clark and Clark, 1977).

Clark (1973) suggested that for the child all of the referents of a particular word share one or more defining features, but more recent studies suggest that children do not always use their first nouns as systematically as the theory maintains. From a detailed study of the language development of her two daughters, Christy and Eva, Melissa Bowerman (1977) concluded that many of their early word uses were "complexive." By this she meant that the children did not consistently regard any single attribute as critical for the word's use; rather, they shifted from one feature to another in successive uses of the word. For example, the child might learn the word *doggie* to refer to dogs, but then extend it to other furry things, such as woolly blankets; to other four-legged things, such as horses; and to other things that move by themselves, such as spiders or beetles. As the best example or prototype of the reference category, the child seems to learn the item first or most frequently named by a particular word by the adults around him. From this he extracts not just one, but many, properties or attributes and extends the word to cover other objects that share any one of these attributes, if he does not already have names for the objects.

This kind of complexive categorization of word meanings had been noted earlier by Vygotsky (1962), Brown (1965), and Bloom (1973). They suggested that it represents a primitive stage of word meaning and is later supplanted in the child's semantic knowledge by the more systematic use of sets of defining features that apply to all instances named by the word. However, Bowerman (1977) points out that both types of word meanings are present from the start in the child's vocabulary development. In fact, the complexive type of organization, with referents of a word resembling each other by one or more different features rather than having a set of defining properties in common, is typical of many adult word meanings (Rosch and Mervis, 1975).[1]

Overextensions in Comprehension

If a child identifies the meaning of a word with a single defining feature, let us say *doggie* with [four-legged], he should not only overextend the use of that word in his own speech, but also overextend it in his comprehension of what other people say. He may call dogs, horses, cows, and cats all *doggie,* and also be unable to pick out *the doggie* from a set of animals. A

---

[1] Clark has recently revised her account of overextensions to include both pure overextensions, in which a single feature underlies all uses of the word, and complexive overextensions (which she calls "mixed overextensions") (Clark 1975).

few children do overextend their early words in comprehension as well as production, but in most cases overextensions are far more frequent in, and sometimes confined to, the child's production of speech (Hutten-locher, 1974; Thomson and Chapman, 1975; Gruendel, 1976). For example, one two-year-old studied by Thomson and Chapman overextended *apple* in her speech to balls, tomatoes, biscuits, and other round objects, but had no difficulty in correctly picking out *the apple* from a set of pictures of spherical and round objects. What might account for the discrepancy between comprehension and production?

The complexive nature of many overextensions provides a possible explanation (Clark and Clark, 1977). A child who uses *doggie* to refer to all four-legged creatures, but also overextends it to furry objects like rugs, has as his meaning of doggie at least the two features [four-legged] and [furry], and possibly others. In comprehension he will have no difficulty in distinguishing *the doggie* from other furry objects unless they are also four-legged. In speech, on the other hand, the child, in his desire to draw the adult's attention to an object or to communicate with the adult, appears to use the word in his vocabulary that most closely fits the object concerned, even though he may know that it is not quite right (Clark, 1975). Children may also employ this strategy to discover the correct words for objects, since overextensions of a word frequently elicit a correction from the parent.

Underextensions

According to the semantic feature hypothesis, the learning of nouns consists of the acquisition of features or attributes of object classes that distinguish them from other classes, accompanied by the gradual narrowing-down or differentiation of the meanings of the words. The direction of semantic development ought therefore to be from word meanings that are too broad toward more and more specific meanings. The initial overextension of words supports this theory of development.

However, early terms of reference are not only overextended but also underextended. Anglin (1977) points out that diary studies, by their very nature, only capture the overextensions. It is obvious to the parent when the child overextends a word to an inappropriate object. But when the child fails to name an object, the parent cannot tell whether he doesn't know the object's name or merely chooses not to say anything. In this way parents keeping a diary of the language development of their child note when he calls a cow a *doggie* but not when he fails to call a chihuahua a *doggie*.

We can name an object at several different levels of generality (Anglin, 1977). Snoopy is appropriately called *Snoopy,* a *Beagle,* a *dog,* a *mammal,* an *animal,* a *living thing,* or an *entity,* depending on what information we wish to convey. Semantic development therefore progresses in both horizontal and vertical directions. Horizontal development refers to expanding or narrowing a word's range of application at a given level of generality; vertical development refers to the acquisition of words at higher or lower levels of generality. In the course of horizontal development of the meaning of a word, both underextensions and overextensions are usually found. For a given level of generality, either underextension or overextension may predominate, but often both processes exist concurrently. For example, many children go through a stage in which they overextend the word *alive* to inanimate objects like clouds or rivers, on the grounds that they move by themselves; yet at the same time they deny that trees and flowers are *alive,* thus underextending the word (Piaget, 1972; Laurindeau and Pinard, 1962). On the other hand, the term *animal* is typically first acquired with a meaning close to that of *mammal.* Children aged two or three often deny that some birds, fish, or insects are *animals,* or that people can be called *animals.* Acquisition of terms of reference therefore consists of the differentiation or narrowing down of the meaning of some words, and the generalization or expansion of the range of application of others, while for many words both processes operate at the same time.

Learning the names for categories of objects is closely related to the conceptual development of the child in forming those categories or concepts in the first place. Misuse of the adult word for a category (for example, *animal*) could be due to inadequate control of the range of meaning of the word; that is, the child might think it appropriately named only a part of his concept, or that its range of application was actually wider than his own categorization of those objects. But it could also result from his underlying concept or object categorization being different from that of adults. The young child may not yet know that insects, worms, and fish all breathe, eat, and reproduce, and so not include them in his concept of animal. On the other hand, whereas he knows that people share these important properties with other mammals, he may deny that the word *animal* applies to people. Conceptual and linguistic development interact. It is easier for the child to learn the range of application of a word if he has already categorized that group of objects together on the basis of perceptual or functional similarity; but being supplied with a word for a group of objects may lead the child to class them together in a way he has not done before. The semantic development of the child thus depends on both his developing ability to classify objects as similar in some way, and on the category words provided for him.

Behavioral Equivalence and the Acquisition
of Category Names

Objects can be named at different levels of generality: how general are the child's first terms of reference? Anglin (1977) investigated this question in a thorough study of the preschool child's early category naming. In one procedure, children were shown three posters, each containing a set of four pictures. One poster showed four different collies, a second showed four different dogs (one of which was a collie), and the third showed four different animals (one of which was a dog). The children were asked to name not only the individual dogs and animals, but also each set; for example, they might be shown the set of four collies and asked, "What are all of these together?" For an adult the three different sets call for category words at different levels of generality—*collies, dogs,* and *animals.* Anglin discovered that children first acquire category names at intermediate levels of generality. For example, the two- to three-year-old children named all of the collies and dogs as *dogs,* and named the four different animals with their individual names. But they could not come up with the name of the specific type of dog or with the general category name *animal.* In the same way, for posters containing pictures of four roses, four different flowers, and four different plants, the youngest children used the intermediate-level word *flower.* Only some of the four- and five-year-olds knew the names of the specific flowers and the general term *plant.* At first, the child does not generally learn names for objects at the most specific or most general level; rather, he initially uses an intermediate word. Vocabulary development proceeds in both directions, towards more specific and more general class names. Why is this the case?

Anglin demonstrated that parents name many objects differently for adults than for two- to three-year-old children. A mother may name coins as *dimes* or *nickels* for an adult but as *money* for the child. Similarly, she will name cars as *Chevrolets, Fords,* and *Dodges* for an adult, but as *cars* for her young child. Brown (1958, 1965) pointed out that this naming practice of parents is a very practical one. Parents name objects at the level of behavioral equivalence for their children. A two-year-old has no need to make distinctions between different coin denominations until much later. He only need know that they are all money, that class of objects that are regarded as having some value by adults, can be exchanged for other goods, but must not be eaten or thrown away. In the same way, the young child has no need of the distinction between roses and tulips: flowers in general are those things that are to be smelled, are pretty to look at, but must not be trampled on or eaten. In this sense flowers are more behaviorally equivalent for a two-year-old than plants: some plants (like grass) can be trampled with abandon, others (like salads) can be eaten with relish. Anglin asked nursery-school teachers and parents to rate category names according to the behavioral equivalence of the objects in those categories for the two-year-old child. Their ratings accurately predicted the naming practices of parents and the child's first terms of reference for seven of the eight semantic domains (for example, animals, vehicles, plants, foodstuffs, and furniture) that Anglin investigated. Parents therefore provide the child with the semantic distinctions he is most likely to need at that age.

To summarize, objects are named for the child by his parents or other adults at an intermediate level of generality, usually at the level at which the objects are behaviorally equivalent for him. It is at this level that the child therefore first acquires the common names for objects like cars, dogs, cats, chairs, tables, and flowers. More general categorizations or more specific names are only learned later on. Finally, many of the child's first terms of reference are both overextended to inappropriate objects that share one or more attribute with central referents of that term, and underextended by leaving out other appropriate referents. When a term is underextended the child typically uses it first for prototypical exemplars of the category and leaves out more dubious members even when they are familiar objects to him (Anglin, 1977).

Verbs and Simple Adjectives

There has been somewhat less systematic study of the child's acquisition of simple verbs and adjectives than of his acquisition of nouns. Most of the early verbs in a child's vocabulary seem to refer to changes in the objects that he plays with: for example, *broke, fell, open;* or to his own actions: *jump, run, throw,* and so on (Nelson, 1973). Bowerman (1977) noted overextensions of her children's first verbs to inappropriate actions. As in their overextensions of nouns, the children seemed to have a prototypical referent for a word, often the action most frequently named by that word by the parents and usually the first usage by the child. But the children soon overextended the word to actions that shared some property with the prototype. Thus, Eva first used the word *kick* at the age of seventeen months as she kicked a floor fan with her foot, and thereafter she usually used it to refer to the action of kicking an object with the foot so that it was propelled forward. But over the next three months she used it for many actions that shared one or more of the features: a waving limb, a sudden sharp contact, especially between a body part and another object, and an object being propelled by the contact. Hence she said *kick* when watching a moth fluttering on a table (a waving limb?), while watching a row of cartoon turtles on television doing a can-can, just before throwing something, and as she made a ball roll by bumping it with the front wheel of her kiddy car. Similar processes therefore occur in the early acquisition of verbs and nouns; the child extracts a set of attributes from the actions or objects that are typically named by adults and then extends the words to other actions or objects that share one or more of those attributes. Only as he learns the names of more and more actions does he limit their use to appropriate referents.

How does the child come to learn the names of the various attributes of the objects he is learning to label? Among the earliest adjectives in children's vocabularies are color words, yet young children are notoriously bad at using color words appropriately (Istomina, 1963; Johnson, 1977). Any complete account of children's acquisition of color words will have to relate their conceptual and linguistic development to each other. Such an account is not yet available, but some progress has been made.

First of all, the child at a very early age responds to the same focal colors as adults—red, green, yellow, and blue—and it has been suggested that these are specified by the nature of the human perceptual system (Heider, 1971; 1972). Bornstein (1975) has shown that as young as four to five months, infants spend more time looking at primary colors than at intermediate colors. Heider (1971) also found a preference for focal colors among three-year-olds, accompanied by better recognition of those colors.

In acquiring the color words, the child first seems to learn that a certain set of words go together as *colors*. When asked "What color is the car?" he responds with a color word, though usually the wrong one, and not with words for another dimension, like *round* or *big*. Asked "Do you know the names of any colors?" he can list several (Bartlett, 1977). Yet at the same time it is not clear whether he has mapped the color words onto the dimension of color as opposed to shape or size, and he certainly does not yet connect the particular color words with their respective colors. The latter mapping is not usually complete even for basic colors for some time, but rapid development takes place between 2½ and 3½ years (Johnson, 1977). Heider (1971) and Johnson (1977) both observed a fairly stable order of acquisition of basic color terms, with *red, green, black, white, orange, yellow, blue, pink, brown*, and *purple* being learned by most children in that order. While many of the early color words that are appropriately used are words for focal colors, that alone does not seem to explain the ordering, since *orange* is not a focal color, yet is learned earlier. The early acquisition of *orange* may come about because it is the name of a familiar fruit as well as a color. What is needed is more information about the frequency with which the colors are named for the child as well as any other possible influences at home or school, since frequency of naming may also determine the order of acquisition. Nevertheless, the general primacy of the focal color words suggests a powerful influence of the physiological basis for color perception on their early acquisition. Furthermore, the frequency of use of the different color words could also reflect the physiological primacy of those colors.

Nelson (1976) has traced the development of different types of adjectives in early child language. The first form to appear is the predicate adjective of the type "it's *broken*" or "it's *open*." In fact, even in the one-word stage, expressions like *broken* or *allgone* are used. These early modifiers generally describe a change in state or a transitory state of objects or people. Somewhat later to develop are attributive adjectives that are used to classify or to subdivide a category of objects. Typical instances of these adjectives in child speech are attributes of size (*big, little*) or evaluative descriptions (*bad, pretty*). Nelson suggests that the child begins by focusing on the states and relationships of the particular objects that he interacts with and only later focuses on more invariant properties that can be used to categorize or specify one out of several objects.

The Basis for Early Semantic Categories

Much of the child's early semantic development consists of the acquisition of names for concepts or categories of objects and actions, these categories being formed on the basis of similarities in perceptual or functional attributes. Clark (1973) has stressed the primacy of perceptual features as the basis for children's early semantic categories; Nelson (1974) has stressed the primacy of function- or action-based categories. In fact, semantic categories based on both types of feature seem to occur from the beginning in child's vocabulary development. A child studied by Gruendel (1976) used the word *bep* to denote objects that were round and the word *hat* to denote any object he could put on his head, regardless of its form. Rings marbles, lollipops and so on were *bep;* keys, a newspaper, and a box that he placed on his head were *hat.* Other types of similarity or constancy in subjective experience are also recognized by children and form the basis for categories to which they apply words. For example, Bowerman's children, Christy and Eva, both used the word *heavy* between the age of twenty-one and twenty-four months to refer to situations involving any physical exertion with an object, whether or not it was actually heavy. From twelve to seventeen months of age Eva used the word *there* in situations where some project had been completed, such as when her mother had finished dressing her, or she had hammered the last peg into her pounding board, or when she had succeeded in opening a box after considerable struggle. Eva also used the expression *too tight* in several situations involving either physical restriction or interference by her mother: for example, when her mother held her chin to give her medicine, pulled her sleeves down, or washed her ears (Bowerman, 1977). The similarities being extracted by the child from these situations are far more abstract than the narrowly perceptual or functional attributes that we considered earlier. Yet in each case the child forms a category of situations, objects, or experiences with some element or set of elements linking them together. In some cases this category will be broader than that to which adults apply a particular word, and semantic development will consist of narrowing the word's range of usage; in other cases, the category will be too narrow and the range of situations to which the word is correctly applied will gradually expand to match the wider adult usage.

RELATIONAL WORDS

Words that specify relationships between people, objects and events occur quite early in child language, but the meanings of most relational words are not acquired in all their complexity until the child is four or five, or even older. For example, the word *more* often appears among the first fifty or so words in a child's vocabulary, but it is first used as a sort of all-purpose demand, a means of obtaining a repeat of what had gone before, for example, *more meat, more tickle.* Later the child may use it to comment on the recurrence of an object or event, but only much later will he use the word in its full comparative sense, as in "this glass contains *more* than that one," or "*more* than it did before."

One of the earliest relational adjective pairs to appear in child speech is *big* and *little,* but it takes some time for the child to master the way in which the size standard for their use shifts with the context. An ingenious game that illustrates the child's developing ability to take the context into account in using these terms was developed by Susan Carey. The child and investigator play a "tea party" game with a set of little toy people sitting around a tiny table. After introducing and setting up the toys (or preferably having the child set them up), the investigator points out that the little girl (or boy) doll has no glass from which to drink her juice. Thereupon he produces a small shot glass and puts it down on the table, saying "What about this one?" When shown to the child separately, out of the context of the doll's tea party, the shot glass invariably elicits the judgement that it is "a little glass," but on the doll's table it looks ridiculously large. After playing tea party for a while, with much drinking and pouring of imaginary juice and tea, the investigator points to the glass and asks the child: "Is this a big glass or a little glass?" (or vice versa). Two- to three-year-olds generally answer "a little glass," just as they do when the glass is in isolation. Even if the investigator specifies, "For *these dolls* is this a big glass or a little glass?", the two-year-olds stick with "a little glass." They seem unable to switch from their own standard for the size of glasses, and *for them* a shot glass is indeed "a little glass." Four-year-olds, on the other hand, often exclaim as soon as the glass is placed on the table, "That's too big!", and they usually judge it to be "a big glass" in the context of the tea party. When it is specified, "For *you* is it a big glass or a little glass?", they revert to "a little glass." Or, as one astute little girl told us: "It's a little glass, big glass . . . a little glass for me and a big glass for them . . . and a *largerger* glass for her!" (as she stretched over and pointed at the smallest doll). This shift from an egocentric standard at age two to a context-sensitive one at age four is typical of a general decentering of viewpoint that occurs throughout the child's intellectual and social development. The importance of this process in the development of the child has been stressed by Piaget (1970), and we will later examine its role in the acquisition of deictic expressions.

Spatial Adjectives

Considerable research into semantic development has been focused on the set of spatial relational adjectives: *big/little, tall/short, high/low, long/short, wide/narrow, fat/skinny, thick/thin,* and *deep/shallow.* The reasons for this interest are threefold: first, these adjectives constitute an important way of describing and identifying objects; second, many studies have revealed a consistent ordering in their acquisition and in the difficulty children have with them; and third, children make interesting errors and substitutions in acquiring the full set of adjectives, errors that are suggestive of the way in which semantic development proceeds.

The Order of Acquisition

In children's spontaneous descriptions of objects, *big* and *little* are the first of the spatial adjectives to appear, well before any of the other contrastive pairs (Brown, 1973). Four- and five-year-olds still tend to use the general adjectives *big* and *little* to refer to the specific dimensions of height, length, and width (Sinclair-de Zwart, 1969). The adjective pair that refers to size in general and not to size along any specific dimension thus appears before, and is employed as a substitute for, the more specific dimensional adjectives.

Several studies have devised language games to test children's knowledge of the spatial adjectives. A particularly entertaining game for four- and five-year-olds is an opposites game played with hand-puppets. The child is introduced to a deliberately contrary puppet who "always says just the opposite" of what the other puppet says. Models of opposites are given—*good* versus *bad, happy* versus *sad,* and so on—and the child is then invited to operate the contrary puppet and produce the opposite of the word or phrase said by the experimenter's puppet. There is a consistent order of difficulty of the spatial adjectives in the opposites game (Clark, 1972; Carey and Considine, 1973). All of the youngest children in Clark's study (mean age 4.4 years) could produce semantically appropriate responses to *big* and *small,* whereas only eighty-two percent and eighty percent could give appropriate responses to *long/short* and *tall/short,* respectively. (A semantically appropriate response was one that reflected at least part of the meaning of the experimenter's word, for example, *up* or *big* as the opposite of *low.*) For the other pairs of spatial adjectives, the percentages of appropriate responses dropped off precipitously: to 45 percent for *high/low*, 12 percent for *thick/thin*, 7 percent for *wide/narrow*, and only 2 percent for *deep/shallow*.

Similar results come from studies in which preschool children were presented with sets of objects that differed along the appropriate dimensions and asked to identify "the *X* one," where "*X*" was a spatial adjective. *Big/little* was the earliest pair mastered. *Tall/short* and *long/short* were easier than *high/low*, which was in turn easier than *thick/thin* and *wide/narrow* (Wales and Campbell, 1970; Tashiro, 1971; Eilers et al, 1974; Bartlett, 1974; 1976).

What might account for this order of difficulty? One possible determinant is the conceptual complexity of the terms. Bierwisch (1967) and H. Clark (1973) both pointed out that some of the spatial adjectives are more general than, or logically prior to, the others, in that their meaning is presupposed by the more specific adjectives. All of the dimensional adjectives refer to the measurement of physical extent along one or more dimensions, but *big* and *little* are the simplest and most general of the set since they refer to degree of physical extent along any or all of the three dimensions. The other adjectives each specify the particular dimension along which the physical extent is measured, requiring the child to distinguish and identify the separate dimensions. While a *big* box can be big along any dimension, a *tall* box must be extended along the vertical dimension. Of the horizontal dimensions, Bierwisch and Clark suggest that length is primary or perceptually salient since it refers to the most extended dimension in the horizontal plane. Furthermore, we normally order the specific dimensions when we describe objects. A door is described in terms of its height, then its width, and last its thickness; a table by its length and then its width. This analysis suggests that the adjective pairs can be partially ordered in terms of generality and salience:

Big and *little* require no specification other than physical extent; *tall/short* and *long/short* require the further specification of the vertical or horizontal dimension; and *wide/narrow* and *thick/thin* require the still further specification that they apply to the secondary horizontal dimensions. Eve Clark (1972, 1973) has shown how this conceptual or logical analysis translates directly into the semantic feature hypothesis when each specification is considered as a component of the meaning of the term. The more specific the pair of adjectives, the more components of meaning the child must master to distinguish it from the other pairs. *Big/little* would have the semantic feature [physical extent] associated with it, *tall/short* the features [physical extent] and [vertical], and *long/short* the features [physical extent] and [horizontal]. *Wide/narrow* would have [secondary] associated with it in addition to [physical extent] and [horizontal]. In this way the relative difficulty of the adjective pairs for children would be predicted, at least partially, by their cumulative semantic complexity, that is, the cumulated number of semantic components associated with each pair.

A second, perhaps simpler, explanation of the order of acquisition and difficulty of the adjective pairs is their frequency in the language that children hear. Carey and Considine (1973) have noted that the relative frequency with which each pair appears in the language of adults (Kučera and Francis, 1967) and in the speech of five-year-olds (Wepman and Hess, 1969) also partially predicts the order of difficulty of these adjectives for children. Several researchers have suggested that frequency of occurrence in adult speech may determine acquisition of lexical items by children (Brown, 1958; Anglin, 1977). However, an appeal to frequency of occurrence alone is not a particularly satisfying explanation of acquisition: the question of what determines the differential frequency of those words in adult language remains to be answered. Indeed, it may be that the conceptual complexity or salience of the dimensional adjectives determines their frequency of usage in the description of objects by both adults and children, and thus indirectly their order of acquisition in child speech.

Positive and Negative Poles

Another characteristic of the dimensional adjectives is that they come in antonymous pairs, one referring to the most extended, or positive, end of the dimension, the other to the least extended, or negative, end. For three related reasons the word for the positive pole seems to be primary and that for the negative pole secondary. First, the names for the spatial dimensions are usually derived from the positive-pole word: *height* (high), *length* (long), *width* (wide), and *thickness* (thick). The positive-pole word can therefore be used in two senses: in a nominal sense, simply to name the dimension being talked about, for example, "How *long* is the table?"; or in a contrastive sense—"The table is *long*" as opposed to *short*. Note that the nominal use is neutral with respect to the actual size of the object. The question "How long is the table?" does not suggest that the table is either long or short. On the other hand, "How *short* is the table?" is only asked when there is the presumption that the table *is* short. So the negative-pole word only has a contrastive sense.

Second, since the positive-pole word refers to the most extended end of the dimension it represents the best instance of that dimension. *Tall* is the best example of "having height," *long* the best example of "having length" (H. Clark, 1970). Finally, the positive-pole adjectives are considerably more frequent in adult speech than the negative-pole words for all of the spatial-adjective pairs except *big/little*. For these reasons, linguists call the positive-pole adjectives unmarked terms and the negative pole adjectives marked. H. Clark (1970, 1973) has suggested that since the unmarked forms appear to be primary in a linguistic and psychological sense, they should be acquired before the marked forms in child speech.

However, a close examination reveals that practically as many studies of dimensional adjectives contradict this prediction as support it. It is true that positive-pole adjectives are much more frequent in the speech of five-year-olds (Wepman and Hess, 1969), and they are more frequently provided by young children as descriptions of objects than are the corresponding negative-pole adjectives (Wales and Campbell, 1970). One possible reason for this could be that the children do not yet understand the negative-pole words. However, the same asymmetry in frequency is found in adult speech and it would clearly be false to conclude from this that adults do not know the meaning of the negative-pole adjectives (Carey and Considine, 1973). Stronger support for Clark's prediction that the unmarked or positive terms should be acquired first comes from several studies of preschoolers' comprehension of dimensional adjectives. The children in these studies understood most of the positive-pole adjectives better than the corresponding negative-pole words (Wales and Campbell, 1970; Tashiro, 1971; Bartlett, 1976).

On the other hand, other studies have produced evidence counter to the prediction that the positive pole should be understood before the negative pole of dimensional adjectives. In Eve Clark's opposites game, the youngest children were as adept (or inept) at giving appropriate opposites for the negative-pole as for the positive-pole adjectives. Clark argues that this result is constrained by the nature of the game—one cannot give an opposite without knowing both words. However, Carey (1976) points out that since Clark recorded "semantically appropriate" responses, not just correct adult opposites, her task should still reflect any differential acquisition of the two poles. The children gave semantically appropriate responses to the positive pole (for example, *little* or *down* as the opposite of *high*), showing that they understood at least part of its meaning. At the same time they should either have not responded or have given an inappropriate word for the opposite of the negative pole. Yet this did not occur, suggesting that the children learned the two members of each pair at about the same time.

In Clark's study each child received both dimensional adjectives, and the results were averaged over the whole group. Carey (1976) repeated the opposites game with a group of thirty-two three- and four-year-olds, with each of them getting both members of the adjective pairs but on different occasions. For the sixteen children who were able to play the game with any success, only in the case of *wide/narrow* and *deep/shallow* were there a significant number of children who could give a semantically appropriate opposite for the positive word but not for the negative. There was no difference for *big/little, tall/short, long/short, high/low, thick/thin,* or *fat/skinny,* so this task provides only weak support for the hypothesis that the positive pole should be acquired first.

In nearly all cases where a difference between the positive- and negative-pole words has been reported, the children were presented with an array of objects differing along one or more dimensions and asked to pick one out, for example, the *tallest* or *skinniest.* So Carey tested her group of preschoolers on a single object at a time, such as a pencil, a piece of string, or a shoe, asking them, "Is this a *long/short* piece of string," and so on. Using appropriate objects for each adjective, the children were asked about both positive and negative members of each pair. Half the time the correct answer was *yes* and half the time it was *no,* and a child never saw both the long and the short pencil or long and short pieces of string. The children were generally as good at answering correctly for the negative pole as for the positive pole. Only for *long/short* and *deep/shallow* did a few children understand the positive-pole word but not the negative-pole word.

Why might children be better at understanding the positive-pole adjectives when there is a comparison with other objects involved, but not when the adjectives describe a single object? Carey suggests that adults and children perceive and encode a set of objects in terms of the positive

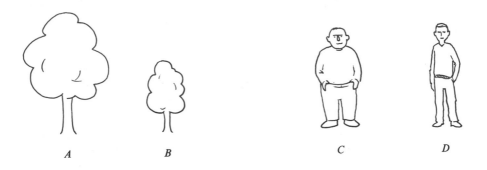

A   B   C   D

pole. The arrays are seen and remembered as "*A* is *taller* than *B*" and "*C* is *fatter* than *D*." not "*B* is *shorter* than *A*" and "*D* is *skinnier* than *C*." If an adult is asked to make a comparison between objects in terms of the negative pole, it takes him longer than if the positive poles are used (H. Clark, 1974), since there is a mismatch between the way he encodes the array and the question that is asked. Children could not only take longer but also make more errors when such a mismatch occurs. In this way, even if children learned both adjectives as a pair at about the same time, they could still respond differently to the positive- and negative-pole descriptions in a comparison situation. The way the child perceives and organizes his experience of the world could interfere with his ability to demonstrate his understanding of the meaning of the negative-pole adjective.

The problem could also be related to the age of the child. Bartlett (1974) and Eilers et al. (1974) did not find any difference between members of the adjective pairs for two- to three-year-olds, though Bartlett did observe some asymmetry in favor of the positive-pole adjectives for older preschoolers. Perhaps the encoding of an array of objects with reference to the positive pole develops with age.

Semantic Confusions

According to the semantic feature hypothesis, the feature [physical extent] is more general than and prior to [vertical] or [horizontal], since the latter two specify the dimension along which physical extent is to be measured. Similarly [vertical] and [horizontal] are logically prior to [positive/negative pole], since the polar feature specifies which end of the dimension is being referred to. H. and E. Clark suggest that the semantic features are acquired, in order, from the general to the specific (E. Clark, 1973; H. Clark, 1973). Thus, the child will first learn that the spatial adjectives are all concerned with the measurement of physical extent, then the dimensions referred to, and last of all the polarity of each adjective. This implies that, for a period of time in the semantic development of the child, *tall, long, wide,* and *thick,* or some subset of these, may mean the same thing as *big*—that is, [physical extent]. Similarly, *tall* and *short* might both mean [physical extent] [vertical] without reference to polarity. During these periods of development the child should substitute *big* and *little* for the other dimensional adjectives and confuse polar opposites.

As we mentioned earlier in this chapter, *big* and *little* are much more frequent than the other adjectives in descriptions of objects by young children, often occurring when a more specific dimensional adjective would be used by adults (Wales and Campbell, 1970; Sinclair-de Zwart, 1969; Ehri, 1976). In the opposites game, four-year-olds often give *little* or *small* as the opposite of *tall, long, wide,* and *thick;* and *big* as the opposite of *short, narrow,* and *thin.*

If [positive/negative pole] is the last aspect of the meaning of spatial adjectives learned by the child, the antonymous pairs should be regarded as synonyms for a period of time. *Tall* and *short* would both be used to refer to height, but they would not be differentiated, since the child would not know their polarity. However, three- and four-year-olds very rarely confuse dimensional adjectives with their polar opposites (Ehri, 1976; Townsend, 1976). The errors that children make in comprehending these adjectives typically confuse the dimensions, not polarity—for example, indicating the *skinniest* object when asked for the *shortest* (Carey, 1976, 1977a; Brewer and Stone, 1975).

The most reliable case in which young children confuse polar opposites does not involve spatial adjectives at all, but rather the confusion of *less* with *more* (Donaldson and Balfour, 1968; Carey, 1972; Palermo, 1973). When three-year-olds are presented with a glass of water and a jug and asked to "Make it so that the glass of water has *less* to drink in it," they frequently add *more* water instead of pouring some out of the glass. The semantic feature hypothesis suggests that the children know that both *more* and *less* mean [amount] but not that they are opposites. Since *more* is the best example of "having some," that is of [amount], the meaning of less is assimilated to that of *more*.

However, this confusion may have less to do with children's representations of the meanings of the words than with nonlinguistic strategies employed by them in the testing situation (Carey, 1977b). When Carey substituted a nonsense word for *less* and asked the children to "Make it so that the glass has *tiv* to drink in it," many of the children who added water for *less* again added water. It seems unlikely that the child's representation of the meaning of *less* leads to his adding water in this task, since he does the same for *tiv* and he clearly has no meaning for that word. The apparent confusion of *less* with *more* may rather result from a response bias or strategy of the child in the context of the testing situation. As long as they interpret the command as having to do with changing the quantity, children appear to be predisposed to add rather than to subtract when manipulating objects or water. Townsend and Erb (1975) also argue that when young children do not understand an instruction involving a spatial adjective they choose the object with the greatest extent along the varied dimension. This represents a nonlinguistic strategy rather than the possession of identical partial meanings for the polar opposites along that dimension.

To summarize our discussion of the acquisition of spatial adjectives:

(1) There is a well established order of difficulty of the set of adjective pairs, from the easiest to the hardest:

This ordering is quite well predicted by two factors that may themselves be related: the frequency of occurrence of the adjectives in adult and child language, and their conceptual (and semantic) complexity, as spelled out by H. Clark (1973) and Bierwisch (1967).

(2) Clark also suggested that the positive-pole adjective in each pair should be easier to comprehend and should be acquired earlier than the

negative-pole adjective. Some studies support this, but the findings seem to be confined to cases in which the child has to compare two or more objects differing along the relevant dimension (Carey, 1976). It also depends on the age of the children, since two- to three-year-olds do not show any better comprehension of the positive pole than of the negative pole (Eilers et al., 1974; Bartlett, 1974).

(3) The semantic feature hypothesis, as elaborated by Eve Clark (1973), maintains that children learn the components of meaning of spatial adjectives in order, from the general to the most specific. A great deal of evidence indicates that *big* and *little,* the most general of the terms, are acquired before, and for a time regarded as meaning the same as, the more specific dimensional adjectives. H. and E. Clark (H. Clark, 1970, 1973; E. Clark, 1973) also assert that the polarity of the adjectives is the last feature acquired, with the result that young children treat some antonyms as if they were synonyms. But the findings of several studies contradict this assertion by demonstrating that children understand the polarity of spatial adjectives before they know the specific dimensions to which they refer (Carey, 1977a; Brewer and Stone, 1975).

Verbs of Possession

Like the spatial adjectives, the verbs *give, take, pay, trade, spend, buy,* and *sell* form a set of relational words that are linked together by common components of meaning. For their comprehension they also require reference to the relationship between the interactors in the transaction. The difference between *X paid Y* and *X gave the money to Y* lies in the notion of obligation that is understood in the first case but not in the second. Gentner (1975) divided these verbs into three levels of complexity based on the semantic features that underlie their use. *Give* and *take* both mean roughly "transfer of possession from X to Y," where the transfer is initiated by one of the interactors. The difference between them lies in who initiates the action, X or Y. *Pay* and *trade* are more complex in that they involve notions of an obligation to transfer money (*pay*) or a mutual contract to exchange goods (*trade*), as well as transfer of possession. Finally, *buy, sell,* and *spend* incorporate all three components—transfer of possession, an obligation involving money, and a mutual contract (to transfer an object in one direction and money in the other)—so they are the most complex.

Children master these verbs in order, from least complex to most complex. Asked to make two dolls act out sentences involving these words, such as "Make Bert buy a car from Ernie," preschoolers not only found the least complex verbs like *give* and *take* the easiest, but they also assimilated the meaning of the more complex words to the least complex.

Thus they acted out *buy* and *sell* as if they meant *give* and *take*, leaving out the obligation to transfer money as well as goods. This suggests that children acquire the semantic component "transfer of possession" and the direction of transfer before they add the component concerning obligation.

DEICTIC EXPRESSIONS

As we pointed out at the beginning of the chapter, deictic expressions, like *here* and *there, this* and *that,* can be extremely complex. To comprehend them one must understand the viewpoint of the speaker relative to one's own as well as a distance standard that varies with the context. For example, if the speaker is on one side of a tree and the listener is on the other side, *this* side of the tree for the speaker is *that* side of the tree for the listener. The speaker indicates the location of any object relative to its proximity to himself. The prepositions *in front of* and *behind* provide an interesting contrast to *this* and *that.* Locational information in terms of *in front of* and *behind* is usually given relative to the intrinsic front or back of the object: "in front of the horse" has a fixed spatial referent. Children first learn their own fronts and backs, and are able to place an object *in front of* or *behind* themselves. They then extend that information to the fronts and backs of objects like cats, dogs, cars, ovens, televisions, and even spoons (Kuczaj and Maratsos, 1975). H. Clark (1973) suggests that the intrinsic front of an object is that side which is most prominent in some way, often the side that we interact with or manipulate (on a stove or typewriter, for example). In cases where the reference object has no intrinsic front or back, however, locational information is given relative to the hearer, not the speaker. "In front of the wall" means between the hearer and the wall, regardless of the speaker's position. The speaker takes the hearer's point of view, the hearer takes his own, so in this respect the rules governing the use of *in front of/behind* are the opposite of those governing *this, that, here,* and *there.*

Spatial deictic expressions appear very early in child speech but it has proven difficult to determine the extent to which young children understand the full meaning of these expressions. Informal observation suggests that even two-year-olds understand the switch of perspective involved in the comprehension of *here* and *there.* Told by his mother from a distance that his toy is "over here," a child does not begin searching in his immediate vicinity but goes over to where his mother is standing. However, parents typically accompany such expressions with all sorts of gestures, so it is uncertain how much the child is responding to the words themselves.

We devised a hide-and-seek game to investigate more systematically children's early mastery of the perspective shifts involved in understanding the deictic terms *my/your, this/that, here/there,* and *in front of/behind* (de Villiers and de Villiers, 1974). The game began with one experimenter sitting opposite the child. Between the experimenter and child stood a Styrofoam wall with an upturned cup placed on either side of it. The child closed his eyes while the second experimenter concealed a chocolate candy or a raisin (for cavity-conscious parents) under one of the two cups. The child then opened his eyes and was told the location of the candy in terms of one of the eight deictic expressions, for example, "The M&M is on *this* side of the wall" or "the M&M is over *there*". To find the candy when *my/your, this/that,* or *here/there* provided the clue, the child had to translate the investigator's viewpoint into his own—*this* side of the wall for the investigator was *that* side of the wall for the child. To comprehend *in front of/behind,* the child had only to maintain his own viewpoint. In another version of the game, the experimenter sat with the child on the same side of the wall, so that they shared the same viewpoint.

Two-year-olds were best able to understand the contrasts that did not require a shift of perspective. By the time they had turned three, however, children were adept at translating from the speaker's perspective into their own. Strangely enough, the four-year-olds overextended this translation of perspective to *in front of* and *behind,* so their performance on that contrast was actually worse than the two-year-olds'. This overgeneralization of a frequent linguistic rule to cover exceptions is a common observation in language acquisition.

For all the children, the easiest contrast was *my/your.* This is the simplest of the set since it never involves any distance rule, only a switch from the speaker's viewpoint to the hearer's. It is interesting to note that the failure to master this most basic distinction between speaker and hearer is characteristic of many autistic children. The autistic child typically refers to himself as *you,* an echo from the speaker's reference to him. We will consider the speech of autistics more fully in a later chapter, suffice it to point out here that the simplest of the switches in perspective that underlie many deictic expressions appears to be beyond the grasp of many autistic children.

Our language game illustrates the child's understanding of these deictic expressions when there is a fixed reference point, the wall, but not mastery of the standards of relative distance involved in the use of *here/there* and *this/that* when there is no fixed reference. These conventions are complex and not easily stated for adult usage and there has been little study of their emergence in child speech. Many researchers have merely noted that the words *this, that,* and *there* (usually pronounced as *dis, dat* and *dere*) appear early and seem to be used appropriately. In fact, *dere* plus a pointing gesture may be among the child's first verbal communications. *Dere* is also used to denote the completion of a task and may start out as a rather all-purpose word to direct the attention of the parents to any object or state of affairs. *Here* is somewhat less frequent in child speech, often appearing first in the routine phrase *here 'tis,* and it is not clear when the child first understands the distance contrast between *here* and *there.* Webb and Abrahamson (1976) found that preschoolers correctly restricted their use of *this* to near objects, but when there was no fixed reference point they had great difficulty in comprehending *this* and *that.* Half of the seven-year-old subjects in their study were still unable to understand the distinction between *this* and *that* when they did not share the experimenter's perspective. So the full understanding of these spatial deictic expressions is not achieved until some years after they first appear in the speech of the child (see also E. Clark, 1977).

THE PROCESS OF WORD LEARNING

We have traced the development of word meaning in child speech from the simplest referential uses of proper and common nouns to the most complex of relational expressions, the use of which depends on complicated standards of comparison and shifts in viewpoint. In each case children usually pass through identifiable stages in their mastery of word usage, and the semantic complexity or adult frequency of the words affects their order of acquisition. Our discussion has concentrated on general trends in development that may be true of most, if not all, children learning English as a first language. But another important question remains to be considered: What is the process by which the child learns new words? By the age of six the child has a productive vocabulary of between 8,000 and 14,000 words (Carey, 1977a). This means that he learns some five to eight words a day between the ages of one and six years—a prodigious feat. How is this achieved?

It is now well-established that Western middle-class parents indulge in elaborate naming rituals with their babies from the time the child produces his first approximations to a word (Ninio and Bruner, 1976). In what Roger Brown (1958) called "the original word game" the parent names objects and corrects the child's attempts to produce those names. Our eleven-month-old son has a very effective routine for eliciting object names. He points a stubby little finger in the general direction of an object and says "Dis?", to which we reply with the name of the object. But we do not yet know about the universality of these naming rituals across different cultures and social strata, so their importance for the acquisition of early words remains uncertain.

A common account of word learning suggests that the child imitates the new words that his parents say to him. In a general sense this must be true, since the child does come to produce the words that he hears from adults, but immediately mimicking part or all of the adult's sentence containing a new word does not seem to be necessary for the acquisition of words. Some children do imitate utterances containing new words before they use those words spontaneously in their own speech (Bloom et al., 1974; Lieven, cited by Ryan, 1973), but most children do not (Leonard and Kaplan, 1976). Just hearing a word used on a few occasions, usually to refer to an object, action, or some property of an object in his immediate environment, is sufficient for the child to attach at least some appropriate meaning to the word and to begin using it himself (Leonard, 1976; Carey, 1977a). In fact, in his first spontaneous use of the new word, the child may use it in a different semantic or grammatical role in the sentence from the one in which he heard it (Leonard, 1976).

The Use of Linguistic and Nonlinguistic Context

Two sources of information about the meaning of a word are normally available to the child: the linguistic context in which it appears, and the nonlinguistic situation in which the utterance occurs. From grammatical markers appended to the word and from its role in the sentence, three- and four-year-olds can tell whether it is a noun or a verb, and even whether it is a count or mass noun (Brown, 1958). The semantic selection restrictions that govern the combination of words in sentences (Katz and Fodor, 1963) also delimit the meaning of a new word. Some verbs, like *drink,* can only be used with an animate subject and an inanimate object; others, like *tickle,* take an animate object (unless they are used metaphorically). Children are sensitive to these selection restrictions surprisingly early in their language development, and in fact they seem more aware of these semantic constraints on word combination than they are of syntactic constraints (de Villiers and de Villiers, 1972). Werner and Kaplan (1952) showed how the ability to use the information from verbal context increases throughout childhood. They presented children with a series of sentences containing a new word, asking them after each sentence to define what the word meant. For example, given the following set:

> A *corplum* may be used for support.
> *Corplums* may be used to close off an open place.
> A *corplum* may be long or short, thick or thin, strong or weak.
> A wet *corplum* does not burn.
> You can make a *corplum* smooth with sandpaper.
> The painter used a *corplum* to mix his paints.

it soon becomes clear that a *corplum* is a stick or a piece of wood. In this study the children were required to give a full verbal definition of the word, and the concepts were generally quite abstract so the children were only able to complete the task successfully at about eleven years of age. However, with simpler contexts and concepts, it can be shown that four-

and five-year-olds can extract a great deal of information about the meaning of a new word. In particular, a child learns a great deal about the properties of the object or action referred to by the word, even if he cannot define the word (Madigan, 1975).

However, the child rarely has to work from verbal context alone; the verbal context is normally supported by the nonlinguistic context of the utterance. Since adults generally speak to children about the here and now, the young child assumes that the new words he hears refer to some aspect of his immediate environment. In forming a hypothesis about what is being referred to he is assisted by the gestures and actions of the adult—pointing to an object, picking it up, giving it to the child, and so on. However, this process is far from foolproof. Children sometimes come up with the wrong hypothesis—like the young child whose mother, when wheeling him out of the house in his pushchair, would often look up to the sky and say, "What a lovely afternoon!" For some time the child thought that *afternoon* was the name for the complex television aerial on the roof. (Appropriately, he grew up to be an electronics engineer.)

Children use their knowledge of the world and the cues in the immediate context to derive strategies for interpreting and using certain words (Clark and Clark, 1977). Sometimes there appears to be considerable uniformity in the strategies that children adopt. At an early stage in the acquisition of words for temporal relations in English, French, or German, children seem to rely on order of mention as a cue to relationship in time (Clark, 1971; Ferreiro and Sinclair, 1971; Schöler, 1975). In their own speech they describe sequences of events in the order in which they happened, and in comprehension they interpret the first event mentioned as having happened first. Thus they make errors on sentences like:

> Before the boy washed his face, he cleaned his teeth.
> The boy washed his face after he cleaned his teeth.

At other times individual differences in strategies appear. In the comprehension of *always* and *never,* some children go through a stage in which they regard both words as positives, but other children at the same age systematically interpret both words as negatives (Kuczaj, 1975). Some of these strategies seem to be limited to particular contexts or tasks, so the view that one gets of semantic development frequently depends on the type of task the child is asked to perform. The children's expectations of the situation and materials they are being asked about interact with their understanding of the words that are being tested (Donaldson and McGarrigle, 1974; Wilcox and Palermo, 1975; Carey, 1977b).

Partial Meanings

Several researchers have argued that when the child first uses a word he understands only part of its meaning. Given the rate at which new words enter children's speech, this is a plausible suggestion. The semantic feature hypothesis represents one such partial-meaning theory of early semantic development. These theories claim that the child initially identifies the meaning of a word with only one, or perhaps a few, of its components of meaning for adults. As he hears and produces the word in a wider range of contexts and has to distinguish it from other related words, the child gradually adds components to his meaning for the word. So *tall* might initially be identified with only [physical extent] and perhaps [positive pole], and only later have added to it the feature [vertical] that distinguishes it from *big* and from the other dimensional adjectives.

If this is a correct characterization of the growth of word meaning, then children should go through stages in which they confuse words that have the same partial meaning. *Tall* might be used interchangeably with *big, wide,* or *long,* and confused with these same words in comprehension, since they could all mean [physical extent] [positive pole] for the child. As mentioned earlier, several studies did report the use of *big* in place of *tall, wide,* and *long,* and the confusion of dimensional adjectives with each other (Wales and Campbell, 1970; E. Clark, 1972; Brewer and Stone, 1975; Ehri, 1976). However, most of these studies only looked at the child's performance on one task or analyzed each task separately. If an individual child is tested on several tasks involving the production and comprehension of spatial adjectives, a slightly different picture emerges. If the theory outlined above is correct, a child who gives *big* as the opposite of *short* has as his meaning for *short* only the components [physical extent] and [negative pole], and he regards *short* as a synonym of *little.* He should therefore frequently confuse *short* with other dimensional adjectives for which he gave *big* as an opposite. A child who confused *tall* with *fat* in a comprehension test should have the partial meaning [physical extent] [positive pole] for these two adjectives, and therefore be likely to give *little* as their opposite. But Carey (1977a) found that individual children's error patterns on five tasks testing the production and comprehension of spatial adjectives were inconsistent with such a theory. A child who confused *tall* with *fat* on one comprehension task did not confuse these dimensions on a similar task using different objects or in the opposites game. A child who gave *big* as the opposite of *short* in the opposites game showed no confusion of dimensions in any other task.

Carey argues that the child must have a fuller meaning for these terms than the semantic feature hypothesis suggests. The child seems to extract not only a subset of the components of adult meaning for the word but also more specific information about the typical objects to which that word applies. Thus, the child may understand not only that *tall* means [physical extent] [positive pole], but also that it applies to people and refers to the distance from head to toe. But he may not know in what respect it applies to buildings or blocks or towers. Similarly he might learn that *deep* and *shallow* are opposites and apply to the ends of swimming pools, but he might not yet have learned that *deep* applies simply to distance downward from a surface, so that holes and bowls and canyons can be *deep*. Thus, if he were asked about the depth or shallowness of holes he might not know what dimension was being referred to. Only as he hears the word in a wider range of contexts does the child come to extract the common features of those objects or relations that make the word applicable, and so refine his representation of the meaning of the word.

In short, a great deal of evidence suggests that between the ages of two and six children acquire productive use of many words after minimal exposure to them, and that they begin to use these words before they possess the full adult meanings. But there remains some question as to the exact nature of the child's incomplete meanings. Future research must explore the interaction between the child's linguistic knowledge, the nonlinguistic context, and the strategies that the child adopts in understanding or using a word. A major question is the generality of the strategies used by children and where these strategies come from. Which of them are fairly universal and reflect general aspects of cognitive development? And which are more idiosyncratic and are derived from the child's particular experience? One aim of any complete theory of semantic development must be to trace the developing linguistic knowledge of the child. But at the same time the theory must account for how that knowledge interacts with the child's beliefs about the world to determine what he says and how he understands what is said to him.

6

Discourse and Metalinguistics

Emir (aged 4): I can speak Hebrew *and* English.
Danielle (aged 5): What's English?

Language serves complex social functions: a competent conversationalist uses a vast number of cognitive and social skills in addition to his knowledge of language as we have described it so far. He can talk about events distant in time and space, hence bring them into the experience of his listener; he can gauge his listener's needs for specificity or repetition; and he is sensitive to the implications of his and his listener's utterances.

Higher mental activities like memory, problem solving, and imagination seem enhanced or sometimes bounded by our language skills: we often hear it said that language is a tool for thought, or even that thought *is* inner language. It is as if the symbols and rules we acquired for the purposes of social interaction can be freed of that role for more individual use in our private mental life. For adults, language has many uses apparently divorced from its social function: witness dictionaries, spelling bees, puns, crossword puzzles, and Scrabble games, to name a few.

The two-year-old child differs from the adult in his use of language in two fundamental ways: he is not a good conversationalist and he does not appreciate language for its own sake. By the time he is six, however, he not only will have learned how to talk better, but also will have become aware of that which he talks, namely language. It is our belief that these two lines of development are inextricably interwoven. The two paths are roughly concurrent in time, but it would be very difficult to prove that one was necessary for the other to occur. All we can do is offer some suggestions for how these new properties of language emerge towards the end of the preschool years, and speculate a little about their basis. We do not wish to claim that language use ever becomes totally free from context; but, the influences on what we say and how we say it become increasingly remote from the stimuli of the immediate physical and social environment. We shall trace this progression first.

DISCOURSE

The Broadening Functions of Language

The very first words children utter do not seem to "stand for" an object, event, or relation independent of the goal of the communication. For example, one Russian child used the word *kat* only when she had thrown her toy cat out of the crib. She never pointed to it and labeled it under other circumstances, nor did she demand it, if someone else had it, by saying *kat* (Svachkin, 1973). Her use of the word was therefore quite rigid and narrow in purpose. Another child cited by Halliday (1975) also used two-word expressions for distinct, special purposes. He used *more meat* only in the sense of "give me more meat," never to describe meat. Such children seem to have a label for a whole complex situation that includes their personal wishes, rather than having a vocabulary at hand to use for various purposes. Needless to say, the period when the child behaves in this way is quite brief. Halliday reported that within a few months the child could extend his originally restricted use of expressions such as *more meat* to fulfill other purposes, such as remarking on the world. This shift from special purpose to multipurpose use of language seems singularly important to us because it makes our language quite different from animal communication systems like bird songs or the cries of apes, where one sound typically has a special communicative function. There is no possibility in animal communication for sound to be used as a symbol, whereas for the child the word acquires a freedom from one particular communicative goal. This important but unheralded achievement is the first step in the progression toward adult linguistic competence.

Language in the Here and Now

The two-year-old child talks very much in the here and now. His simple sentences involve objects and events that take place within his immediate personal experience. As we shall discuss in Chapter 7, it is probably vitally important in the early stages that the child share the encoding of these experiences with a linguistically mature adult or older child, in order to acquire the rudiments of language.

Before long, however, the child is making reference to objects not physically present. He is soon able to ask for *milk* or *cookie* even when his parent has put them out of sight. Once again, the child is developing a certain freedom from the stimuli that surround him in producing words in the absence of their referents. Slightly later, he can talk about events that happened in the past. Both of these achievements rely on nonverbal developments: the child's growing memory and appreciation that objects continue to exist when out of sight.

The result of these accomplishments is that the child is increasingly competent at communicating with people outside his immediate family. He is not dependent on being provided the cues for requests like *milk* or *potty* by an obliging parent; he can request these objects under any circumstances. He can also provide some orientation in time by using tense markings, crucial for distinguishing whether he sees a bear behind you right now or saw one last night on TV.

The other aspect of being able to represent absent objects and events through language is that the child can pretend in more and more complex ways. Again, this is not just a linguistic development, for very small children engage in imaginative play with objects, for example, using a blue rug as a ocean for a toy boat. But language extends this to a new level. Brown (personal communication) has suggested that words are first used in reference to real, three-dimensional objects, such as *table* for a real table; the child is then able to extend this word to a version of a table that shares some but not all of the properties of the original. For example, he may correctly name a two-dimensional picture or a very shrunken version in a doll's house. Later, he may use the word for something quite unlike the real object, such as a matchbox around which he seats some tiny dolls, and eventually children can say, "let's pretend we have a table" with no referent there at all. Children seem to vary enormously in their tolerance for "degraded" stimuli, with some perfectly bright children refusing to engage in such foolishness, and others with an imaginary playmate in every corner. One day we watched three-year-old Mandy take the head off a toy cow and peer inside. "Ooh!" we squeaked, "What's in his tummy? What can you see?" "Dirt," she said solemnly.

The Needs of the Listener

Nonlinguistic Discourse

Once the ability to refer to unseen objects and events is firmly established, the child has some of the linguistic apparatus necessary to take account of his listener's needs. There has been increasing interest in the last few years in the child's acquisition of the rules of conversation beyond grammar and vocabulary. Some aspects of discourse are independent of the content of language. For example, people have to take turns at speaking, they have to recognize their turn to speak, not dominate the interaction exclusively, not interrupt, and make eye contact or other non-verbal signs of attention and willingness to continue the interaction. The young child may learn these aspects of social interaction in the first months of life; that is, perhaps the roots of conversation lie in the non-verbal interactions the infant and his caretaker engage in. Bateson (1975) proposes that routinized turn-taking in games such as peek-a-boo provides the basis for later conversational turn-taking. Other nonlinguistic aspects of discourse are gaze-coupling, the use of eye contact to elicit and maintain an interaction, and gaze aversion to terminate it. Bruner (1975) sees the precursors to shared linguistic reference in the infant's following his mother's gaze to an object. Many of these aspects of social interaction may be unlearned, and by the end of the first year the infant is aware not only that other persons can be agents and do things for him, but also that he can engage their attention through gestures and eye contact to indicate what he needs. At this point the infant is proficient at regulating the content of nonverbal discourse with people he knows well.

Given this complex set of precursors, what is added by language? In our opinion, a great deal. Not only is it a lot more convenient to make an explicit reference or comment by linguistic means than by elaborate gesturing, it is also possible to engage attention and appropriate action from persons out of sight or visually distracted. Quite apart from this design advantage of human speech, there is the necessity for maintaining continuity of theme across the dialogue. There is an analogy in nonverbal interaction but language develops this to a new level. Pointing, after all, is very ambiguous compared to linguistic reference. The parent can comment verbally on a wide variety of aspects of a single situation, maintain attention by introducing novel linguistic forms, and teach through language. There is evidence from Keenan (1975) that the two-year-old child is able to maintain continuity in conversational topic over longer and longer periods of time, in contrast to the staccato quality of the eighteen-month-old child's discourse. Nevertheless, the language is still bound to the immediate present and will therefore fluctuate with the circumstances in a way that adult conversation does not; the two-year-old is still a captive of his environment. Even in a restricted play situation, however, the topics are infinite, and by 2½ years the child is indicating his willingness to direct his attention toward the same aspects as his interactor. The older and more skillful this interactor is, the more sustained will be the dialogue.

Linguistic Discourse

(1) *Articles*. The more attention the child pays to the content of his interactor's conversation, the more he will learn about the specifically

linguistic rules of discourse. Some we have had occasion to mention already; for example, the child has to learn that certain words shift meaning depending on the speaker, such as *my/your, here/there, this/that.* The use of the definite and indefinite articles in English also requires taking the listener's perspective and knowledge into account. The course of article acquisition has been partially mapped out by both Maratsos (1974) and Warden (1976) in a series of very interesting experimental tasks.

In Maratsos' study the children ranged in age from thirty-two to sixty months and each child was told several stories designed to elicit either definite or indefinite articles. For example, one story went as follows: "Once there was someone who wanted to have an animal. He went out to a pond. He saw two bunches of animals, lots of frogs and lots of turtles. He went up with his box and he put one of them into his box. What did he put in?" Since there has been no mention of a particular frog or turtle, the listener should answer "*a* frog" or "*a* turtle," since it is the first mention of a unique referent. In a second version of the story, the line is changed to "he saw two animals, a frog and a turtle." This sentence establishes the unique referent for the listener so the child should now reply "*the* frog" or "*the* turtle," in accordance with the discourse rule.

In another variant, no particular referent was established in the story, not even in a group, for example: "A man went to the jungle to look for a lion or a zebra. He looked all over to see if he could find a lion or a zebra. He looked for a lion or a zebra everywhere. He looked and looked. Suddenly, who came running out at the man?" This time the answer is "*a* lion" or "*a* zebra."

Maratsos found even the youngest children performed significantly better than chance on these tasks; that is, they had some notion of the rules for making definite and indefinite reference depending on what had been introduced in previous discourse. However, the younger children made frequent errors such as assuming a shared referent with the experimenter when it did not exist. For example, they would reply "the frog" to the story that introduced the group of frogs without identifying a unique member. To the younger children, it was sufficient that they themselves had a particular frog in mind.

Warden (1976) used a slightly different procedure in which the child had to initiate use of the articles rather than respond appropriately to them. The children received a story in cartoon form and had to tell the story to another child who could not see the pictures because of a screen. Each story involved four referents, two of which appeared twice, allowing for a first and a second mention. For example, in the first picture there might be a dog chasing a hen. In the second, a cow stops the dog and the hen is hiding behind the cow. Finally, the hen has laid an egg. Warden tested children aged three, five, seven, and nine years and adult college students. Adults always used an indefinite article to introduce the noun the first time, then in subsequent occurrences used the definite article, just as we did in the description of the cartoon. Clearly then, despite the fact that all the referents are concrete for themselves, adults take into account their listener's perspective. Three-year-olds, in contrast, were equally likely to use *a* or *the* on first mention, but they did prefer *the* for second mention. Table 6 shows the increasing tendency in this age range to take into account the listener's ignorance.

Both studies document the child's growing awareness of the perspective of the other person, as revealed by his use of articles. No doubt future research will elaborate on the contextual and task influences on this developmental course beyond the glimpse we have provided here.

(2) *The contingent query.* A more complex example of discourse is the contingent query, studied by Garvey (1975). The speaker in this case must be skilled at turn-taking in conversation as well as being attentive to his listener's needs. Garvey points out that almost any utterance can serve as the trigger for an unsolicited query from one's listener, in the form of a demand for clarification before the conversation continues. What is interesting is that the query episode can be slotted into an ongoing conversation without disrupting the overall sequence. After the query episode is completed, the turn at speaking reverts to the first speaker and the listener is obliged to respond appropriately to the clarified message. We can illustrate the process with a hypothetical example: on the left is a conversation containing three contingent queries; on the right is the same conversation without them:

I saw Harry, you know.	I saw Harry, you know.
What?	Yeah? How is he?
I saw Harry.	
Who?	
Harry.	
Where?	
Downtown.	
Yeah? How is he?	

The queries were deliberately chosen to illustrate the variety of functions they serve. The first, *What?,* is a straight request for repetition of the whole utterance, and would normally have a rising intonation to indicate this. The second, *Who?* alerts the speaker to a specific portion of the utterance that needs repetition or clarification. The final *Where?* does not request repetition, for the basic proposition has been communicated, but the listener requests further, previously unspecified, information. Once this is provided, the dialogue can proceed as before, with the listener responding to the initial utterance.

Table 6. Definite and indefinite referring expressions.

	First mention (percent)		Second mention (percent)	
Subject group	Definite expression	Indefinite expression	Definite expression	Indefinite expression
Adults	—	100	100	—
Nine-year-olds	18	82	100	—
Seven-year-olds	39	61	100	—
Five-year-olds	38	62	90	10
Three-year-olds	54	46	92	8

To be an ideal conversationalist, one must recognize both the rules of turn-taking in the whole dialogue and the signals, often intonational, that indicate the function of the query. This is obvious if we violate the rules and notice the havoc that results from an incompetent first (on the left) or second (on the right) speaker:

I saw Harry, you know.	I saw Harry, you know.
What?	Where?
You know.	Downtown.
Know what?!	Who?
Harry.	I told you, Harry!
	Was it a good one?

Garvey studied pairs of children aged between two and four years in natural interactions, and she kept a tally of the appropriateness of their responses to queries from their peers. Most queries were successful; that is, children answered specific queries with specific information, repeating whole utterances on request and generally attending to the intonational cues signaling the function of the query. Only the youngest age group was comparatively inattentive, not bothering to respond at all to 40 percent of the queries addressed to them. Because each member of the pair was the same age, it was not clear who should take the blame for this. Did the questioner fail to modulate the query correctly, or did the first speaker fail to understand a well-formed query? However, even the youngest children did not answer at random, suggesting that they already knew many of the conversational rules. Garvey also found clear evidence of different responses to falling intonation and rising intonation, although some of the children misinterpreted the function of a query on occasion. The same question-word can signal different queries, depending on whether the intonation is falling or rising:

I'm going to California on Sunday.	I'm going to California on Sunday.
Where ↘?	Where ↗?
Los Angeles.	California.

This is a rather fragile cue and we suspect it is usually bolstered in conversation by other signals, for example, a "filler" acknowledging that the content has been received:

I'm going to California on Sunday.
Oh, where ↘?
Los Angeles.

It is fascinating that children in the age range of two to four years exhibit these complex conversational skills. It is not yet clear whether they depend on nonverbal cues such as eye contact or facial expression to disambiguate the function of the query. For example, can the same children talk so skillfully in telephone conversations?

(3) *Negation*. Another aspect of discourse tnat has come under scrutiny recently is the notion of the presupposition. Negation is a useful example here, for one fundamental truth is that we cannot deny what no one has asserted. A person who walks into a room and says "this ceiling isn't blue" or "you don't have three heads," without any prior context, would rightly be considered mad. There has to be a reason for supposing the affirmative before we can negate; that is, a presupposition must be established. However the assertion does not have to be explicit for the negation to sound acceptable, in fact, it can be buried in a long chain of inference. When President Nixon made the historical statement "I am not a crook" it was not in response to a heckler shouting "crook!", yet neither could he have made the statement before Watergate without sounding very bizarre.

When are children aware of this property of negative sentences? Antinucci and Volterra (1973) claimed that children between 1½ and 2 years are aware of the rule and make sophisticated use of presuppositions. They do not, in fact, make negative statements out of the blue. The problem in proving that to our satisfaction is this: if we look at production data from children, select out all the negative sentences and search for the assertions that provided the occasion for them, we are almost bound to find them. The difficulty is twofold, for not only can the assertion be implicit in the discourse rather than explicit, but the assertion may be nonverbal in nature. Imagine watching your friend squeeze shaving cream onto a toothbrush and raise it to his lips. We hope you would not hesitate to shout, "That's not toothpaste!" even though he never explicitly stated that it was!

So the post hoc analysis of production data is too biased toward what we want to find, given the freedom we have to invent presuppositions. Comprehension data can mitigate this problem: one could devise a situation in which the child heard an unsupported negative statement and see if he recognized it as a rule violation. We (de Villiers and Tager-Flusberg,

1975) set up an experimental situation meeting these requirements, modeled after a task used by Wason (1965) with adults. We presented children with a visual display consisting of seven identical objects and one odd one, for example, seven horses and a cow. Now it is very natural to point to the cow and say "that's not a horse," because there is an expectation that the items should all be the same. We call this a plausible negative. The implausible negative is to point to one of the horses and say "that's not a cow." Why would anyone suppose it was? We had several different displays that we showed to two-, three-, and four-year-old children, asking each child to complete sentences of the sort "That's a _____" or "That's not a _____" when we pointed either to an odd item or one of the set of similar items. We kept a check of errors in completing the sentences and the time taken to complete them. Both measures revealed a large difference between plausible and implausible negatives. For example, some of the youngest children could complete the plausible negatives, but made errors on the implausible ones. So when we pointed to a horse and said "that's not a _____" they would reply "horse!" Older children also made more errors on implausible negatives than on plausible ones, and they took longer to reply to them when they did succeed in answering correctly. By four years of age the children were still slower at completing the implausible negatives, but the plausible negatives were completed almost as fast as the affirmative statements. This implies that, given appropriate context, the added grammatical complexity of negation is psychologically unimportant by the age of four.

In this very simple task we have evidence that even two-year-olds are highly sensitive to the plausibility of negative statements. It is not yet clear how skillful they are at reconstructing the lines of inference behind negatives in real discourse. Adults can generally make the presuppositions explicit if their listener looks bewildered; we have no evidence that two-year-olds can do this at all. The assertion behind a negative proposition can be more or less explicit. The most explicit is the case where a previous statement is denied, for example:

It's raining.
No, it's not raining.

Slightly more complex is an instance where what is denied is directly implied by the first statement:

I saw John's wife.
He's not married.

Anyone with a knowledge of English would be able to reconstruct the source of the affirmative that is being denied: to be married is part of the meaning of *wife*. However, some negatives rely on shared knowledge between the speakers that could not be reconstructed with the aid of a dictionary:

> The Williamses have gone to Maine.
> Jane hasn't left.

Here it would be necessary to know that Jane is a Williams, which is personal knowledge. There are cases where more than one proposition is required as an intermediary; in the following dialogue there are several shared inferences unspoken:

> I thought I'd invite Jim to the party in October.
> He didn't get tenure.

This is a very indirect way of denying that Jim will be here in October, since on superficial consideration what is being denied looks tangential to the proposition by the first speaker.

We would predict that very young children might have more trouble understanding the more indirect negatives than the simplest kind, because they do not have sufficient knowledge of the implications of words and phrases, and because their knowledge of the world is so limited. It is difficult to know what to predict about production. The same considerations would lead us to propose a similar progression from simple, direct denials to the more obtuse kind. However the alternative is equally plausible: perhaps on hearing an utterance the young child has all kinds of idiosyncratic associations that he uses as the basis for his negative sentences, in which case they will seem not at all direct to us, in fact they will be opaque. Until a method is developed to study this phenomenon unambiguously the debate can not be resolved.

(4) *Indirect speech acts.* To review the argument up till this point: the child slowly moves beyond the influence of immediate circumstances toward language that is increasing under his own control; that is, his vocabulary becomes more flexible, he becomes able to invoke past or distant events, and his use of various terms is increasingly molded by his broadening awareness of his listener's knowledge. As he becomes cognizant of these social aspects of discourse he is able to see beyond the surface forms of language to presuppositions of an increasingly complex kind. Having introduced the idea that language in discourse can involve inferences beyond the propositions themselves, we can turn to another important theoretical idea in discourse analysis: the illocutionary force. The term comes from a tradition in philosophy called speech act analysis, associated with philosophers such as Austin, Grice, and Searle. It has long been recognized that there are occasions when the function or goal of an utterance must be distinguished from its propositional content. To take an example, if someone said to you:

> Would you mind telling me the time?

it is inappropriate to simply say, "no, I wouldn't." The aim of the speaker is to find out the time, not question your affability. The sentence means something other than what it says, to use the broadest sense of *meaning* The illocutionary force of the utterance is a request, not a question. Similarly, the illocutionary force of:

> How many times do I have to tell you to get that frog out of here!

is a rather firm demand for action that is not fulfilled by the answer "seven!" Of course, in many simple declarative sentences the gap is not so wide: the aim of the speaker may be to convey the propositional content, plain and simple. But English is particularly rich in the devices it contains for modulating the politeness of requests for action by adding phrases to disguise the direct purpose. All this seems very unfair to the child, who has spent so much time just learning to decode the propositional content of the speech he hears.

Ervin-Tripp (1977) has proposed that children understand direct requests before they understand indirect ones. They would of necessity have to master the propositional content of sentences, but they would later learn that all sentences do not mean what they say. Shatz (1974) set out to test this possibility by looking at the responses of two- to four-year-olds to requests from their mothers. To her surprise, there were very few erroneous reactions to the mothers' indirect requests. The children seemed to understand from an early age that the forms were to be interpreted as commands, and they did not reply inappropriately to them. They were more likely, however, to give a verbal reply to an indirect command—in addition to obeying it—than to a direct command. Holzman (1973) looked at interrogatives that the parents of Adam, Eve, and Sarah spoke to their children, and she found many indirect forms present from the earliest transcripts, but few misinterpretations by the children. Garvey (1975) in her study of pairs of nursery school children found similar results. Nevertheless, there is the possibility that at an early age children have merely mastered certain forms as idioms or routines, and it is these forms that give the impression of a mastery of indirect requests. For example, children may learn that commands are frequently posed as questions beginning "can you . . ." A strong possibility is that very young children only process the core of the proposition, hence never detecting the ambiguity. At a stage when one of the children studied by Brown and his associates clearly did not understand "why" questions, his mother said to him:

> Why don't you put your toys away?

He probably heard only:

> Put your toys away.

There has not been sufficient research yet on children's understanding of even more indirect requests; for example, when someone shivers and says:

It's cold in here.

to get his listener to close the window. However even in these cases, there is ample opportunity for nonverbal cues to the speaker's meaning, which could disambiguate the illocutionary force. Shatz reported that only some of the very youngest children responded to the indirect commands as if they were direct. So the evidence that comprehension of direct commands precedes that of indirect is rather weak.

Bates (1976a) presents evidence that in the child's own speech production, direct commands precede the indirect by a substantial margin. Unfortunately, the indirect forms are often grammatically more complex also, so it is not completely clear how we should interpret the delay. One of the most interesting findings comes from an experiment reported by Bates on children's judgments of politeness. The children listened to two different puppets requesting candy, and had to decide who asked most nicely for it. For example, one puppet might say:

Give me candy.

and the other:

I would like some candy.

or:

May I have some candy?

Bates found that children three years old thought the puppet that asked indirectly was more deserving of the candy, but they could not explain this choice. If pressed for an explanation, they often said "this puppet said 'please'," although none of the puppets did! So it seems as though recognition of polite forms precedes the ability to produce them.

Speech Style

It is interesting to note that parents modify this aspect of language in talking to children of different ages. They address more direct commands to two-year-olds, perhaps in recognition of the fact that the indirect forms may be misinterpreted (see Chapter 7). However, there are variables other than age that enter into choice of speech style. We have noticed in the records of our play sessions with two-year-olds and their parents that we are much more polite and indirect to the children than their mothers are to them. This was brought home vividly to us by an interchange with a particularly awkward little girl who began crumbling Playdo and rubbing it onto her baby sister. Revealing his true colors as a parent rather than a playmate, then rapidly reverting to his indirect form, Peter snapped:

Don't do that! I wouldn't . . . should you?

So status and role are also important influences on speech style. We talk differently to two-, four-, and ten-year-olds, to teachers and pupils, to policemen and professors. There are different codes or registers that speakers use in different circumstances. For the child to be able to modulate his speech depending on his listener, he must have mastery of the following:

1. Enough flexibility of grammar and vocabulary to be able to choose among speech codes.
2. A recognition that different listeners have different needs in conversation; for example, that a stranger will need more explicit information than a close family member.
3. A recognition that certain modes of address are more polite than others.
4. The ability to tell which audience deserves, or will demand, a more polite or formal style.

Shatz and Gelman (1973) studied four-year-old children teaching a game to two-year-olds, to their peers, and to adults. The four-year-olds were surprisingly adept at modifying their speech style to their audience. They were more direct with the two-year-olds, and they addressed more indirect requests and questions to the adults, just as adults would do.

Social-class differences in speech codes have been researched extensively in Britain by Basil Bernstein and his colleagues (Bernstein, 1966). This research suggests that middle-class children have mastery of two registers: one a restricted code for use in the family situation, when there is extensive shared knowledge, another, called the elaborated code, for more formal occasions such as school. The codes differ in the proportion of content words versus pronouns, the politeness of forms of address, and so forth. Working-class children, in contrast, had only the restricted code, which put them at a disadvantage in formal situations. Bates (1976b) reports that Italian children by the age of two years showed a class difference: the middle-class group apparently already conversed in such a way that adults depended less on context to understand them than to understand a working class group of the same age.

A question that has not yet received a satisfactory answer is: What component skill do these working class children lack? Going back to our analysis of what is necessary for adopting different speech registers, there are at least three possibilities:

1. They do not have the flexibility of vocabulary or grammar to demonstrate modifications.
2. They fail to recognize their listener's needs.
3. They have not realized that certain groups require different forms of address.

Any of these three possibilities could be the result of either delayed development or a lack of social opportunity, making it difficult to evaluate the significance of the social-class difference for school performance or remediation.

To review the argument so far: the proposal is that as children grow older they become less and less dependent on context in producing and understanding language. In their vocabulary, they gain this flexibility early; by the age of three they can make reference to absent persons and events. This enables them to carry their language to new circumstances and new audiences. At around age four they become increasingly sensitive to their listener's needs in conversation, and they can now make explicit what is not shared knowledge. They gradually learn to make use of the implications and presuppositions that underlie much of adult discourse but have no surface cues in the environment or the speech itself; rather they are buried in the shared history and knowledge of the speakers. Finally, at around four or five years, children are capable of modifying their style of speech depending on their audience, showing sensitivity to the poorer understanding of two-year-olds and to the power and status of adults.

Becoming a Good Liar

What might be the ultimate achievement of this line of progress? We will make a scandalous claim: it is to lie effectively, for "only men can be fools and liars" (Olmsted, 1971). However offensive it may seem to regard lying as the culmination of a developmental trend, just consider the skills inherent in lying. The liar cannot be bound by circumstance or he would uncontrollably blurt out the truth. He must be aware of his listener's knowledge or he would be caught out. Finally, he has to be aware of what information would best convince his listener, and even the style to adopt to convey it most effectively.

Of course few psychologists have dared investigate lying in young children (but see Hartshorne and May, 1928). Some observations we have made informally suggest there may be several immature forms of lying before mastery is achieved. One story was told to us of a woman who had placed several small cans of ant poison around her house. A friend and her small boy came to visit, and after a time the woman noticed one of the cans was displaced from its original position. Not wishing to alarm the child unnecessarily, she put on her sweetest and calmest voice to ask, "Did you touch this little can?" Her young visitor beamed back and said "Yes!" At this point the woman became noticeably ruffled and her manner changed abruptly to a sharp "What did you do with it?" "Nothing," said the child, shutting up like a clam and disavowing all! There was simply no way to ask the question neutrally! The story illustrates how two-year-olds may appear to take into account their listener's wishes in giving an answer, but it is by relying on tone of voice and manner rather than the content of the message.

We have on numerous occasions witnessed older children, of three or four years, with an equally disastrous strategy for getting out of trouble. Such a child will rush forward as his mother arrives and say determinedly, "I didn't break the lamp!" before anyone has claimed he did, thus giving away the fact that the assertion to be denied was true! Real lying is much more subtle: it is the deliberate use of language as a tool to escape reprimand, with the content of the message unsupported by context, and designed to mislead the listener.

METALINGUISTIC AWARENESS

This talk of language as a disembodied entity, to be used for various purposes, leads us to the next question: When are children consciously aware of language? We have talked a great deal about language rules but have never claimed they were conscious rules, yet it is clear that we as adults can reflect on language as a system, or else a book like this would be impossible.

Inspection of various lines of evidence leads to the conclusion that children around the age of five are aware of language as something that can be turned around on itself, played and joked with, and used as a tool in lying, in reasoning, and in memory. The area of *metalinguistics* is a very rich one for further study. The little that is known now can be reviewed under the headings: (1) awareness of component sounds (2) awareness of word-meaning correspondence, (3) awareness of rules of grammar and semantics, and (4) awareness of ambiguity.

Awareness of Sounds

Weir's recordings of her son in his crib (Weir, 1962) reveal his preoccupation with the sounds of language for their own sake:

    back please
    berries
    not barries
    barries
    not barries
    berries

Yet it is only much later, at around five years, that children can consciously recognize that words are made up of component sounds. In 1964, Bruce tried to get children to play a game by asking: "Take the word *address*. Take off the *a* sound. What's left?" Children under the age of six were baffled by the task. Yet Bruce had deliberately chosen words that could be subdivided into other real words, to try and maximize their success. These same children had for years been making distinctions on the basis of these component sounds, yet the rules were not in conscious awareness.

Similar work was done with Russian children by Zhurova (1973), who set up a clever game for preschoolers. She placed a sentry on a little bridge over which different toy animals had to cross. The experimenter played the role of the sentry, the child played the role of each animal in turn. The sentry asked each animal to say the first letter in its name as a password. The child was supposed to say *b* for *bear* (or its Russian equivalent), *d* for *dog*, and so forth. The following delightful dialogue shows that the task was as opaque to small Russians as Bruce's task was to English-speaking children:

> (Child approaches bridge with a toy billy goat)
> Experimenter: What's the first sound in your name?
> Child: Bill-ee-goat
> Experimenter: But what's the first sound?
> Child: Me-eh-eh-eh!
> Experimenter: No, now listen—b-b-billy goat
> Child: B . . b . . b?

The children were unable to perform as asked until age four and could not do it readily until age five or six.

Awareness of Words

Vygotsky (1962) wrote, "The word, to the child, is an integral part of the object it denotes." By this he meant that children find it difficult to see words as arbitrarily connected to meanings. A preschooler explains the names of objects by the attributes they possess, for example, "a cow's called *cow* because it has horns." If the child is asked, "Could you call a cow *ink* and ink, *cow*?" (admittedly a bizarre question) the child will reply, "No! Ink is used for writing and a cow gives milk." The attributes cling to a name, and move with it.

Interestingly, some work with young bilingual children (Ianco-Worrall, 1972) shows that they develop an appreciation that words are arbitrary earlier than monolingual children do. This is presumably because their exposure to the two languages reveals that different people can use different words to refer to the same thing, that vocabulary is a matter of custom rather than necessity.

Preschoolers have a very restricted notion of what can count as a word (Papandrapolou and Sinclair, 1974): at first it is only concrete nouns and verbs and they will not admit such words as *if, is, for,* and *and*, rejecting them as readily as *oople*. One child we saw even denied that *ghost* was a word, "because it's not real." Here again we see the confusion of word and referent. Until the child can separate words and things, he is likely to have problems learning to read and write. Imagine the child's perplexity if we point to a mark on paper and tell him "that says *the*." To the child who has no conception of a word disembodied, that must seem as weird as it still seems to us to say "let $x = \sqrt{-1}$."

Fortunately, the age at which formal schooling begins coincides with the age at which most children reach a certain level of metalinguistic awareness. Cazden (1976) reports overhearing a kindergartener in her classroom staring at words in wonder and saying "*little* is a big word, and *big* is a little word!" The extent to which reading difficulties can be traced to a failure to reach this level is still a matter of speculation and research.

Awareness of Rules and Grammar

The child's ability to reflect on the grammatical rules of his language is of great interest. In the chapters on grammar we often had occasion to debate whether the rules were "psychologically real" or not for children. Rules were proposed that fitted the observed speech quite adequately, but the rules were open to the criticism, "But children can't know a rule like that, they just talk, they don't construct sentences!" This is a very thorny problem for psycholinguistics, and one that will continue to perplex. The fact is that it is not unique to linguistic behavior: the rules a physiologist would write for an activity like walking would include very complex factors that we certainly are not conscious of as we put one foot after the other. But language is different because we have some awareness of its components, and linguists have provided a way to represent its structure. We can tell when something is inappropriate or ungrammatical. This in turn gives linguists another source of evidence for determining rules: they are not limited to writing down speech and then trying to write parsimonious rules. Typically, an anthropological linguist can find an informant from a tribe, present him or her with alternative sentences, and say, "Can you say this in Umbimboto?" or "Would anyone ever say that?" In this way, the investigator can narrow down the possibilities among the rules he writes much more readily than by collecting vast samples of spontaneous speech.

Developmental psycholinguists have been enthusiastic about tapping the young child's metalinguistic ability, because, instead of waiting around to collect several hours of tape, the researcher can merely ask the two-year-old, "Which is better, *two shoe* or *two shoes*?" and so on. In this way the child's rule system can be revealed. Ursula Bellugi tried this question on Adam early in the research project. Adam's response is a classic; he said triumphantly, "Pop goes the weasel!"

However, in 1970 there appeared a research report (Gleitman, Gleitman, and Shipley, 1972) describing elicited judgments of grammaticality from two-year-olds. Admittedly there were only three children, and the sentences were extremely simple, but the report was enthusiastically received because the technique sounded so promising. The investigators introduced the task in the form of a game for mothers and children to play together. First the researcher and mother played it and then the children were invited to join in. The mother read some simple imperatives that were either correct, for example:

Eat the cake.

or reversed:

Box the open.

and the researcher either said "good" and repeated the correct sentences, or said "silly" and corrected the reversed sentences. After a few examples all three children were eager to become the "judge." The three children, all aged about thirty months, could tell the difference between the deviant and the well-formed sentences. However, they accepted over 50 percent of the reversed imperatives as "good," so their discrimination, although significant, was far from perfect.

To determine what the children thought was silly about the sentences, it is crucial to examine the corrections they offered. Unfortunately, the children were more reluctant to offer a correction than they were to judge, but it is interesting that the corrections they suggested changed meaning rather than just grammar. For example, *box the open* was changed to *get in the box*. Of the nineteen corrections obtained, only three of these changed word order alone.

We used a modification of Gleitman's procedure with several children whose linguistic ability we measured by MLU, since at least one of Gleitman's three subjects seemed to us very verbally precocious for her age. Our subjects played a game with two puppets, one of which said things "all the wrong way round." The child was asked to help the teacher puppet teach the backward puppet how to talk properly. The children were enthusiastic about this task; one little boy, whom we visited twice, said on seeing the puppet again, "I remember him! I teached him how to talk!" The backward puppet spoke imperatives with correct (for example, *pat the dog*) or reversed word order (*cake the eat*), and the child had to judge whether he was right or wrong. We chose *right* or *wrong* instead of *good* or *silly* because the latter have semantic connotations. We also asked the child to tell us "the right way to say it" instead of asking him to "fix it up", to try and maximize the chance of the child's responding to grammar rather than meaning.

In a second session, we gave the same children nonsense sentences like *tickle the table* or *drink the chair,* to see if they could judge and correct them. When we arranged the children according to their MLU, we found the following developmental sequence:

(1) The least advanced children could not discriminate between the reversed and correct sentences. Furthermore, their behavior suggested they saw through the faulty grammar to the meaning and judged that instead. For example, when the puppet said "teeth your brush," one child immediately pretended to brush his teeth and said, "that's O.K." Nevertheless, these same children rapidly rejected the nonsense sentences, showing that the game itself was not beyond their grasp. However, they could offer no corrections.

(2) Slightly more advanced children could reject the reversed imperatives but not offer suggestions as to how to correct them. These children did offer corrections for the nonsense sentences, showing again that the task demands were understood.

(3) The next children in the sequence offered corrections for the reversed imperatives, but like Gleitman's subjects, they seemed guided more by considerations of meaning. So they changed *house a build* to *live in a house,* for example.

(4) Only children with an MLU of over 4.0, which is beyond the average two-year-old level, could offer direct word-order corrections for the reversed imperatives. In a subsequent study we further documented the shift from predominantly semantic corrections to word-order corrections with increasing linguistic maturity (de Villiers and de Villiers, 1974).

In a television documentary that we made, we were keen to capture on film the phenomenon of judgment. In the glare of the camera lights, we patiently explained to a three-year-old girl that one of our puppets "has a terrible problem. He can't talk properly. He keeps saying things the wrong way around. Can you help us teach him how to talk?" Alas, she was too quick for us. She replied, "*My* puppet has almost as bad a problem, 'cept he says everything *sideways,*" at which point she twisted her puppet at a peculiar angle! Since the cameraman collapsed at the same time we did, this gem never made it into the finished documentary.

We are not optimistic about using judgments as a means of determining the psychologically real rules for child speech. Metalinguistic awareness comes many months or even years after the child appears to use such rules systematically in his own speech and in understanding others. We are not going to tap this awareness in the average two-year-old, but it is the two-year-old whose rules are most often in doubt. Nevertheless, the emerging awareness of syntax and semantics is a fascinating area of study in its own right and promises to be an exciting one in the future, particularly as it relates to other aspects of cognitive development.

Awareness of Ambiguity

One of the more subtle linguistic skills is the appreciation of ambiguity—that certain words, phrases, or sentences can mean different things depending on the context. To recognize that possibility is to suspend the influence of a particular context and see the hypothetical alternative. Several different levels of ambiguity are possible: *lexical* ambiguity, where a single word has two or more meanings, for example, *board, glasses,* or *stick;* surface-structure ambiguity, in which the groupings imposed reveal various possibilities, for example, *thin boys and girls;* and deep-structure ambiguity, where the double meaning is not a property of the surface form, for example;

The shooting of the hunters was terrible.

Bever (1968) has speculated that children first appreciate surface-structure ambiguity and only later recognize deep-structure ambiguity. He held that five-year-olds' jokes capitalized on surface tricks, like:

Why can you never starve in the desert?
Because of the sand which is [sandwiches] there.

Ten-year-olds, in contrast, appreciate deep-structure tricks as in:

I can jump higher than the Empire State Building.
How come?
The Empire State Building can't jump!

This interesting proposal has not been supported in the studies conducted so far. Kessel (1970) undertook a thorough investigation of children's understanding of lexical, surface-structure, and deep-structure ambiguities. The children, aged between five and ten years, were asked to select a picture depicting a spoken sentence; two of the four pictures presented were appropriate if the child recognized the double meaning. For example, the sentence "the eating of the chicken was sloppy" was presented with four pictures: some people messily eating a chicken, a chicken slopping its own food, and two "dummy" pictures. Kessel found that as early as kindergarten the children could pick out two appropriate pictures for a lexically ambiguous item, like *pen* as both a writing implement and an enclosure. However, clearly this result would not hold for all lexical ambiguities, for we continue into adulthood to learn new meanings for old words like *grass* and *fence* that we hope are not in the five-year-old's vocabulary.

When given a sentence like "the eating of the chicken was sloppy," the six-year-olds tended to choose two appropriate pictures but for the wrong reasons; for example, they would say "these both have chickens in them." Older children would reject one alternative, with a justification such as "no, the people are eating, not the chicken." By third grade the children could accurately detect both meanings. Surface-structure and deep-structure ambiguity were detected equally early; if anything, there was a slight lag in recognizing two meanings for surface-structure ambiguities, which is the reverse of Bever's prediction. In speech we distinguish the meanings of surface structure ambiguities by intonation or pausing:

They fed her dog . . . biscuits.
They fed her . . . dog biscuits.

Kessel read the sentences to his subjects, so he was forced to read each one twice, once with each intonation pattern. Deep structure ambiguities like:

The eating of the chicken was sloppy.

cannot be distinguished by intonation. It would be interesting to see the effect on the pattern of development of presenting the sentences in written form or without intonation.

Jokes

At around the same time that children begin to recognize ambiguity, there is a huge change in their appreciation of puns and jokes that rely on ambiguity. To refer back to our discussion of indirect requests, the six-year-old may now delight in replying to

Can you tell me the time?

with

Yes, I can.

demonstrating that both direct and indirect meanings are now available to him.

Compared to lying, joke-telling is a more light-hearted culmination of the skills that form the theme of this chapter. For discourse rules are just as important an influence on effective joking as is the appreciation of word play. Four-year-olds have often learned a couple of jokes but not that jokes grow stale when told over and over again. They find them uproariously funny to tell to their mother a hundred times a day. Similarly, they may retrieve something of the form of a joke but not the rules that make it funny, for example, the fact that an ambiguity must be set up and then revealed, or that there should be a connection between the first and second parts of a dialogue. We told one four-year-old the Empire State Building joke and watched him destroy it in telling his friend: "Hey! Guess what! The Empire State Building can't jump as high as I can!" Or Elizabeth, at four, who had the routine format, "What did the X say to the Y?" but had no conception of how to make the reply funny. So she would generate hundreds of "jokes" a day like:

I say, what did the guitar say to the violin?
What?
Buttons! (screams of laughter from Elizabeth *only*)

Telling jokes and riddles is as sophisticated as lying in terms of discourse rules, but it is perhaps even more advanced when one considers the subtle ambiguities and relationships on which the humor depends. Most of us never reach the level where we can create good new jokes, but we can at least recognize that failing. Most young children cannot!

SUMMARY

Over the first five years, language becomes a very flexible medium. In the beginning, the child's language is dominated by the immediate situation. With time, the child becomes less and less reliant on physical cues from the here-and-now in order to speak. By the age of four or five years, the child is able to modulate the content of his speech depending on his listener's likely state of knowledge, and he has already started to adopt different speech styles for different listeners. The increasing flexibility has its origins in the communicative demands made on the developing child to learn to converse with wider audiences about topics remote in space or time. Moreover, the choice the child now exercises in speaking may render the object of choice available for conscious consideration, for by the age of five or six years the child has become aware of the sounds, meanings, and grammar of his language, and can appreciate jokes that rely on verbal trickery. The debate has raged for years over whether language in the human species evolved for primarily social communicative purposes or to serve the intellect. At least for the ontogenesis of language in the child, the two may be inseparable.

7

A Structured Child
or a Structured World?

LANGUAGE UNIVERSALS

Language, it is claimed, is unique in two respects: unique as a form of behavior and unique to man. Its special properties have led many writers to propose that the capacity for language must be innate in humans; that we genetically transmit to our offspring the ability to acquire a human language, a feat out of reach of any other species. The present chapter will explore the various ways in which language has been held to be qualitatively different from other forms of human behavior as well as animal communication.

Certain distinctive features of language have been found in all human societies studied to date. All normal human beings communicate with an oral-aural code. Furthermore, language is a system of symbols that stand for real-life referents, but which symbol stands for which referent is arbitrary; otherwise, all languages would have identical vocabularies. Language has a syntax; that is, combinations of elements mean something different from the sum of the parts. *John hit Mary* conveys a different message from *Mary hit John*. Given this potential for combining elements, the range of meanings that can be expressed is infinitely large. This brings us to the property most often underlined in current linguistics: human language is creative, for most sentences that we speak have never been heard or spoken before. From the communicative standpoint, we can use language to talk about events remote from us in space and time, bringing them second-hand into the experience of our listener. Brown (1973) argues that it is this characteristic that makes possible the transmission of culture from generation to generation, alleviating the necessity for a human child to recapitulate the experiences that led to that culture.

The use of an oral-aural code is hardly unique in the animal kingdom, though many animals use other media of communication such as vision or scent. However, the units in animal communication systems do not function as symbols to the same extent as words do. Usually, the vocabulary is shared by all members of a species, though in bird song there are distinct dialects for different regions (Marler, 1952). In many cases a signal is a degraded version of the behavior it suggests; for example, a dog may bare its teeth to communicate a threat rather than to bite. In other cases the relation of signal to message is arbitrary: bees returning to the hive execute a complex dance to convey the distance and direction of a source of honey (von Frisch, 1967). Although the relation is arbitrary, it would be hopelessly inefficient if bees had to learn it, for young bees could hardly fly all over the countryside at random until they learned the vocabulary of their elders. Instead, the vocabulary is part of the genetic make-up of the species. Human languages may have developed flexible vocabularies to allow for potential expansion to new events, objects, and experiences. The range of meanings expressed by lower animals is very restricted compared to human language. Many of their signals convey messages about threats, predators, sexual excitement, or territoriality. Dingwall (1975) has surveyed the physiological evidence showing that these forms of communication are mediated by the limbic system, which is a very old part of the brain in evolutionary terms. Man still has a limbic system and there is some evidence that emotional ''language''—swearing, cries of pain, and so forth, can be elicited by electrical stimulation of that region (Penfield and Roberts, 1959). However, most of language in man is controlled by the cortex. Emotional communication may be on a continuum both behaviorally and anatomically with animal communication, but the rest of language is not.

Katz (1976) believes that it is at the semantic level that the uniqueness of human language is most in evidence. He argues that human languages are all intertranslatable (which is a point of dispute); any proposition has a counterpart in a sentence in any natural language. In other words, we can express in language any conceivable thought.

The most important characteristic of human language is syntax, which is the organization of the units of language to convey meaning. Psychology long ago gave up the notion that we open our mouths and one word triggers the next in line, for such a model of speech production fails to account for the hierarchical structuring of language. Instead, language is organized in advance of speaking, as was pointed out by the physiologist Karl Lashley in a famous paper in 1951. He argued that many actions require movement sequences that are executed too rapidly to consist of a small chain of responses. Playing the piano, for example, requires transitions from one muscle movement to the next that occur faster than the time it takes a nerve impulse to travel from the hand to the brain and back again, so one movement could not be acting as the stimulus for the next to occur. Instead, whole patterns must be planned in advance and structure the movements. Language is not unique in possessing pre-arranged structure. The order of actions clearly makes a difference, just as the order of words does in language. The result achieved may be quite different if the order is scrambled. Some patients who suffer brain damage have disorders that encompass the syntax of action as well as of words, and they behave in a bizarre fashion. They may confuse the most ordinary actions; for example, a patient might seal an envelope before inserting a letter, or strike a match and put it to his lips before opening his cigarettes.

Now we come to the question of creativity. There is no question that action is infinitely various: no tennis shot is ever repeated exactly; no spider builds the same web twice. Both are adaptive to circumstances and so are in that sense creative. But if action has a syntax, can the units be combined indefinitely to produce an infinity of different meanings or goals? The difference may be one of magnitude. To return to our example of the letter and envelope, a different arrangement of those subunits would have a different end result but it would not be a meaningful one, it would not be an action that served any useful purpose. It would be analogous to an ungrammatical sentence like *Mary John hit*. It would count as a failure to achieve the goal, rather than a different goal. Something similar is true of animal communication, even the most elaborately structured, like bird song. Some birds sing songs in which the order of trills is of vital importance, but the importance lies in distinguishing the song as the song of that species. Scientists have played birds tape recordings with the song rearranged, and found that changes in order result not in a different message, but in a rejection of the song as meaningful. Again, permutation of the units results in the equivalent of a nonsentence, not a new message. Since research of this kind is in its infancy we do not wish to rule out the possibility that some permutations for some species may be new messages, in which case we would reexamine the uniqueness of language syntax. At present, though, the syntax of human language does seem a distinctive characteristic.

What of the proposals made in Chapter 6, that children increasingly talk of events remote in space and time, and take into account the needs of their listener? Could animals do that? It appears that a creature as lowly as the honey bee can! The dance upon returning to the hive conveys the distance and direction of a source of nectar. This certainly counts as a remote event, one that is not immediately present to trigger the response. Bees even modify their dance according to the reception they get from their audience in the hive. One aspect of the dance varies with the quality or concentration of nectar found at the source. In very hot weather the hive becomes dehydrated, and the hive bees are less enthusiastic about highly concentrated nectar. A bee that returns boasting of a strong source will get a cool reception and modify its dance accordingly, while a bee returning from a dilute nectar source is encouraged to amplify its claims. It is fun to anthropomorphize about these accomplishments but of course the difference is that bees learn none of this. Instinct has solved the problem of inference about one's audience for the bee. The scale of both achievements is vastly different from human language even in the two-year-old. Nevertheless, it is clear that neither the ability to refer to remote events, nor a sensitivity to one's audience, are unique to human communication.

The very general characteristics of human language mentioned earlier can be seen to have some continuity with other behavior and with animal communication. However, linguists have catalogued other features that are purported to be universal in human languages and unique to them. For example, languages have an implicit hierarchy of grammatical classes. In a 1964 paper, Chomsky contended that there are degrees of grammaticality in natural languages, rather than sentences being completely acceptable or unacceptable. As an illustration, native speakers can accept the sentence *John plays golf* but reject *golf plays John*. Yet this latter has some meaning compared to *golf plays aggressive*. McNeill (1966) imagined a hierarchy in which the top of the tree would be all the words of English, which would then divide into nouns and verbs, and then the nouns would be divided into, say, animate and inanimate, and so on down to all the distinctions that make a difference grammatically. The more of these distinctions that are violated, the less acceptable a string of words would be to a native speaker. *Golf plays John* has at least a noun object, even though animate things are not usually played by inanimate things, but *aggressive* is not even a noun, never mind something not usually played.

Furthermore, all languages have a means of expressing the basic grammatical relations *subject and predicate, modifier and noun,* and *verb and object*. It will be remembered from Chapter 3 that these are not superficial properties of sentences but are defined in the deep structure of a sentence. Subject, for example, is not the first noun, nor is it consistently identifiable with a semantic role like agent. It is the noun phrase that branches directly from the sentence node in the abstract underlying structure proposed in transformational grammar. According to this grammar, transformational rules operate on these deep-structure relations to permute and delete them to arrive at the surface form of the sentence. The rules are thus structure-dependent, and this dependency is also supposed to be universally true, though considerable dispute still rages as to the form of deep structure and transformations themselves.

As explained earlier, the abstract deep structure was introduced as the input for transformational rules to reduce the number of rules needed for deriving passive sentences, for example. Instead of several rules to generate passives from their corresponding actives, the necessary transformations were allowed to operate on an abstract deep structure, but in a specified order (see Chapter 3). So if one accepts that version of transformational grammar as a correct model of language, *rule ordering* is another putative universal. We simply do not have sufficient knowledge of the structure of nonlinguistic behavior to be able to identify analogs to these properties—that is, analogs of an abstract deep structure on which rules operate in a specified order to produce the surface arrangement of units.

More recently, Chomsky (1976) has formulated the argument that there are universal constraints on the form that grammars of natural language can take. He argues: suppose a language has an abstract property, *P*, that all speakers respect and behave in accordance with, and yet it can be demonstrated that nothing in their environment would make it likely for them to select *P* as a hypothesis; then, that property must be part of the innate knowledge that they bring to language learning. As such, P must be a language universal, even though it may have been described in only one language. Chomsky presents several candiates for a property such as *P*, one of the most convincing being related to the constraint on complex noun phrases (Ross, 1967). For example, take the transformation that moves *wh*-words to the front of sentences and relates sentences (*a*) and (*b*) below:

(a) John saw whom?
(b) Whom did John see?

The *wh*-word can be deeply embedded in the sentence from which it is extracted, as in:

(c) Mary believed Bill wanted her to see whom?
(d) Whom did Mary believe Bill wanted her to see?

However, in certain cases the transformation is not allowed. For example, although (*e*) is understandable, (*f*) is recognizably peculiar:

(e) Mary believed the claim that John saw whom?
(f) Whom did Mary believe the claim that John saw?

What is special about such cases? When the *wh*-word is embedded in a noun phrase, it cannot be extracted from that noun phrase. Chomsky believes this and many other facts can be incorporated in one general requirement that transformational rules are bounded and cyclic, that is, they cannot operate across certain syntactic boundaries. Speakers of English recognize that (*d*) is acceptable but (*f*) is not, yet it is unlikely that they were exposed to type (*d*) with any great frequency, nor is it probable that they have made errors like (*f*) and been corrected. Yet to produce (f) would be a perfectly reasonable generalization were it not for this very general constraint. Properties such as this, Chomsky reasons, must be part of the knowledge we share as human beings, limitations on the form of grammars that human languages can take.

Since it would be unreasonable or unethical to control the environment of children to see what form their language would take, it is difficult to know how such a claim could be proved or disproved. Fortunately, there is another avenue of proof: if any human language turns out not to have a putative universal constraint, then that constraint could not be a candidate as an innate property of the language faculty. The example given above highlights the close interaction between findings in linguistics and language acquisition.

Universals are open to question on two grounds: are they indisputably true of all human language and if they are, are they unique to language? As we shall see, however, proposals for language universals have provided the major logical underpinnings for the argument that man must have an innate capacity unique to language and unique among animals.

THE LANGUAGE ACQUISITION DEVICE (LAD)

One of the most influential theories of language acquisition, propounded by Chomsky (1965), Katz (1966), and McNeill (1966), claims that the human child is in much the same position as a linguist trying to discover the grammar of an unknown language. Each is confronted with a haphazard collection of sentences, some of them incomplete, full of slips of the tongue and grammatical errors, from which he must construct a theory of the language. Since rules based simply on surface-structure regularities will ultimately fail, it is necessary to discover the base structure from which each sentence is derived, for only then will the underlying system be revealed in its simplicity. How can the child, or linguist, discover the base structure when he receives as input only surface structures? The argument goes: only by being equipped already with some theories about language. In the case of the child, this means innately.

McNeill (1966) conceived of the problem in the following way: imagine building a device that would receive as input a collection of English sentences, and its task is to learn the rules of these sentences to generate novel ones of its own. What properties must the device have to achieve this goal? McNeill argued that in order to make sense of the input the device would need to be equipped with information about the structural characteristics common to all languages. For example, it would need to know that a hierarchy of grammatical classes exists, that a sentence consists of a subject and predicate, that transformations operate on underlying rather than surface structure, and so forth. McNeill argued that these properties are not given by the input itself and yet they are critically important prerequisites for coming up with the right theory of language. By equipping the device with these hypotheses he attempted to narrow the possible grammars it might invent on the basis of the input.

To supplement the logical argument, McNeill collected evidence that the child from the start demonstrates knowledge of grammatical classes and basic grammatical relations. He suggested that Brown's subject Adam already respected adult grammatical distinctions in a pivot grammar (see Chapter 3 for definition). He claimed that the class of words that would count in adult speech as adjectives all occurred in Adam's pivot class, so they already formed a distinct category. At a later time this group subdivided into modifiers versus articles versus demonstratives, each with distinct privileges of occurrence, as if Adam were starting near the top of the implicit hierarchy of grammatical classes and working his way down as he acquired the finer distinctions. Unfortunately, this finding has been considerably weakened by Brown (1973), who has pointed out that Adam had nothing like a pivot grammar at the time of these observations, and those children who did have a real pivot grammar (Braine, 1963a) showed no respect at all for adult grammatical categories! So Gregory, for instance, had some verbs as pivots and some in the open class. The adjective *pretty* was a pivot, *hot* was an open word. More recently (1970a) McNeill himself abandoned the idea of an innate hierarchy of classes.

McNeill (1966) also argued that the earliest sentences of Brown's three subjects contained the basic grammatical relations. Although subject and predicate did not occur together in the children's first sentences, McNeill explained this as a performance limitation, pointing to the occurrence of modifier and noun plus verb and object constructions as evidence. We argued in Chapter 3 that describing child speech in such abstract categories has fallen into disfavor since the grounds for distinguishing, say, *subject* from *agent* are missing from child speech. We conclude that the empirical evidence is extremely weak for either grammatical classes or grammatical relations being present from the start to guide children's language learning.

Quite aside from lack of empirical evidence, it is difficult to imagine how the child might be equipped with substantive universals. What form would they take? As Fodor (1966) argued in reply to McNeill, how would it help the child to know that "there exist nouns," when he would still have the problem of identifying them in the input? Slobin (1966) had an alternative proposal to McNeill. He preferred to believe that the substantive universals are not given in the child's genetic make-up but are, rather, the result of the way he processes the world. He pointed out that the child is not learning language divorced from reality, and there are real-world correlates of such categories as nouns and verbs, animacy, plurality, and so on. Perhaps all the child needs is the ability to learn conceptual categories, that are necessary for purposes other than language. Then he simply learns the grammatical forms corresponding to these categories. However, in the standard transformational account, there can be no real-world correlates of abstract categories like subject. On the other hand, we have seen in Chapters 3 and 4 that the psychological reality of that notion for the child is open to question. We will have occasion to return to this issue in a later section of this chapter.

The basic question then is: To what extent is the language-learning ability specific to language, and to what extent is it a consequence of the way we process the world in general? Could grammatical knowledge of the kind proposed by Chomsky be built upon the division of reality into conceptual categories like property, thing, and action? If so, are there specifically human ways of processing reality that preclude the learning of language by other species? Is that why human languages have similar structural properties?

McNeill, in a later paper (1970b), designated this kind of universal, namely, one founded on adult cognition in general, as a *weak* universal. In contrast are *strong* universals specific to language and having no analog in other behavior or in the world. An an example he chose the fact that nouns and verbs have asymmetrical properties in adult language, since verbs can more readily be used as nouns,

Skiing is good exercise.

than nouns can as verbs,

Let's basket these strawberries.

Furthermore, verbs are inflected to agree with noun properties such as plurality or gender, but nouns remain uninfluenced by the tense or aspect of the verb. This independence of nouns is not easily explained by the way we divide up reality, but seems peculiarly linguistic and qualifies as a strong universal. What evidence is there that the child comes equipped with this bias? McNeill uses an observation by Braine (1971), who taught his young daughter two nonsense syllables, *niss* and *seb*. *Niss* was used for a kitchen utensil; *seb* for the action of walking with the hands. Neither was used in a sentence by Braine. His daughter spontaneously produced sentences with both words, using *niss* as a noun in *that niss* and *more niss,* and *seb* as a verb in *seb Teddy*. However, she also used *seb* in sentences like *more seb, that seb,* where it apparently functioned as a noun. *Niss* was not used as a verb. This asymmetry was also present in her own language at the time. Unfortunately, it is not clear that she was inventing this bias herself, for the input may have had this property and she could have been simply incorporating the new words into established structures. It would be nice, but probably impossible to carry out, to do the same experiment with a child who heard *no* uses of verbs as nouns before he himself produced them. In support, we must add that no one has reported any child having the false hypothesis that nouns should be inflected to agree with verbs.

The constraints on grammar described by Chomsky (1976) would similarly qualify as strong universals. No one has claimed that any of the constraints are initially violated in child speech, but then perhaps no one has looked, for the construction types in question are very late to appear.

LANGUAGE IN CHIMPANZEES?

The question of language specificity might also be answered by looking at other animals who seem to share our way of processing reality. Our visual and auditory systems are not much different from those of the higher primates, so could they learn a human language? In nature they do not, but it may be an accident of evolutionary pressure that they developed a simpler communication system for their needs. We are asking a slightly different question, which is: What are the limits of the ape's language learning capacity? Could we train a chimpanzee to use a language having the universal features proposed above?

We are well aware of the failings of this approach in answering the question of whether man has an innate capacity for language. First, we may be able to train an ape to use language much the way we can train a dog to walk on its hind legs, neither achievement having any bearing at all on the question of the basis of the equivalent human propensity (Fodor, Bever, and Garrett, 1974). However, the argument in favor of a language acquisition device has been that without one, a child could not acquire human language. It was claimed to be a logical *necessity*, not just a short cut provided by evolution.

Second, if we fail to train a chimpanzee to use language, it may be inadequacy of our training techniques rather than the incapacity of the chimpanzee (Premack, 1971). It is difficult to ascertain the true limits of ability of another species. Premack has noted that some animal species have made substantial gains in intelligence over the last century of experimental testing!

Finally, if our chimpanzee subject fails despite the superiority of his education, there could be reasons for his failure having little to do with his lack of a language acquisition device with the requisite universals. Chimpanzees, though charming, are not as bright as children. Their memories, their attention, their reasoning, are all inferior and may set limits on the language they can acquire. If this is the case, it should also be true of severely retarded children. Their languages also should be different qualitatively from normal children. Yet, in arguing for the innate basis for language, Lenneberg (1966) claimed that the language learning of retardates was slower but not different in kind from that of normal children (see Chapter 9).

The initial problem confronting experimenters who wish to train chimpanzees to use language is that the vocal apparatus of the chimp is unsuited to the rapid articulation required for human speech (Lieberman, 1973). The Hayeses (1951) spent many years trying to teach their chimpanzee Viki to speak, at the end of which she could laboriously mouth a few single syllable words like *cup*. So the oral-aural code had to be abandoned before progress could be made.

Washoe

The Gardners (1969) noticed the manual dexterity of chimpanzees and decided to exploit it rather than the speech organs. There is a naturally occurring human language that uses this medium of communication, namely the sign language of the deaf, the American Sign Language (ASL). In this system, a particular hand configuration and movement is the equivalent of a word in spoken language, and Klima and Bellugi (1975) have argued that it also has the equivalent of phonemes. Evidence is accruing that it is as rich as any other human language in the meanings it can express, though the expressions are often quite different (see Chapter 9). It was a natural choice for researchers seeking a non verbal equivalent for chimpanzees.

The Gardners reared an infant chimpanzee named Washoe in the company of human signers. Her upbringing was similar to that of a human child, except that she slept in a trailer in the backyard of the Gardner's home. She was given constant attention and her human companions continuously communicated with her and each other. She was coaxed to produce signs and given food and social rewards for doing so, though training was not rigidly organized. The Gardners preferred to arrange Washoe's life so that if she chose to "talk," she would have interesting things to talk about and congenial people to converse with. The results of the program are quite remarkable, yet many psychologists and linguists have reacted in violent opposition. We once heard it said that there is a predictable pattern of reactions to any scientific discovery: the first is to deny the finding is real, the second is to claim one knew it all along.

It was therefore quite expected that the first reports that Washoe was making signs and understanding them would be greeted with disbelief. The Gardners kept diaries of her progress and also films, so interested psycholinguists could view them and decide for themselves. By the end of twenty-two months and at the age of three years, Washoe had control of some thirty-four signs. To the uninitiated observer viewing the films, it looks like so much hand-waving. It is difficult to separate the signs as units without knowing what one is looking for, and this is made especially difficult by Washoe's incredible baseline activity. It is hard to pay attention to the right thing when watching a chimpanzee hang by one toe from the branch of a tree, scratch herself with one foot, and casually place one hand to her chin for the sign *dirty*. Nevertheless, her ability to use these signs is no longer in doubt, nor is her ability to understand them, for the Gardners have completed extensive and well-controlled tests.

How similar are Washoe's signs to human words? Might they not simply be responses made to the various stimuli surrounding the chimp? They might indeed, but then we would have to conclude the same thing about the child. For Washoe uses her signs as creatively as a child uses words, spontaneously generalizing a sign to a new instance of a class of objects. *Dog* for example, was used for all dogs, including pictures in a picture book. *Open* was used for doors, boxes, and a briefcase, and even extended to turning on faucets. In fact, her use of words is uncannily like the descriptions of complexive overextensions by children discussed in Chapter 5.

> Washoe learned the sign for *listen* for an alarm clock which signals meal time. She used the sign for other bells, for the sounds of people walking outside her trailer door, and for watches and clocks. She signed *listen* spontaneously when she found a broken watchband, and then when she saw a flashlight that blinks on and off. Washoe has a sign for *hurt* which she learned first with scratches or bruises. Later she used the sign also for red stains, for a decal on the back of a person's hand, and the first time she saw a person's navel. (Klima and Bellugi, 1973, p. 99)

One exciting aspect of Washoe's sign use was her invention of new signs for objects. For example, she spontaneously coined the conjunct expression *water-bird* for a duck. Human languages use combinations of signs for more extensive purposes than the coining of new words. Very near to the start of Washoe's signing, when she had about six signs, the Gardners reported that she spontaneously combined signs in sequences. They felt that they could distinguish these sequences from two separate signs rapidly following each other by the fact that Washoe relaxed her hands after a sequence. This relaxation is the sign equivalent to intonation in speech signaling the end of an utterance. Washoe punctuated her sequences with this gesture, giving credence to the proposal that the signs were meant to be related. The sequences themselves certainly seemed appropriate to the situation, as these examples illustrate:

open drink (for the water faucet)
key open please blanket (at the bedding cupboard)
listen dog (at the sound of barking)
more tickle (for her companion to resume tickling Washoe)
Roger Washoe tickle (for Roger to tickle Washoe)

Brown (1970) has concluded that Washoe's sequences look very much like the simplest sentences of the Stage I child. The same range of meanings seems to be expressed: agent-action-object, action-locative, recurrence, and so forth (see Chapter 3). The primary reason for attributing these rich meanings to young children's sequences is that the children use a formal means, word order, to encode contrasts in meaning. So *bite cat* means something different from *cat bite*. In contrast, Washoe at the start had flexible sign order. She was as likely to say *tickle you* as *you tickle* when she wanted to be tickled. The randomness of her sign combinations led Brown (1970) and Fodor, Bever, and Garrett (1974) to conclude that while Washoe may be expressing the semantic relations she is not encoding them syntactically. This makes her linguistic achievements less impressive than those of a two-year-old child.

This conclusion may have brought sighs of relief to those who like an orderly world with humanity safely out of reach of its primate relatives. It is not possible for us to end the story there, however. The first complication is that ASL is not a sequential language to the same extent that speech is. Spoken language does things with order that ASL accomplishes by other means. For example, by different positions in space, a signer can establish the subject and object of a stentence simultaneously. It is not clear whether Washoe was taught normal ASL or a version of Signed English, which is more like English sentences translated into sign and retaining English syntax. So it is possible that sign order was much freer in the language seen by Washoe than it is in the language heard by hearing children. Furthermore, young deaf children learning ASL may not consistently use sign order either, but learn different means of encoding contrastive meanings. Brown (1970) made the point that there is little communication pressure operating on Washoe as long as she is conversing in the here-and-now, for her companions have context to disambiguate her meaning. Perhaps if order became crucial for her message to be understood, she would learn to use it.

Moreover, there are conflicting reports about Washoe's sign orders. In the fifth and sixth diary summaries of the Gardners, they reported that the signs in combination tended to occur in all possible orders (Brown, 1970). This information must have led to the conclusions about Washoe's lack of syntax in Klima and Bellugi (1973) and Fodor, Bever, and Garrett (1974). But the film of Washoe released by the Gardners shows that she uses sign order consistently to signal different meanings! Dingwall (1975), citing Linden (1974), wrote "In some facets of syntax, Washoe demonstrates greater ability than her human counterparts. The Gardners report that Washoe makes fewer reversals of word order and that she performs at a much higher level of accuracy (90% versus 50% correct) in matching reversible strings such as 'cat bit dog' versus 'dog bit cat' to pictures" (pp. 41–42). Evidently we shall not be able to reach any firm conclusions until the Gardners publish all their data.

Before we leave Washoe, we need to raise the issue of the extent to which she uses language like a human child. We mentioned that the meanings she expresses look similar to Stage I meanings, but is signing a true communication system for her? Fodor, Bever, and Garrett (1974) do not equivocate: "Washoe's signing, like that of domestic animals, appears to have remained resolutely nonconversational. Washoe didn't chatter with her trainers in the way that children chatter with their parents, nor did she use her language to make spontaneous reports of the state of her nonlinguistic environment" (p. 442). This opinion is in sharp contrast to Brown's (1973) report: "The ASL functioned between Washoe and her trainers as a genuine medium of communication. She did not simply respond to the initiative of her trainers but she herself constantly initiated communication. The number of signs she produced at suppertime, for instance, came to average about 150." The first authors must have been around some extraordinarily talkative children to reach the conclusion they do. Certainly the film of Washoe shows her engaging in spontaneous descriptions and requests, and not merely responding to questions. It also documents a further aspect of Washoe's language that had been denied by all other reports: her production of questions. The Gardners claim they can distinguish Washoe's questions from her statements by a difference in duration of the sign, as well as a questioning look. We described previously how Washoe would drop her hands after a sequence of signs to mark the end of a statement. In the case of a question, Washoe would look at her companion and hold the final sign for a longer duration. In the film Washoe is seen making the signs *time eat*?, holding the *eat* sign until her companion signs *yes,* and then signing *time eat* in the normal declarative fashion. Unfortunately, a spontaneous situation like this does not convince us that Washoe intends a question. We need evidence that Washoe lacks information, seeks it, and then acts in accordance with it. It is puzzling that, for all the thousands of times Washoe was asked *What's this?* about an object, there are no reports that she asked for the name of a new object. Yet that is the first, and for years the most prevalent, question that children typically ask. Washoe appears to have the rudiments of language. She has progressed to about the same level as a Stage I child, but Brown (1973) adds the caution that we only call the Stage I child's accomplishments *linguistic* because of the system he eventually acquires. That is rather unfortunate for Washoe.

Sarah

Although Washoe's syntactic and logical accomplishments are meager at present, in another recent study a chimpanzee called Sarah went much further. Like the Gardners, Premack (1971) was interested in circumventing the requirement that a linguistic ape must be able to speak, but the similarities in the studies stop there. Premack had no interest in approximating the natural environment of the child to see what the chimpanzee might pick up and choose to say. Instead, he was interested in the limits of the chimp's logical and linguistic capacities. He employed the rigorous training techniques of operant conditioning, which basically involves dividing the most complex task into its simplest components and applying systematic rewards contingent on responses until the requisite complex behavior is built up. Premack formulated recipes for teaching various language forms. The language was not a naturally occurring one like ASL, but consisted instead of magnetic-backed plastic tokens that could adhere to a board between Sarah and the experimenter. Each token was arbitrarily associated with a single object or relation—for example, a green triangle might be chosen as the "word" for apple.

The fundamental principle of the training procedure was to make a change in the language coincident with a change in the chimp's environment. Premack first exploited an exchange scheme in which Sarah was required to place a plastic token on the board to receive a favorite food, say a fig. Sarah was easily trained to do this, and Premack introduced different tokens for different foodstuffs like bananas, chocolate, and so forth. Now discrimination training was begun. Sarah was shown a food item and had to choose, among several tokens to be placed on the board, the token previously associated with it. On being shown an apple, for example, she would have to choose the green triangle. This again is a very trivial task for a chimpanzee and no one at this point could claim the tokens constituted a vocabulary.

At this point, Premack kept the foodstuff constant for a time, while varying the experimenter who offered it to Sarah. Sarah learned to place two tokens on the board: one corresponding to the foodstuff and another one for the experimenter. This two-step discrimination having been attained, different actions were introduced. Sarah had to notice the agent or experimenter and respond appropriately by using tokens for the action he was performing, whether it was *giving* or *pointing* or *inserting* or whatever, and the object he used. At this stage one might argue that Sarah was using the equivalent of simple sentences like *Mary give Sarah fig, Joe point apple, Roger insert apple dish,* and so forth. Sarah was trained to comprehend sequences of tokens in similar fashion, until she could respond to commands as complex as:

If Sarah take square then Mary give Sarah candy.

versus

If Sarah take triangle then Mary not give Sarah candy.

But Sarah's "language" needs to be examined with a more critical eye. First, what gives us the right to call these bits of plastic "words" or "symbols"? They are certainly used appropriately, but is there any evidence that they "stand for" objects in the way human words do? Premack has been most interested in this question of symbolism, and reported one intriguing experiment with Sarah. It proved very easy to teach Sarah to choose tokens corresponding to properties of an object she was shown. She had a vocabulary of tokens for modifiers like *yellow, green, big, small, round,* and *square* and she could choose from among them to "describe" a banana, for example. After establishing this skill, Premack tried a fascinating variation. Instead of a real object, he showed Sarah the plastic token corresponding to apple, namely a green triangle. How did she describe it? As round, red and edible. Sarah had distanced herself from the token's immediate physical properties and was using it as a symbol for the real object.

At later stages of training, Sarah could be taught new words without a correspondence between object and token having been systematically trained over many trials. A piece of plastic was introduced to mean *name of* and it could be placed between a new token and object, for example, in English equivalents:

pear name-of

Moreover, Sarah could now correctly answer questions about the names of objects, as in:

What name-of

Therefore, Sarah had a rudimentary metalinguistics.

Syntax

The question of syntax is a knottier one. Can lines of plastic tokens be called sentences? First, it is clear that Sarah did not merely respond to each token in turn: the tokens interacted to convey the meaning, and the whole sequence was important. Second, Sarah did not just produce the sequences on which she was trained, but generalized her training to new sequences not previously seen. Fodor, Bever, and Garrett (1974) contend that Sarah's productivity seemed limited to substituting new words or phrases into established syntactic frames, rather than generating novel constituent sequences. They write "it has the striking consequence that the 'language' that Sarah has mastered is fundamentally nongenerative" (p. 449). Their criticism may need to be modified in the light of the recent report by Premack (1976) that in three cases Sarah showed mastery of a structure on which she had never been trained. These cases did not merely involve transfer of lexical items or phrases across constructions. They were as follows:

(1) *Adjectives and demonstratives.* Sarah was first trained on sentence frames like the following:

> Sarah take red.
> Sarah take green.

and sentences such as:

> Sarah take dish.
> Sarah take pail.

However, she had no training in the use of color terms as modifiers of an object. She was then presented with sentences such as:

> Sarah take red dish.

and she performed correctly. Premack argues this is evidence for Sarah understanding a novel sentence structure without prior training. Unfortunately, it can be criticized on the grounds that she may not have needed to understand the relation between *red* and *dish* in order to act correctly—she may have responded to the words individually. Premack rules out this possibility for adjectives in general by including rigorous tests such as:

> Sarah take red dish blue pail.

To understand that sentence it was necessary for Sarah to understand that *red* modified *dish* and *blue* modified *pail*. Clearly, at this level she understood adjectives, but it is not pertinent to the novelty argument. It would be more impressive if Sarah, confronted with a large set of dishes and other objects varying in color, had spontaneously coined:

> Give Sarah red dish.

to request one in particular of her listener. Production of the novel sentence would indicate that she understood that it would be ambiguous for her listener if she produced only a form like those she had been taught. Data are not available for the spontaneous production of adjectives but there are data for the demonstratives *this* and *that*. Sarah had received training on the demonstratives *this* and *that* in the frames:

> Sarah take this.
> Sarah take that.

After the distinction was mastered in both production and comprehension, two cookies were placed on the table, one larger and more desirable than the other. Sometimes the large one was near her, sometimes near the trainer. Without further training she was required to produce:

> Give Sarah this cookie.

or

> Give Sarah that cookie.

depending on the location of the large cookie. She performed with only three errors on fifteen trials, none in the first five trials. Premack contends that this is further evidence of her mastery of novel syntactic structures. It is not clear, however, at what point in her overall training this event took place. It is likely that it occurred after the training on adjectives, quantifiers, and so forth, so there were plenty of existing models for the frame:

> Give Sarah [property] cookie.

and the demonstratives, though having the distinctive feature of deixis, may have been to Sarah just another property to insert in the frame. Lest we seem overly critical, it should be noted that the demonstration of Sarah's spontaneous mastery of novel syntactic structure involving modifiers, weak though it is, has not even been attempted for young children! No one has done the experiment of restricting a baby's experience with modifiers used with nouns, to see if they would use them spontaneously!

(2) *Conjunction*. The second example provided by Premack concerns sentence conjunction. Sarah had been trained to write whole sentences such as:

> Mary give Sarah banana.
> Mary give Sarah chocolate.

However, when both foodstuffs were present she spontaneously coined the conjunct sentence:

> Mary give Sarah banana chocolate.

Hence, she literally deleted the redundant elements! In like fashion she conjoined verbs, as in:

> Wash cut apple.

Since conjunction is one of the major devices for generating novel syntactic structures it is impressive that Sarah hit upon it by herself. Fodor, Bever, and Garrett (1974) dismiss this achievement because conjunction is not truly *recursive:* it is a list-like structure that does not require hierarchical organization. In contrast are relative clause constructions such as:

> The man wore a hat.
> The man who wrote the letter wore a hat.
> The man who wrote the letter that the newspaper published wore a hat . . .

These forms are truly recursive in that each noun phrase can be expanded indefinitely to form new constituent structures that are hierarchical in form. Of course it would be more impressive if Sarah were to invent this generative schema after, say, exposure only to sentences with one relative clause. It would be especially impressive since we again have no evidence that young children spontaneously create sentences involving more than a single relative clause. If Sarah were to do it we should probably let her out of the cage and put the children in.

(3) *Transfer across syntactic role*. The third example discussed by Premack is a more basic requirement for language: the ability to transfer a phrase into a different syntactic role. Sarah received training on the metalinguistic form *name-of* only in nominative position:

X name-of Y

Nevertheless she was able to understand the term when it appeared for the first time in accusative role in sentences such as:

Sarah insert name of cracker in cup.

versus

Sarah insert cracker in cup.

Now the novelty of propositions would be severely restricted if phrases or words were tied to their original sentential roles. Sarah, like children, proved able to generalize beyond the boundary of the sentence frames on which she was trained.

Clever Hans or Clever Sarah?

Some of Premack's critics have questioned not Sarah's linguistic accomplishments so much as her credibility. For example, Brown (1973) remains unconvinced that possible artifacts were ruled out by Premack's procedures. He draws a comparison with a circus horse of apparently extraordinary arithmetic talent, appropriately known as Clever Hans. Hans would tap his forehoof the correct number of times in answer to a problem of addition or multiplication. His ability astounded the naive and learned alike, until he was finally exposed as a sham. His trainer would quite unconsciously relax when Hans reached the right number of hoofbeats, and Hans would promptly stop and receive his reward. Brown cautions that Sarah's trainers also might have given unwitting cues about the right response.

To answer his critics, Premack brought in a naive trainer who did not know the language and had him pose Sarah questions. Sarah's performance dropped from her usual 80–90 percent correct to around 70 percent correct, but that was still way above chance for the problems posed. Brown argued that the "dumb" trainer might have learned enough of the language to begin giving nonlinguistic cues, but Premack (1976) presents the data on the extent of the dumb trainer's learning and shows that he actually mislearned more than he learned, so that Sarah would have been foolish to follow his advice! A second objection to the control was that

Sarah might have learned the answers initially by using nonlinguistic cues from her trainers, then committed to memory the answers to particular problems. She received fifty-eight problems from her dumb trainer, and it is conceivable that she could have memorized fifty-eight answers. However, she had received at that time 2,600 problems, and had no way of guessing *which* fifty-eight she would receive, so she would have had to have learned 2,600 answers (Premack, 1976). It is difficult to believe that feat more likely than her learning some simple linguistic rules. Also, her performance on novel problems in the dumb-trainer situation was not significantly poorer than her performance on problems she had seen before, which removes most of the appeal of the memory explanation. Interestingly, Sarah also became quite slapdash in her placement of the tokens. Such effects might be equally expected if a child were suddenly required to converse with his parents via a foreigner who did not comprehend the messages!

New Developments

The third study of a chimpanzee's capacity for language acquisition was designed to get around the objection of artifact, at least in so far as computers are infallible. For Lana, a chimpanzee at Yerkes Primate Research Center, is in communication with a computer. She types messages onto a keyboard and receives them back via a console above the keyboard, which is situated in her room. Also in the room are small trays that deliver candy, or fruit, or other items she requests from the benevolent machine. She can get access to other events rewarding to man's closest relative: movies and slides, a window to stare out at a sunlit scene, and someone to walk in and tickle her!

The language uses visual symbols consisting of arbitrary hieroglyphics. These are painted on the keyboard, and the keys are frequently randomized in position so Lana must attend to the symbols on them. Reports of this study are still scanty, but evidence so far suggests that Lana performs comparably to Sarah on at least the elementary sentence forms (Rumbaugh and Gill, 1976). When the computer begins a sequence of symbols, Lana can complete it, showing that it is the end product she attends to rather than a sequence of responses. Moreover, occasionally she has hit a wrong key and then erased the sequence and begun again, thus spontaneously correcting her errors. Also, for the first time we have clear evidence of a chimpanzee requesting the name of an object that no one had named for her.

This line of research is still too new to be evaluated throughly, and there are all kinds of possibilities on the horizon. As the chimps catch up on humans, we anticipate that the demands made upon them will be all the more stringent. At least one study (Fouts, cited in Fleming, 1974) plans to test whether chimpanzees taught sign language will transmit their knowledge to their offspring or resort back to natural chimp communication. Everyone has his own preference for what he would try; some tests that would be useful from the perspective of child-language acquisition are: (1) a check on the ability of the chimpanzee to understand and produce recursive structures and embeddings; (2) an attempt to introduce displacement in time through the introduction of past and future verb tenses; (3) a demonstration that chimpanzees can modify a message depending on the knowledge of their listener; and (4) stronger evidence that the chimpanzee spontaneously asks questions of all varieties.

This diversion into studies of chimpanzee language was an attempt to find an answer to the difficult question: Could one learn a human language without a specifically linguistic innate ability? The language acquisition device was proposed to solve the problem of discovering an abstract deep structure from the input of surface structures. Nothing in the reports so far suggests that apes have learned a language that requires the postulation of a deep structure/surface structure distinction plus ordered transformational rules or any of the other universals proposed to be uniquely human (Chomsky, 1976). If those are held to be a necessary part of the definition of human language (Chomsky, 1967), the answer to the above question must, so far, be "no." Let it be said, however, that the psychological reality of the linguistic model for humans is still in doubt, and as Brown so aptly phrases it: "Chomsky's 'essentials' will certainly leave the animals 'out,' but what is the use of that if it is not clear that we ourselves are 'in'?" (1973, p. 58).

THE INPUT TO THE CHILD

The other half of the argument that a strong innate component is required for language learning is the contention that the input to the child is not helpful to him in discovering latent structure. The last ten years have witnessed a substantial shift in our knowledge of the context of child language learning. At the start of the modern enterprise, many researchers took notes on the context of children's utterances only if it helped disambiguate meaning. The corpus of utterances was meant to stand alone as a model of what the child was acquiring. Children appeared to learn language at a rate that astounded some writers ((for example, Miller, 1965), especially since the data on which children had to base their hypotheses about language, the speech addressed to them, were "defective," "degenerate," full of slips of the tongue and grammatical errors (Chomsky, 1965). The speech of adults was held to be a very poor reflection of their linguistic knowledge for two reasons. First, because all sorts of confounding factors like lapses of memory or attention, false starts, and slips intervene to distort the sentences they speak. Second, adults speak in surface structures, with many transformations distorting the base structure. Yet the argument was that the child had to have the base structure of a sentence revealed to him before he could understand its meaning. These were not empirical claims about adult speech to children, for no one had systematically studied it, but Fodor (1966) guessed that "the language environment of the child does not differ in any useful way from that of an adult."

As early as 1964, however, Brown and Bellugi pointed out that the utterances of parents to young children were short, syntactically and semantically simple, well-formed, and repetitive. Subsequent research has confirmed and extended these findings (see Table 7). For example, most studies have found that the mean length of utterance in adult-child speech, measured in either words or morphemes, is considerably shorter than in adult-adult speech (e.g. Drach, 1969; Newport, 1975). In fact, a mother's utterances become even shorter when her child first begins to produce intelligible words (Phillips, 1973; Lord, 1975). Mothers usually speak to eight-month-old children to catch and maintain their attention, or for their own amusement, and so the MLU of their speech is as long as it is to twenty-eight-month-olds. However, once the child starts to respond with a word or two, much of the mother's speech is concerned with eliciting a verbal response from the child. The speech of a mother to an eighteen-month-old thus has a shorter MLU, with more single names and phrases like "What's that?" or "say 'ball'."

As well as being short, parental speech is remarkably grammatical. Newport (1975) studied the speech of fifteen mothers to their children and found the incidence of ungrammatical errors to be only one in 1,500 utterances. Moreover, their speech was highly repetitive, 34 percent of their utterances being full or partial repetitions of one of the previous utterances. These features—brevity, completeness, and repetitiveness—must surely narrow the gap between adult knowledge and performance that was held to cause difficulties for language learning.

How general is this phenomenon of the modification of speech directed at young children? Similar findings come from studies of black (Drach, 1969) or white (Snow, 1974) mothers, of different social classes (Snow et al., 1974), and even of different language communities and cultures (Blount, 1972). Furthermore, parents and nonparents perform similarly (Sachs et al, 1972), mothers being only slightly better at predicting the linguistic needs of their children than women without children (Snow, 1971). Even four-year-old children produce simpler speech to two-year-olds than to adults, whether they themselves have two-year-old siblings or not (Shatz and Gelman, 1973), and they can switch to the appropriate speech mode if told that a doll is a baby or a grownup (Sachs and Devin, 1973). These findings with four-year-olds gain further importance from the fact that particularly in non-Western cultures the primary caretakers of

Table 7. Differences between adult-child and adult-adult speech.

Type of difference	Source
Phonological differences	
Higher pitch and exaggerated intonation	Drach, 1969; Phillips, 1970; Remick, 1971; Sachs et al., 1972
Clear enunciation, slower speech, and distinct pauses between utterances	Drach, 1969; Newport, 1975; Sachs et al., 1972
Phonological simplification, distinct consonant-vowel combinations, and frequent syllable reduplication	DePaulo and Bonvillian, 1975; Ferguson, 1964, 1977b
Syntactic differences	
Shorter and less varied utterance length (MLU), shorter mean preverb length	Brown and Bellugi, 1964; Drach, 1969; Lord, 1975; Moerk, 1972; Nelson, 1973; Newport, 1975; Phillips, 1970, 1973; Sachs et al, 1972; Shatz and Gelman, 1973; Snow, 1971, 1972; Vorster, 1974; Cross, 1977
Almost all sentences well-formed and intelligible	Broen, 1972; Brown and Bellugi, 1964; Drach, 1969; Newport, 1975; Phillips, 1970, 1973; Remick, 1971; Snow, 1971, 1972; Cross, 1977
Many partial or complete repetitions of own or child's utterances, sometimes with expansion	Brown, Cazden, and Bellugi, 1969; Kobashigawa, 1969; Newport, 1975; Snow, 1971, 1972
Fewer disfluencies or broken sentences	Broen, 1972; Newport, 1975; Snow, 1972
Many constituents uttered in isolation	Broen, 1972; Newport, 1975; Snow, 1971, 1972
Transformationally less complex	Drach, 1969; Pfuderer, 1969
Fewer verbs per utterance, fewer coordinate or subordinate clauses, fewer embeddings	Drach, 1969; Newport, 1975; Phillips, 1970, 1973; Shatz and Gelman, 1973; Snow, 1971, 1972; Vorster, 1974
Rarity of modifiers and pronouns, more content words and fewer functors	Newport, 1975; Phillips, 1970
Subject nouns or pronouns and auxiliary in *yes-no* questions often deleted	Newport, 1975; Remick, 1971
More imperatives and questions to young children, particularly occasional questions	Blount, 1972; Brown, Cazden, and Bellugi, 1969; Drach, 1969; Gelman and Shatz, 1975; Newport, 1975

Table 7 (*Cont.*)

Type of difference	Source
Increasing number of declaratives with increasing age of child	Brown and Hanlon, 1970; Newport, 1975
Semantic differences	
More limited vocabulary use, but with unique words for objects and many diminutives	Blount, 1972; Drach, 1969; Ferguson, 1977b; Phillips, 1970
Reference invariably to the here and now; words have concrete referents and there are few references to the past	Phillips, 1970; Remick, 1971; Shatz and Gelman, 1973; Snow, 1971; Cross, 1977
Different level of generality in naming objects	Anglin, 1977
More limited range of semantic relations	Snow, 1974
Pragmatic differences	
More directives, imperatives, and questions	Blount, 1972; Gelman and Shatz, 1975; Newport, 1975; Shatz and Gelman, 1973
More deictic utterances	Newport, 1975

young children are often their older siblings (Slobin, 1968). Vorster (1974) puts it best when he writes: "In the spirit of Cole Porter one may say that women do it, men do it, adults do it, children do it, parents and non-parents do it; and the recent investigation mentioned above shows that indeed 'the Dutch in old Amsterdam do it'—in essentially the same way at various socio-economic levels."

How might the special aspects of adult-child speech assist the child in acquiring the conventional forms of his language? Several recent investigators have suggested that the corpus of speech provided by adults to children represents an input well-suited for the learning of linguistic structure and form, an input carefully graded in complexity to the child's capacities and containing many teaching devices (Snow, 1972, 1974; Vorster, 1974).

Of the phonological aspects mentioned in Table 7, several might play a role in facilitating language acquisition, but others seem to be more a reflection of adults' conceptions of the way babies talk. The adults' utterances are clearly pronounced and have distinct pauses between them, so the child can easily tell where they begin and end. The exaggerated, sing-song intonation could also be important, since du Preez (1974) has shown that children in the one-word period typically imitate the word on which the major stress falls, called the *tonic* word. That stress is greatly exaggerated in adults' speech to children. The tonic word often falls at the end of the utterance, but when it appears earlier in the utterance, the child tends to imitate that word plus some of the words following it.

With respect to the intonation patterns of adults when speaking to young children, researchers have reported that the fundamental frequency is typically higher and the contour more exaggerated than it is in adult-adult speech, but no one has studied whether particular patterns are also more consistently tied to particular pragmatic functions. While rising and falling intonation patterns in adult-adult speech do not always signal queries and statements or imperatives, respectively, they may do so in adult-child speech. This would be a considerable help to the child in learning to use intonation to signal his communicative intent.

The phonological simplification and reduplication that is typical of adult-child speech provides a clearly enunciated model for phonological development but little else, and these factors may simply reflect imitation of the child's own forms by the adult (Weir, 1962; Moerk, 1972).

The most general of the syntactic features of parental speech, well-formedness and short utterance length, are likely to be helpful to the language-learning child. Glanzer and Dodd (1975) observed that mothers are more likely to get a response from their children when they shorten their utterances. Shipley, Smith, and Gleitman (1969) reported that children are most likely to respond to short, well-formed instructions, and may simply not respond at all when the input becomes too complex. So these general features do appear helpful to the language-learning child.

Nevertheless, Fodor had something other than simplicity in mind when he presumed that adult-child speech does not differ from adult-adult speech in any *useful* way; he meant *useful* in the sense of better displaying deep structure relationships. Is there any evidence that parental speech is useful in this respect? The more transformations involved in a sentence, the more distant is the deep structure from the surface form. It is therefore to children's advantage in discovering deep structure that parent-child speech generally has fewer transformations than adult-adult speech (Pfuderer, 1969). Drach (1969) showed that it is transformationally less varied and contains fewer transformations, hence there is less distortion of the deep structure in the surface form. Pfuderer (1969) demonstrated that parents' speech becomes transformationally more complex as their children go from an early to a late stage of linguistic development, measured in MLU. It is a finding typical of recent studies that mothers' sentences to young children contain only a single clause (Newport, 1975), with subordination and coordination much less frequent than in adult-adult speech (Vorster, 1974).

On the other hand, Newport (1975) argues that in some respects mothers' speech to very young children can be considered more complex in terms of a standard transformational grammar, since mothers delete many deep structure constituents. Their speech to young children contains many imperatives that, in the conventional transformational account, have the deep structure subject *you* deleted. There are also a large number of *yes-no* questions in which the mothers delete the auxiliary and the pronoun *you* thus: *Want a cookie?* Newport's study revealed that the auxiliary + pronoun are more frequently supplied by the mothers in their speech to older children, when they also use fewer imperatives. Furthermore, Newport found that *wh*-questions were fairly frequent and declaratives less frequent in speech to younger children (less than two years old). She concludes that since the underlying propositional form is syntactically much deformed in *wh*-questions and these questions are transformationally quite complex in adult terms, mothers' speech provides a somewhat more complex input to younger than to older children. It then becomes difficult to see how the mothers' speech helps young children to acquire syntactic categories.

However, several arguments can be raised against this conclusion. First, consideration of the pragmatic context of utterances suggests that the subject *you* in imperatives is given by the communicative context. The adult is usually making eye contact with the child and using gesture to indicate what needs doing. Even domestic dogs understand that imperatives are addressed to them. The child clearly need not derive the syntactic role of *you* in underlying linguistic structure in order to understand or produce imperatives correctly. Second, deletion of auxiliary + *you* makes *yes-no* questions shorter and perhaps easier to process for the young child. Again, the subject of the question is apparent from the conversational context and such nonlinguistic factors as direction of regard. In the case of *wh*-questions, it is not clear that the child need possess the knowledge of linguistic structure that we attribute to adults when they understand such questions. There is so much redundancy in the situational context that the child can interpret the question with knowledge of only a few key words. Such *wh*-questions as "What's that?" are clearly unanalyzed routines for young children, and they begin by using them as routines (Brown, 1973). Other questions may be interpreted on the basis of the *wh*-word and other stressed words in the utterance.

In fact, some question forms do appear to provide an important teaching experience. Brown, Cazden, and Bellugi (1969) pointed out that a very common type of question asked of young children is the *occasional question,* a request for the child to supply a missing answer or repeat a word or phrase. Thus, in the interaction:

Child: I want milk.
Mother: You want what?
Child: Milk.

the child is asked to repeat a constituent. Similarly, the child is prompted in the following interaction (Brown et al, 1969, p. 71):

Mother: What do you want?

Child: (no answer)
Mother: You want what?

Such promptings and recastings of *wh*-questions might assist the child in inferring the constituent structure of the questions. Both Brown et al. (1969) and Moerk (1972) report that the child is more likely to answer an occasional question than a regular question, and use of occasional questions by parents correlates positively with the syntactic development of the child.

Snow (1971, 1972) has emphasized the importance of sentence constituents uttered in isolation by mothers in making the grammatical structure of sentences transparent to the child. These incomplete sentences must be clearly distinguished from the "broken sentences" present in adult-adult speech. In the incomplete sentences of mothers, complete constituent units, usually noun phrases or prepositional phrases, are repeated following the full utterance. For example, the mother says: "Put the red truck in the box now. The red truck. No, the red truck. In the box. The red truck in the box" (Snow, 1972, p. 562). Snow suggests that these are tailor-made lessons in phrase structure, since by isolating phrases the hierarchical structure of the full sentence is revealed.

For all these lessons in phrase structure and the like, is adult speech useful in Fodor's sense of revealing deep structure? It is true that having only heard language of this kind, one would be hard pressed to derive underlying meanings. Luckily, the child is not in this position. He is not in a dark room listening to language through a loudspeaker and attempting to understand it; he is engaged in interaction with the world and the helpful people in it. To a large extent, the underlying meaning relations of the simple speech he hears are given by the world, for the child and the adults who converse with him are tied very much to the here-and-now. An event happens, an adult makes an appropriate comment, and the child's task is to map his reading of the situation onto the adult linguistic form. Adults oblige by being sensitive to the child's level of comprehension and by restricting their use of complex transformations such as passive or embedded sentences. Even in a language where word order is relatively free, namely Hebrew, Buium (1974) reports that the father she studied limited himself almost exclusively to a subject-verb-object order for a variety of construction types.

The discussion in Chapter 3 on what rules and categories are psychologically real for child speech now achieves a new importance. If the child is exemplifying abstract notions like *subject* in his speech, we have to build in a great deal of prior knowledge because subjects do not correspond to any real-world categories like *agent,* and thus the fact that the child is listening to speech in context becomes irrelevant. But if the child's speech begins with quite concrete categories like *agent,* the importance of context is highlighted and one needs to impute correspondingly less in the way of innate structure.

8

Processes and Constraints

Clearly, language learning is an interactional process between adult and child. However, we have not yet provided any explanations of how the child makes use of adult speech in developing his own speech. How do the conventional forms make their way into his language? We turn now to some traditional explanations: imitation, feedback, and reinforcement, to see if they can shed light on this process.

IMITATION

If someone were to stop people on the street and ask them how children learn language, there would be one predominant answer: children imitate the speech they hear. What could be more obvious? English children speak English; Zulu children speak Zulu. Yet the role of imitation in language acquisition is a source of considerable dispute among psychologists. The problem can be stated simply enough. To speak or understand a language it is no good having a repertoire of sentences for all occasions, like a tourist phrase book. The child, like the tourist, needs to extract the rules of the language in order to produce sentences appropriate to his changing situation. Children who fail to formulate rules and instead use stock phrases are labeled psychotic (see Chapter 9, section on autism). By definition, to generalize beyond what is imitated involves more principles than imitation alone. Furthermore, the transformational grammarians claim that the rules operate on deep structure, which is not evidenced in the surface forms and hence cannot be imitated.

Language acquisition is more than simple imitation, but perhaps imitation plays some facilitating role in the internalization of rules. What is the status of the evidence bearing on this weaker claim? Is there any empirical evidence that the child copies the adult language he hears and in doing so increases his linguistic knowledge? Whitehurst, Ironsmith, and Goldfein (1974) contend that they have experimental evidence of this phenomenon. Whitehurst and Vasta (1975) made the point that imitation should not be considered superficially, that is, as an exact copy of the sentences heard. Instead, they propose that more general aspects of the model may influence the child's productions, as, for example, a child asks a lot of questions because his parents do, though not necessarily the same questions. This is the same point we have been making: that imitation must be supplemented by the child's extracting rules and generalizing to new instances. Whitehurst, Ironsmith, and Goldfein proposed to test whether exposing children to passive sentences, normally rarely heard, would increase the children's spontaneous production of these forms.

The twelve subjects ranged in age from 4 to 5½ years, an age range when spontaneous production of the passive is virtually zero, and comprehension usually poor. The children were shown pictures of animals in action, for example, a mouse squirting a turtle. The experimental group heard passive sentences spoken by the experimenter, of the kind:

The turtle is being squirted by the mouse.

Interposed among these were probe pictures of a similar variety, which the child was asked to describe. The control group of children had to describe all of the pictures, with no models being spoken by the experimenter. The experimental group produced many more passive forms than the control group during the probe trials. This is not in itself convincing, for the children may have already known the passive construction and have just figured out how to play the game rather than having learned the passive from the model. However, the experimenters included a comprehension test after the modeling, in which they presented the children with passive sentences and asked them to point to the appropriate picture in a set. The experimental group performed significantly better than the control group, implying that their knowledge of the passive was superior, and that they had not just adopted the construction as an option during the game. So Whitehurst et al. conclude that modeling a form can change a child's linguistic knowledge.

There are some problems with this conclusion however. First of all, with only six children in each group it is hard to be certain that the groups did not differ in their knowledge of the passive before the experiment, in other words, the results may have been purely chance. The study would be more impressive if this equality had been established before the experiment. The groups did perform equally on active sentences but that might not be the best control, particularly since children at this age usually perform accurately on such sentences. An even more convincing design would be to match two groups of children, then expose one to passive sentences and the other to some other difficult construction, say relative clauses, and show a divergence in knowledge of the two groups.

The second problem is that it is not clear whether imitation played a crucial role or whether just listening to the twenty passive sentences improved the children's comprehension scores. A third group should have just listened to the passives, with no probe trials at all.

For the moment, though, let us assume the finding is a robust one and turn to the serious question it raises. The experiment surely did not provide the only experience with the passive construction these children had had, for even the control group demonstrated some comprehension of the passive. Nevertheless, the control group did not spontaneously use the passive to describe the pictures, and probably never had used it. How could the experimental group have learned to construct passives, since we have argued elsewhere that this involves applying ordered rules to an abstract deep structure, not just a superficial manipulation of an active sentence? Nothing in the input, it would be claimed, could reveal this property. Actually, the children in this experiment may have learned a semantically based rule for producing passive sentences from their corresponding actives, by, for example, reversing the positions of *agent* and *patient*. Remember that this strategy would fail for complex sentences, but in Whitehurst et al's experiment the sentences were all of a standard, simple variety. It would be fascinating to repeat the study with more heterogeneous pictured situations on the probe trials, to determine whether the children had adopted a limited scope rule or one that applies across semantic roles.

The same people who so readily invoke imitation as an explanation of language learning would immediately confess that child language does not simply mimic adult language, for why then would one hear telegraphic speech? (See Chapter 3.) Instead, imitation appears to be *selective*. Not everything the child hears gets imitated. For instance, the young child tends to imitate the ends of sentences and selectively imitates the stressed word in an utterance regardless of its position (du Preez, 1974). The child's hearing may be tuned to certain physical parameters of the input. There may be identifying physical characteristics of adult-child speech, such as pitch and rate, that cue the child that he is being addressed, for most children rarely imitate speech that is not directed at them (except for words spoken with a high degree of emotion—those are picked up uncannily well, to the chagrin of parents). So imitation is not random but selective in these physical respects.

There is accumulating evidence that imitation is selective in more complex ways too. Let us return to the question of whether imitation can be a means of introducing new structural knowledge into the child's repertoire. If it is, one would expect imitated utterances to be more advanced structurally than spontaneous utterances. Ervin-Tripp (1964) wrote grammars for both spontaneous and imitative utterances of five children and found the imitated speech involved either the same or simpler rules than the spontaneous speech. She concluded that imitations were not progressive but seemed to use the same knowledge the child already possessed, as if he were filtering the imitations through his own grammar. Kemp and Dale (1973) used an elicited imitation task and found apparently contradictory results: some grammatical features were produced spontaneously but never imitated; others were imitated but not found in the child's spontaneous speech.

Bloom, Hood, and Lightbown (1973) report findings similar to those of Kemp and Dale, though they offer a cogent explanation that removes the contradiction. They kept track of six children in the earliest stages of language acquisition, recording both spontaneous and imitative speech. They examined the children's vocabulary growth and their production of various semantic and syntactic constructions common to Stage I (see Chapter 3), for example, attribution, recurrence, action-object, object-location, and so forth. A fine-grained analysis revealed differences between the children's imitative and spontaneous speech, differences that would be missed by looking only at MLU or word-order rules as did some of the earlier studies.

One of the clearest cases was the child Eric, who selectively imitated words he did not use spontaneously. Over time these words entered his productive vocabulary, suggesting imitation did play a role in the acquisition of new words. Bloom et al. set as a criterion for mastery of a construction the occurrence of five or more different utterances exemplifying the relation at a particular time of observation. Eric tended to imitate new words in constructions he had already mastered, which was an opposite strategy to that of a second child, Peter. Peter selectively imitated constructions he had not yet mastered in his spontaneous speech, but which contained words familiar to him. These constructions entered his productive repertoire in subsequent sessions, suggesting imitation helped grammatical learning also. It is as if the children would not imitate totally novel sentences, nor did they try to imitate sentences they could have produced themselves.

Once again, imitation is shown to be selective, but the selectivity is not on physical grounds. The child is actively processing speech he hears in the light of his current knowledge and apparently paying special attention to those aspects currently under mastery. In fact, though, there are two competing interpretations of these interesting observations. One is that by imitating at one time the child learns forms that are productive at a later time. The second possibility is that the child at one time gives evidence by imitation of what he is in the process of learning by quite different principles and has mastered by the later time. Bloom et al. do not strictly decide between these alternatives but they give a highly plausible account of the process. The very fact that imitation is selective demonstrates that the child knows something about the utterance before imitating it: it is neither entirely new nor under complete control. By imitating it he can experience verbally encoding an event in front of him, helping to strengthen whatever he previously knew about mapping forms onto meanings. In this way his productive competence improves and imitation declines.

However plausible this process sounds, it is clear from Bloom et al,'s own data that imitation is not the only means available to children learning language. The six children varied enormously in the extent to which they imitated, from 6 percent to 29 percent of their utterances, yet this was not correlated with their rate of acquisition. Furthermore, some spontaneously productive forms in the imitating children had no observable history of imitation, so imitation is clearly not a necessary process for language learning.

EXPANSION

The data from Bloom et al. suggest that children pay attention to and learn from input that is slightly more advanced than their own speech. Shipley, Smith, and Gleitman (1969) reported the same phenomenon in studying the child's ability to act out commands. Holophrastic children responded best to telegraphic commands; children with telegraphic speech acted out simple but complete imperatives most successfully. It is interesting, therefore, to note that parents indulge a great deal in what Brown and Bellugi (1964) called *expansions* of their child's speech. For example, a child who says *mommy eat* will often be answered with: *yes, mommy's eating her lunch*. If he says *truck fall*, he will hear, *oh dear, the truck fell over*. The expansions supply the missing grammatical information while retaining the same content, and since they are delivered contingent upon the child's utterance they would seem to provide an ideal learning experience. It has proven very difficult to demonstrate that this is indeed the case.

Brown, Cazden, and Bellugi (1969) noticed that the mothers of Adam and Eve responded with expansions some 30 percent of the time, but Sarah's mother expanded her utterances much less. Sarah was also the slowest at language development. However, Sarah's mother also talked less in general, so it was not clear whether the lack of expansions or the lack of speech was the contributing factor. Cazden (1965) undertook an experiment to tease apart these variables. Her subjects were twelve black children, aged twenty-eight to thirty-eight months, in a daycare center in Boston. The children were assigned to three groups, matched according to initial language level, age and talkativeness. For a period of three months, one group (expansion) received forty minutes per school day of intensive and deliberate expansions of their speech by a specially trained tutor; a second group (modeling) was talked to by a tutor who provided an equal amount of speech but made no attempt to expand the children's sentences. As an example of the difference, a child in the expansion group who said *dog bark* might hear *yes, the dog's barking*. In the modeling group the tutor might say instead *he's mad at the kitty* or something equally appropriate. A third group received no treatment but remained familiar with the materials and tutors throughout the three months.

Cazden used six measures of language ability. One was a test of the child's ability to repeat sentences, and the others were indices of the complexity of spontaneous speech. Contrary to the hypothesis that inspired the research, the expansion group did not gain in grammatical development relative to the group that received no treatment. In general, the differences between the groups did not reach statistical significance, but the groups did differ in overall growth: modeling best, then expansion, then the no-treatment group. On one task, sentence imitation, the modeling and control groups were significantly better than the expansion group!

One explanation offered was that the tutors may have misinterpreted the children's utterances and thus expanded them incorrectly, which might have confused rather than helped. So Feldman (1971) added another control to a repeat of Cazden's experiment in which only unambiguous utterances were expanded. However, again there was no difference between the groups on a sentence imitation task.

One weakness in both the Cazden and Feldman studies concerns the use of lower-class black children as subjects. The expansions provided by the white student experimenters probably did not take into account differences between so-called Standard English and the black English dialect spoken in the homes of the children (DePaulo and Bonvillian, 1975). On the other hand, DePaulo and Bonvillian point out that a study by Gonzales (1973) in which the utterances of two Mexican-American children were expanded by their mothers also failed to find differences between these children and two controls on four measures of language development.

Cazden (1965) and Brown et al. (1969) suggest two reasons for the failure of expansions to enhance acquisition in Cazden's study. First, richness and variety of linguistic input may be the most important determinant of rate of language acquisition. Cazden's modeling group received a syntactically more varied and semantically richer input from the experimenters than the expansion group. Second, the function of occasional expansions for the child may be to confirm for the child the relationship between his utterance and the situational context. But the continued expansions of every utterance by the experimenters may have led to the loss of effectiveness of that confirmation, and the children may have ceased to pay attention to the expansions.

These two explanations are supported by the results of an experiment by Nelson, Carskaddon, and Bonvillian (1973). In this study, the experimenters expanded the children's incomplete sentences, but they also recast their complete utterances into sentences with a different syntactic form but the same semantic reference. For example, a declarative uttered by the child might be followed by a question concerning the same semantic information. This recast-sentence group later performed significantly better than a control group on a sentence imitation test and also produced more complex predicate forms. On two measures of verb phrase complexity they were also more advanced than a group that heard new sentences modeled by the experimenter but did not have their own sentences recast. In this study, when the child commented on some aspect of the verbal or nonverbal context of the interaction, the experimenter kept that shared aspect of the context constant but provided the child with an alternative syntactic means of encoding it.

Nelson (1975) provided an even stronger demonstration of the efficacy of recasting complex questions and verb forms in facilitating the acquisition of those forms in twenty-eight- to twenty-nine-month-old children. Children who on a pretest showed no productive use of either complex question forms such as tag questions and negative questions, or verb forms like future or conditional tense or two verbs in a sentence, were exposed to one of two intervention conditions. In both conditions the experimenter attempted to recast the child's sentences, but in one the recastings were in the form of complex questions while in the other they were in the form of complex verbs. At the end of the treatment period, Nelson found that significantly more of the children exposed to the complex questions showed use of those forms in their own speech than did children exposed to complex verbs. Similarly, significantly more children in the latter group had begun to use complex verb forms. On more general measures of language development, MLU, and number of elements per noun phrase, the two groups of children showed the same advances. Increased exposure through recasting thus seems to have selective effects on syntactic progress. Nelson suggests that the recastings attract the child's attention to the comparison between his own utterance and that of the adult. Since the mothers did use these forms, though infrequently, in speech to the child, the experimenter's recastings did not introduce altogether new forms, but did tend to draw attention to the form.

The possibility exists that a moderate degree of novelty, tied closely to what the child currently produces, may be the most efficacious way of enhancing grammatical development (Brown et al., 1969; dePaulo and Bonvillian, 1975.) The phenomenon of moderate discrepancy commanding the most attention from a child has been noticed in domains other than language (Kagan, 1970). One would expect, if this were the case, that simply correcting children's grammatical mistakes would result in improvement, yet the literature abounds with anecdotes to the contrary (Bellugi, 1970), where a child appears oblivious to his parent's attempts to correct his errors. The process may be much less direct than that, with the child alert at certain times for information pertinent to the rules he is working on. That is, the child may set the pace. Since the literature is mostly anecdotal, we don't mind offering one of our own. One child we recorded at the age of thirty months had the common overgeneralization error *mines* in her speech, which she used consistently in the first half of our play session. In the following dialogue with Peter, she is playing with Playdo and engaged in a running argument over which grimy pieces belong to whom:

> Katie: Don't crush mines up!
> Peter: What was yours? What was it?. Had you made it into something?
> Katie: Dis is mines.
> Peter: That's yours, O.K.

Notice how this exchange offers support to Katie's apparent hypothesis that all truncated possessive forms end in *s*. But wait:

> Katie: Dat's yours.
> Peter: That's mine. O.K. I'll keep that. Is that as well? I have lots of pieces now, don't I?
> Katie: Dis is mine.
> Peter: Hm-mm.

Here she seems to have correctly noticed the exception. Unfortunately her rules are never static for long:

> Peter: Did you steal some more? You stole some more! Keep stealing all mine, don't you?
> Katie: I keep stealing all your.

The exception has now been accepted as the rule!

REINFORCEMENT

Another favorite explanation of language learning is that parents reinforce or reward their children for speaking correctly, so grammatical sentences get strengthened and ungrammatical, ill-formed sentences drop out of the child's repertoire. What kind of rewards might these be? One simple possibility is approval or disapproval, for they typically work as rewards and punishments for behavior other than language. Brown and Hanlon (1969) examined the records of Adam, Eve, and Sarah and their parents for familiar expressions of approval and disapproval contingent on the children's speech. Expressions like *that's right* or *very good* or *that's wrong* or *no* were quite rare in the records, but each occurrence was listed together with the child's utterance it followed. The researchers then contrasted the population of utterances followed by signs of approval with that followed by signs of disapproval, to determine whether the latter was less syntactically correct than the former. They scored an utterance incorrect if it did not contain obligatory morphemes, as in the sentence *He not walking,* or if a morpheme was erroneous, as in *I throwed it.* Although the numbers were quite small, Brown and Hanlon conclude: "In neither case is there even a shred of evidence that approval and disapproval are contingent on syntactic correctness." Instead, the parents attended to the *truth* value of the children's utterances rather than their grammaticality. So Eve, for example, said truthfully, "Mama isn't boy, he a girl," and her mother said, "That's right." Adam said, grammatically but falsely, "And Walt Disney comes on Tuesday," and his mother said firmly, "No, he does not."

It is as if parents see through the ungrammatical speech of their children to the meaning behind it, and attend to that. Nevertheless, the possibility remains that such a broad definition of grammaticality was too gross to detect the subtle shaping that might occur in interaction between parents and children. It is quite possible, though it has not been demonstrated, that parents are sensitive to their children's linguistic ability and demand only slightly better syntax than they currently produce. We suspect that a five-year-old who lapsed back into telegraphic speech would hear disapproval loud and clear, and at the other extreme, a long sentence from an eighteen-month-old would bring shrieks of joy from his listeners, quite independent of the meaning. Fortunately also, truth and grammaticality are not orthogonal in normal language. The child is more likely to get his meaning across if he speaks correctly, and more likely to be misinterpreted if he speaks ungrammatically.

This brings us to a more refined notion of reinforcement than simply approval/disapproval. Surely that is not what keeps us talking as adults. Instead, if reinforcers operate at all in maintaining adult speech, they are quite subtle and differ for different speech acts. Joking, for example, is hardly maintained by people saying *that's right,* nor are insults encouraged by approval from the person insulted. Very generally, we expect to be understood by our listener, to get our message across whatever its intent. Could that be a force for change in child speech? Brown and Hanlon searched the records for instances of certain constructions such as tag questions, negatives, and questions, that had both immature and mature forms coexisting in the child's speech. For example, an immature *wh*-question might have the auxiliary and subject uninverted, as in *What time it is?* Brown and Hanlon looked at the adults' responses following both well-formed and immature forms to see if there was evidence that they understood well-formed utterances more consistently. For example, in response to "What time it is?" the adult replied, "Uh, huh, it tells what time it is," which was a fairly clear misunderstanding. Unfortunately for the hypothesis but fortunately for the children, that was the only instance of a misunderstanding in the records! There was no evidence that parents selectively understood the mature forms over the immature forms.

This study is often cited as evidence that communication pressure cannot be a force for change in child language learning, though Brown and Hanlon draw a much weaker conclusion. They point to the difficulty in doing research on communication failures, since the experimenter, a stranger in the situation, must be better at detecting the child's messages than the parent! In addition, the age range of the children in this study and the limited set of constructions studied mitigates such a strong conclusion. The set of immature *wh*-questions, negatives, and the like are highly redundant in context; for example, *yes-no* questions carry rising intonation, and negatives typically contain *no,* so it is hard to miss the messages even if they are not completely correct syntactically. Studying younger children and a wider range of constructions in situations where the child's goal can be unambiguously determined by the experimenter may result in quite different conclusions, but this research enterprise has not been undertaken.

We have discussed reinforcement in this section from a highly simplified standpoint. We hoped to identify the consequences of children's speech that would make immature forms drop out and mature forms enter the children's repertoire. Reinforcers, however, are defined in terms of their effects: a reinforcer is that consequence which strengthens the behavior on which it is contingent. Yet we have proceeded back-to-front, by examining the parents' speech for certain responses thought to be rewarding, and then examining the forms on which they were contingent. Admittedly, Brown and Hanlon were aware of this problem and proceeded only with caution to consider events as reinforcers on the basis of plausibility.

However, it seems likely that the rewards for language change dramatically over the course of its development, so events perceived by the child as reinforcing at one time might no longer motivate him at a later time. For the tiny infant, it may be enough to have someone loom into his field of vision as he coos. Later on, a smiling adult who makes a variety of sounds in reply may maintain a high level of babbling from the child. When the child begins to use his first words, merely repeating them may be reinforcing to him. As he develops a simple syntax, the most important consequence may be to be understood, to have a parent expand his sentences or fulfill his requests appropriately. After grammar is fairly well established, it might be important to have feedback in the form of maintained attention or repetition to confirm that his sentences sound like an adult's. If this change in reinforcers over time has any validity, it would be impossible to observe in any single study at any one time. It would require longitudinal studies that would extend observation by controlling the interactions between parents and their children to show that suspected reinforcers do affect the child's speech. For reasons of complexity as well as ethics, such a study has not been forthcoming with normal children. We will discuss the use of rewards in training language with developmentally disordered children in Chapter 9. What might cause difficulties for such intervention is the possibility that the child determines which events are reinforcing, depending on his level of development, and the appropriate reinforcers may not be readily invented by a well-meaning teacher. The difficulty of transferring motivation for language use from arbitrary food rewards to the natural environment is a pervasive problem with these training programs.

The role that reinforcement plays in learning, beyond attracting the attention of the organism and providing the motivation for behavior, is an open question (Brown and Herrnstein, 1975). Rewards may change the relative frequency of already established aspects of behavior, or motivate changes in the behavior, without influencing the pattern that these changes take. In the field of animal behavior there is a substantial interest in this question of constraints on learning (Seligman and Hager, 1972; Hinde and Stevenson-Hinde, 1973). It has become evident, for instance, that there are limits to the degree to which reinforcers can shape behavior, and they are of a more subtle variety than that no one has yet taught pigs to fly. For example, pigeons readily peck at a lighted disk associated with food, but it is extremely difficult to teach them to peck at a disk to avoid electric shock. Why? Because a pigeon's natural response to an unpleasant stimulus is to fly away, not to peck. Rats will readily learn to run to another place to escape shock, but have great trouble learning that pressing a lever will just as rapidly remove the shock (Bolles, 1970). There are thus intrinsic biases to behavior that reinforcers cannot overcome.

It is a fundamental tenet of cognitive approaches to behavior that the organism itself has a contribution to make, that it is insufficient simply to take note of the stimuli impinging on it and the responses it makes. Just as we speculated that the child defines what is reinforcing at different stages of his knowledge, we now introduce some further constraints to the rate and sequence of acquisition of that knowledge: biological maturation, linguistic complexity and cognitive preparedness. We propose that these may define and limit the course of language acquisition to a greater extent than the rewards provided by the environment.

BIOLOGICAL CONSTRAINTS

The Critical Period Hypothesis

In biology there is a phenomenon known as the *critical period* for the acquisition of a behavior. For example, shortly after hatching, the young of Mallard ducks will follow the first moving object they see. It is usually the mother duck, but in her absence they might become attached to a bird of another species, a prying human naturalist, or as unlikely a parent as a colored balloon. This following behavior only occurs within a certain time period after hatching, after which point the ducklings develop a fear of strange objects and retreat instead of following. Within these time limits is the *critical period* for the following behavior. Another example is provided by the chaffinch, whose adult song is highly intricate. It is crucial for development of that song that the young bird hear an adult singing the full song within a certain time period. If it hears only its own immature song, or if it is deafened before it hears an adult, the full song will never appear, even if at a later time the deafness is reversed.

Lenneberg (1967) has been the major proponent of the idea that there is a critical period for language learning in humans. His evidence has been collected from a great variety of sources and ingeniously woven together to suggest a period of maximum sensitivity beginning around age two and brought to a close by the physiological changes of puberty. The proposal is intuitively appealing as an excuse for those of us who struggled to learn a second language after that point. In particular we recall a foreign visiting professor with years of instruction in English, who struggled to make himself understood while his five-year-old child, starting from scratch, acquired English rapidly enough to giggle at the father's mistakes!

Lenneberg first pointed to the universality of the course of language acquisition in its grossest aspects. Children in our culture begin to coo at around three or four months, babbling reaches a peak at nine months or so, the first words appear at twelve to eighteen months, and two years usually marks the beginning of the simplest sentences. Lenneberg draws a parallel with other behaviors such as grasping, crawling, standing, and walking, which also make their appearance on an invariable timetable, the onset of each being a consequence of physical maturation rather than environmental shaping. Interestingly, the onset of language behaviors seems to be synchronized with these milestones of motor development, since retarded children are slowed in both respects. Moreover, the synchrony is preserved in societies whose language and child rearing practices are vastly different from our own. Lenneberg explains that the synchrony is not due to a dependence of the speech milestones on the maturation of the speech musculature, for some children suffering from impaired muscular development nevertheless learn to speak on schedule, though clumsily.

The possibility exists, then, that the onset of language is independent of particular environmental contingencies, and dependent instead on biological maturation. The claim is not that the environment is irrelevant after onset, for as we saw in Chapter 2, although deaf babies begin to babble at the same time as normals this babbling drops out in time as they fail to get the feedback of their own sounds that normal babies do (see also Chapter 9).

Thus, the onset of the critical period may be set by biological growth rather than because the need to communicate develops at a constant point in time or because all parents begin shaping language as the child reaches a certain age.

What sets the end point of the critical period? Lenneberg used several kinds of evidence to draw the conclusion that brain maturity at puberty marks a limit to normal language acquisition. A major premise of his argument was that the human brain begins with bilateral representation of language functions, but by puberty language becomes lateralized in the dominant (usually left) hemisphere.

This hypothesis was supported by a review of cases of traumatic aphasia in childhood. It suggests that a child who suffers damage to the right, nondominant hemisphere should have a greater chance than an adult of suffering language interruption, since language is more diffusely represented in the brains of children. Lenneberg claimed that in the clinical data he reviewed, the children aged nine or younger had a higher incidence of right-hemisphere lesions causing aphasia than the adults.

Furthermore, if the hemispheres of the brain are more or less equipotential for language early in life, children who suffer damage to the left hemisphere should be able to compensate by using the right hemisphere for language skills. But if lateralization is complete at puberty, and hemispheric functions are then fixed, compensation by the minor hemisphere should be less likely after that time. Lenneberg maintained that children who suffer aphasia before puberty have a much more rapid and complete recovery than older children, whose prognosis for complete recovery after a few months of severe language disturbance is, like that of adults, regrettably poor.

Subsequent evidence and interpretation has cast Lenneberg's hypothesis into doubt. The major attacks have been directed at the proposal that lateralization determines the end of the critical period, while not denying that language recovery is more difficult with increasing age. The criticisms come from several sources: first, arguments that the original data Lenneberg used would be just as much in keeping with the hypothesis that lateralization is complete by age five; second, and even more severe, that the reports on childhood aphasia are unreliable and inaccurate; third, the final blow, that accumulating evidence from such tasks as dichotic listening show that language functions are lateralized from birth!

Krashen (1973) took a new look at the major source of clinical data reviewed by Lenneberg: a series of cases of childhood aphasia reported by Basser (1962). He found that in all the cases that showed complete recovery of language, the child was younger than five years, a rather early age to be pubescent. There was no clear evidence that the minor hemisphere could take over language functions after age five. The percentage of cases of children older than five with aphasia due to left hemisphere damage, compared to right hemisphere damage, was about the same as it is in adults.

Kinsbourne (1975) goes one step further than Krashen in his criticism of the data used by Lenneberg. He maintains that to unequivocally prove the case that a right-sided brain-injury has impaired language function, two demonstrations are required: one, that only the right hemisphere was damaged, and two, that language was affected as a result. In most of the cases reviewed by Lenneberg, it remains an open question whether the left hemisphere was affected as well as the right. For example, some cases involved a virus infection that resulted in seizures and a partial one-sided paralysis, but this provides no guarantee that only one hemisphere was affected. In only one series of cases was there unambiguous evidence that only the right hemisphere was involved, but in this series there were no reports of aphasia!

Moreover, in the case reports of language disturbance, the disturbance is rarely documented by speech and language testing. Instead, as Kinsbourne puts it, "Usually the report amounts to no more than the observation that the child was not speaking to the clinician" (p. 246). He believes the data are consistent only with the weaker claim that the brain is less adaptable with the increasing age of the patient.

Finally, Kinsbourne reviews the evidence on dichotic listening, the task (discussed in Chapter 2) in which different stimuli are delivered simultaneously to the two ears. We reported there that for verbal stimuli there is a moderate right-ear advantage, since information from the right ear goes first to the language-dominant left hemisphere. According to the latest reports, there is no evidence of an increasing right-ear advantage with increasing age of the child, although this would be predicted if lateralization is an ongoing process until puberty. Instead, the most recent evidence from Entus (1975) (reported in full in Chapter 2) would suggest that two-month-old infants have a right-ear advantage for speech stimuli, in keeping with the picture of anatomical asymmetry of the brain found at birth (Witelson and Pallie, 1973). However, in a speculative article, Krashen (1975a) attempts to wed these findings with the picture of possible bilateral representation of language until age five that he derived from childhood aphasia studies.

For our present purposes, however, we can see that the notion of lateralization at puberty has come under increasing attack, and hence the claim that it sets the limit of the critical period may no longer be valid. There are also some doubts cast on the proposal that children's brains are relatively adaptable up until puberty: the data are equivocal as to the exact time period beyond which aphasia due to traumatic brain damage cannot be overcome.

Nevertheless it remains true that language recovery is increasingly difficult with age, but what of language learning itself? Although first-language learning seems to be complete well before puberty, Lenneberg presented data from retarded children to suggest that puberty marks the end of their progress in language development. Lenneberg, Nichols, and Rosenberger (1964) followed fifty-four Down's Syndrome children for a period of three years, and tested each one two or three times per year. Although the measures used were rather gross by modern standards, they reported that children made no progress through the language milestones after the age of fourteen, while younger children continued to progress. Lenneberg argued (1966), therefore, that puberty sets a ceiling on the retardate's language development much as it does on the aphasic's recovery. We know of no data from the natural language acquisition of retarded children that would argue against this finding, though many language training programs continue after the children are adolescent and they are, one hopes, not in vain. (See Chapter 9 for evidence from Cromer [1974b] that retarded adolescents employ different language strategies from younger normal and retarded children.)

Finally, Lenneberg maintains that second-language learning after puberty must proceed by different means than language acquisition in childhood. The argument has two facets: first, that the pattern of acquisition should differ in adults, and second, that the process itself should differ. Krashen (1975b) has reviewed the relevant evidence. Error analyses by Richards (1971) demonstrated that adult second-language learners make similar errors to child first-language learners, so there seem to be certain inevitable pitfalls inherent in the language learned, like the error of overgeneralizing irregular verbs. But the prevalence in the second language of errors caused by interference from the first language versus developmental-type errors does not answer the question of whether adults and children acquire a second language in the same way when their first language is held constant. Several attempts to answer this question have used a test of oral production of the obligatory grammatical morphemes described in Chapter 3. Although there are reservations to be made about the validity of the test employed (Porter, 1975; Rosansky, 1976), it appears from the data that adults and children learning English as a second language have a similar ordering of difficulty of these morphemes. More studies of this type but employing a wider variety of language measures are needed before the issue can be settled either way.

Krashen (1975b) also presents findings that purport to show that formal instruction in a second language is superior to mere immersion in the language after puberty. For example, he finds that years of formal instruction is a better predictor of English proficiency for adults than years spent in an English-speaking country. It would be extremely difficult to prove that the reverse is true for children, yet that would be the only demonstration relevant to the question of whether adults differ from children in second-language learning. Krashen merely states that formal instruction is not necessary for children, a finding that is consistent only with the plausible, weaker hypothesis that children are better at language learning than adults, not different.

In our opinion none of these data are conclusive and so this aspect of the question of a critical period for second-language acquisition must remain open to debate. Lenneberg also observed that persons who acquire a second language after puberty almost invariably keep a foreign accent, in contrast to bilingual children. We must all know individual exceptions to this rule, but nevertheless the observation is well supported by data. Asher and Garcia (1969) and Oyama (1973) found that immigrants who arrived in the United States earlier than puberty either had more convincing American accents, or thought they had (Seliger, Krashen, and Ladefoged, 1975), than those who arrived when they were older. Intriguingly, the same may be true of the acquisition of dialects within a language. Labov (1970) claims that New York speech is only acquired by non–New Yorkers if they move to New York prior to puberty! In all these studies the number of *years* of exposure has no effect compared to the age at exposure.

It is at the phonological level that the boundaries of a critical period seem most difficult to deny: namely, that environmental influence is irrelevant to the onset of babbling, and accent is relatively immutable at puberty. The arguments for a critical period for higher levels of language are much less conclusive. Further research is necessary to determine whether articulatory development alone has a critical period for maturation, much like bird song.

The Curious Case of Genie

Much of the evidence for a critical period for first-language acquisition is maddeningly indirect: what one needs is a child who was raised until puberty with no opportunity to learn a language; the course of first-language acquisition after puberty could then be studied in the absence of confounding factors like foreign languages, retardation, and the like. There are scattered reports throughout history of so-called wolf children, children who were found living like animals in the wild, usually savage and uttering animal-like cries instead of speech. Unfortunately, in every case there have been doubts about whether the child was normal before he or she was abandoned, and documentation is lacking about the number of years spent in that state and about subsequent educational attempts and successes. A most complete account of teaching language to such a wild child is provided by Jean-Marc-Gaspard Itard in the book *The Wild Boy of Aveyron* (1932), dramatized in a wonderful film by François Truffaut called *The Wild Child*. No wolf-child has been successfully taught a language, but the social deprivation and probable retardation of the children renders this evidence worthless for the critical period hypothesis.

One would have thought wolf children belonged to another era of mankind and hence that the critical data provided by their tragic stories was forever lost to science. Yet in November 1970 a child came to the attention of the Los Angeles authorities: a child whose isolation and neglect matches that of any wolf child. She was at the time thirteen years, seven months old, and already past puberty, though she appeared much younger due to malnutrition, weighing just over sixty pounds. She could not stand erect, was incontinent, unable to chew food, and mute. Yet the evidence revealed this gross behavioral retardation was not due to brain damage or abnormality but most likely to the unbelievable circumstances of her life to that point.

Genie's first months seemed to have been medically unremarkable, at least as revealed by scanty pediatric records. However, from the age of about twenty months until she was discovered, Genie was kept in a small closed and curtained room, either tied to a pottychair or laid in a covered infant crib, confined from the waist down. Her mother, who was almost blind, visited her for only a few minutes each day to feed her with soft infant food. There was no opportunity for Genie to hear television or radio, for there was neither in the house. If she made noises she was liable to be beaten by her father, who could not tolerate noise. The father and elder brother of Genie did not speak to her but were wont to bark at her like dogs. It was the father's belief that Genie was hopelessly retarded, based on the fact that she was delayed in starting to walk because of a congenital hip dislocation that was treated during her first year.

It is unnecessary to explain that such circumstances did not leave Genie intact in body and mind. However, although she was malnourished, there was no evidence of physical abnormalities sufficient to account for her behavior, for she had adequate hearing, vision, and eye-hand coordination. She was severely disturbed emotionally, having frequent but silent tantrums, yet there were no other symptoms of childhood autism (see Chapter 9 for description). The most likely explanation of her behavior was the chronic social deprivation she had suffered for those twelve years (Fromkin, Krashen, Curtiss, Rigler, and Rigler, 1974).

Shortly after her rescue, Genie was tested on a series of language comprehension tests. Although within a very short time she began imitating words and learning names, her comprehension of grammar was completely absent. So Genie qualifies as the most satisfactory case to date to test Lenneberg's critical age hypothesis for first-language acquisition.

After her emergence into the world, Genie was placed in a foster home, where she began to acquire a first language primarily by exposure rather than training, like a normal child. Her progress in this undertaking can be assessed with an eye to two questions:

(1) Has Genie acquired enough to count as language?
(2) Is the process like normal first-language acquisition?

Phonology

At first, Genie's utterances were often either silent articulations or whispers. She had great difficulty controlling the flow and volume of air and she spoke in a monotone. In all likelihood these difficulties stemmed from the punishment she received for vocalizations prior to her rescue. In a later report (Curtiss et al., 1975) her spontaneous articulation remained impaired but she performed better when she was imitating speech than when she was speaking spontaneously. Her speech had increased in loudness and was beginning to vary in pitch toward more normal sentence intonation, with one stressed syllable per utterance. However, strangers still found her speech hard to understand.

Genie's phonological development has not differed markedly from that of normal children. Her earliest words consisted of consonant-vowel monosyllables, with longer words entering her speech later. She has now produced, either spontaneously or imitatively, all the consonants of standard American English. Like young normal children, she originally simplified consonant clusters, reducing initial /sp/, /st/, and /sk/ clusters by deleting /s/, and she either deleted or simplified final consonant clusters. Nevertheless, she demonstrated on comprehension tests that she could distinguish between final simple consonants and consonant clusters, so the problem existed at the articulatory level. The articulatory difficulties Genie displayed are in keeping with our earlier speculation that the critical period for language acquisition is best borne out in the area of phonology.

Semantic Development

Genie from the start generalized words for specific objects to the class of objects. For example, the word *dog* was learned for a specific pet but generalized immediately to all other dogs. There is no mention of over- or under-extensions of her early words. In fact, Genie needed no training on semantic classifications: she knew which objects counted as *clothes* without being taught each member of the class; she recognized that a toy that moved was nevertheless inanimate. Furthermore, color words and numbers occurred in her early vocabulary though they appear relatively late in normal children. So her conceptual development seemed considerably in advance of her linguistic development.

Most peculiar of all, Genie understood all *wh*-question words at about the same time: this is in contrast to young normal children who acquire *why, when,* and *how* much later than *what* and *where* (Blank, 1975; Ervin-Tripp, 1970). It is difficult to imagine how Genie could determine these meanings so rapidly, as they depend on linguistic exposure.

It is equally puzzling that she had no difficulty with concepts like *more* and *less,* again suggesting an independence of cognition and language, if by language we mean syntactic sophistication.

Genie had a vocabulary of two hundred words at the point where she began making two-word combinations, a figure that far outstrips normal children, who begin syntax with a vocabulary of around fifty words. Genie began producing single words spontaneously about five months after her liberation, and two-word utterances three months after that, so the period of single-word utterances was by no means abnormally protracted.

Grammatical Development

Genie's earliest two-word utterances expressed the relations attribute + entity, and possessor-possessed, much like those of a normal child. Soon afterwards she produced agent-action and action-object forms, and then three-word utterances that combined these relations. The two-word phrases became constituents in larger strings in a manner identical to normal development. As in the primitive negative sentences of normal children, Genie appended *no* to the beginning of an utterance, but almost four years after her release she did not use any negative auxiliaries (Fromkin et al., 1974).

In terms of morphemes, she began with the progressive *ing* and plural markers, and her mastery of the article came later. Her mastery of tense after five years was less than complete; although she understood strongly marked forms like *the girl finished opening the umbrella,* she was unable to use the usual *ed* ending as a cue to tense. The picture may be complicated by the fact that Genie's articulation problems mask her true grammatical knowledge. The sequence reported above parallels normal acquisition but the published details remain insufficient to judge the completeness of the parallel.

Genie composes novel utterances and also demonstrates a minimal form of recursiveness. But her achievements here are identical in scope to those of the chimpanzee Sarah, for her recursive sentences are conjunctions like *cat dog hurt* (Fromkin et al., 1974) which might be claimed to have minimal hierarchical structure (Fodor, Bever, and Garrett, 1974). Indeed, there is another parallel with Sarah and Washoe: five years after she began learning to speak, Genie had asked no spontaneous questions, only those she was specifically trained to ask.

Strategies and Errors

Many pieces of evidence suggest that Genies' language acquisition has approximated normal acquisition. Her errors were in many instances typical ones, as the following examples show:

(1) When presented with a relative-clause sentence such as:

The boy who is looking at the girl is frowning.

Genie interpreted the noun closest to the verb as its agent, that is, that the girl is frowning. Normal children do the same.

(2) She had difficulty with sentences in which the order of mention was not the order of events, as in:

Touch your nose after you touch your ear.

or

Before you touch your nose touch your ear.

in contrast to:

Touch your nose before you touch your ear.

or

After you touch your nose touch your ear.

(3) Her confusions of preposition pairs like *over* and *under, in front* and *in back* were revealing, as she confused the members of a pair with each other.

In contrast to these examples, however, Genie demonstrated peculiar inconsistencies in word order. Her own sentences were unfailingly correct: modifier-noun, agent-action-object, possessor-possessed, and so on. But in comprehension tests she did not correctly interpret simple NVN sequences as meaning agent-action-object, doing as poorly on active sentences as on passives. This is certainly out of keeping with the normal pattern of acquisition and at variance with her own use of an NVN strategy to decode relative-clause sentences and with other tests involving pronouns that appear to impose identical requirements (Curtiss et al., 1975). There seems to be no good explanation of her inconsistency in this area.

Lateralization

In terms of the anatomical representation of language in the brain, Genie is an anomaly. Instead of the usual pattern of language dominance in the left hemisphere, Genie uses her right hemisphere to process speech sounds. A dichotic listening task showed her left-ear bias to be very strong. However there is still confusion about her cerebral organization. Initially, Fromkin et al. (1974) speculated that Genie was using her right hemisphere almost exclusively, that the lack of language input had somehow caused the left hemisphere to stop developing normally while the right hemisphere had received sufficient visual and tactile stimuli to promote relatively normal development.

More recently, the evidence has supported a reversal of normal dominance, with Genie's left hemisphere dominant for spatial tasks and her right hemisphere for verbal processing (Curtiss et al., 1975). Until all the tests are completed we can only point to the possibility that the underlying language representation is abnormal in Genie, for what reason we shall never know.

In sum, Genie represents a case of first-language acquisition after the critical age of puberty. To be sure, her development is laborious and incomplete, but the similarities between it and normal acquisition outweigh the differences. We can only wait to see how far Genie will progress along the road to a normal life after such an incredible childhood. With luck she will be the last "wild child."

LINGUISTIC CONSTRAINTS

We will now consider other sources of constraint on the course of language acquisition. As discussed in Chapter 7, Chomsky has contended that there are constraints on the forms that languages can take, constraints that are not provided by environmental influences but by the nature of our innate endowment. These delimit in advance the possible hypotheses a child will adopt in discovering the grammar of his language, and thus the argument bears a resemblance to ethologist's claims about the constraints on learning in other species.

In addition, the characteristics of the language being learned provide a constraint that is presumably not amenable to alteration by contingencies of reward or punishment. The claim is that the fewer or simpler the rules involved in a construction, the easier it will be to learn, and thus a simpler construction would inevitably precede a more complex construction, provided such factors as frequency of exposure are held constant. The clearest example is provided by the two bilingual children studied by Mikeš (1967) and mentioned in Slobin (1973). They concurrently learned Hungarian and Serbo-Croatian, and showed a much earlier use of locative prepositions in Hungarian than in Serbo-Croatian. The explanation offered was that in Hungarian the prepositions are simple, systematic, and consistent, whilst in Serbo-Croatian they involve an inflection on the corresponding noun, which may or may not be redundant. Furthermore, the inflection varies with gender and final sound of the noun, making the final realization much more complex grammatically and phonologically. One can see that the prior acquisition of the Hungarian forms is highly likely if the frequency of exposure is matched.

However, there is a more troublesome sense in which structure within a language might predetermine the order of acquisition (discussed at length in Chapter 4). Many constructions have been considered to be simpler than related forms on the basis of the number of transformational rules involved. This highly plausible claim has not, however, been successfully borne out by the data on child speech. Either the failure is due to a faulty analysis, which would mean that the linguistic model is psychologically unreal, or one has to propose that the real relative difficulty of the constructions is being disguised by such factors as unequal frequency in the input. There are, however, two instances in which the linguistic analysis has predicted the order of acquisition. One of these is the order of acquisition of fourteen grammatical morphemes, the other the learning of larger-scale constructions such as *yes-no* questions, negatives, and tag questions. In each case, the linguistic analysis in terms of cumulative knowledge has accurately predicted the order of controlled use of the forms in children's speech.

So, for these forms at least, the natural order of acquisition seems to be constrained by their linguistic complexity, for in neither case was there a shred of evidence that rewards had shaped the order of emergence. But does invariability of sequence mean *inevitability?* One cannot conclude that from natural observation alone. For instance, could one train tags to a child who had none of the natural precursors in his speech? Perhaps if one tried to do that, the child would show spontaneous use of negatives, *yes-no* questions and the like without having been trained to use them, whereas he would not demonstrate spontaneous use of tag questions if he was trained to form negatives. That would be a clear demonstration that the natural precursors are logical prerequisites. It would not surprise us, however, if in this hypothetical experiment the child knew only what he had been trained and components of that knowledge proved inaccessible for other functions. But it is doubtful that either outcome could be adequately demonstrated, for a normal child who was too young to have any of the forms would also be too young to participate, and to teach an abnormal (or retarded) child would be to invite criticism of the design on the grounds that it would tell us nothing about normal acquisition.

COGNITIVE CONSTRAINTS

On Onset

According to Lenneberg (1966), the age of onset of language is limited by the brain's maturation. Piaget (1967, 1970) and Sinclair (1971) would argue that it awaits the acquisition of certain cognitive prerequisites, the outcomes of the sensorimotor period of development. One example is the concept of object permanence, which is basically two realizations: that an object stays the same over changes in position, distance, orientation, and so forth, and that it continues to exist if it is hidden or otherwise moved from sight. The first component of object permanence has been called object identity, and it is clear that a child who had not developed that notion of constancy would have difficulty learning names since there would be nothing for him to stick his labels onto; the world of objects would be in a state of flux. Recent research (Bower, 1974) has purported to show that object identity may not develop at all but be innate in the human infant. In that case, it would be a less interesting constraint on the onset of language acquisition, for no one has yet argued that language may begin before birth!

The other component of object permanence, namely, that concealed objects continue to exist, may not constrain the very beginnings of language but would certainly affect the onset of talking about objects and people that are not immediately present. Language input might even play a role in fostering this development.

Another example of cognition setting the pace for language acquisition is the development of *symbolic representation.* It is noted by Piaget (1970) that this normally begins at the end of the sensorimotor period of development, with make-believe play, in which the child makes one object stand for another. For example, he may pretend a block is a car, or place a cup on his head as a hat. This is seen as the forerunner of the use of an arbitrary sequence of phonemes, a word, to stand for an object. The claim is a convincing one to us, but it is possible that the first words are not symbols in this sense. It has been observed that a few children begin speaking with routines used for social purposes, like *hi, bye-bye,* and so forth. Furthermore, many children have words that stand for whole situations, like the child in Chapter 6 who said *kat* every time she threw her toy kitty out of her crib, but only then. As it is often difficult to know when these meanings narrow down in function and reference, it is equally arbitrary to decide at which point they should qualify as symbolic representations of an object. Yet, why should make-believe constitute a prerequisite for social greetings or the like? We suspect there are several developments at the end of the first year of life, both cognitive and social, which together make possible the onset of language in all its senses.

On Rate of Acquisition

We have mentioned several times the idea that language learning involves the mapping of linguistic forms onto already established concepts. If this is indeed true, then conceptual development will determine the rate and sequence of language acquisition. However, Schlesinger (1975) has pointed to some problems with this simple formulation of the relation between concepts and language.

For example, one popular notion is that the child learns linguistic concepts like *agent* or *patient* by utilizing the categories of experience that are an outcome of the sensorimotor period of development. He learns to class together all persons who can help him achieve a goal: this provides the basis for the linguistic category of agent. Similarly, he groups together things that are affected by action, and this is the foundation for the patient category. Schlesinger uses this latter example as an illustration of the insufficiency of the analysis:

> Similar considerations are pertinent in regard to the patient (goal) concept. In discussing the acquisition of the notion of the transitive verb, Macnamara (1972) argues that the child must perceive that something happens to the object, that the object is affected by the action denoted by the verb. But how much affected does it have to be if it is to be considered the object of a transitive verb? Suppose you hit a wall with your head—is the wall "affected" without showing it? And when you sit on a bed that has just been made and the bed shows it very much, should it be considered a patient (and hence *sit* as a transitive verb), contrary to what is suggested by the sentence *I sit on the bed?* Cognitive development will not furnish the clue to this problem of where the boundaries are to be drawn. There seems to be nothing in the child's extralinguistic interaction with the environment which shows him where the boundaries are to be drawn. (Pp. 7–8)

Schlesinger maintains that the child may learn to interpret the world before he is a linguistic being, but the division of events into specific agents, actions, and patients does not solve the larger problem, which is, how does his particular language class these things together? That can only be determined by hearing the language in conjunction with the events. Schlesinger provides another illustration from the domain of possession. In Chapter 3 we noted that English makes no distinction linguistically between alienable possession (my hat) and inalienable possession (my arm), yet other languages do. So the nonlinguistic environment offers the child no clues as to whether he should classify these situations similarly or not: he must learn through hearing his particular language.

Thus, while some aspects of conceptual development must precede the acquisition of forms, it is logical to suppose that language and cognitive development interact, rather than nonlinguistic classifications always providing the foundation for the linguistic classes. Linguistic forms may serve to draw attention to events and categorizations that the child would not otherwise heed, such as the similarity between inalienable and alienable possession, or the distinction between proper and common nouns (see, for example, Chapter 5).

Blank (1975) supplies a fascinating example of a child being dependent on the language for discovering meanings, in the acquisition of *why* and *how* questions. Blank argues that languages contain many words that have no perceptual correlates in the world, but instead have intangible meanings. For example, *why* questions cover a huge range of meanings. One can question actions, as in:

Why did he try to carry three cups at once?

or states of affairs:

Why are people living so much longer?

or functions:

Why do men's jackets have spare buttonholes?

or causes:

Why did the rug catch fire?

There is an equally baffling number of answer types that depend on one's theories of motivation, explanation, justification, and so on; so the question above about action might receive an answer about motives:

Because he was trying to impress his girlfriend.

or justification:

Because he had too many trips to make.

or attributes:

Because he has a very good sense of balance.

How is the child to learn what constitutes a sensible *why* question or answer, given this array of possibilities? Blank maintains that children learn by asking the questions as early and as often as possible, a fact familiar to anyone who has spent any time around a three-year-old. Only by testing the listener's reaction to his questions, and by observing reactions to his answers, can the child gradually home in on the varieties of explanation that his language expresses. Blank reports some results of a study of the development of *why* questions and answers in a child named Dusty. At around eighteen months of age, Dusty began asking *why* questions in response to a negative statement from an adult, but appeared not to know whether the answer was what she wanted:

Adult: The cat has a body but no head.
Child: Why?
Adult: Why? I don't know why. Did someone break it?
Child: (no reaction)

By twenty-six months, Dusty had attached her word *why* to phrases, seemingly at random, as in:

> Adult: That's the garage door.
> Child: Why the garage door?

Question words like *where* and *what* would be appropriate in such contexts. She now reacted to *why* questions with "I don't know."

At twenty-eight months, Dusty had gone a step further and no longer used *why* just with nouns, but with whole predicates:

> Adult: He's reading a book.
> Child: Why he reading a book?

This allowed much more reasonable responses from the adult. In reply to *why* questions, Dusty now offered an attribute of the situation, but it was often inappropriate as an explanation:

> Child: I can't wash this.
> Adult: Why not?
> Child: In here.

This phenomenon led to the observation by Ervin-Tripp (1970) that young children often respond to *why* questions as if they were other forms like *when* or *where*. The child cannot come by knowledge about explanations without offering answers and watching his audience react, or by listening to complex dialogue between other persons. Blank speculates that this is one reason that children from socially impoverished environments do especially poorly when presented with *why* questions. They simply lack the experience with sufficiently sophisticated conversations.

The case of *why* questions is a good example of how language may be in the service of cognitive growth. Without adequate linguistic experience, the child would be incapable of formulating and understanding explanations. Nonetheless, there are some instances where language development seems to wait upon cognitive growth, and Cromer (1974a) uses the example of the *hypothetical,* whose acquisition he studied in Brown's subjects Adam and Sarah. Hypothetical statements involve reference to two future events, one dependent on the other, for example:

> If it is windy we shall fly the kite

In more complicated examples called counterfactuals, a possibility counter to the fact in past time is expressed, with an event contingent, as in:

> If it had snowed we would have lost our way.

Both types thus require an ability to conceive of possibilities rather than actualities, and an ability to shift time reference.

Cromer speculated that the earliest forerunner of expressions of possibility may be make-believe, as in:

> Dis could be the mother.

in playing with dolls. Only when the children were 4½ or older did true expressions of possibility appear:

> Someping might come out my pocket.

At the same time the first hypotheticals appeared, such as:

> If you keep going it's gonna get bigger on this side and bigger on that side, right?

Cromer maintained that all the component linguistic forms were available in the child's repertoire much earlier than this, but they were not used for hypothetical statements until a comparatively late stage. Slobin (1966) observed that the hypothetical in Russian is extremely simple grammatically, though it makes its appearance quite late in Russian children's speech, again suggesting it is conceptual rather than linguistic requirements that delay its emergence. In this respect, then, cognitive development sets the pace for language acquisition.

COGNITIVE CONSTRAINTS ON SEQUENCE

Some conceptual developments are said to delimit the time of language onset; others may constrain the rate of language acquisition. Still others may affect the *sequence* of acquisition. Slobin (1973) proposed that there are inherent biases that the child brings to the language-learning task, and these determine the linguistic forms and constructions he will find easiest. This is not the same as arguing that the constructions themselves are more or less complex in terms of the number of rules they might involve, but rather it suggests that the child approaches language with certain general cognitive-processing strategies. Slobin drew on a large body of data from many different languages to search for regularities in the learning process. These regularities he formulated as a set of *operating principles,* as if they were statements of beliefs the child holds as he begins to learn any language. We will only provide a single illustration of his evidence for each principle, for Slobin believed that they should be thought of as directions for future research rather than proven facts.

The Operating Principles

(1) *Pay attention to the ends of words*. This bias was attributed to children on the basis of evidence that they learn postpositions and suffixes more readily than prefixes or prepositions. In pure form, this bias would be independent of the meaning attached to the postposition or preposition form and of the number of rules involved in its use or its derivation, though for any given language these factors would be confounded. Slobin argued that children learning Bulgarian acquire the ar-

ticle quite early, and articles in Bulgarian are suffixes. This is in contrast to children acquiring either English or German, where the pronominal article is mastered comparatively late.

(2) *The phonological forms of words can be systematically modified.* Children often engage in a great deal of playful modification of words, and Slobin cites instances where children experiment with reduplication, diminutive endings or inflections before learning the meanings of those modifications.

(3) *Pay attention to the order of words and morphemes.* As evidence, Slobin pointed to the tendency of children to mimic the word order of the input language, a phenomenon readily seen in English where violations of order in child speech are quite rare.

(4) *Avoid interruption or rearrangement of linguistic units.* This principle was used to account for the difficulty children encounter with inversions of major constituents, as in *yes-no* questions, which they initially mark by intonation alone (but see Chapter 4 for complications).

(5) *Underlying semantic relations should be marked overtly and clearly.* Slobin maintained that children would have difficulty with an underlying semantic relation that had an obscure or absent surface form. A rather bizarre sounding example, at least to an English speaker, is provided by the Arabic plural marking. In Arabic the singular has no extra morpheme; any number between two and ten requires an inflection, but for numbers greater than ten, there is, again, no inflection. In English the parallel would be something like: *one duck, two ducks . . . ten ducks* and then *many duck*. Egyptian children, however, prefer to use the plural for all instances in which there is more than one item; they have difficulty with the absence of plural marking when there are many items. It also follows from this operating principle that children should have more difficulty with sentences in which there are constituents that are deleted in the surface structure but are necessary for meaning. However, see Chapter 4 for some disconfirmations of this prediction.

(6) *Avoid exceptions.* There are hundreds of examples of children overgeneralizing linguistic rules to the exceptional case: the English past tense *-ed* ending is the commonest example.

(7) *The use of grammatical markers should make semantic sense.* Slobin supported this principle by pointing to the difficulty children have with grammatical markers that have purely formal selection restrictions, for example, agreements that involve *gender* when this is an arbitrary feature. In contrast, markers that correspond to a real-life quality like plurality, earlierness, duration, and so forth, are much easier to master as the cues to their use are more than intralinguistic: the environment at first assists their acquisition.

These principles provide a fascinating first attempt to summarize the inherent biases of the young language-learner, though much more research is needed to ensure their generality. For instance, some of them may be redundant: *avoid exceptions* may incorporate the more specific principles without any loss of predictability. Nevertheless, they are a useful guideline for documenting future findings on many languages.

We must always, however, delve deeper than a summary description. As we described earlier, recent research on animal learning has documented the inherent biases in animals, for example the relative difficulty of training a pigeon to escape shock by staying still and pecking a key, rather than flying away. This research might be summarized by saying that organisms use a principle like: "Try species-specific responses before arbitrary ones." But this would not suffice as an explanation of the phenomenon. For the explanation, one looks to the evolutionary history of the particular species. Where do we search for the explanation of the operating principles for language acquisition? The first requirement is to ensure that they are not somehow provided by the language input; for example, in the case of principle (1) we must make sure that the ends of words are not systematically stressed or otherwise made salient by people speaking to the child, but that instead he notices them more readily regardless of their salience. Only then can we be sure that the child actually brings the biases to the language-learning situation.

Once that is established, there is a need for research on the generality of these principles. Some of them, for example (3) and (6), may have much wider utility than just for language learning. Others, such as (2), (4), or (7), may be rephrased to expose more general principles. For instance (7) may simply mean: it is easier to learn behaviors when there is a wide variety of supporting stimuli than when there is only a single cue. Alternatively, the biases may be specific to language learning. In the latter case, one would need information on the universality of the easier forms in the world's languages. For example, are the ends rather than the fronts of words usually more informative? If so, why did language evolve with this characteristic? All these questions remain open for the future, for we do not yet have in psychology a learning theory sufficient to the task of incorporating the biases organisms share.

9

Language in Developmentally Disabled Children

Just as they vary in physical growth and temperament, children show substantial individual variation in their language development. For reasons of biological maturity as well as experience, children differ in the age at which they begin to talk, in the rate at which linguistic development proceeds, and in the strategies they may adopt at various stages of development. Marked individual differences are also reported in the prevalence of the typical errors that children make: phonological omissions and substitutions, overgeneralization of syntactic rules, and over- and under-extensions of word meanings.

Yet in most of the cases of individual variation that we have so far considered, adult native speakers of the language would not regard the children's development as in any sense abnormal or disordered. We now turn to instances, most of them fortunately rare, in which the delay in acquisition or the frequency and peculiar nature of errors lead native speakers to characterize the child's language as deviant or disordered. What we have already described of normal language development will illuminate the different points at which the process can be disrupted.

(1) In the second chapter we outlined how the child must analyze the complex stream of speech he hears into the functional speech sounds of his native language and learn how to combine them into meaningful units. Any failure to segment the input into morphemes or to distinguish between the phonemes that make up morphemes will lead to a breakdown in oral language acquisition at a very basic level. As we shall see later in this chapter, some children suffering from developmental aphasia cannot discriminate between certain consonant sounds, while some autistic children seem unable to segment whole utterances into words and conse-

228

quently fail to develop productive speech. On the other hand, we will argue that use of the auditory channel is not essential to language. Profoundly impaired hearing that would seem to preclude any analysis of incoming speech does not hamper the development in deaf children of a sign language as complex and flexible as spoken English. Furthermore, a significant proportion of them learn to read and write English even though their spoken language is greatly impaired.

(2) In Chapter 5 we discussed the child's acquisition of the meanings of words for objects, actions, qualities, and relationships. Since these words label regularities in our environment, lexical development depends heavily on the child's ability to abstract such invariances from his experience. At even the simplest level of nouns, a delay in learning about the permanence of objects across perceptual transformations would severely hamper lexical development, since each time the child heard a word it would seem to refer to a different object. Delayed or deviant conceptual development might also be expected to retard semantic development to the extent that the child was unable to categorize his experience in the same way as the adults providing the labels for those categories.

(3) Chapters 3 and 4 examined the acquisition of syntax: rules for the combination of morphemes in order to communicate different underlying meanings. Several aspects of this process could pose difficulties for children. An important property of language is the application of a limited number of syntactic rules to a finite set of linguistic units to generate meaningful new combinations. The child must learn which units of utterances are operated on by the rules—words, phrases, clauses, and so on—and how they are combined to form various syntactic structures. He cannot simply learn utterances by rote; the memory load would be too great. Yet the speech of some autistic children seems to be limited to sentences and phrases that they have learned as unanalyzed wholes in particular situations.

A particularly important syntactic rule in English is the use of word order to signal different meanings, so an inability to sequence auditory events or remember their order would also severely disrupt a child's comprehension and production of the language. Both of these handicaps have been attributed to developmentally aphasic children.

(4) Finally, we have stressed the pragmatic and social aspects of language (Chapters 2 and 6). One basic purpose of language is social—to communicate one's feelings and desires and to pass on information about the world to others. And it is within this context of social interaction that language is acquired. At the simplest level this requires an awareness of oneself as separate from others and a desire to enter into communication with them. Withdrawal from social interaction leads to impoverished language development. At a higher level of discourse, communication requires consideration of the state of knowledge of the listener, so a delay in

the ability to decenter one's viewpoint will also result in impaired verbal communication. The classic case of social withdrawal is that of the autistic child, and a severe disorder of language acquisition is typical of these children.

Delay and Deviance

There are several senses in which language can be delayed or deviant. Onset of intelligible speech may be late; the rate of development after onset may be abnormally slow; or the final level of competence achieved may remain below that of normal adults. Of course, all three types of delay could occur in the same child, and often do, as in the severely retarded (Lenneberg, 1967). The question of mere delay or true deviance in the form and process of language acquisition has guided many descriptive studies of the developmentally disabled child. Language development may be simply slowed down but still follow the same pattern or sequence as normal development, or it may be truly deviant in the sense of differing in *what* is acquired or *how* it is acquired. Of crucial importance in answering this question is to decide what is to count as a real difference, and we will have to consider that problem in some detail as we proceed.

At a more general level, the perceived deviance of a child's language depends partially on his linguistic maturity compared to his age, but also depends on the number of aspects of his language that differ markedly from normal (Menyuk, 1971). The speech of a child with an articulation problem does not appear as disordered as it would if that problem were combined with deviant grammar, and so on. In addition, the several aspects of language can themselves be ordered, based perhaps on their importance for communication or on the degree to which children normally have difficulty with them. A child with impaired articulation does not seem nearly as disordered as one whose speech is perfectly pronounced but often noncommunicative and inappropriate to the situation.

Incidence of Language Problems

Some 5 percent of all school-age children show delayed or deviant language, most of these (about 88 percent) suffering from articulation problems or stuttering. The reader should note that a dialect or other accent is not generally considered an articulation problem, as long as the child's speech is intelligible at school. Articulation becomes a problem when the child persists with a pattern of pronunciation that obscures the distinction between some phonemes, blurring sound distinctions that make a difference for meaning. From what we know of phonological development it is apparent that different kinds of articulation problems can occur. One might simply be a difficulty in producing some of the speech sounds (phones) of the language in any context or in isolation; another might be a problem with those sounds in context, though they can be accurately produced on their own, that is, a problem in blending sounds together in words. A more specific example of the latter would be a case in which certain sounds were consistently misarticulated only in particular combinations. In this case the child might actually have a perfectly coherent and consistent set of phonological rules that described his speech production, only they would deviate from those of adults and other children in his community. All of these problems could lead to the child not making speech sound distinctions that are crucial for meaning differences in his language. Most of the descriptive studies of articulation problems in children have concentrated on specifying the particular speech sounds with which the children experience most difficulty, or on cataloguing the typical errors of omission or substitution that they make. These studies are well summarized in Winitz (1969). Only recently have any attempts been made to study these children's phonological systems to see if their persistent errors might be captured by one or more phonological rules not employed in adult language (Compton, 1975, 1976; Lorentz, 1976).

Our major concern in the remainder of the chapter will be with the other 12 percent of language-delayed children, whose problem is not just one of articulation, but is apparently more fundamental. In a thorough survey of 278 such children, Telford and Sawrey (1967) reported that some 40 percent were deaf, 26 percent suffered from developmental aphasia, 25 percent were mentally deficient, and 1 percent were diagnosed as mentally ill. For these four main categories of developmental disorder, we will consider how what is known about the underlying disorder illuminates the children's problems with language, and how a careful characterization of the children's language increases our understanding of the more general disorder.

Most studies of language-delayed children have investigated a given aspect of their speech production or comprehension at one specific time, often employing some standardized experimental test. The performance of children with a particular disorder has then been compared to that of normal subjects on the same test or to the corresponding performance of a different group of disordered children. Usually, the different groups have been matched on mental age by an intelligence test, but very few studies have compared several aspects of the linguistic functioning of one child, or related them to other aspects of the child's cognitive and social functioning. Increasingly, however, researchers have come to realize that much more detailed cross-sectional and preferably longitudinal studies of a wide range of linguistic abilities in the same children are needed if we are to understand their difficulties with language rather than just document them.

DEAFNESS

Since human languages almost all use the oral/aural mode of communication, a deficit in hearing has a severe effect on language acquisition. Yet, within the general category of deafness, there are considerable differences in the degree and type of hearing impairment that children can have. In many cases the child is unable to hear high-frequency sounds, but can hear low frequencies practically normally; just the opposite may also occur, with low sounds differentially affected. Other children may have a general hearing loss right across the range of audible sound frequencies. In all likelihood, then, deaf children's perception of speech will be different not only from that of their normal peers, but also from each other. One should therefore not expect a common defect in the comprehension of speech by all deaf children.

Our discussion of the language acquisition of the deaf will be divided into three sections: (1) the acquisition of oral speech; (2) comprehension and production of written English; and (3) the acquisition of manual sign language.

Oral Speech

Deaf children are typically severely handicapped in their development of oral speech, and many do not acquire much more than the rudiments of oral communication. Like hearing infants, even the profoundly deaf begin to babble around four-to-six months of age. But at the end of that period, as auditory feedback from others and from his own vocalizations becomes important for the normal child, the deaf infant ceases babbling and usually does not develop intelligible speech. He lacks feedback from his own sounds as well as vocal stimulation from others that so often elicits babbling from an infant. Indeed, if the deaf child does continue to babble for a while it is because he can see the adult who is speaking to him; the sounds produced do not gradually approximate those of the language being spoken. The social reinforcement of the adult's presence is sufficient to maintain the motor movements that produce sounds, but the child does not hear the sounds he should imitate. An analysis of the continued babbling sounds of these deaf children could show how much the course of speech sound development is constrained when adult speech is not heard. However, we know of no such systematic investigation; most reports of the babbling of deaf babies are impressionistic in nature, usually concluding that the babbled sounds are "similar in nature" or "a little more monotonous" than those of normal children.

If the young deaf child is provided with hearing aids that can significantly correct his impairment, babbling continues to run its normal course. In fact, in several cases in which the child was not diagnosed as deaf until after the babbling stage, it was found that babbling began again spontaneously some time (even up to a few months) after the hearing aids were fitted (Fry, 1966). The development of approximately normal speech requires that the child be able to hear himself and others so that links between the motor activity of speech and auditory feedback can be established at the right time.

Despite their hearing problems, some deaf children do learn to speak remarkably well if they hear enough clear speech. The Nuffield Hearing and Speech Center in London has reported many instances of children with profound hearing loss who have nevertheless acquired quite adequate speech (Fry, 1966). Fry suggests that success or failure in acquiring speech does not depend on the degree of hearing impairment per se, though of course a child with *no* effective hearing could not comprehend any oral language. Rather, in the case of most moderate hearing impairments, it depends on the amount and clarity of the speech that the child hears and the use that he makes of his remaining hearing. Figure 8 reproduces the audiograms of several children; these measure their hearing loss (in decibels) across different frequencies of sound. As indicated in the figure, some of these children were at schools for the deaf but had learned practically no speech; others, though similarly or even more severely impaired in hearing, had perfectly intelligible speech and were in normal schools (Fry, 1966). Although the latter children differed among themselves in patterns of hearing loss (see audiograms *D, E,* and *F*), and all of them had different hearing from normal children, they were still able to hear and produce appropriate distinctions between phonemes. So, as long as the child has enough residual hearing and sufficient verbal input for him to hear distinctions between speech sounds, even though these distinctions may be based on acoustic cues different from those normally used, he seems to be able to acquire adequate oral communication. This is interesting from the perspective of acoustic phonetics, for it suggests that there are probably multiple acoustic cues to distinguish many of the phonemes that we use in English.

Fry maintains that some of the difficulty experienced by deaf children in learning to understand speech results from the failure of adults around them to provide sufficient clear input at important periods of development, either because they do not know the child has a hearing problem, or because it is easier to communicate with him in gestures. Mothers of deaf preschoolers do in fact talk less in interaction with them than do mothers of hearing children, presumably because the deaf children do not respond as often to speech. Furthermore, in comparison with mothers of hearing children, mothers of deaf children are more inclined to give suggestions and directions and less inclined to ask for information and opinions from their offspring: they give less praise to the children and show less agreement with them (Kenady and Proctor, 1968; as reported by Lowell and

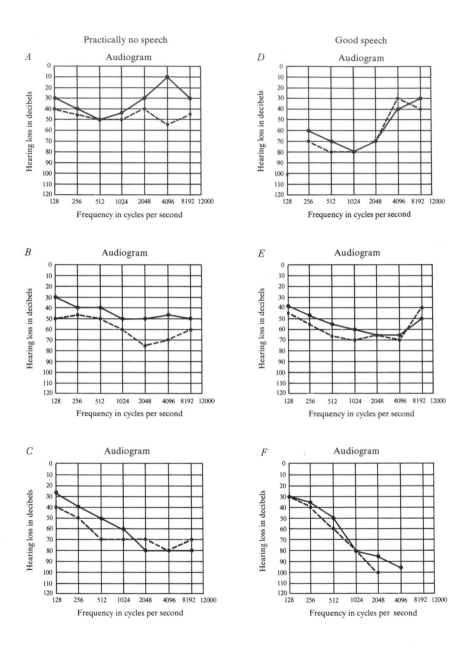

Figure 8. A, B, C: Audiograms of three children in schools for the deaf who had practically no speech. D, E, F: Similar audiograms of three children who had developed excellent speech and were being educated in ordinary schools.

Lowell, 1976). Comparative studies of large groups of mothers and a wide range of age groups, especially children younger than three or four years, are called for, but it does appear that the typical deaf preschooler has to contend with less input and less encouragement to use speech than a hearing child of the same age.

The importance of the parents and the quality of their speech to the deaf child is also stressed by a clinical program at the Wilkerson Hearing and Speech Center in Nashville, Tennessee, under the direction of Kathryn Horton and her associates (Horton and McConnell, 1970; Horton, 1974). At the heart of this program are the early assessment of hearing loss, preferably within the first year, and the use of two methods to maximize the deaf child's opportunities to develop his residual hearing: first, binaural hearing aids are fitted as soon as possible; and second, attempts are made to upgrade the child's auditory and linguistic environments by training his parents. In addition to being taught about the stages and sequences of normal language development, parents learn how to direct the child's attention to environmental sounds and their sources, and to reward with praise and attention any of the child's responses to sound. With respect to language input, the parents are trained in the following (Lillie, 1972): to reinforce the child's vocal and verbal behaviors by verbal and nonverbal means; to provide constant feedback and expansion of the child's utterances, lexically, syntactically and semantically; and in their own speech to emphasize relevance to the immediate situation and interest of the child, redundancy in semantic and syntactic aspects, and the correct use of intonation and stress. In even the simplest aspect of interaction, making sure the child can hear you, parents need to be alerted to the problems of having a deaf child. For example, when the child wanders away during play, the parent has to raise his or her voice or remain close to the child. In this way the amount and quality of the linguistic input to the child is upgraded along the lines of the ideal mother-to-child speech (outlined in Chapter 7).

When the language growth and auditory development of the children who had been in the program for a period of three years was assessed and compared to that of normal and deaf children who were not identified before two years of age, they proved to be much more like the normals than the other deaf children. Eighteen of the early participants in the program were able to enter regular first and second grades when they reached school age, and they performed successfully—a remarkable achievement for any deaf child. Although the number of severely deaf children who acquire adequate oral English is still distressingly small, the success of programs that attempt to train both the parents and the children, and the increasing stress by federal programs on techniques for early identification of deafness, suggest an optimistic outlook, at least for the moderately deaf infant.

Written Language

Up to a few years ago, most of the studies of deaf children's language investigated their comprehension and production of written linguistic material. These studies suffered from several limitations: first, only a select proportion of deaf children achieve functional literacy (estimated at 35 percent of the deaf population in 1967 [Vernon, 1967]); second, the children tested must be somewhat older than the age at which most normal children learn language; and third, the outcome of the test may be as much a function of the particular sequence and method in which the child was taught to read and write as it is of the natural pattern of acquisition.

The practically universal finding has been that the deaf lag well behind hearing children of similar age and intelligence on several aspects of written English. For example, Cooper (1967) studied the comprehension and production of morphological forms (for example, plurals, comparatives, and superlatives) by a large number of deaf and hearing children aged seven to nineteen years, all of whom could read at second grade level or above. In the comprehension test the children had to pick out a picture that corresponded to a morphological form appended to a nonsense word (for example, mups); in the production test they had to complete a written sentence (for example, "Here are two gutch_____")(Berko, 1958). The patterns of difficulty in comprehension and production of the items were similar for hearing and deaf children, but the deaf children were significantly worse even when the groups were equated for mental or chronological age. In fact, mental age and chronological age were not nearly as closely related to linguistic performance for the deaf as for the hearing group. In a similar variety of pencil and paper tasks that tested comprehension and production of active-declarative, negative, passive, and passive-negative sentences, Schmitt (1968) found that normal eight-year-olds obtained better scores than seventeen-year-old deaf adolescents. In some respects the performance of the deaf children was most unlike that of normal acquisition: for example, the eight- and eleven-year-olds sometimes reversed the word order of active-declarative sentences, but word order in English active sentences is mastered in the earliest stages of language development by normal hearing children (de Villiers and de Villiers, 1973a). Similarly, the present progressive morpheme, acquired early by hearing children (Brown, 1973), was often deviant in the deaf group. Many of the young deaf children had difficulty with the negatives, often treating them as affirmative sentences, and even the seventeen-year-olds had not completely mastered all the forms of the negative in English. Moores, Weiss, and Goodwin (1973) also reported that young (six and seven year old) deaf children tended to overlook the negative marker in sentences presented orally or in written form.

In short, then, deaf children are significantly impaired in their understanding and production of written English and in some respects seem to differ from normals in the relative difficulty they have with certain syntactic aspects of the language. But it is not clear to what extent these differences can be attributed to the way in which the language was taught and to what extent they are due to the deaf child's knowledge of sign language systems, which differ in some aspects from spoken and written English, particularly in having a freer word order. The differences may relate to the peculiar difficulty of learning to read and write English without the benefit of substantial oral mastery of the same language beforehand. In the past, in some programs emphasizing oral and auditory skills, teaching of reading and writing was not encouraged for younger deaf children, since it was thought to detract from early oral language learning (Moores, 1974). But it has now become a central part of most training programs, so the number of literate deaf persons should multiply.

Sign Language

Recent years have seen an upsurge of interest in the sign languages of the deaf. Small groups of deaf children who are exposed to only oral speech at home or at school spontaneously develop gesture "languages" in an attempt to communicate with each other (Tervoort, 1961; Goldin-Meadow and Feldman, 1975), even when such gestures are frowned upon by their parents and teachers (Lenneberg, 1967). These signs are frequently esoteric and unintelligible to adults or other groups of deaf children, even within the same school (Tervoort, 1961). Such self-made communication systems have generally been approached from the perspective of the degree to which they might interfere with the later learning of English, whether in spoken, written, or more formal signed form (Moores, 1974). But Furth (1975) recently raised the possibility that the inherent structure of these "natural" sign languages, which have developed with little, if any, adult input, might provide some insight into innate constraints on human language systems. Deaf children who create their own languages in this way not only devise signs for objects and actions, but also combine gestures in rule-governed ways to specify relations between objects and actions (Goldin-Meadow and Feldman, 1975). The fact that some of the gesture languages of small groups of deaf children are not intelligible to other groups suggests that the children are not just pantomiming but are developing arbitrary signs. The learning or creation of arbitrary symbols for objects and events during an individual's lifetime may be unique to human languages (see Chapter 7).

Several standard sign languages are used by large groups of deaf persons in different countries, manual languages that share many of the properties of spoken languages, such as a relatively abstract referential vocabulary and generative syntactic structure. These languages are quite distinct from each other and are not simply a reflection of spoken English; hence, a deaf person signing in American Sign Language (ASL or Ameslan) cannot be understood by a person who only knows the sign language most widely used in England, and vice versa. In fact, since the roots of ASL lie in the sign language developed by de l'Epee in France to reflect French syntax, a signer of ASL can converse quite successfully with French signers, though he knows no spoken French and they know no English. Stokoe (1972) reports that at the 1968 meeting of the World Federation of the Deaf in Paris, no fewer than six manual interpreters translated oral and signed speeches into the various sign languages.

Over the past several years ASL has been subjected to extensive linguistic analysis (for example, Stokoe, 1958, 1972; Klima and Bellugi, 1975). Apart from the fact that it is produced by the hands (aided by facial expressions and body posture) rather than orally, and perceived visually rather than auditorily, or perhaps because of this fact, ASL differs in two main respects from spoken language.

First, many signs are quite iconic in nature and seem to have developed from pantomime, so they lack the total arbitrariness of most words. Yet most are not so iconic that a nonsigner could immediately guess their meaning. Historically, signs have become less pantomimic over time, becoming more systematically related to each other and assuming more arbitrary shapes and positions. In fact, signs are not stored as holistic gestures but are made up of a limited set of formational parameters (Klima and Bellugi, 1975), much like the distinctive features of speech sounds (Stokoe, 1958). In ASL these are: (1) the place where the sign is made; (2) the distinctive configuration of the hand; (3) the characteristic movement of the hand or hands; and (4) the orientation of the hands (Klima and Bellugi, 1975). These parameters are of course arbitrary with respect to meaning, much like speech sounds. The evidence for the psychological reality of these parameters comes from studies of short-term memory for signs (Bellugi, Klima, and Siple, 1975) and "slips of the hand" (Klima and Bellugi, 1975). The intrusion errors that deaf people make when recalling a list of signs are structurally related to the signs that are presented. All except one or two of a sign's formational parameters are preserved. For example, errors for the sign CAT, which represents the whiskers of a cat, do not include "iconic" errors such as signing other aspects of a cat (for example, CLAWS, PURR, FUR, for which there are other signs). Instead, a frequent error was the sign INDIAN. Each sign is made with one hand on the cheek, with the same handshape, but they differ in movement—CAT involves a brushing movement of the hand, INDIAN two successive points of contact. Figure 9 shows two other typical intrusion errors, the first involving only the place at which the sign is made, the second involving only movement. These errors seem comparable to the acoustic confusion

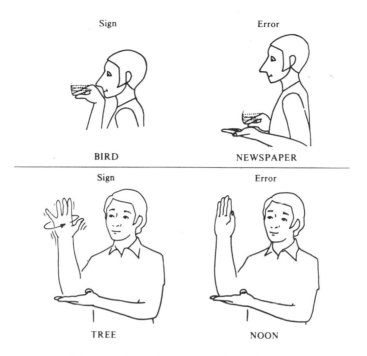

Figure 9. From Klima and Bellugi, 1975.

errors made in verbal short-term memory, such as *feast* for *beast,* or *posterior* for *posterity.*

Slips of the hand reflect the organizational parameters of signs, just as slips of the tongue reveal the organization of oral language (Fromkin, 1973). Most slips do not replace whole signs, but interchange one or more formational parameters. Figure 10 depicts one such case from Klima and Bellugi (1975), in which just the hand configurations of the two signs were transposed.

The second difference between ASL and spoken language concerns the simultaneity of elements in signs as compared to the sequential arrangement of elements in speech. While words are made up of a temporal sequence of phonemes, signs simultaneously employ a particular combination of the four formational parameters. Similarly, modulations of word meaning that are accomplished by suffixes in spoken English are frequently realized in Sign by simultaneous changes in movement or some other parameter. For example, *blue* becomes *bluish* in English; to mark the same modulation of meaning in ASL, the sign for BLUE is simply made with increased laxness of handshape and hesitancy of movement (Klima and Bellugi, 1975). Another example of simultaneity in the modulation of meaning is the use of a headshake concurrent with a signed sentence to negate that proposition, or with an already negative

Figure 10. From Klima and Bellugi, 1975.

sentence to emphasize its negativity. The headshake, which we will transcribe as NEG, can also be used as a sign in sequence with other signs, usually in initial or terminal position.

Sign, unlike spoken language, has the potential for producing two signs at once and indicating their grammatical relation by some spatial cue. In practice, however, two lexical signs are not made at the same time in everyday speech, only in poetic plays on words. Although signs are generally produced in sequence, the order appears to be quite free, with location in space rather than temporal order serving to distinguish subject from object in most cases (Klima and Bellugi, 1975).

To summarize, American Sign Language appears to be quite as complex and flexible a language as spoken English, sharing some aspects with it and differing in others perhaps unique to its manual and visual form.

The Acquisition of ASL

Deaf children do not usually learn ASL until they reach school (and then only if the school uses Sign), since their parents usually have normal hearing and do not know a formal sign language. But the deaf child of deaf parents often acquires ASL in interaction with them, just as a normal child learns to talk. What is that acquisition like? Researchers have just recently begun detailed longitudinal studies of the natural acquisition of ASL, so only a few children have so far been studied. However, the early observations suggest that in many respects the acquisition of ASL parallels the acquisition of oral language in hearing children, but with some interesting differences that seem to follow from the special nature of sign language. For example, because of the iconic nature of many signs, the first words may be signed by deaf children of deaf parents at an earlier age than words are spoken by hearing children (Moores, 1974). The signs for EAT, SLEEP, DRINK, CRY, HUG, WASH, TABLE, CAT, and BIRD, all likely to be salient in the world of the infant, resemble the corresponding actions or objects in some way. This makes them easy for the child to understand, and since children gain control of their hands and arms earlier than their articulatory apparatus, they can produce signs earlier than spoken words. Nevertheless, children's production of early signs tends to be simpler and sloppier than the full adult signs; for example, the hand configurations may be simplified or the signs made in a different orientation. In fact, scenes in the Gardners' film of Washoe show the chimp producing some of her early signs in forms remarkably similar to the signing child's simplifications.[1] One is reminded of sound simplifications in the baby talk of hearing children and parents, though we know of no report of signing parents using simplified signs when conversing with an infant.[2]

When they first combine signs, deaf children begin by signaling in telegraphic form the same limited set of semantic relations as the normal hearing child (Bellugi and Klima, 1972; Schlesinger and Meadow, 1972). Function words like auxiliaries appear quite late in the grammatical development of the signing child, as they do in oral language acquisition.

The progressive formation of negative sentences by children learning Sign also resembles that of hearing children. As we saw in Chapter 4, children learning English begin by using *no* or *not* as an all-purpose negative marker. Adults use *no* as an interjection or, in an anaphoric way, to negate a previous utterance or assumption, as in *No, that's an aardvark*, denying that the beast in question could be anything else. *No* also functions as an emphatic to reinforce the negativity of an utterance, as in:

No, you can't ride on the elephant.

It is always used in initial position or alone, and never negates the sentence that it precedes. Bellugi claimed that hearing children also use *no* in initial position at first, but they use it as a negative operator to negate the following proposition; anaphoric use of *no* develops later (Bellugi, 1967; Bloom, 1970). Still later they use *no* in an internal position in the sentence, as in:

Johnny *no* want to read.

---

[1] Actually, Bellugi (personal communication) remarks that Washoe produces all her signs with a marked "chimpanzee" accent.

[2] In fact, we know of no study of the sign language adults use with deaf children as opposed to what they use with other adults. One wonders when deaf parents begin signing to their offspring and whether that input is simplified as the speech of parents to hearing children is simplified (see Chapter 7).

Finally, the adult use of *not* is acquired, along with other more specific negatives like *can't* and *don't,* and *no* is limited to its correct position and function. The auxiliaries are learned as unitary negative words, not in opposition to their positive form; thus *can't* is used well before *can* is acquired (Bellugi, 1967).

Bellugi and Klima (1972, citing the work of Lacy) report that a signing deaf child began by using two signs, NO and NEG (a headshake), as all-purpose negatives. Both are frequent signs in adult ASL. Like the English *no,* NO occurs alone or first in a sentence and is used anaphorically and as an emphatic or interjection. NEG can occur first or last in the sentence, or simultaneous with it; it has many functions, but never negates a sentence that it begins. The child studied by Lacy used NO and NEG in initial position to negate signed sentences, like hearing children's early use of *no* but unlike signing adults' use of initial NO and NEG. The two negative signs did not at first occur within signed sentences, but were in either first or last position. Later, the child dropped NO as a general negative marker as she acquired more correct and specific negative signs like NOT, CAN'T, and DON'T, these signs also appearing more frequently internal to her sentences. CAN'T was again acquired before CAN, as with hearing children.[3]

A longitudinal study of the deaf daughter of deaf parents by Ellenberger, Moores, and Hoffmeister (1975) produced similar observations of the acquisition of ASL negatives. NO was rare in Alice's signing, but she went from using NEG as a general negative operator in initial or final position to production of a variety of more specific negatives in their appropriate positions in the sentence. Unlike normal hearing children or the deaf child studied by Lacy, however, Alice seemed to use NEG anaphorically from the beginning.

Taken all together, these patterns of acquisition of sign language look remarkably like the normal acquisition of oral English, except for aspects in which Sign itself differs from oral language, such as iconicity and simultaneity. The ability of young deaf children to use appropriate negative forms in Sign sharply contradicts the work on much older children's understanding of written negative sentences. It suggests that the latter's difficulties are with specific grammatical rules of written English learned without adequate verbal input, not with the understanding of negation per se.

The Use of Signs in Training Programs for the Deaf

Since the late 1960s, a heated debate has raged among educators of the deaf about the value of sign languages in programs dedicated to teaching

---

[3] This is less surprising in ASL than in English, since the sign for CAN'T is not derived from the sign for CAN (Ellenberger, Moores, and Hoffmeister, 1975).

deaf children oral communication skills. The argument does not concern the ultimate aim of training programs; all agree that it is to develop as far as possible the deaf child's ability to speak and understand the spoken word. To that extent all programs favor the early identification of hearing loss and fitting of hearing aids. The disagreement arises over the best method of achieving the goal of adequate oral communication.

Up until the 1960s many educators of the deaf attempted to repress any form of manual communication on the part of the child, at least until the age of eleven years or so. After that age some programs exposed children who failed to develop oral language to finger spelling, in which each letter of the alphabet has a corresponding hand sign and English words are spelled out,[4] or to sign language, in which whole words or ideas are expressed by each sign. The arguments given for this practice seem plausible enough. The deaf child had to learn to function in a "hearing" world, so he needed to develop oral communication; use of sign language might interfere with or detract from the acquisition of a spoken language (Kates, 1972). Since ASL constitutes a different language with its own syntax, it might interfere with simultaneous or subsequent acquisition of English. Furthermore, once the child possessed an effective means of communication with his peers his motivation to learn spoken English might decrease.

On the other side of the argument, an increasing number of psychologists, linguists and educators have advocated that the deaf be exposed to sign as well as oral speech as early as possible in order to develop *language* skills, regardless of the channel of communication (Lenneberg, 1967; Moores, 1974). As we have already seen, ASL constitutes just as rich a communication system as oral languages. More formal types of sign language, like Signed English, employ English syntax and supplement signs with finger spelling for some function words like *of* or *the,* for which no sign exists in ASL. Programs that employ oral input plus sign language and finger spelling with very young children are commonly called total communication programs.

Despite the dire warnings of oral-only advocates, there exists no evidence that possessing a sign language does interfere with oral language development. If this were the case one would expect deaf children of deaf parents, who receive mainly signed input and little early exposure to speech, to be impaired in oral language accomplishments relative to the deaf offspring of hearing parents, who have received mainly speech input and have not usually acquired a standard sign language. Yet several studies that have made just this comparison reveal that the children of

---

[4] To the reader not familiar with finger spelling this may appear a particularly slow and laborious process. But a fluent finger-speller can maintain a rate of presentation of around a hundred words per minute, not an unreasonable rate of speech and comparable to the speed of an expert typist.

deaf parents are equal if not superior in educational achievement and such linguistic skills as reading, writing, and lip-reading. Typically, no differences in speech are observed (Moores, 1974). Perhaps more importantly, one of these studies (Meadow, 1966) found that teachers and counselors rated the deaf children of deaf parents higher in social and personal adjustment. Hence, the manual communication of these children with their parents certainly did not harm their later development of language skills. On the other hand, deaf children of deaf parents play a much more normal role in their families than the deaf child of hearing parents, who is an anomaly in the family group, and this alone could enhance their relative adjustment and motivation.

In a more direct comparison of oral-only with oral-plus training programs, Moores and his associates conducted a thorough longitudinal evaluation of seven preschool programs for the deaf in the United States, each containing children of roughly equal hearing impairment. Two of the programs employed oral-only instruction, two employed total communication, and the remaining three used intermediate or variable methods. Language understanding was tested in five different modes of communication: speech alone, written material, speech plus lip-reading, speech plus lip-reading plus finger-spelling, and speech plus lip-reading plus sign. The children in the total communication programs were as good as any of the other children in comprehension of speech alone or written material. In addition, their comprehension of speech when it was supplemented by finger-spelling or sign greatly exceeded any child's comprehension of speech or written material alone. These children's experience with sign language clearly did not impair their acquisition of oral skills and provided them with an additional effective means of communication.

In short, while total communication methods have not been shown to enhance the development of oral language, they do not harm it; and they provide a better overall system of communication for the deaf child. In this way the child's general facility with language and social interaction may be improved. Consequently, total communication programs, coupled with emphasis on upgrading the child's oral linguistic environment, are becoming more prevalent in the education of the deaf in the United States.

DEVELOPMENTAL APHASIA

We have already discussed the occurrence of traumatic aphasia in adults and children, the severe loss of the understanding or production of speech, or both, following a brain lesion. In children, provided that the lesion occurs early enough and leaves one hemisphere of the brain undamaged, recovery is practically complete. The child regains language and the undamaged hemisphere of the brain compensates for the loss or impairment of the other hemisphere.

However, there exists a second type of aphasia in children, usually called *developmental aphasia* or *dysphasia,* in which the prognosis is not as optimistic. In this case the child fails to develop adequate language from the start rather than losing it at some later point due to brain trauma. A major problem in studying developmental aphasia lies in defining exactly who counts as a developmentally aphasic child. Much of the research in the field does not clearly define the criteria used in diagnosis but talks generally about "language-delayed children" or "children with a specific language problem." While the obvious criterion is severe delay in the development of receptive or expressive language, that does not distinguish the dysphasic child from deaf, autistic, or retarded children. In practice, developmental aphasia is defined by exclusion.

Generally accepted criteria (Eisenson, 1972) include: exclusion of traumatic brain damage, although it is agreed that dysphasics suffer from some neurological dysfunction; absence of severe hearing loss or physical articulation problems; and elimination of mental retardation or infantile autism. In many cases the diagnosis is a difficult one to make. Some dysphasic children exhibit withdrawal from social interaction, a defining characteristic of autism; nevertheless, it is not typical and most of the children do attempt to communicate with others by means of gestures and sounds. Some dysphasics show impairment in hearing high frequency sounds, but unlike deaf children, most dysphasics have oddly fluctuating thresholds for sound. Tested with several different types of auditory stimuli or repeatedly with the same stimulus, the dysphasic children's thresholds varied much more over trials than those of either deaf or normal children (Reichstein, 1964). At times they seemed to hear the sounds quite normally, at others their hearing seemed impaired. In general, though, their language difficulty is out of all proportion with audiometric assessment of their hearing.

Another defining characteristic of dysphasic children is their near-normal performance on nonverbal intelligence tests, provided that the tasks do not require verbal mediation. Mentally retarded children score poorly on both verbal and nonverbal tests. Differences in the severity of the disorder increase the difficulty of diagnosis. Some children are practically mute at age five or six and show little language improvement thereafter; others make significant progress by puberty. Children who are nearly mute are difficult to test and may consequently appear to be retarded though they are not.

Language Development in Dysphasia

Whether the course of language development in developmental aphasics is truly deviant rather than simply delayed or slower is a matter of dispute. Indeed, there may be considerable individual variation within a group of children diagnosed as dysphasic (Menyuk, 1975a). Some may have difficulty only in producing language, while others have difficulty in both comprehension and production. In some cases language will be merely delayed, in others it will be truly disordered. Different aspects of language may also display different patterns of impairment.

For example, the acquisition of basic syntactic structures, such as declaratives, questions, and negatives, seems delayed but in the same order as normal acquisition (Menyuk, 1974). The difficulty ordering of several grammatical morphemes, like the present progressive -*ing* and third person -*s,* plural, articles, copula, and auxiliary, appears to be the same in language-delayed children as it is in young normal children's speech (Kessler, 1975).

On the other hand, Menyuk (1974) reports several syntactic differences between language-delayed and normal children. The former do not use the major linguistic categories like nouns and verbs in as many different syntactic contexts as normals. Unlike normal children, they make more errors of omission than errors of overgeneralization in the generation of sentences (Menyuk, 1964; Leonard, 1972).

Menyuk and Looney (1972a, b) investigated sentence and syllable imitation by children diagnosed as having a specific language disorder. All of the children used appropriate intonation or *wh*-words and negatives to indicate the modality of the sentences. In contrast, many of them showed severe phonological disorders. Some children seemed to have acquired unique phonological rules, substituting or deleting sounds unlike any normal child; others employed phonological rules like those of younger normal children. The children who had unique phonological rules also performed worst on repeating the sentences. Thus, some children were simply behind in their phonological development while others were truly deviant.

Other researchers have concentrated on the phonological processing of dysphasic children, since this is the most basic level at which the language disorder could occur. In several respects these children have deficient perception of speech sounds. While they can sometimes discriminate between phonemes in isolation, as soon as the phonemes are placed in context in real or nonsense words their performance disintegrates (McReynolds, 1966). Similarly, they have difficulty judging whether phonemes embedded in nonsense syllables are the same or different, even though they previously articulated the phonemes correctly (Monsees, 1968). Eisenson (1972) suggests that the dysphasic child may form phoneme categories that are either broader or narrower than normal, leading to confusions, particularly when the input is a little degraded, as it is when the phonemes are in context.

A critical aspect of phoneme perception, especially in ongoing speech, is the speed at which one can identify rapid changes in sound frequency, since these are often important cues to the different phonemes.

As we indicated in Chapter 2, stop consonants in particular are distinguished by very rapid sound transitions, lasting approximately 40 to 50 milliseconds. Voiced and unvoiced stop consonants are identified at least in part by differences in the time of onset of the various components of sound that make up the consonant, differences of the order of 40 milliseconds.

It is in just this aspect of sound discrimination, rapid processing of changes or differences, that dysphasic children have great difficulty. They require an inter-stimulus interval of around 350 milliseconds to determine the correct order of two sounds; normal children require only 36 milliseconds to perform at the same level of accuracy (Lowe and Campbell, 1965). Since the typical rate of speech hovers around 80 milliseconds per phoneme, it becomes apparent that the dysphasic child will have difficulty in understanding speech.

Recent research by Tallal and Piercy in Cambridge, England, has confirmed the dysphasics' problem with rapid sound changes and illustrated how that problem selectively impairs their identification and discrimination of consonants. The group of dysphasic children they studied could readily distinguish between two steady-state vowels of 250 milliseconds duration, but they could not discriminate between two consonant-vowel syllables, *ba* and *da*. These syllables also lasted for 250 milliseconds, but the sound transition that distinguished the initial consonants was only 43 milliseconds long (Tallal and Piercy, 1974). It was not just sound transitions per se that posed a problem: vowel-vowel syllables without transitions but with brief duration vowels were just as difficult for the children to distinguish, whereas consonant-vowel syllables in which the initial transitions had been artificially lengthened to 250 milliseconds were readily discriminated (Tallal and Piercy, 1975).

The consonant phonemes that dysphasics have trouble identifying are also the speech sounds they have most difficulty with in speech production. Dysphasic children who failed to learn a discrimination between stop-consonant–vowel syllables with 43 millisecond initial transitions also experienced great difficulty in producing stop-consonant–vowel or consonant-consonant combinations. Isolated vowels or nasal consonants that have long steady-state portions of sound were the easiest for these children to hear and articulate (Tallal, Stark, and Curtiss, 1976).

The dysphasic child's problem with rapid sound changes is not confined to speech sounds, however. In tasks involving the discrimination of sequences of tones, the performance of dysphasics deteriorated when the duration of the tone or the time between tone presentations was shortened (Tallal and Piercy, 1973). In fact, 7- to 9-year-old dysphasics performed worse than 4½-year-old normal children with rapid sequences of tones, although they were similar to normal children of their own age when the time between tones was long. Even with long tones well-spaced in time, however, the dysphasic children could not easily remember sequences longer than four tones, suggesting that they suffer from an auditory short-term memory deficit as well as a speed constraint. A similar deficit in short-term memory for speech was proposed by Menyuk (1971) to account for dysphasic children's language impairment.

These results suggest that the primary deficit in children with developmental aphasia is not specifically linguistic, but is a general auditory problem. It affects speech sounds in particular, since rapid changes in sound are functionally important in speech. The greater the speed constraint on the child's auditory processing, the more speech sounds he would confuse. This could account for the difference in dysphasic's phoneme categories suggested by Eisenson (1972). The dysphasic child's auditory memory limitation should also prove debilitating to language processing, since identifying sequences of phonemes is crucial for distinguishing between words.

Together, these deficits explain why speaking slowly to dysphasic children does not dramatically improve their comprehension. Slower speech only lengthens the steady-state portions of words and extends the pauses between words; it does not significantly change the duration of stop consonant transitions. It also increases the period for which the sound sequences must be held in short-term auditory memory.

Finally, since the ability to process nonverbal sounds rapidly and to discriminate between phonemes improves with age, reaching asymptote at around eight years in Tallal and Piercy's tasks, developmental aphasia may not result from any permanent deficit but from delayed development of this processing ability. The fact that a considerable proportion of dysphasic children eventually achieve near-normal language proficiency supports this possibility (Tallal and Piercy, 1974).

Several questions remain, however. The generality of Tallal and Piercy's finding must still be established. Their studies are based on twelve children who were extensively tested, but it is not clear how typical those children are of the larger population of dysphasics. Second, the extent to which variations in language acquisition amongst dysphasic children can be explained by such a general auditory deficit remains uncertain. The variations may arise from differences within the population of dysphasics, or from the particular teaching methods or materials that these children were exposed to in language training programs.

Ultimately, this raises the question of diagnosis again. Although the diagnosis of developmental aphasia carries with it the assumption of an organic condition, operationally it turns out to be a behavioral classification. Thus, we could define as developmentally aphasic all children with a developmental delay specific to language, as is the current practice. The problem with this approach is that there seems to be nothing that all these children have in common, though it is still possible that a single, as yet undiscovered, general deficit underlies all the different manifestations of language disorder. Alternatively, one could define as dysphasic only those children with a particular problem, for example, the rapid auditory processing limitation. Other children with delayed language would be classified separately. The value of this approach is that it defines a relatively homogeneous group, so that treatment or training could be directed towards their specific problem. The reason why this latter approach has not been widely adopted has been partly the hope that a single underlying cause could be found for most dysphasics' problems, and partly the lack of techniques for identifying fairly specific and concrete deficits that would account for the language difficulties of at least a sizable number of dysphasics. Perhaps the Tallal and Piercy procedures will provide such a technique.

One can draw an analogy between the practice of classing together for treatment all children with a delay in language and attempting a single kind of physiotherapy with all persons complaining of severe pains in the leg. Admittedly, they all have the same trouble getting around, but true advances in their treatment only come with accurate diagnosis into varicosity, arthritis, war wounds, broken bones, and the residual category exemplified by the favorite British comedy line:

I can't do that, not with my bad leg!

MENTAL RETARDATION

The defining characteristic of the retarded child is that he lags behind normal children in his intellectual development. Yet included within this general category are a wide variety of different disorders that impair intellectual functioning. Mental retardation applies to children with metabolic disorders like phenylketonuria (PKU) or hystedenemia and chromosomal disorders like Down's syndrome (mongolism); to various brain-damaged children, such as encephalopaths; and to so-called familial retardates, children who simply score particularly low on standard intelligence tests and generally have low IQ parents and come from poor environments. In some cases there is clear evidence of organic disorder, while in others the classification is purely a behavioral one based largely on test scores. The common element seems to be delayed development of problem-solving, memory, perceptual inference, and language skills.[5]

The question that has dominated much of the research into the language development of retarded children is the one we raised early in this chapter: Is their language development just slower than normal but in the

[5] In fact, a few researchers have suggested that in some retardates the development of problem-solving and other cognitive skills may actually deviate from normal as well as being delayed (see Inhelder, 1966; Das, 1972).

same sequence, or is it actually deviant in what is acquired or when and how it is acquired? There are several things that we should bear in mind as we consider these studies. First, given the variety of disorders grouped under the category "mentally retarded," it is somewhat naive to expect the language development of all these groups to be the same. In fact, to talk about "the language development of the mentally retarded" may well be something of a misnomer. The separate disorders differ with respect to several behavioral problems, such as the prevalence of hyperactivity or difficulties with fine motor movements, and are likely to differ in their effects on language behavior as well.

Second, much of the research on retardates has been confined to children older than six years of age who reside in institutions; fewer studies have looked at retarded children reared at home or at younger children (Ellis, 1971). Yet differences in cognitive processes have been reported between retarded children who are institutionalized and retarded children who are not, even when they are equated for mental age (MA) (Hagen and Hale, 1973). In addition, the typical subject falls into the range of "educable" retardates, with an IQ between 50 and 75, and less attention has been paid to more severely retarded individuals.

Third, most studies have concentrated on a limited aspect of language comprehension or production and have compared the performance of retarded children with that of normal children of comparable mental age. Studies comparing a wider range of language skills in the same group of children, or longitudinal studies of the course of acquisition, are practically nonexistent. Furthermore, we must remember that mental age simply represents the child's score on a particular test and may vary with the type of test employed or the context in which it is given. In particular, an eight-year-old retarded child with a measured MA of three years clearly differs in many respects from a normal three-year-old, if only by virtue of his greater experience with the world.

Finally, a factor that greatly complicates any interpretation of the language development of retardates is the difficulty of determining the range of individual variation in normal development. Large differences in age of mastery of a particular aspect of language are easy enough to identify, but the degree of normal variability in the pattern or sequence of development has simply not yet been established.

General Studies

Two very general early studies of language development in retardates reported that their language acquisition, like their motor development, was similar in pattern but just slower than normal. In a study of fifty retarded children living at home, Karlin and Strazzulla (1952) found that the lower the IQ of the children the more delayed the onset of babbling, first words, and sentences. The same held true for motor milestones like sitting up, crawling, and walking. Lenneberg, Nichols, and Rosenberger (1964) followed the development of fifty-four Down's syndrome children, aged three to twenty-two years, over a period of three years. The rate and level of language development was best predicted not by the MA of the children, but by chronological age and the passing of motor milestones. This led them to suggest that language development is paced by the physical maturation of the brain, which is slowed in Down's syndrome children. On the basis of the retarded children's performance on sentence imitation tests, as well as their spontaneous speech, Lenneberg et al. concluded that the language of these children is in no way bizarre but merely slowed down or arrested at a primitive but normal stage of development. Unfortunately, these studies employed somewhat gross measures of spontaneous speech, with categories like "mostly babble," "first words," "mostly words," "primitive phrases," and "sentences," and a more detailed linguistic analysis of the utterances of the children may have turned up deviations from normal acquisition. It is to such detailed studies of selected aspects of retardates' speech that we shall now turn.

Phonological Studies

The speech of between 70 percent and 90 percent of all moderate and severely retarded children suffers from defective articulation, many of the errors being omissions of phonemes (Yoder and Miller, 1972). Two studies, one of a mixed group of institutionalized, severely retarded children aged six to fifteen years (Bricker and Bricker, 1972), the other of two smaller groups of children with Down's syndrome and other severely subnormal children (Dodd, as cited by Cromer, 1974b, and Smith, 1975), have recently approached this problem from rather different perspectives. Bricker and Bricker compared the imitation of consonant-vowel syllables by retarded and normal children from the perspective of the types of errors made and the relative difficulty of English speech sounds (phones) for the two groups. The retarded children made significantly more errors than the three-year-old normal subjects, but the types of errors and relative difficulty of the different sounds were practically the same for the two groups. The relative frequency of the phones in adult and infant speech (Miller, 1951; Irwin and Chen, 1946) accurately predicted their hierarchy of difficulty in the children's imitation, the most frequent sounds being easiest.

Dodd examined the spontaneous and imitated naming of pictures by ten normal and ten Down's syndrome (mongoloid) children who were matched for mental age and social background. She found that a set of twenty-three phonological rules captured both the correct and "erroneous" word pronunciations of the normal children. These rules were common to most of the children and seemed to be applied consistently by the individual children. An example was the systematic deletion of [1] and [r] following a consonant; so *flower* became *fower,* and *train* became *tain.* (See Chapter 2 for a full account of this type of approach to phonological development.) The same set of rules described many of the word productions of the Down's syndrome children, but they seemed to apply them inconsistently, and many of their errors could not be accounted for by any general phonological rule. They typically repeated syllables in a word, so *dentist* became *denten,* and they often deleted large portions of words, as in *e-e* for *elephant* and *wiers* for *whiskers.* Finally, many of their sound substitution errors were inconsistent: on different occasions the same child might replace [p] and [b] with [m], [f], [sh], [n], or [ch] (Cromer, 1974b). When Dodd subsequently tested another group of severely subnormal children, who were matched with the Down's syndrome children on mental age but were not themselves mongoloid, she found that they performed like the normal children. Their errors were consistently in accordance with the phonological rules she had written for the normal group.

What could be different about the Down's syndrome children? Down's children generally have been shown to lack muscle tone when compared with other subnormals, and this might affect their motor feedback from articulation (O'Connor and Hermelin, 1963). But Cromer (1974b) denies that this could account for Dodd's phonological results. Unlike the normal children, the Down's syndrome group made significantly fewer errors in imitation than in spontaneous production (see also Lenneberg, 1967), suggesting that they were able to produce the sounds. Cromer proposes instead that the Down's children are deficient in the long-term motor planning that goes into generating a phonological sequence (Lashley, 1951). In the imitation task, the amount of planning needed would be reduced because the sound sequence to be matched has just been provided.

To summarize, these studies reveal differences between Down's syndrome and other retarded children, and suggest that, in their case at least, phonological development differs from that of normal children in more than just rate. The other retarded groups appeared to be merely slowed in their development.

Semantic Relations

We saw in Chapter 3 that young normal children in the two-word stage mostly speak about the same limited set of relations among persons, objects, and actions (Brown, 1973; Bowerman, 1973a, 1976). Do older retarded children who are just combining words also talk about the same semantic relations, despite their longer exposure to the world of people and objects? Two recent doctoral dissertations, one a longitudinal study of two children (Dooley, 1976), the other a cross-sectional study of four children (Coggins, 1976), have provided a detailed analysis of the early multiword utterances of Down's syndrome children.

Dooley noted that his retarded subjects made extremely slow progress in such measures of linguistic development as mean length of utterance (MLU), percentage of multiword sentences, and frequency of different sentence types. One of them actually showed no increase in MLU over the year of the longitudinal sample, although she improved by about the equivalent of one month of normal development on other measures. The other child also showed the linguistic advancement in a year that normal children make in a month during this stage of acquisition. Despite the tremendous slowing down of development and the greater age of the Down's children (four to six years), however, in both studies the set of semantic relations studied by Brown (1973) accounted for approximately the same percentage of their two-word combinations as Brown reported for normal children of similar MLU (1.00 to 2.00 morphemes per utterance). Furthermore, the relative frequency of the various semantic relations was very similar for the normal and retarded children. This is in keeping with the suggestion that the child's intellectual development in the sensorimotor period determines what he is able to talk about at this stage (Sinclair, 1971). Since the Down's syndrome children are slowed in cognitive development, they should also be able to communicate only a limited set of relationships in their early speech.

Grammatical Studies

The great majority of language studies with retardates have looked at some aspect of syntax. Grammatical analyses of the spontaneous speech of retarded children of mixed diagnoses reveal many similarities to the speech of normal children (Lackner, 1968; Graham and Graham, 1971). Sentence length increases with mental age and is comparable with that of normal children of similar mental development. Transformational grammars written to describe retarded children's utterances are in keeping with normal usage. The relative difficulty and order of acquisition of different constructions and grammatical forms matches that reported for normal children. Finally, a sentence of given transformational complexity does not occur in the speech of the retarded child unless all of the less complex types are also present, as is the case in normal acquisition (Brown and Hanlon, 1970). What is still in question, however, is the adequacy of a standard transformational grammar in accounting for the pattern of normal acquisition, let alone that of retarded children. In several respects a transformational grammar of the type used by Lackner and the Grahams may not provide the best description of early child language (see Chapter 4 for a full review of this question).

In tests of sentence imitation and comprehension the performances of subnormal and normal children also correspond. The grammatical complexity of sentence types they can successfully imitate or comprehend increases with MA (Lackner, 1968), and their imitation of grammatical forms is generally better than their comprehension, which is in turn better than their production (Lovell and Dixon, 1967; Fraser, Bellugi, and Brown, 1963). Several studies of retardates' productive use of the morphological rules of English have employed some modification of a test devised for normal children by Berko (1958). In this test the child might be presented with a catchy picture of a man performing some unusual action and told: "Here is a man who knows how to *bing*. Yesterday he _____." In completing this sentence the child demonstrates his mastery of past tense form. Similar examples test the present progressive, plural, possessive, comparative, and superlative morphemes. In general, the relative difficulty of these word-endings is the same for retarded children as for normal children (Lovell and Dixon, 1967; Newfield and Schlanger, 1968; Dever and Gardner, 1970). Both groups do better at supplying the morphemes for real words than for nonsense words, but the retarded subjects are relatively more impaired at extending the rules from familiar English words to nonsense words. Newfield and Schlanger (1968) and Menyuk (1971) suggest that retardates may generally be less able to generalize grammatical rules to new instances, but it is also possible that their greater impairment on nonsense words stems from a lack of understanding of what is required in the test situation (Dever and Gardner, 1970). Retarded children often display quite different behavior in a test situation than they do in their natural environment, and their scores on the Berko test may bear little relationship to their use of English morphology in spontaneous speech (Dever, 1972).

These studies have reported that the language of retarded children is delayed but still in keeping with their mental age. Others note that they lag further behind than one would expect from their MA. While their vocabulary equals or even surpasses (Spreen, 1965) that of normal children of similar MA, retardates may evidence a small lag in such measures as sentence length and complexity and in the variety of contexts in which they use nouns, verbs, and adjectives (Spreen, 1965; Bartel, Bryen, and Keehn, 1973; Semmel, Barritt, and Bennett, 1970).

We have already mentioned some of the limitations of studies that administer a single language test at one time or make comparisons on the basis of MA. For a start, the relationship observed between MA and language performance depends on which intelligence test is used. Some, like the Peabody Picture Vocabulary Test, already involve some aspect of language that may or may not correlate with the particular task employed in the study; others, like the Columbia Mental Maturity Scale, assess visual concepts and perceptual inference, so are largely language independent.

The Stanford-Binet employs both verbal and nonverbal items. Further-more, by their very nature most of these studies cannot detect differences in the *processes* by which normal and subnormal children acquire lan-guage. Rather, they describe the product of those processes at some stage of development. But very similar final outcomes or patterns of develop-ment could result from different processes, and group studies that average results over many children would obscure such differences. In short, while most of the studies so far reviewed have failed to establish any substantial difference between the language of retarded and normal chil-dren, besides delay and slow development, they have lacked the experi-mental design necessary to pick up more subtle differences.

Studies on Process

Two of the investigations that we have already mentioned suggest a dif-ference in the processes of early language acquisition in children with Down's syndrome. First, the inconsistency and peculiarity of their pho-nological errors, when compared to those of normal and other sub-normal children at roughly the same stage of mental development, may reflect a marked deviance in the phonological process underlying their speech (Smith, 1975). Second, both of the children in Dooley's (1976) longitudinal study made extensive use of routine phrases that were ap-parently learned as unanalyzed chunks, like separate lexical items. Ex-amples of these are:

> Here it is.
> Here they go.
> I got it.
> I do it.
> Another one.
> What a mess.
> What is it.
> Come here.

Several features mark these as routines. They are used in a stereotyped fashion, so they are not modified in accordance with semantic restrictions like animacy, number, person, and case, and the grammatical morphemes in them are not used contrastively. Thus, combinations like:

> *I got it* car.
> *Here it is* kitty.
> *Another one* dog.

occur. Furthermore, some lexical items appear only in such routines and not on their own or in other combinations.

In addition, Dooley notes that both children employed a remarkable number of pronouns and other proforms in their multiword utterances, even when these appeared to be constructions rather than routines. Proforms are words like *one, some, this, that, here, there, do,* or *get,* and are far less specific than substantive lexical items. A large proportion of the children's expressions of the basic semantic relations—agent-action, action-object, agent-action-object, and entity-attribute—consisted of the forms pronoun + verb, verb + pronoun, pronoun + verb + pronoun, and pronoun + adjective. In this respect, the sentences of Down's syndrome children are much more general than those of normal children. A construction in which both terms of a semantic relation are expressed by substantives, like *Draw rabbit,* places more demands on the semantic and possibly the syntactic processing of the child than one like *Do it,* in which both are proforms (Dooley, 1976).

It is difficult to assess how much the acquisition of these features by children with Down's syndrome deviates from normal acquisition, because there are insufficient data to establish the prevalence of the same features in normal acquisition. Several researchers have noted the incidence of unanalyzed routines in the early speech of normal children (Brown, 1973) or foreign children learning English as a second language (Hakuta, 1975), but they seem to occur only during a very brief stage. Bloom, Lightbown, and Hood (1975) have suggested that there may be different strategies for acquiring syntax in the two-word stage. Of the four children that they studied, two used pronouns far more frequently than nouns to express the roles of agent, object, and location in the basic semantic relations, although their productive vocabulary contained the relevant nouns. The other two children almost always used nouns. The pronominal strategy of the first two children simplified the task, since many semantic features of the objects being talked about did not need to be specified. Furthermore, pronouns were as prevalent in the early word combinations of these two children as they were for Dooley's two Down's syndrome children at the same MLU (Dooley, 1976). Nelson (1975) has also observed sizable individual differences in the way in which normal children use pronouns in their early multiword combinations.

The Down's syndrome children's extensive use of routines and proforms may therefore not represent any real deviation from the way in which normal children acquire language but only the persistence for a long period of time of one simplifying strategy for combining words to express semantic relations. The two retarded children made only about one month of normal progress in a year, and this stretching out of the process may also have made their use of routines and proforms easier to spot. Since their linguistic progress was so slow, they would have produced many more instances over a longer period of time. Normal children might have routines for only a short period of time before breaking them up into their separate elements, and their speech might not be sampled at just that point. Dooley does report that routines and proforms were much less frequent in the speech of one of the retarded children at the end of the year of study.

Cromer (1974b) has suggested that the linguistic strategies that retarded children employ at a much later stage of language development differ from those of their normal counterparts. He investigated the comprehension of complex sentences like:

The duck is keen to bite.
The wolf is easy to bite.
The duck is fun to bite.
The wolf is willing to bite.

The underlying meanings of these sentences differ, although their surface form is the same. Sometimes the named animal is the agent of the action, sometimes it is the object. Normal children only master sentences like these at around ten years of age. In Cromer's study the subjects had two puppets, a duck and a wolf, and had to indicate who was the biter and who was the bitten for each sentence. Up to a mental age of 6½ years, normal children always showed the named animal as the agent. This strategy was limited to these kinds of sentences, however, because the children correctly indicated the unnamed animal as the agent for passive sentences like "The wolf was bitten." From 6½ to 9 or 10 years the children were inconsistent. They knew that different interpretations were possible, but they did not know which interpretation fit which adjective. After ten years of age, when the children had learned more about the different adjectives, the sentences were correctly understood.

Educable retarded children only acquire the correct understanding of these sentences between fourteen and sixteen years of age, but they go through the same stages in getting there. They too employ the named-animal-as-agent strategy until they achieve a mental age of 6½.

Cromer (1974b) hypothesized that children learn the differences between these adjectives from the other types of sentences in which they can occur. Adjectives like *glad, keen,* or *willing* can appear in sentences such as "I am always _____ to read to you," but adjectives like *fun, easy,* or *hard* are ridiculous in these contexts. On the other hand, the adjectives in the second group occur in contexts such as "Reading to you is _____," whereas those in the first group make no sense in these sentences. Cromer presented nonsense words to normal and retarded children in sentence frames like the above, and then tested what the children had learned about the words by using the words in test sentences like "The wolf is _____ to bite." Some of the nonsense words had been placed in the appropriate context for an adjective like *glad* or *willing,* in which case *the wolf* would be the agent; others had been placed in the contexts for adjectives like *fun* or *easy,* making *the wolf* the object of *bite.* Many children adopted systematic strategies to deal with the nonsense adjectives presented in the test sentences. For the normal children a progressive change in strategy occurred. Children under MA 6½ years, who all used an agent strategy with the real adjectives like *glad* and *easy,* continued to do so with the nonsense adjectives, presenting the named animal as the agent for all of the sentences. Normal children of nine or ten, who comprehended the real adjectives correctly, were far more likely to use an object strategy, presenting the named animal as the object and the unnamed animal as the agent. For the retarded children, however, there was no such change in strategy: all of the children who used a systematic strategy adopted the agent strategy. Even when these retarded children understood the real English adjectives correctly, they tended to present the named animal as the agent for the nonsense adjective sentences. Surprisingly, normal adults given the same training on the nonsense words in sentence frames also all used the agent strategy on the test sentences.

Cromer concludes that the strategies adopted by children do not determine whether they will come to understand these sentence forms or not, since the retarded and normal children adopted different strategies but both eventually understood the forms. But he suggests that people who are learning linguistic tasks beyond puberty, the possible critical period for normal language acquisition, adopt different strategies in those tasks than those used by children immediately prior to puberty. If the strategies adopted in this task reflect the processes by which children and adolescents actually acquire new linguistic forms (and that is not proven in Cromer's experiment), a delay in language acquisition in retarded children that forces them to learn new forms beyond puberty may lead to differences in the way they approach these forms.

In conclusion, the bulk of the descriptive research on the language of retarded children does not show them to be different from normal children, except that they are slower by varying degrees. The patterns or sequences of development of speech sound production, semantic relations, and many aspects of syntax seem to fall within the range of normal variation. The only substantial differences seem to occur in children with Down's syndrome and subnormal children who are past puberty (and the latter perform like normal adults on certain sentences!). But there have been few studies that reveal the processes of acquisition in either retarded or normal children (see Chapter 8). The various impairments of selective attention, perception, memory, inferences, and motor control that may beset the different types of mentally retarded children (O'Connor and Hermelin, 1963) could well lead to differences in the way they learn language.

AUTISM

It is now more than thirty years since Leo Kanner first described a syndrome in children that he called early infantile autism (Kanner, 1943). Despite its low rate of incidence, four out of every ten thousand children, this disorder continues to fascinate researchers and laymen alike, inspiring popular books, television documentaries, and considerable clinical study. Part of the fascination lies in the mystery of a child who is physically beautiful and graceful, yet seems totally inaccessible and unresponsive to the people who should be closest to him. It was this striking absence of interest in others that led Kanner to label the syndrome "autism"—a preoccupation with oneself. The severely autistic child treats other persons as if they were just inanimate objects, making no meaningful eye contact and often responding to only a part of the person, perhaps manipulating a hand, an arm, or a sleeve.

Kanner reports that this social unresponsiveness may even show itself in early infancy. The smiling response to the mother and other adults that normally appear in the second or third month of life may simply not develop in the autistic child. He does not reach out to people or adopt an anticipatory posture when picked up, and may actively resist holding and cuddling. Parents of autistic children frequently report that the children appeared quite content when left alone as babies, making no response to their mother's comings and goings. Most normal children, on the other hand, demand entertainment and vehemently protest any separation from their mother beginning at the age of six to eight months. The universality of these early signs of autism should be viewed with some caution, however, since some autistic children may not show them (Wing, 1966). Furthermore, the parents' descriptions of the child's infancy come from retrospective reports made some time after the child had been diagnosed as autistic, and the diagnosis itself could have influenced their recollections of the child's early years.

Several other behavioral symptoms that tend to cluster with the social withdrawal led Kanner to distinguish autism from disorders like mental retardation, developmental aphasia, and childhood schizophrenia. First, the autistic child typically shows an obsessive insistence on sameness in his environment. He panics when there is the slightest change in some aspect of his daily routine: a change in the clothing in which he is dressed each day or in the arrangement of familiar household objects, or a new route taken when he goes out for a walk. Paradoxically, given their lack of attachment to the people around them, many autistic children are enthralled with particular inanimate objects, such as bottles or flags or records. They will play with them for hours, arranging them in long rows or patterns and becoming quite distraught if one of the set is lost or displaced.

The autistic child frequently exhibits repetitive or ritualistic motor behavior, endlessly rocking back and forth in his chair, flapping, or twisting his hands about in front of his face, or walking about with a strange gait. This repetitive behavior may also become self-destructive, with the child rhythmically striking his head or arm against an object.

There often appears to be a strange incongruity or flatness to the autistic child's emotions. The moods of those around him do not seem to affect him, but he may suddenly break into inconsolable crying or a screaming tantrum for no apparent reason. He exhibits sudden and irrational fears: of any exposed light bulb or a particular toy, for example. Yet at the same time he may climb about on a high wall or walk into the street in front of the traffic with complete unconcern for personal safety.

The child's abnormal response to sights and sounds often leads parents to assume that he is deaf or blind or both. He may ignore loud sounds and seem unable to recognize large objects that are pointed out to him; but he will discriminate surprising minute details, the rustle of a candy wrapper or the rotation of just one block in a long row. He explores objects by means of his proximal senses of touch, taste, or smell, or he may twist them about in his peripheral vision.

Autistic children usually score very low on standard intelligence tests, and before Kanner's characterization of the disorder they were frequently institutionalized as mentally retarded. But Kanner pointed out several inconsistencies in that diagnosis. First, autistic children do not look retarded; in fact, they are often remarkably handsome and intelligent-looking, and unlike retardates their motor development and manipulative skills are usually unimpaired. Second, some of them exhibit paradoxical flashes of higher intelligence. Their manipulation of puzzles can be quite skilled, and despite the impairment of their speech, some autistics learn to read and write. Their feats of rote memory are legendary. Kanner mentions a child who could recite all of the United States presidents plus their vice-presidents, a task that has plagued many a generation of American schoolchildren. We know an autistic child who after returning from a visit to a Baskin-Robbins ice cream parlor proceeded to write down all thirty-one varieties for that month, complete with the correct spelling of dacquiri ice!

Perhaps the most characteristic symptom of autism besides social unresponsiveness is a severe disturbance of language acquisition. The degree of language impairment in autistics varies considerably, from children who remain mute to those who speak fluently but still show peculiar syntax and word usage. Indeed, the severity of the child's problem with language constitutes one of the best prognostic indicators; children whose language improves substantially between the ages of three and ten years also show greatly improved social interaction and affect. Children who remain seriously deficient in language typically fail to make any recovery in other areas of behavior. Such observations have led researchers like Rutter (1968) and Churchill (1972) to suggest that the underlying deficit in autism is language-related, much like a severe form of developmental aphasia. What are the characteristics of the language of autistic children?

Phonological Aspects

In general, the autistic child's articulation of speech sounds does not appear to differ from normal (Fay and Butler, 1968), but there have been practically no detailed phonological studies of autistics' speech. On the other hand, their use of intonation reveals several aspects that are not typical of normal speech. In particular, the timbre of the autistic child's voice often sounds peculiar, either shrill or hollow. Some autistics seem unable to rephrase the intonation patterns of utterances they have heard, repeating them without modifying the intonation to suit any change in the context or function of the utterance (Simon, 1975). The stress and rhythm of their utterances therefore appear strangely inappropriate. Simon argues that they simply fail to perceive the use of stress emphasis and therefore cannot break a sentence up into its important units. In contrast to this, Frith (1969) found that autistic children did respond differentially to stress in the speech input. They recalled stressed words better than unstressed words in a sentence, particularly if the content words were stressed, a finding that parallels the performance of normal children. This suggests that they may have trouble with stress only in producing speech, although it is also possible that Simon and Frith were looking at different populations of autistic children and some of them neither perceive nor produce stress appropriately. Other autistic children do employ intonation quite appropriately in their spontaneous speech, although it sometimes appears sing-song or monotonous (Aug, 1974; Shapiro and Huebner, 1976).

Echolalia

A frequent characteristic of autistic children's speech is their tendency to echo back sentences addressed to them. Some normal children also imitate much of the speech that they hear, but they are usually more selective as to what types of utterances they imitate (Bloom et al., 1974), and they have a substantial amount of productive speech as well. For many autistic children, echoed utterances are nonselective and constitute almost all of their verbal behavior. Echolalia takes two forms, immediate and delayed. Immediate echolalia refers to the repetition, frequently word for word, of the utterance that the child has just heard. It is particularly noticeable in response to questions, where the child simply echoes the question and does not answer it.

But an echolalic utterance can also occur some time (even as long as a few years) after the child first heard the sentence. Then it will often be produced in a context in which it appears irrelevant and bizarre to the listener. Kanner mentions a five-year-old autistic boy who produced the utterance: ''Don't throw the dog off the balcony,'' when it had no apparent relevance to anything in the situation. Careful inquiry of the parents revealed that some three years previously the family had stayed in a hotel room with a balcony. At that time the child was admonished by the mother not to throw his toy dog off the balcony. Kanner suggests that the boy had come to use the whole sentence to express the meaning *no* or *don't,* and in that sense it was appropriate when he used it.

The mother of an autistic boy told us of an incident that further illustrates this phenomenon and also highlights the problems experienced by parents of an autistic child. She had taken her son shopping at a local supermarket. During the course of the shopping he noticed all of the tiny national flags stuck in the cheeses in the international section of the delicatessan. Since flags were his abiding interest, he began to collect them all. Seeing a perfectly normal-looking ten-year-old removing all of the flags from the cheeses, the store attendant came out from behind the counter to intervene, saying in a loud voice: ''Hey kid, what do you think you're doing?'' At this, to the dismay of his mother, the autistic boy took a handful of chocolate eclairs from a nearby shelf, smeared them down the front of the attendant's tunic and said: ''Do you want me to take your shoes off!'' To say the least, this caused a stir in the store, and the mother found herself making an impromptu lecture on autism to the crowd of curious shoppers that had rapidly gathered. Once again the autistic child had repeated in a most inappropriate context an entire sentence he had heard previously. His mother recalled occasions on which he had lain on the bed in his room kicking his shoes against the wall, and she had shouted up to him, ''Do you want me to take your shoes off!'' It appears that the child took this whole sentence to mean threat or anger directed towards him, and repeated it in situations that shared that emotional meaning.

Delayed echolalia also reveals itself in the way autistic children ritually repeat phrases of commercial jingles picked up from television or radio. Sometimes these seem to be addressed to people; more frequently they are said to no one in particular.

Pronoun Reversal

Several psychologists have related autistic children's difficulty with personal pronouns to the prevalence of echolalia in their speech. Many autistics confuse these pronouns, the most characteristic confusion being the reversal of *I* and *you*. The child might say ''*You* get hurt'' as he jerks his hand away from a hot stove, or ''*You* want to take a walk'' when he is clearly expressing his own and not his listener's desires. Some normal two-year-olds also refer to themselves as "you" or by their first name, but in normal development this represents a very brief stage, and *I* and *you* (with *me/you* and *my/your*) are the first set of personal pronouns that they master (Arboleda, 1976). In contrast, the *I/you* confusion persists in autistic children's speech and may never be resolved.

If much of the child's speech consists of echoes of the sentences he hears, the consistent reversal of *I* and *you* becomes understandable; the speaker addresses the child as *you* and refers to himself as *I*. But the autistic also often uses *he* or *she* where he should use *you*. This suggests that he not only echoes back the speech addressed to him, but also fails to distinguish the persons in verbal interaction from other persons in a situation. This failure has been described in psychoanalytic terms as a breakdown in the child's development of a sense of personal identity, a self, so that he does not distinguish himself from others (Bettelheim, 1967). For whatever reason, many autistic children cannot determine the different roles of interactors in a conversation and do not acquire the appropriate semantics of person deixis.

Segmentation and Productive Rules

Many autistic children seem unable to analyze utterances into smaller units or to extract any general syntactic rules by which these units can be combined into new meaningful sentences. In a sense they represent a caricature of a discredited theory of language acquisition, which held that the child learns entire sentences by rote rather than learning generative rules (Brown and Herrnstein, 1975). While normal children begin by combining content words and omitting function words like prepositions, articles, and other grammatical morphemes (Brown, 1973), the early utterances of some severely autistic children look remarkably complete by comparison. These autistics do not appear to go through the stage of telegraphic speech; rather, they supply full sentences from the start (Simon, 1975). Furthermore, they do not make overgeneralization errors on morphemes like the regular past tense *-ed* ending, which is so characteristic of normal development (Brown and Herrnstein, 1975). When viewed in context, however, the nonproductive nature of these sentences is revealed. They may seem grammatically well-formed when compared to the telegraphic speech of normal children, but unlike normal speech they are not adapted to changing circumstances and are often inappropriate. It is as if the child had stored complete sentences from past interactions rather than rules for producing appropriate new sentences. Language learning cannot proceed like this, for the child's rote memory capacity would soon be exceeded, and such a system makes no provisions for communicating about the new situations one might encounter.

Memory

A similar failure to extract regularities or rules of combination character-izes the autistic child's short-term memory for verbal and visual material (Hermelin and Frith, 1971; Hermelin and O'Connor, 1970). Given mean-ingful sentences or random word strings to remember, many autistic chil-dren recall only the last few words. Unlike normal or retarded children they do not remember more of the sentences than the random sequences. When a normal child is given a sequence of colors like *red, red, blue, blue, red, red, blue, blue,* he readily extracts the regularity underlying it and can then use that rule (aabb) to remember lengthy sequences that are well beyond his memory span for random items. In contrast, autistic chil-dren do little better on rule-governed visual sequences than on random ones.

However, a strange incongruity in the autistics' behavior appears when they are allowed to generate their own sequences of sounds or colors. They do not produce random sequences, but instead impose strictly ordered patterns. In keeping with their appreciation for music, these patterns are more complex and less repetitive for tones than for colors. The autistic child therefore imposes order and regularity on the se-quences of behavior that he produces—witness his play with objects and his ritualized motor behavior—but he cannot extract order from sequen-tial visual or speech input (Frith, 1970a and b).

Later studies suggest that autistics have greater trouble with tem-poral than with spatially ordered sequences (Hermelin and O'Connor, 1973, 1975). They are far more likely to pick up a spatial regularity (such as left to right) than a temporal regularity in the presentation of visual stim-uli. Given the importance of temporal sequencing in the production and comprehension of speech, their difficulty with oral language acquisition becomes understandable. However, this finding suggests that they might do better with a visually presented symbol language like that used by Pre-mack with the chimpanzee Sarah, in which the syntactic ordering is spa-tial. Some success at training such a symbol language to severely autistic children has been reported by deVilliers and Naughton (1974).

Severity of the Disorder and the Use of Syntax

All of the above evidence supports Simon's contention that autistic chil-dren do not analyze sentences into smaller units or extract the rules that combine them, and further suggests that the problem with sequencing rules pervades much of the children's cognitive processing. On the other hand, several recent studies indicate that this deficit varies with the sever-ity of the disorder, and may not even be present in some children who are nevertheless diagnosed as autistic.

Zufall and Weiss (1975) demonstrated that the autistics' failure to recall sentences better than lists of random words depends on their lack of comprehension of the sentence material. Their comprehension of simple active sentences like "the truck bumped the car," revealed in their ability to act them out with toys, predicts whether they will remember sentences of this type better than the same words presented in random order. Only the youngest autistic children (aged five to nine years), who could not use the word order rules of English to understand these sentences, recalled them as a list of random words, the last few words first. The older autistics (ten to fourteen years) could comprehend the sentences and performed like normal children of similar immediate memory span, remembering the sentences better than the lists of random words.

Autistic children's inability to use syntactic structure in remembering sentences longer than their memory span also depends on their degree of general intellectual and social impairment. In a study by Voeltz (1976) five echolalic autistics imitated sentences or random strings of words that exceeded their immediate memory span. The higher the general level of functioning of the child, the more the syntactic structuring of the material facilitated imitation.

Fay and Butler (1968) studied twenty-two echolalic three-year-olds and a group of normal children matched for IQ. The echolalic children were defined as those who gave ten or more echoic responses to fifty consecutive utterances in an interview. They were divided into "pure" echoers and "mitigated" echoers, the latter group containing those children who modified the input sentences, usually by deleting elements (for example: "I sleep?" for "Where do I sleep?"). Modification of the input sentence by deletion typifies the imitations of normal children, and the mitigated echoers were much more like normal children on several tests of language comprehension and production than were the pure echoers. The extent to which an autistic child breaks down an utterance into its elements therefore provides an indication of the severity of his language problems.

Simon (1975) has suggested that autistic children do not go through the normal stage of telegraphic speech, but several other researchers report early stages of language acquisition in autistics that look much like those of normal children. Cunningham (1966) traced the development of language in one autistic child between six and eleven years of age. Over the first six months of observation the child's mean utterance length increased from 1.9 to 3.0 words per sentence and then remained at that level. As in the telegraphic speech of normal children, the grammatical morphemes were frequently absent from the child's speech. Similar observations of autistics' speech have been made by Wing and Wing (1971) and Pierce and Bartolucci (1976). The latter two researchers found that the older autistic children they studied did not differ from normal and retarded children of equal nonverbal mental age in terms of their use of complex transformational rules. However, they more frequently omitted function words, pronouns, and articles. Language development in these children therefore seems delayed or arrested in the telegraphic stage rather than deviating from normal development in the way suggested by Simon.

In conclusion, we must stress that there is a considerable range of individual variation in language and other behavioral impairment among children diagnosed as autistic. We have outlined the classic symptoms of autism and the most striking characteristics of autistic language, but the child who is "classically" autistic in the sense that he exhibits all or even most of these symptoms and characteristics is rare indeed. Far more usual is the autistic child who reveals some subset of the symptoms, in particular the social unresponsiveness and some disruption of language acquisition. The nature of the language disruption may vary, though. In a study of five autistic adolescents between the ages of twelve and nineteen years, Shapiro and Huebner (1976) described marked differences among them in their spontaneous speech. The utterances of three of the autistics were severely limited in length, with an MLU of around 3.0 words per utterance; but these three differed among themselves in several other aspects of their speech. Only one was noticeably echolalic; another was not echolalic but only 60 percent of his utterances were deemed communicative by the investigators. The third produced simple telegraphic utterances that were almost always communicative and appropriate to their context, much like a mentally retarded child's. Only one of the three appeared to have any problems with intonation. Of the two adolescents who produced long utterances, only one showed disordered syntax or spoke many utterances that seemed bizarre in the context in which they were uttered. Thus, although all these children were diagnosed as autistic in early childhood, eight to thirteen years later, in adolescence, their language disorders differed in both severity and nature.

Detailed study of larger samples of autistic children might determine if we are dealing with different groups of autistics, distinguished by language impairments of a different nature, or if these children differ only in the severity of a unitary disorder. Some autistic children rarely use language productively or appropriately, their speech being composed almost exclusively of immediate or delayed echoes; others seem to develop language in the normal sequence, yet are delayed or arrested at some stage in that development.

LANGUAGE TRAINING PROGRAMS

Answers to the question, To what extent is language acquisition in the developmentally disabled merely delayed or actually deviant from normal? do not have merely academic interest, since they supply the clinician with helpful information for planning treatment. If development proceeds in the normal sequence, but more slowly, several options are available to the clinician: (1) He can simply leave the child to develop at his own pace; (2) he can attempt to enrich the environment of the child in ways that may enhance normal development (to the extent that these are known); (3) he can attempt to train particular language skills in the order in which they are normally acquired, beginning one stage above that which the child has reached. If the course of development differs from normal and it can be established how and why it is different, the clinician may wish to tailor his training program to take advantage of or to compensate for those differences (Menyuk, 1975b). Other important information for the clinician would come from determining the point of breakdown in the child's language, be it phonological, syntactic, semantic or pragmatic, or some combination of these. He could then concentrate on that aspect of language in treatment, or find some way to avoid that problem in training other language skills.

Questions of what aspects of language to train and the best way to teach them have dominated language treatment programs. The goal of any such program is to teach the child communication skills that will be effective in his daily life—ways of making his needs and desires known, of requesting information and regulating social interaction. Yet much of the information that could be important for planning the specific content of training programs is simply not available. Our knowledge of the different points of breakdown in the language of disordered children, and their physical or environmental basis, remains woefully incomplete. At the same time, our understanding of the course of normal acquisition, though fuller, is not sufficient to dictate the best order or way to teach language to an impaired child.

But the clinician must attempt to alleviate the problems of the language deficient child now; he cannot wait for the researcher to discover all the answers. As a result, several programs have recently been proposed that differ somewhat in the aspects of language that they stress and the order in which they train them. Since there exists at this time no empirical evidence as to the relative effectiveness of these alternative programs, we will merely outline three such programs, pointing out common features and contrasts in their content and training methods. The programs we will consider are those proposed by Bricker and Bricker (1974), Miller and Yoder (1974), and Guess, Sailor, and Baer (1974), each designed for use with mentally retarded and autistic children who are mute or suffer from severe language disturbances.

Like many others, these three programs employ operant conditioning techniques to establish verbal behavior in nonverbal children or to modify their existing verbal repertoire. While there are minor variations in the way the techniques are applied, the basic pattern of early language training remains much the same in most studies. In dealing with a mute child, especially with an autistic, the first step is to train him to pay attention to the therapist—more specifically, to make eye contact. To achieve this the therapist first rewards the child with such things as favorite foods, verbal praise, or an affectionate hug, for any spontaneous eye contact or for eye contact following the command, "Look at me!" Sometimes the child needs to be prompted by the food reward being placed near the therapist's face to attract his attention, but the eye contact is soon brought under the control of the verbal command and maintained by intermittent reward.

Usually, the therapist then trains nonverbal imitation: initially of gross motor movements like clapping, standing up or touching toes; later of more refined movements of the mouth, like opening and closing it or pursing the lips. The tacit assumption is that this motor imitation will facilitate later training of verbal imitation, but there is presently little empirical support for this (Guess, Sailor and Baer, 1974; Harris, 1975). It may well be just as effective to begin with verbal imitation.

The next step is to establish imitation of speech. Most clinicians employ some variation of the procedure outlined by Lovaas et al. (1966). At first, any vocalization by the child receives reward, then only vocalizations following within a few seconds of the therapist's model sound, and finally only vocalizations that sufficiently resemble the model sounds. The therapist introduces new sounds interspersed with those the child has already mastered and gradually progresses until the child is imitating complete words. At this stage the object or action to be named is frequently presented as an added cue for the child. Many published studies have reported success at establishing verbal imitation in previously mute retarded and psychotic children by following this procedure (see Harris, 1975, for a review). Food and praise have been the most common rewards employed, but physical contact, music, colored lights, and the opportunity to play games have also proved successful in initiating and maintaining the nonverbal child's imitation of speech.

However, imitative speech has no communicative value, so the crucial next step is to train functional language. Most programs begin by teaching lexical items like nouns and verbs and later introduce syntactic features like plural or tense markers, or train the children to combine words into simple sentences. It is in the training of functional language that the three programs we have selected for closer consideration differ most.

Bricker and Bricker (1974) emphasize the possible cognitive prerequisites for the acquisition of referential language, as proposed by Sinclair (1971) and other Piagetians. They therefore organize their program around the initial assessment and subsequent training of cognitive skills from the late sensorimotor period of development (Piaget, 1970), such as object permanence, classificatory behavior, imitation, and representational play with objects. Only when the child has mastered these basic cognitive skills does language training proceed. In general, we have two reservations about this program: first, it has yet to be established that training cognitive skills on nonverbal tasks actually facilitates later language acquisition; second, the length and complexity of such a program may make it prohibitive to implement.

Miller and Yoder (1974) base their program on four principles: (1) The content of the program should be taken from what is known about the course of normal language acquisition. (2) The program should concentrate on teaching the basic semantic relations in the same sequence as they are normally acquired. (3) A single, frequently occurring experience should be used to teach a semantic relation; thereafter, that semantic relation can be extended to other familiar or novel experiences. (4) The first expansions to two-word utterances should be of semantic relations previously expressed by a single word, for example from *more* to *more juice*. Thus, while Bricker and Bricker base their program on current theories of the cognitive prerequisites for language acquisition in normal children, Miller and Yoder stress the description of early language development in terms of underlying semantic relations (see Chapter 3). Both programs emphasize the importance of research and theory on normal acquisition for the planning of training procedures.

In contrast, Guess, Sailor, and Baer (1974) place more stress on the functional aspects of language than on the normal sequence of acquisition. They concentrate on building up a small set of specific linguistic repertoires that the child can use to control his environment. Examples of these are: (1) labels for persons, things, properties and actions; (2) questions like "What that?" and "What (are) you doing?" by which the child can extend his lexicon; and (3) demands like "I want (thing)," "I want (action)," and later "I want (action) with (thing)" or "I want you to (action) with (thing)." The child is taught first to produce these utterances in imitation of the therapist and then to use them spontaneously in appropriate circumstances. He is also taught to respond appropriately when they are produced by others. In the process of learning these functional repertoires, the child acquires the basic operations of reference; the distinction between *yes* and *no,* and *I* and *you;* the ability to combine nouns, pronouns, and verbs into sentences; and the ability to produce various forms of request. In short, he is taught a simple but effective linguistic means of affecting his environment. An attractive aspect of this program, especially for training nonverbal children, is its simple step-by-step nature and its relative brevity.

It is not known to what extent the determinants of the order of acquisition of various linguistic forms in normal children also constrain the sequence in which they should be taught to disordered children. We would like to think that research on the course of normal acquisition and the processes underlying it will ultimately benefit the development of effective language-training programs for the developmentally disabled. Such pure research clearly provides assessment techniques and norms for the evaluation of the existing language behavior of the disordered child and valuable insights into the appropriate components of a given linguistic skill. Some normal sequences of development may also represent the easiest or even the necessary order in which to acquire those forms, particularly in cases where the normal acquisition order seems to be determined by cumulative syntactic or semantic complexity (Brown, 1973; Brown and Herrnstein, 1975; see also Chapters 3 and 4). But the extent to which this is true must be empirically established. On the other hand, it is dangerous for a clinician to follow slavishly the current trends (dare we call them fads) in theories of normal acquisition. All too frequently clinicians take a *description* of the course of normal acquisition as a *prescription* for the way language must be taught. But trends change, and what was once proposed as a necessary, universal stage of development can become just one of several alternative strategies for acquiring language or merely an anachronism in theories of acquisition.

Generalization of Trained Language Skills

A major problem that faces language-training programs is the question of whether the child transfers language learned in the training situation to his natural environment. Most language-training studies have tested the generalization of acquired linguistic rules to new instances of the rules, but few have tested transfer of those forms to the everyday speech of the child.

Even limited generalization can be difficult for retarded and autistic children. For example, Guess and Baer (Guess, 1969; Guess and Baer, 1973) trained severely retarded children on plural endings but found little or no generalization from expressive training (production) to receptive use (comprehension) and vice versa. Similar failures to transfer trained grammatical forms from one modality to the other have been reported by other studies of retarded and autistic children (Harris, 1975). For normal children, on the other hand, comprehension usually precedes production of a form, and productive training rapidly transfers to comprehension.

Few studies have even tested whether a disordered child can extend functional speech learned in therapy to other persons besides the therapist and to other settings besides the therapy room. An exception is the study by Garcia (1974), who trained a simple conversational sequence to severely retarded children and then looked for generalization of that sequence to other persons. He found that the child had to be trained with several different conversational partners before a transfer could be obtained. Koegel and Rincover (1974) similarly report that language learned in a one-to-one setting did not readily carry over to a one-to-eight classroom setting. Generalization of trained language skills therefore seems considerably more restricted in disordered children, and training in a wide variety of settings may be necessary for any transfer of functional speech.

Most of the data on the transfer of language from the training situation to the natural environment come from case reports, and in general the long-term carry-over to the children's everyday speech has been distressingly small (Harris, 1975). In some cases, the initial improvement in the children's language has been rapidly reversed when their environment failed to maintain the same demands on their behavior as the training situation (Lovaas et al., 1973).

Part of the problem may be the use in training of arbitrary primary rewards such as food; the child must then shift to the natural rewards for speech—social communication, gaining information, obtaining what one desires, and similar functions (Ferster, 1972). Yet in many programs the children are never taught to accomplish these functions by means of speech. If they have other means of communicating their needs and getting them fulfilled in their everyday environment, they may never transfer the language they have learned to accomplish those and other functions. It is also possible that some rewards for language (to the extent that we can specify them for normal children) simply do not operate for some disordered populations. Autistic children, for example, are unresponsive to social contact, but so much of language function depends on the maintenance of social interaction.

All this suggests that simply training a given language skill in a variety of situations may not help the transfer of that skill to a natural setting if arbitrary rewards continue to be used. Even if there are linguistic forms that the disordered child can only learn in a strict training procedure with powerful primary rewards, he must still learn what that language is good for when the artificial rewards are no longer provided. In short, to be successful in establishing truly functional speech in the retarded or autistic child, any language training program must at some point create a context in which the child has something to say, in which communicative effectiveness can serve as the reward, and it must make provision for transfer of the acquired language skills to the child's environment.

10

Conclusion

At this point it is appropriate to return to the themes of the introduction, to ask, "So, how does a child learn language?" The ambiguity of the word "how" provides a most convenient escape route, for it has two senses and we can deal with one more readily than the other. If we take the question to mean, What knowledge does the child have at various stages? then we can give a reasonable, if lengthy, reply. Our reader may feel vaguely unsatisfied, but will come away with the impression that, indeed, academics know quite a lot about language acquisition. The dissatisfaction arises because we have not answered the other sense of the question, namely, What is the process by which the child acquires a language?

NATURE VERSUS NURTURE

First, we must ask what would be required of a theory of learning. An adequate theory must provide us with a list of the necessary and sufficient conditions for there to be a change in a person's knowledge that is reflected in behavior, and furthermore, specify the constraints on the form that change in knowledge will take. In Chapter 8 we saw how certain time-honored learning principles—imitation, correction and reinforcement—have not yet been proven necessary for language acquisition to proceed. Children who imitate very little learn to talk just as rapidly and as well as the frequent imitators; furthermore, a reasonable description of how imitation might facilitate the acquisition of language rules does not yet exist. Parents do not systematically provide corrective feedback for their children's syntax but rather for the truth of their state-

272

ments. In addition, while extrinsic reinforcements like approval may determine how much the child talks, to whom he speaks, and even some of the content and form of his utterances, it has not been easy to determine what should count as reinforcement for the acquisition of grammatical rules. It is possible to save the theory by postulating intrinsic reinforcers such as "sounding like an adult" or "mastery of rules," but then the theory becomes true by definition and the links to principles of reinforcement derived from laboratory experiments become more tenuous.

The context of language learning has come in for much more research in recent years, for it appears that children, in our culture at least, learn language under a rather special set of circumstances. For example, recent work suggests that adults' speech to children is much simpler and more complete than had been presumed, but the determinants and consequences of these simplifications have not yet been firmly established. Three related questions must be distinguished. First, what leads the adult to alter his speech? Some of the modifications appear to reflect social factors such as attitudes toward children (Blount, 1972), and others pragmatic considerations like the desire to direct the child's actions (Shatz, 1974). Other sources of influence are the cognitive and linguistic capacities of the child; for example, Cross (1977) observed that several measures of the complexity of parental speech were highly correlated with the child's level of language comprehension. Correlations with measures of the child's production were somewhat less impressive (see also Newport, 1975), suggesting that the parents tailored their speech more to what their child could understand than to what he could express. Finally, several typical characteristics of baby talk show up in other contexts as well—in speech to pets or foreigners, and in the endearments of lovers (Brown, 1977).

In Chapter 7 our discussion was directed mainly at a second question: What aspects of baby talk could be helpful to the child in discovering the rules of his language? Yet without a more complete description of the child's own phonology, grammar, and semantic knowledge at different stages of development, it is difficult to define what might be helpful at each stage. Although the specifics of one's language *must* be learned from the language one hears, it has not yet been demonstrated that the speech of adults could reveal to the child the fundamental properties of language structure. In particular, the input to the child remains opaque with respect to crucial features of classical transformational grammar. For this reason, the theory one entertains about the end point of language development has important ramifications for one's view of the contribution of the linguistic input in acquisition. Nevertheless, the more the input reveals to the child, the less one needs postulate as innate.

This leads to the third question, the most critical of the three, yet the one about which we have least information. To what extent does the child's linguistic development actually depend on the special properties of the speech addressed to him? Are any of the modifications present in our speech to children really necessary for normal language development, or do they even facilitate acquisition? A very reasonable doubt exists that children would learn to talk if they were exposed only to television, but it remains to be determined which particular characteristics of adult-child interaction—verbal, contextual, or social—are the critical ones for language learning to proceed. Studies correlating children's rate of language development with differences in the speech they hear are just now being completed, but their interpretation will be difficult. The rate of language learning and the way parents speak to their children may vary with social class or educational level, so the determination of cause and effect becomes problematic unless these other variables are controlled. Cross-cultural studies may shed some light on the importance of simplified input, but the same confounding of determinants must be guarded against.

ACTIVE VERSUS PASSIVE LEARNING

The preceding discussion has concentrated almost exclusively on the environmental conditions for language learning, but we have had occasion time and time again to talk of the child's contribution to the process, that he appears not to be a passive recipient of external influence. This contribution takes various forms: first, for any language learning to take place there must be not only the appropriate environment but also a certain perceptual and cognitive readiness in the child. Nevertheless, it has proven difficult to establish that certain precursors of language are indeed prerequisites. Second, the child's level of development may limit the regularities he can extract at any one time, in other words, constrain the form of the change in knowledge that can take place. For instance, it has been suggested that the early multiword utterances encode the limited set of relationships among people, objects, and events that the child can understand at that time. The child's use of the input is therefore selective, making it important to distinguish *input* from *intake*.

When regularities in the child's behavior do not coincide with our adult knowledge, many writers refer to the child as possessing "strategies" of one type or another. At best, the term highlights the active nature of the learning that is taking place, but at worst it may masquerade as a theory of learning. We must still ask where the strategies themselves come from, and research is scanty on this question. One possible avenue of explanation is to relate the strategies to other abilities the child has at the time, or to his experience. Some strategies may even derive from the special nature of parental speech to the child at some earlier time, though here the chicken-egg problem becomes particularly acute. For instance, might the child's strategy of interpreting noun-verb-noun sequences as agent-action-object derive from the preponderance of that form in parental speech to children? Or are the parents modifying their speech to take into account a bias that stems initially from the child? If different children use different strategies, then it becomes doubly important not merely to document their occurrence but to relate them to the child's level of cognitive development, or his parents' child-rearing practices, or his particular linguistic input—whatever factor might account for the variation. Without fundamental answers like these, the significant generalizations so far discovered are threatened with burial under a voluminous literature on idiosyncrasies.

Chomsky has argued that certain hypotheses that the child entertains about language are not the product of any experience, nor could they derive from other areas of knowledge because they are specifically linguistic. He contends that they come instead from the genetic make-up of the child, that is, they are innate constraints on the form that language learning will take and they are a consequence of species membership rather than individual life history. This relates to the question of the uniqueness of human language.

MAN VERSUS ANIMAL

The linguistic model proposed by Chomsky posits abstract features of syntax that are unparalleled in natural animal communication or in the language that has been acquired so far by chimpanzees given special training. But if abstract structures, transformations, and recursiveness are required in order for a communication system to qualify as a language, most of early child speech is eliminated. But, if the uniqueness of man's language arises from a special innate capacity, particularly if it is specific to language and not a general purpose cognitive capacity, what selection pressures could have operated in evolution to produce it? What possible reproductive advantage could it have conveyed to *homo sapiens?*

Study of the languages, natural and artificial, that the great apes are able to learn may provide us with insights into the forerunners and possible cognitive bases of our linguistic ability. The limitations of those languages are also instructive for establishing the crucial design features of a natural language as well as the uniquely human aspects of our linguistic capacity. For example, are the apes limited as to the propositions they can express? In what respects is their syntax impoverished, and how does that impede communication?

Finally, work by ethologists on the range of meanings and communicative functions expressed by lower organisms in their natural communication promises to help us understand the conditions under which creativity, of vocabulary or syntax, might become useful to a species.

NORMAL VERSUS ABNORMAL BEHAVIOR AND THOUGHT

The analyses of language acquisition at the level of speech perception, phonology, semantics, syntax, and discourse reveal the many points at which the acquisition process may go awry, and how such a disturbance might manifest itself. The extent to which pure research on language acquisition can help in intervention programs remains to be seen. Evidence is lacking as to whether programs based on current theories of normal acquisition are more beneficial for the language-deficient child than any other approach. At the very least, a knowledge of what normal children can do will provide guidelines about the content of language training programs. It is less clear that we know enough about the process of acquisition to give advice about content sequencing, optimum training procedures, reasonable rewards, or methods of achieving generalization to either novel materials or novel social settings.

INTERACTIONS AMONG LANGUAGE DOMAINS

Some major areas of investigation have not yet received their due share of attention, partly because they involve overlap between traditionally distinct areas of investigation. Three examples follow.

Syntax and Suprasegmental Aspects of Phonology

Little attention has been directed toward understanding the interactions between syntax learning and the intonation, rhythm, and timing of speech. For example, it appears that children recognize the natural rhythm of adult sentences before they learn the function of all the morphemes that the rhythm encompasses, since even two-year-olds notice the peculiarity of telegraphic utterances spoken by an adult (Gleitman, Gleitman, and Shipley, 1972). At an unidentified later stage in language learning, stress and pause patterns come to serve as cues to the correct parsing of a sentence into constituent structure, for as adults we use this information to resolve surface-structure ambiguities in the speech we hear. How do children come to recognize such cues?

In speech production, research has begun on the question of how the child learns to control the rhythms of speech (Branigan, 1976a,b). It has been shown for adults that the stress and timing of particular words depend not just on adjacent words but on the entire configuration of the utterance (Martin, 1972). For instance, when we say the two sentences:

(a) John saw Mary
(b) John saw Marie

the verb *saw* has different durations, being typically shorter in (*b*) than in (*a*) to allow for the different stress pattern of the word that *follows* it. The example illustrates that sentences are planned in advance of their execution, and that there are certain constraints on the rhythms we produce. It is important to discover whether these principles hold also for child speech, and how they interact with the learning of syntax. The suprasegmental aspects might provide the researcher with cues about the length and complexity of the units that a child is capable of planning in advance of opening his mouth to speak.

Syntax and Semantics

In standard transformational grammar, syntax and semantics are considered to be independent. More recently, the trend has been to incorporate more information about meaning into a specification of the syntactic rules, increasing the interdependence of the two analyses. Work in child language acquisition reinforces this shift in linguistics, for several lines of evidence suggest that children's early syntactic rules operate on only a limited domain of words or semantic relations, and more abstract rules appear only later (for example, rules for word order, Braine, 1976; for inflections, Tanouye, Lifter, and Bloom, 1977; for the passive construction, Maratsos, 1977). Children appear to define more narrowly than adults do the domain of words that can enter into a particular syntactic relationship. For children, at least, syntactic rules at first are not independent of the meanings expressed. Yet it has been customary to design tests of syntax comprehension to measure the percentage a child gets correct out of a number of sentences containing different words or semantic relations. An individual child is then characterized as developing a knowledge of, say, the passive, as his percentage of correct responses rises. Such a procedure ignores the process that should be of primary interest, namely, how the child might come to realize that a construction he heard in a single sentence context can be used with new words and in new circumstances. For example, the child hears a picture described as:

The tiger is being chased by the lion.

How many instances of the passive must he hear before he can spontaneously produce a novel example, such as:

The dog is being bitten by the cat.

What further experience, if any, is necessary before he will generalize the passive rule to describe an event in which the verb is not an action that affects anything, such as:

The book is being read by John.

After the child has learned several rules, first over a limited semantic domain and then more broadly, does the process of generalization become speeded up, so that less experience is necessary for him to try the new rule in very different circumstances? All of these questions remain for future research to address.

Syntax, Semantics, and Pragmatics

Two perspective shifts have occurred in the past decade of language-acquisition research (de Villiers and de Villiers, 1977). Early research was concerned with the grammatical forms the child could use at different stages, but it was soon recognized that this provided a misleading view of development. The child is not reciting sentence types but is conveying meanings, and an analysis at a semantic level reveals more cross-cultural similarities in acquisition, particularly at the early stages, as well as exposing the continuities with prelinguistic cognitive development.

The second shift in outlook occurred with the recognition that the child does not describe events in a social vacuum. Instead, he is using language for a variety of social purposes, such as demanding, questioning, blaming, denying, and the like. A pragmatic perspective looks not at the forms, not at the propositions they encode, but at the functions language serves in social interaction. As a consequence, the continuity with prelinguistic social development is highlighted. Each of the three viewpoints—syntax, semantics, and pragmatics—has its own engrossing and difficult questions. However, it is evident now that any researcher must master all the vocabularies and methodologies in order to understand language acquisition, for the child, unlike a textbook, does not view his task as a series of stepping stones labeled "phonology," "syntax," "semantics," and, finally, "discourse": he is simultaneously involved in each enterprise.

REFERENCES

INDEX

References

Anglin, J. M. 1977. *Word, object, and conceptual development*. New York: Norton.

Antinucci, F., and Volterra, V. 1973. Lo sviluppo della negazione nel linguaggio infantile: uno studio pragmatico. In Studi per un modello del linguaggio, *Quaderni della Ricera Scientifica*. Rome: CNR.

Arboleda, C. 1976. The acquisition of pronouns: a test of the semantic complexity hypothesis. Senior honors thesis, Harvard University.

Asher, J., and Garcia, R. 1969. The optimal age to learn a foreign language. *Modern Lang. J.* 53: 334–341.

Aug, R. G. 1974. The language of the autistic child. In *Language and language disturbances,* ed. E. W. Straus. Pittsburgh: Duquesne University Press.

Bartel, N. R.; Bryen, D.; and Keehn, S. 1973. Language comprehension in the mentally retarded child. *Except. Child.* 39: 375–382.

Bartlett, E. J. 1974. How young children comprehend some relational terms and comparative sentences. Ed. D. diss., Harvard University.

———. 1976. Sizing things up: the acquisition of the meaning of dimensional adjectives. *J. Child Lang.* 3: 205–219.

———. 1977. Acquisition of the meaning of color terms. Paper presented to the Biennial Conference of the Society for Research in Child Development, New Orleans.

Basser, L. S. 1962. Hemiplegia of early onset and the faculty of speech with special reference to the effects of hemispherectomy. *Brain* 85: 427–460.

Bates, E. 1976a. *Language and context: the acquisition of pragmatics*. New York: Academic Press.

———. 1976b. Pragmatics and sociolinguistics in child language. In *Normal and deficient language,* ed. D. M. Morehead and A. E. Morehead. Baltimore: University Park Press.

281

Bateson, M. C. 1975. Mother-infant exchanges: the epigenesis of conversational interaction. In *Developmental psycholinguistics and communication disorders,* ed. D. Aaronson and R. W. Rieber. *Ann. N.Y. Acad. Sci.* 263: 101–113.

Bellugi, U. 1967. The acquisition of negation. Ph.D. diss., Harvard University.

_____. 1970. Learning the language. *Psychol. Today* 4: 32–35, 66.

Bellugi, U., and Klima, E. S. 1972. The roots of language in the sign talk of the deaf. *Psychol. Today* 6: 60–64, 76.

Bellugi, U.; Klima, E. S.; and Siple, P. 1975. Remembering in signs. *Cognition* 3: 93–125.

Berko, J. 1958. The child's learning of English morphology. *Word* 14: 150–177.

Bernstein, B. 1966. Elaborated and restricted codes: their social origins and some consequences. In *Communication and culture,* ed. A. G. Smith. New York: Holt, Rinehart and Winston.

Bettelheim, B. 1967. *The empty fortress: infantile autism and the birth of self.* London: Collier-MacMillan.

Bever, T. G. 1968. Association to stimulus-response theories of language. In *Verbal behavior and general behavior theory,* ed. T. R. Dixon and D. L. Horton. Englewood Cliffs, N.J.: Prentice-Hall.

_____. 1970. The cognitive basis for linguistic structures. *In Cognition and the development of language,* ed. J. R. Hayes. New York: Wiley.

Bever, T. G.; Fodor, J. A.; and Weksel, W. 1965. On the acquisition of syntax. *Psychol. Rev.* 72: 467–482.

Bierwisch, M. 1970. Semantics. In *New horizons in linguistics.* ed. J. Lyons. Baltimore: Penguin Books.

Blank, M. 1975. Mastering the intangible through language. In *Developmental psycholinguistics and communication disorders,* ed. D. Aaronson and R. W. Rieber. *Ann. N.Y, Acad. Sci.* 263: 44–58.

Bloom, L. M. 1970. *Language development: form and function in emerging grammars.* Cambridge, Mass.: MIT Press.

_____. 1973. *One word at a time: the use of single word utterances before syntax.* The Hague: Mouton.

_____. 1974. Talking, understanding and thinking. In *Language perspectives: acquisition, retardation, and intervention,* ed. R. L. Schiefelbusch and L. L. Lloyd. Baltimore: University Park Press.

Bloom, L. M.; Hood, L.; and Lightbown, P. 1974. Imitation in language development: if, when and why. *Cognitive Psychol.* 6: 380–420.

Bloom, L. M.; Lightbown, P.; and Hood, L. 1975. Structure and variation in child language. *Monogr. Soc. Res. Child. Dev.* 40.

Blount, B. G. 1972. Parental speech and language acquisition: some Luo and Samoan examples. *Anthro. Ling.* 14: 119–130.

Bolles, R. C. 1970. Species-specific defense reactions and avoidance learning. *Psychol. Rev.* 77: 32–48.

Bornstein, M. H. 1975. Qualities of color vision in infancy. *J. Exp. Child Psychol.* 19: 401–419.

Bower, T. G. R. 1974. *Development in infancy.* San Francisco: W. H. Freeman:

Bowerman, M. F. 1973a. *Learning to talk: a cross-linguistic study of early syntac-*

tic development, with special reference to Finnish. Cambridge: Cambridge University Press.

_____. 1973b. Structural relationships in children's utterances: syntactic or semantic? In *Cognitive development and the acquisition of language,* ed. T. E. Moore. New York: Academic Press.

_____. 1976. Semantic factors in the acquisition of rules for word use and sentence construction. In *Normal and deficient language,* ed. D. M. Morehead and A. E. Morehead. Baltimore: University Park Press.

_____. 1977. The acquisition of word meaning: an investigation of some current conflicts. In *Proceedings of the Third International Child Language Symposium.* ed. N. Waterson and C. Snow. New York: Wiley.

Braine, M. D. S. 1963a. The ontogeny of English phrase structure: the first phase. *Language* 39: 1–13.

_____. 1963b. On learning the grammatical order of words. *Psychol. Rev.* 70: 323–348.

_____. 1971. The acquisition of language in infant and child. In *The learning of language,* ed. C. Reed, New York: Appleton-Century-Crofts.

_____. 1976. Children's first word combinations. *Monogr. Soc. Res. Child Dev.* 41.

Branigan, G. 1976a. Sequences of single words as structured units. Paper presented at the Eighth Annual Child Language Research Forum, Stanford University.

_____. 1976b. Organizational constraints during the one-word period. Paper presented at First Annual Boston University Conference on Language Development.

Brewer, W. F., and Stone, J. B. 1975. Acquisition of spatial antonym pairs. *J. Exp. Child Psychol.* 19: 299–307.

Bricker, W. A., and Bricker, D. D. 1972. Assessment and modification of verbal imitation with low-functioning children. *J. Speech Hearing Res.* 15: 690–698.

_____. 1974. An early language training strategy. In *Language perspectives acquisition, retardation, and intervention,* ed. R. L. Schiefelbusch and L. L. Lloyd. Baltimore: University Park Press.

Broen, P. A. 1972. The verbal environment of the language-learning child. *Amer. Speech Hearing Assoc. Monogr.* 17.

Brown, R. 1957. Linguistic determinism and part of speech. *J. Abnorm. Soc. Psychol.* 55: 1–5.

_____. 1958. *Words and things.* New York: Free Press.

_____. 1965. *Social psychology.* New York: Free Press.

_____. 1968. The development of wh questions in child speech. *J. Verb. Learning Verb. Behav.* 7: 279–290.

_____. 1970. The first sentences of child and chimpanzee. In *Psycholinguistics: selected papers.* New York: The Free Press.

_____. 1973. *A first language: the early stages.* Cambridge, Mass.: Harvard University Press.

_____. 1977. In *Talking to children: language input and acquisition,* C. Ferguson and C. Snow. Cambridge: Cambridge University Press.

Brown, R., and Bellugi, U. 1964. Three processes in the child's acquisition of syntax. *Harvard Educ. Rev.* 34: 133–151.

Brown, R.; Cazden, C.; and Bellugi, U. 1969. The child's grammar from I to III. In *Minnesota Symposium on Child Psychology,* vol. 2., ed. J. P. Hill. Minneapolis: Univ. of Minnesota Press.

Brown, R., and Fraser, C. 1964. The acquisition of syntax. In *The acquisition of language,* ed. U. Bellugi and R. Brown. *Monogr. Soc. Res. Child Dev.* 29: 43–79.

Brown, R., and Hanlon, C. 1970. Derivational complexity and order of acquisition in child speech. In *Cognition and the development of language,* ed. J. R. Hayes, New York: Wiley.

Brown, R., and Herrnstein, R. J. 1975. *Psychology.* Boston: Little-Brown.

Brown, R., and Hildum, D. C. 1956. Expectancy and the perception of syllables. *Language* 32: 411–419.

Bruce, D. J. 1964. The analysis of word sounds by young children. *Brit. J. Educ. Psychol.* 34: 158–159.

Bruner, J. S. 1975. From communication to language: a psychological perspective. *Cognition* 3: 255–287.

Bruner, J. S.; Goodnow, J. J.; and Austin, G. A. 1956. *A study of thinking.* New York: Wiley.

Bryant, B., and Anisfeld, M. 1969. Feedback versus no-feedback in testing children's knowledge of English pluralization rules. *J. Exp. Child Psychol.* 8: 250–255.

Buium, N. 1974. An investigation of the word order parameter of a parent-child verbal interaction in a relatively free order language. *Lang. Speech* 17: 182–186.

Burling, R. 1959. Language development of a Garo and English-speaking child. *Word* 15: 45–68.

Butterfield, E. C., and Cairns, G. F. 1974. Discussion summary: infant reception research. In *Language perspectives: acquisition, retardation, and intervention,* ed. R. L. Schiefelbusch and L. L. Lloyd. Baltimore: University Park Press.

Butterfield, E. C., and Siperstein, G. N. 1974. Influence of contingent auditory stimulation upon non-nutritional suckle. In *Proceedings of Third Symposium on Oral Sensation and Perception: the mouth of the infant.* Springfield, Ill.: Charles C. Thomas.

Carey, S. 1972. Are children little scientists with false theories of amount? Ph.D. diss., Harvard University.

————. 1976. Spatial adjectives. Unpublished working paper, MIT.

————. 1977a. The child as word learner. In *Linguistic theory and psychological reality.* ed. M. Halle, J. Bresnan, and G. A. Miller. Cambridge, Mass: MIT Press.

————. 1977b. "Less" may never mean more. In *Proceedings of Stirling Conference on Psycholinguistics,* ed. R. Campbell.

Carey, S., and Considine, T. 1973. The domain of comparative adjectives. Unpublished working paper, MIT.

Cazden, C. B. 1965. Environmental assistance to the child's acquisition of grammar. Ph.D. diss., Harvard University.

————. 1976. How knowledge about language helps the classroom teacher-or does it: a personal account. *The Urban Review* 9: 74–90.

Chamberlain, A. F., and Chamberlain, J. C. 1904. Studies of a child. *Pedagogical Seminary* 11: 264–291.

Chomsky, C. 1969. *Acquisition of syntax in children from 5 to 10.* Cambridge, Mass.: MIT Press.

Chomsky, N. 1957. *Syntactic structures.* The Hague: Mouton.

————. 1959. A review of B. F. Skinner's *Verbal behavior. Language* 35: 26–58.

————. 1964. Degrees of grammaticalness. In *The structure of language: readings in the philosophy of language,* ed. J. A. Fodor and J. J. Katz. Englewood Cliffs, N.J.: Prentice-Hall.

————. 1965. *Aspects of the theory of syntax.* Cambridge, Mass.: MIT Press.

————. 1967. The general properties of language. In *Brain mechanisms underlying speech and language,* ed. C. H. Millikan and F. L. Darley. New York: Grune and Stratton.

————. 1976. On the nature of language. In *Origins and evolution of language and speech,* ed. S. R. Harnad, H. D. Steklis, and J. Lancaster. *Ann. N.Y. Acad. Sci.* 280: 46–55.

Chomsky, N., and Halle, M. 1968. *The sound pattern of English.* New York: Harper and Row.

Churchill, D. W. 1972. The relation of infantile autism and early childhood schizophrenia to developmental language disorders of childhood. *J. Aut. Child. Schiz.* 2: 182–197.

Clark, E. V. 1971. On the acquisition of the meaning of *before* and *after. J. Verb. Learning Verb. Behav.* 10: 266–275.

————. 1972. On the child's acquisition of antonyms in two semantic fields. *J. Verb. Learning Verb. Behav.* 11: 750–758.

————. 1973. What's in a word? On the child's acquisition of semantics in his first language. In *Cognitive development and the acquisition of language,* ed. T. E. Moore. New York: Academic Press.

————. 1975. Knowledge, context and strategy in the acquisition of meaning. In *Georgetown University Round Table on Languages and Linguistics,* ed. D. P. Dato. Washington, D.C.: Georgetown University Press.

————. 1977. From gesture to word: on the natural history of deixis in language acquisition. In *Human growth and development: Wolfson College lectures 1976,* ed. J. S. Bruner and A. Garton. Oxford: Oxford University Press.

Clark, H. H. 1970. The primitive nature of children's relational concepts. In *Cognition and the development of language,* ed. J. R. Hayes. New York: Wiley.

————. 1973. Space, time, semantics and the child. In *Cognitive development and the acquisition of language,* ed. T. E. Moore. New York: Academic Press.

————. 1974. Semantics and comprehension. In *Current trends in linguistics,* vol. 12: *Linguistics and the adjacent arts and sciences,* ed. T. A. Sebeok. The Hague: Mouton.

Clark, H. H., and Clark, E. V. 1977. *Psychology and language: an introduction to psycholinguistics.* New York: Harcourt Brace Jovanovich.

Clark, R. 1974. Performing without competence. *J. Child Lang.* 1: 1–10.

Coggins, R. 1976. The classification of relational meanings expressed in the early two-word utterances of Down's syndrome children. Ph.D. diss., University of Wisconsin.

Compton, A. J. 1975. Generative studies of children's phonological disorders: a strategy of therapy. In *Measurement procedures in speech, hearing, and language,* ed. S. Singh. Baltimore: University Park Press.

————. 1976. Generative studies of children's phonological disorders: clinical ramifications. In *Normal and deficient language,* ed. D. M. Morehead and A. E. Morehead. Baltimore: University Park Press.

Condon, W. S., and Ogston, W. D. 1966. Sound film analyses of normal and pathological behavior patterns. *J. Nerv. Ment. Dis.* 142: 338–347.

————. 1967. A segmentation of behavior. *J. Psychiat. Res.* 5: 221–235.

Condon, W. S., and Sander, L. W. 1974. Synchrony demonstrated between movements of the neonate and adult speech. *Child Devel.* 65: 456–462.

Cooper, R. L. 1967. The ability of deaf and hearing children to apply morphophonological rules. *J. Speech Hearing Res.* 10: 77–85.

Cromer, R. F. 1974a. The development of language and cognition: the cognition hypothesis. In *New perspectives in child development,* ed. B. Foss. Harmondsworth, Middlesex, England: Penguin Books.

————. 1974b. Receptive language in the mentally retarded: processes and diagnostic distinctions. In *Language perspectives: acquisition, retardation, and intervention,* ed. R. L. Schiefelbusch and L. L. Lloyd. Baltimore: University Park Press.

Cross, T. G. 1977. Mother's speech adjustments: the contributions of selected child listener variables. In *Talking to children: language input and acquisition,* ed. C. Ferguson and C. Snow. Cambridge: Cambridge University Press.

Cunningham, M. A. 1966. A five year study of the language of an autistic child. *J. Child Psychol. Psychiat.* 7: 143–154.

Curtiss, S.; Fromkin, V.; Rigler, D.; Rigler, M.; and Krashen, S. 1975. An update on the linguistic development of Genie. In *Georgetown University Round Table on Languages and Linguistics,* ed. D. P. Dato. Washington, D.C.: Georgetown University Press.

Dale, P. 1973. *Language development: structure and function.* New York: Holt, Rinehart and Winston.

Das, J. 1972. Patterns of cognitive ability in nonretarded and retarded children. *Amer. J. Mental Defic.* 77: 6–12.

Delattre, P. C.; Liberman, A. M.; and Cooper, F. S. 1955. Acoustic loci and transitional cues for consonants. *J. Acoust. Soc. Amer.* 27: 769–773.

DePaulo, B. M., and Bonvillian, J. D. 1975. The effect on language development of the special characteristics of speech addressed to children. Unpublished paper, Harvard University.

Dever, R. B. 1972. A comparison of the results of a revised version of Berko's Test of Morphology with the free speech of mentally retarded children. *J. Speech Hearing Res.* 15: 169–178.

Dever, R. B., and Gardner, W. I. 1970. Performance of normal and retarded boys on Berko's test of morphology. *Lang. Speech* 13: 162–181.

de Villiers, J. G., and de Villiers, P. A. 1973a. Development of the use of word order in comprehension. *J. Psycholing. Res.* 2: 331–341.

————. 1973b. A cross-sectional study of the acquisition of grammatical morphemes. *J. Psycholing. Res.* 2: 267–78.

──────. 1977. Semantics and syntax in the first two years: the output of form and function and the form and function of the input. In *Communicative and cognitive abilities: early behavioral assessment,* ed. F. D. Minifie and L. L. Lloyd. Baltimore: University Park Press.

de Villiers, J. G., and Naughton, J. M. 1974. Teaching a symbol language to autistic children. *J. Consult. Clin. Psychol.* 42: 111–117.

de Villiers, J. G., and Tager-Flusberg, H. B. 1975. Some facts one simply cannot deny. *J. Child Lang.* 2: 279–286.

de Villiers, J. G., Tager-Flusberg, H. B., and Hakuta, K. 1976. The roots of co-ordination in child speech. Paper presented at First Annual Boston University Conference on Language Development.

de Villiers, P. A., and de Villiers, J. G. 1972. Early judgments of semantic and syntactic acceptability by children. *J. Psycholing. Res.* 1: 299–310.

──────. 1974. On this, that, and the other: nonegocentrism in very young children. *J. Exp. Child Psychol.* 18: 438–447.

Dingwall, W. O. 1975. The species-specificity of speech. In *Georgetown University Round Table on Languages and Linguistics,* ed. D. P. Dato. Washington, D.C.: Georgetown University Press.

Dodd, B. J. 1972. Effects of social and vocal stimulation on infant babbling. *Devel. Psychol.* 7: 80–83.

Donaldson, M., and Balfour, G. 1968. Less is more: a study of language comprehension in children. *Brit. J. Psychol.* 59: 461–472.

Donaldson, M., and McGarrigle, J. 1974. Some clues to the nature of semantic development. *J. Child. Lang.* 1: 185–194.

Dooley, J. 1976. Language acquisition and Down's syndrome: a study of early semantics and syntax. Ph.D. diss., Harvard University.

Dore, J. 1974. A pragmatic description of early language development. *J. Psycholing. Res.* 3: 343–350.

──────. 1975. Holophrases, speech acts, and language universals. *J. Child Lang.* 2: 21–40.

Drach, K. M. 1969. *The language of the parent: a pilot study.* Working paper no. 14. Berkeley: University of California.

Dulay, H., and Burt, M. K. 1974. Natural sequences in child second language acquisition. *Lang. Learning* 24: 37–53.

du Preez, P. 1974. Units of information in the acquisition of language. *Lang. Speech* 17: 369–376.

Edwards, M. L. 1971. One child's acquisition of English liquids. *Papers and Reports on Child Lang. Devel.* (Stanford University) 3: 101–109.

──────. 1974. Perception and production in child phonology: the testing of four hypotheses. *J. Child Lang.* 1: 205–219.

Ehri, L. C. 1976. Comprehension and production of adjectives and seriation. *J. Child Lang.* 3: 369–384.

Eilers, R. E.; Oller, K. K.; and Ellington, J. 1974. The acquisition of word-meaning for dimensional adjectives: the long and short of it. *J. Child Lang.* 1: 195–204.

Eimas, P. D. 1974. Linguistic processing of speech by young infants. In *Language perspectives: acquisition, retardation, and intervention,* ed. R. L. Schiefelbusch and L. L. Lloyd. Baltimore: University Park Press.

————. 1975. Developmental studies of speech perception. In *Infant perception,* ed. L. B. Cohen and P. Salapatek. New York: Academic Press.

Eimas, P. D., and Corbit, J. D. 1973. Selective adaptation of linguistic feature detectors. *Cognitive Psychol.* 4: 99–109.

Eimas, P. D.; Siqueland, E. R.; Jusczyk, P.; and Vigorito, J. 1971. Speech perception in infants. *Science* 171: 303–306.

Eisenson, J. 1972. *Aphasia in children.* New York: Harper and Row.

Ellenberger, R.; Moores, D. F.; and Hoffmeister, R. 1975. *Early stages in the acquisition of negation by a deaf child of deaf parents.* Research report no. 94. Minneapolis: Center in Education of Handicapped Children, University of Minnesota.

Ellis, N. R. 1971. *International review of research in mental retardation,* vol. 5 New York: Academic Press.

Entus, A. K. 1975. Hemispheric asymmetry in processing of dichotically presented speech and nonspeech stimuli by infants. Paper presented at the Biennial Meeting of the Society for Research in Child Development, Denver.

Ervin-Tripp, S. 1964. Imitation and structural change in children's language. In *New directions in the study of language,* ed. E. H. Lenneberg. Cambridge, Mass.: MIT Press.

————. 1970. Discourse agreement: how children answer questions. In *Cognition and the development of language,* ed. J. R. Hayes. New York: Wiley.

————. 1977. Wait for me, rollerskate! In *Child discourse,* ed. C. Mitchell-Kernan and S. Ervin-Tripp. New York: Academic Press.

Fay, W. H., and Butler, B. V. 1968. Echolalia, I. Q. and the developmental dichotomy of speech and language systems. *J. Speech Hearing Res.* 11: 365–371.

Feldman, C. 1971. The effects of various types of adult responses in the syntactic acquisition of two to three-year-olds. Unpublished paper, University of Chicago.

Ferguson, C. A. 1964. Baby talk in six languages. *Amer. Anthro.* 66: 103–114.

————. 1973. Fricatives in child language acquisition. *Papers and Reports on Child. Lang. Devel.* (Stanford University) 6: 61–86.

————. 1977a. Learning to pronounce: the earliest stages of phonological development in the child. In *Communication and cognitive abilities: early behavioral assessment,* ed. F. D. Minifie and L. L. Lloyd. Baltimore: University Park Press.

————. 1977b. Baby talk as a simplified register. In *Talking to children: language input and acquisition,* ed. C. Ferguson and C. Snow. Cambridge: Cambridge University Press.

Ferguson, C. A., and Farwell, C. 1975. Words and sounds in early language acquisition: English consonants in the first 50 words. *Language* 51: 419–439.

Ferguson, C. A., and Garnica, O. K. 1975. Theories of phonological development. In *Foundations of language development: a multidisciplinary approach,* vol. 1, ed. E. H. Lenneberg and E. Lenneberg. New York: Academic Press.

Ferreiro, E., and Sinclair, H. 1971. Temporal relations in language. *Internat. J. Psychol.* 6: 39–47.

Ferster, C. B. 1972. Clinical reinforcement. *Seminars in Psychiat.* 4: 101–111.

Fillmore, C. J. 1968. The case for case. In *Universals of linguistic theory,* ed. E. Bach and R. T. Harms. New York: Holt, Rinehart and Winston.

Fleming, J. D. 1974. Field report: the state of the apes. *Psychol. Today* 8: 31–46.

Fodor, J. A. 1966. How to learn to talk: some simple ways. In *The Genesis of Language,* ed. F. Smith and G. A. Miller. Cambridge, Mass.: MIT Press.

Fodor, J. A; Bever, T. G.; and Garrett, M. 1974. *The psychology of language.* New York: McGraw-Hill Book Co.

Fraser, C.; Bellugi, U.; and Brown, R. 1963. Control of grammar in imitation, comprehension and production. *J. Verb. Learning Verb. Behav.* 2: 121–135.

Frisch, K. von. 1967. *The dance language and orientation of bees,* trans. L. E. Chadwick. Cambridge, Mass.: Harvard University Press.

Frith, U. 1969. Emphasis and meaning in recall in normal and autistic children. *Lang. Speech.* 12: 29–38.

———. 1970a. Studies in pattern detection in normal and autistic children: I. Immediate recall of auditory sequences. *J. Abnorm. Psychol.* 76: 413–420.

———. 1970b. Studies in pattern detection in normal and autistic children: II. Reproduction and production of color sequences. *J. Exp. Child Psychol.* 10: 120–135.

Fromkin, V. A. 1973. Slips of the tongue. *Sci. Amer.* 229: 110–117.

Fromkin, V. A.; Krashen, S.; Curtiss, S.; Rigler, D.; and Rigler, M. 1974. The development of language in Genie: a case of language acquisition beyond the "critical period." *Brain and Language.* 1: 81–107.

Fry, D. B. 1966. The development of the phonological system in the normal and the deaf child. In *The genesis of language,* ed. F. Smith and G. A. Miller. Cambridge, Mass.: MIT Press.

Furth, H. G. 1975. On the nature of language from the perspective of research with profoundly deaf children. In *Developmental psycholinguistics and communication disorders,* ed. D. Aaronson and R. W. Rieber. *Ann. N.Y. Acad. Sci.* 263: 70–75.

Garcia, E. 1974. The training and generalization of a conversational speech form in nonverbal retardates. *J. Appl. Behav. Anal.* 7: 137–149.

Gardner, R. A., and Gardner, B. T. 1969. Teaching sign language to a chimpanzee. *Science.* 165: 664–672.

Garnica, O. K. 1973. The development of phonemic speech perception. In *Cognition and the acquisition of language,* ed. T. E. Moore. New York: Academic Press.

Garvey, C. 1975. Requests and responses in children's speech. *J. Child Lang.* 2: 41–63.

Gazzaniga, M. S. 1967. The split brain in man. *Sci. Amer.* 217: 24–29.

Gelman, R., and Shatz, M. 1975. Rule governed variation in children's conversations. Unpublished paper, Univ. of Pennsylvania.

Gentner, D. 1975. Evidence for the psychological reality of semantic components: the verbs of possession. In *Explorations in cognition,* ed. D. A. Norman, D. E. Rumelhart, and the LNR Research Group. San Francisco: W. H. Freeman.

Geschwind, N. 1970. The organization of language and the brain. *Science* 170: 940–944.

Geschwind, N., and Levitsky, W. 1968. Human brain: left-right asymmetries in temporal speech area. *Science*. 161: 186–187.

Glanzer, P. D., and Dodd, D. H. 1975. Developmental changes in the language spoken to children. Paper presented to the Biennial Conference of the Society for Research in Child Development, Denver.

Gleitman, L. R.; Gleitman, H.; and Shipley, E. F. 1972. The emergence of the child as grammarian. *Cognition* 1: 137–164.

Glucksberg, S., and Danks, J. H. 1975. *Experimental psycholinguistics: an introduction*. Hillsdale, N.J: Lawrence Erlbaum Associates.

Goldin-Meadow, S., and Feldman, H. 1975. The creation of a communication system: a study of deaf children of hearing parents. Paper presented to the Biennial Conference of the Society for Research in Child Development, Denver.

Gonzales, J. L. 1973. The effects of maternal stimulation on early language development of Mexican-American children. *Diss. Abstr.* 33 (7-A): 3436.

Graham, J. T., and Graham, L. W. 1971. Language behavior of the mentally retarded: syntactic characteristics. *Amer. J. Ment. Defic.* 75: 623–629.

Greenfield, P. M., and Smith, J. H. 1976. *The structure of communication in early language development*. New York: Academic Press.

Gruendel, M. M. 1976. Concepts, categories and early word use: over-extension reconsidered. Paper presented at the First Annual Boston University Conference on Language Development.

Guess, D. 1969. A functional analysis of receptive language and productive speech: acquisition of the plural morpheme. *J. Appl. Behav. Anal.* 2: 55–64.

Guess, D., and Baer, D. M. 1973. An analysis of individual differences in generalization between receptive and productive language in retarded children. *J. Appl. Behav. Anal.* 6: 311–329.

Guess, D.; Sailor, W.; and Baer, D. M. 1974. To teach language to retarded children. In *Language perspectives: acquisition, retardation and intervention,* ed. R. L. Schiefelbusch and L. L. Lloyd. Baltimore: University Park Press.

Hagen, J. W., and Hale, G. H. The development of attention in children. In *Minnesota Symposia on Child Psychol,* Vol 7, ed. A. D. Pick. Minneapolis: University of Minnesota Press.

Hakuta, K. 1974. Prefabricated patterns and the emergence of structure in second language acquisition. *Lang. Learning,* 24: 287–297.

———. 1975. Learning to speak a second language: what exactly does the child learn? In *Georgetown University Round Table on Languages and Linguistics,* ed. D. P. Dato. Washington, D. C.: Georgetown Univ. Press.

———. 1976. A case study of a Japanese child learning English. *Lang. Learning,* 26: 321–351.

Halliday, M. A. K. 1975. Learning how to mean. In *Foundations of language development: a multidisciplinary approach,* vol 1., ed E. H. Lenneberg and E. Lenneberg. New York: Academic Press.

Harris, S. L. 1975. Teaching language to nonverbal children: with emphasis on problems of generalization. *Psychol. Bull.* 82: 565–580.

Hartshorne, H., and May, M. A. 1928. *Studies in the nature of character: I. Studies in deceit*. New York: Macmillan.

Hayes, C. 1951. *The ape in our house.* New York: Harper.

Hecht, B. F., and Morse, R. 1974. What the hell are dese? Unpublished paper, Harvard University.

Heider, E. R. 1971. "Focal" color areas and the development of color names. *Devel. Psychol.* 4: 447–455.

————. 1972. Universals in color naming and memory. *J. Exp. Psychol.* 93: 10–20.

Hermelin, B., and Frith, U. 1971. Psychological studies of childhood autism: can autistic children make use of what they see and hear? *J. Special Educ.* 5: 107–117.

Hermelin, B., and O'Connor, N. 1970. *Psychological experiments with autistic children.* Oxford: Pergamon Press.

————. 1973. Ordering in recognition memory after ambiguous initial and recognition displays. *Canad. J. Psychol.* 27: 191–199.

————. 1975. The recall of digits by normal, deaf and autistic children. *Brit. J. Psychol.* 66: 203–209.

Hinde, R. A., and Stevenson-Hinde, J., eds. 1973. *Constraints on learning.* New York: Academic Press.

Hockett, C. F. 1958. *A course in modern linguistics.* New York: Macmillan.

Holzman, M. 1973. The use of interrogative forms in verbal interaction of three mothers and their children. *J. Psycholing. Res.* 1: 311–336.

Horton, K. B. 1974. Infant intervention and language learning. In *Language perspectives: acquisition, retardation, and intervention,* ed. R. L. Schiefelbusch and L. L. Lloyd. Baltimore: University Park Press.

Horton, K. B., and McConnell, F. 1970. Early intervention for the young deaf child through parent training. In *Proceedings of the International Congress on Education of the Deaf,* vol. 1. Stockholm.

Hutt, S. J.; Hutt, C.; Leonard, H. G.; Benuth, H. V.; and Muntjewerff, W. J. 1968. Auditory responsivity in the human newborn. *Nature* 218: 888–890.

Huttenlocher, J. 1974. The origins of language comprehension. In *Theories in cognitive psychology,* ed. R. L. Solso. Potomac, Md.: Lawrence Erlbaum Associates.

Ianco-Worrall, A. D. 1972. Bilingualism and cognitive development. *Child Devel.* 43: 1390–1400.

Ingram, D. 1971. Phonological rules in young children. *Papers and Reports on Child Lang. Devel.* (Stanford University) 3: 31–49.

————. 1973. The inversion of subject NP and Aux in children's questions. Paper presented at Linguistic Society of America.

————. 1974. Fronting in child phonology. *J. Child Lang.* 1: 233–241.

————. 1975. If and when transformations are acquired by children. In *Georgetown University Round Table on Languages and Linguistics,* ed. D. P. Dato. Washington, D.C.: Georgetown University Press.

————. 1976. Current issues in child phonology. In *Normal and deficient language,* ed. D. M. Morehead and A. E. Morehead. Baltimore: University Park Press.

Inhelder, B. 1966. Cognitive development and its contribution to diagnosis of some phenomena of mental deficiency. *Merrill-Palmer Quarterly* 12: 299–317.

Irwin, O. C., and Chen, H. P. 1946. Infant speech: vowel and consonant frequency. *J. Speech Disord.* 11: 123–125.

Istomina, Z. M. 1963. Perception and naming of color in early childhood. *Soviet Psychol. and Psychiat.* 1: 37–45.

Itard, J. M. G. 1932. *The wild boy of Aveyron,* trans. G. and M. Humphrey. New York: Century.

Jacobs, R. A., and Rosenbaum, P. S. 1968. *English transformational grammar.* Waltham, Mass.: Blaisdell.

Jakobson, R. 1968. *Child language, aphasia, and phonological universals.* The Hague: Mouton.

Jesperson, O. 1922. *Language: its nature, development, and origin.* London: Allen and Unwin.

Johnson, E. G. 1977. The development of color knowledge in preschool children. *Child Devel.* 48: 308–311.

Kagan, J. 1970. Determinants of attention in the infant. *Amer. Scientist* 58: 289–306.

Kanner, L. 1943. Autistic disturbances of affective contact. *Nerv. Child.* 2: 217–250.

Kaplan, E. L. 1969. The role of intonation in the acquisition of language. Ph.D. diss., Cornell University.

Karlin, I. W., and Strazzulla, M. 1952. Speech and language problems of mentally deficient children. *J. Speech Hearing Disord.* 17: 286–294.

Kates, S. 1972. *Language development in deaf and hearing adolescents.* Northampton, Mass.: Clarke School for the Deaf.

Katz, J. J. 1966. *The philosophy of language.* New York: Harper & Row.

————. 1976. A hypothesis about the uniqueness of natural language. In *Origins and evolution of language and speech,* ed. S. R. Harnad, H. D. Steklis, and J. Lancaster, *Ann. N.Y. Acad. Sci.* 280: 33–41.

Katz, J. J., and Fodor, J. A. 1963. The structure of a semantic theory. *Language* 39: 170–210.

Katz, N.; Baker, E.; and Macnamara, J. 1974. What's in a name? A study of how children learn common and proper names. *Child Devel.* 65: 469–473.

Keenan, E. O. 1975. Conversational competence in children. *J. Child Lang.,* 2: 163–183.

Kemp, J., and Dale, P. 1973. Spontaneous imitation and free speech: a developmental comparison. Paper presented at the Biennial Conference of the Society for Research in Child Development, Philadelphia.

Kenady, K. E., and Proctor, C. L. 1968. A comparison of the language used by mothers of deaf children and mothers of hearing children. M. A. diss., University of Southern California.

Kessel, F. 1970. The role of syntax in children's comprehension from ages six to twelve. *Monogr. Soc. Res. Child Dev.* 35: 1–95.

Kessler, C. 1975. Postsemantic processes in delayed child language related to first and second language learning. *Georgetown University Round Table on Languages and Linguistics,* ed. D. P. Dato. Washington, D.C.: Georgetown University Press.

Khadem, F. V., and Corballis, M. C. 1977. Cerebral asymmetry in infants. Paper presented at the Biennial Conference of the Society for Research in Child Development, New Orleans.

Kimura, D. 1961. Cerebral dominance and the perception of verbal stimuli. *Canadian J. Psychol.* 15: 166–171.

———. 1963. Speech lateralization in young children as determined by an auditory test. *J. Comp. Physiol. Psychol.* 56: 899–902.

Kinsbourne, M. 1975. The ontogeny of cerebral dominance. In *Developmental psycholinguistics and communication disorders*, ed. D. Aaronson and R. W. Rieber. *Ann. N.Y. Acad. Sci.* 263: 244–250.

Klima, E. S., and Bellugi, U. 1973. Teaching apes to communicate. In *Communication, language, and meaning*, ed. G. Miller, New York: Basic Books.

———. 1975. Perception and production in a visually based language. In *Developmental psycholinguistics and communication disorders*, ed. D. Aaronson and R. W. Rieber. *Ann. N.Y. Acad. Sci.* 263: 225–235.

Kobashigawa, B. 1969. *Repetitions in a mother's speech to her child.* Working paper no. 14. Berkeley: University of California.

Koegel, R. L., and Rincover, A. 1974. Treatment of psychotic children in a classroom environment: I. Learning in a large group. *J. Appl. Behav. Anal.* 7: 45–60.

Krashen, S. 1973. Lateralization, language learning, and the critical period: some new evidence. *Lang. Learning.* 23: 63–74.

———. 1975a. The development of cerebral dominance and language learning: more new evidence. In *Georgetown University Round Table on Languages and Linguistics*, ed. D. P. Dato. Washington, D.C.: Georgetown University Press.

———. 1975b. The critical period for language acquisition and its possible bases. In *Developmental psycholinguistics and communication disorders*, ed. D. Aaronson and R. W. Rieber, *Ann. N.Y. Acad. Sci.*, 263: 211–224.

Kučera, H., and Francis, W. N. 1967. *Computational analysis of present-day American English.* Providence, R. I.: Brown University Press.

Kuczaj, S. A. II. 1975. On the acquisition of a semantic system. *J. Verb. Learning Verb. Behav.* 14: 340–358.

Kuczaj, S. A. II, and Maratsos, M. P. 1975. On the acquisition of front, back, and side. *Child Devel.* 46: 202–210.

Kuhl, P. K., and Miller, J. D. 1975. Speech perception by the chinchilla: voiced-voiceless distinction in alveolar plosive consonants. *Science* 190: 69–72.

Labov, W. 1970. *The study of nonstandard English.* Urbana, Ill.: National Council of Teachers of English.

Lackner, J. R. 1968. A developmental study of language behavior in retarded children. *Neuropsychologia,* 6: 301–320.

Ladefoged, P., and Broadbent, D. E. 1957. Information conveyed by vowels. *J. Acoust. Soc. Amer.* 19: 98–104.

Lashley, K. S. 1951. The problem of serial order in behavior. In *Cerebral mechanisms in behavior: the Hixon Symposium*, ed. L. A. Jeffress. New York: Wiley.

Laurendeau, M., and Pinard, A. 1962. *Causal thinking in the child.* New York: International Universities Press.

Lenneberg, E. H., ed. 1964. *New directions in the study of language.* Cambridge, Mass.: MIT Press.

————. 1966. The natural history of language. In *Genesis of language,* ed. F. Smith and G. A. Miller. Cambridge, Mass.: MIT Press.

————. 1967. *Biological foundations of language.* New York: Wiley.

Lenneberg, E. H.; Nichols, I. A.; and Rosenberger, E. R. 1964. Primitive stages of language development in mongolism. *Disorders of communication* (Research Publications, Association for Research in Nervous and Mental Disease) 42: 119–137.

Lenneberg, E. H.; Rebelsky, F. G.; and Nichols, I. A. 1965. The vocalizations of infants born to deaf and hearing parents. *Human Devel.* 8: 23–37.

Leonard, L. B. 1972. What is deviant language? *J. Speech Hearing Disord.* 37: 427–446.

————. 1976. *Meaning in child language.* New York: Grune and Stratton.

Leonard, L. B., and Kaplan, L. 1976. A note on imitation and lexical acquisition. *J. Child Lang.* 3: 449–455.

Leopold, W. F. 1947. *Speech development of a bilingual child: a linguist's record,* vol. 2: *Sound learning in the first two years.* Evanston, Ill: Northwestern University Press.

————. 1949. *Speech development of a bilingual child: a linguist's record,* vol. 4: *Diary from age two.* Evanston, Ill.: Northwestern University Press.

————. 1953. Patterning in children's language learning. *Lang. Learning* 5: 1–14.

Lewis, M. M. 1936. *Infant speech: a study of the beginnings of language.* London: Routledge and Kegan Paul.

Liberman, A. M.; Cooper, F. S.; Harris, K. S.; MacNeilage, P. F.; and Studdert-Kennedy, M. 1967a. Some observations on a model for speech perception. In *Models for the perception of speech and visual form,* ed. W. Wathen-Dunn. Cambridge, Mass.: MIT Press.

Liberman, A. M.; Cooper, F.; Shankweiler, D.; and Studdert-Kennedy, M. 1967b. Perception of the speech code. *Psychol. Rev.* 74: 431–459.

Lieberman, P. 1967. *Intonation, perception, and language.* Cambridge, Mass.: MIT Press.

————. 1973. On the evolution of language: a unified view. *Cognition.* 2: 59–94.

Lillie, S. M. 1972. Principles of parent teaching for language handicapped children under four. *Bulletin* (Division for Children with Communication Disorders) 9: 15–19.

Limber, J. 1973. The genesis of complex sentences. In *Cognitive development and the acquisition of language,* ed. T. E. Moore. New York: Academic Press.

Linden, E. 1974. *Apes, men, and language.* New York: Saturday Review Press/E. P. Dutton Co.

Lindner, G. 1898. *Aus dem naturgarten der Kindersprache.* Leipzig: Th. Ljieben's Verlag.

Lord, C. 1975. Is talking to baby more than baby talk? A longitudinal study of the modification of linguistic input to young children. Unpublished paper presented at the Biennial Conference of the Society for Research in Child Development, Denver.

Lorentz, J. P. 1976. An analysis of some deviant rules of English. In *Normal and deficient language,* ed. D. M. Morehead and A. E. Morehead. Baltimore: University Park Press.

Lovaas, O. I.; Berberich, J. P.; Perloff, B. F.; and Schaeffer, B. 1966. Acquisition of imitative speech by schizophrenic children. *Science* 151: 705–707.

Lovaas, O. I.; Koegel, R.; Simmons, J. Q.; and Long, J. S. 1973. Some generalization and follow-up measures on autistic children in behavior therapy. *J. Appl. Behav. Anal.* 6: 131–166.

Lovell, K., and Dixon, E. M. 1967. The growth of the control of grammar in imitation, comprehension and production. *J. Child Psychol. Psychiat.* 8: 31–39.

Lowe, A. D., and Campbell, R. A. 1965. Temporal discrimination in aphasoid and normal children. *J. Speech Hearing Res.* 8: 313–314.

Lowell, E. L., and Lowell, M. O. 1976. Interaction of assessment and intervention: hearing impairment. Paper presented at the Orcas Island Conference on Early Behavioral Assessment of the Communicative and Cognitive Abilities of the Developmentally Disabled.

McCarthy, D. A. 1954. Language development in children. In *Manual of child psychology,* 2nd ed., ed. L. Carmichael. New York: Wiley.

Maccoby, E. E., and Jacklin, C. N. 1974. *The psychology of sex differences.* Stanford Calif.: Stanford University Press.

Macnamara, J. 1972. Cognitive basis of language learning in infants. *Psychol. Rev.* 79: 1–14.

McNeill, D. 1966. Developmental psycholinguistics. In *The genesis of language,* ed. F. Smith and G. Miller. Cambridge, Mass: MIT Press.

McNeill, D. 1970a. *The acquisition of language.* New York: Harper and Row.

————. 1970b. Explaining linguistic universals. In *Biological and social factors in psycholinguistics,* ed. J. Morton. London: Logos Press.

McReynolds, L. K. 1966. Operant conditioning for investigating speech and discrimination in aphasic children. *J. Speech. Hearing Res.* 9: 519–528.

Madigan, A. M. 1975. The use of verbal context by second and third graders. Senior honors thesis, Harvard University.

Maratsos, M. P. 1974. Preschool children's use of definite and indefinite articles. *Child Devel.* 45: 446–455.

————. 1976. *The use of definite and indefinite reference in young children: an experimental study of semantic acquisition.* Cambridge: Cambridge University Press.

————. 1977. New models in linguistics and language acquisition. In *Linguistic theory and psychological reality,* ed. M. Halle, J. Bresnan, and G. A. Miller. Cambridge, Mass.: MIT Press.

Marler, P. 1952. Variation in the song of the Chaffinch Fringilla coelebs. *Ibis* 94: 458–472.

Martin, J. G. 1972. Rhythmic (hierarchical) versus serial structure in speech and other behavior. *Psychol. Rev.* 79: 487–509.

Meadow, K. 1966. The effect of early manual communication and family climate on the deaf child's development. Ph.D. diss., University of California, Berkeley.

Menn, L. 1976. On the origin and function of rules of child phonology: Interactionist-discovery theory and new evidence for it. Paper presented at Child Language Research Forum, Stanford University.

Menyuk, P. 1964. Comparison of grammar of children with functionally deviant and normal speech. *J. Speech Hearing Res.* 7: 109–121.

————. 1968. The role of distinctive features in children's acquisition of phonology. *J. Speech Hearing Res.* 11: 138–146.

————. 1969. *Sentences children use.* Cambridge, Mass.: MIT Press.

––––––. 1971. *The acquisition and development of language.* Englewood Cliffs, N.J.: Prentice-Hall.

––––––. 1974. The bases of language acquisition: some questions. *J. Aut. Child. Schiz.* 4: 325–345.

––––––. 1975a. The language-impaired child: linguistic or cognitive impairment? In *Developmental psycholinguistics and communication disorders,* ed. D. Aaronson and R. W. Rieber. *Ann. N.Y. Acad. Sci.,* 263: 59–69.

––––––. 1975b. Children with language problems: what's the problem? In *Georgetown University Round Table on Languages and Linguistics,* ed. D. P. Dato. Washington, D.C.: Georgetown University Press.

Menyuk, P., and Bernholtz, N. 1969. Prosodic features and children's language production. *Quart. Progress Rep.* (Research Laboratory of Electronics, MIT) 93: 216–219.

Menyuk, P., and Looney, P. 1972a. A problem of language disorder: length versus structure. *J. Speech Hearing Res.,* 15: 264–279.

––––––. 1972b. Relationships among components of the grammar. *J. Speech Hearing Res.* 15: 395–406.

Messer, S. 1967. Implicit phonology in children. *J. Verb. Learning Verb. Behav.* 6: 609–613.

Mikeš, M. 1967. Acquisition des categoires grammaticales dans le language de l'enfant. *Enfance.* 20: 289–298.

Miller, G. A. 1951. *Language and communication.* New York: McGraw-Hill.

––––––. 1965. Some preliminaries to psycholinguistics. *Amer. Psychol.* 20: 15–20.

Miller, G. A., and Johnson-Laird, P. N. 1976. *Language and perception.* Cambridge, Mass.: Harvard University Press.

Miller, G. A., and Nicely, P. 1955. An analysis of perceptual confusions among some English consonants. *J. Acoust. Soc. Amer.* 27: 338–352.

Miller, J. F., and Yoder, D. E. 1974. An ontogenetic language teaching strategy for retarded children. In *Language perspectives: acquisition, retardation, and intervention,* ed. R. L. Schiefelbusch and L. L. Lloyd. Baltimore: University Park Press.

Miller, R. L. 1953. Auditory tests with synthetic vowels. *J. Acoust. Soc. Amer.* 25: 114–121.

Miller, W., and Ervin, S. 1964. The development of grammar in child language. In *The acquisition of language,* ed. U. Bellugi and R. Brown. *Monogr. Soc. Res. Child Devel.* 29, no. 92: 9–34.

Moerk, E. 1972. Principles of interaction in language learning. *Merrill-Palmer Quarterly* 18: 229–257.

Molfese, D. L. 1972. Cerebral asymmetry in infants, children and adults: auditory evoked responses to speech and noise stimuli. Ph.D. diss., Pennsylvania State University.

––––––. 1973. Cerebral asymmetry in infants, children and adults: auditory evoked responses to speech and musical stimuli. *J. Acoust. Soc. Amer.* 53: 363.

Monsees, E. K. 1968. Temporal sequential auditory expressive language disorders. *Except. Child.* 35: 141–147.

Moore, K. C. 1896. The mental development of a child. *Psychol. Rev. Monogr. Suppl.* 1 (3).

Moores, D. F. 1974. Nonvocal systems of verbal behavior. In *Language perspectives: acquisition, retardation, and intervention,* ed. R. L. Schiefelbusch and L. L. Lloyd. Baltimore: University Park Press.

Moores, D. F.; Weiss, K.; and Goodwin, M. 1973. *Evaluation of programs for hearing impaired children.* Research report no. 57. Minneapolis: Center in Education of Handicapped Children, University of Minnesota.

Morse, P. A. 1974. Infant speech perception: a preliminary model and review of the literature. In *Language perspectives: acquisition, retardation, and intervention,* ed. R. L. Schiefelbusch and L. L. Lloyd. Baltimore: University Park Press.

Moskowitz, A. I. 1973. Acquisition of phonology and syntax: a preliminary study. In *Approaches to natural language,* ed. Hintikka et al. Dordrecht, Holland: Reidel Publ. Co.

Moskowitz, B. A. 1973. On the status of vowel shift in English. In *Cognitive development and the acquisition of language,* ed. T. E. Moore. New York: Academic Press.

Mowrer, O. H. 1954. The psychologist looks at language. *Amer. Psychol.* 9: 660–694.

Nakazima, S. 1962. A comparative study of the speech developments of Japanese and American English in childhood. *Stud. Phonol.* 2: 27–39.

——. 1975. Phonemicization and symbolization in language development. In *Foundations of language: a multidisciplinary approach,* vol. 1., ed. E. H. Lenneberg and E. Lenneberg, New York: Academic Press.

Nelson, K. 1973. Structure and strategy in learning to talk. *Monogr. Soc. Res. Child Dev.* 38, no. 149.

——. 1974. Concept, word and sentence: interrelations in acquisition and development. *Psychol. Rev.* 81: 267–285.

——. 1975. Individual differences in early semantic and syntax development. In *Developmental psycholinguistics and communication disorders,* ed. D. Aaronson and R. W. Rieber. *Ann. N.Y. Acad. Sci.* 263: 132–139.

——. 1976. Some attributes of adjectives used by young children. *Cognition* 4: 13–30.

Nelson, K. E. 1975. Facilitating syntax acquisition. Paper presented to the Eastern Psychological Association in New York, April meeting.

Nelson, K. E.; Carskaddon, G.; and Bonvillian, J. D. 1973. Syntax acquisition: impact of experimental variation in adult verbal interaction with the child. *Child Devel.* 44: 497–504.

Newfield, M. U., and Schlanger, B. B. 1968. The acquisition of English morphology by normal and educable mentally retarded children. *J. Speech Hearing Res.* 11: 693–706.

Newport, E. L. 1975. Motherese: the speech of mothers to young children. Technical report no. 52, Center for Human Information Processing. San Diego: University of California.

Ninio, A., and Bruner, J. 1976. The achievement and antecedents of labelling. Unpublished paper, Hebrew University, Jerusalem.

O'Connor, N., and Hermelin, B. 1963. *Speech and thought in severe subnormality.* Oxford: Pergamon Press.

O'Donnell, R.; Griffin, W.; and Norris, R. 1967. Syntax of kindergarten and elementary school children: a transformational analysis. Champaign-Urbana, Ill.: National Council of Teachers of English.

Oller, D. K.; Wieman, L. A.; Doyle, W. J.; and Ross, C. 1976. Infant babbling and speech. *J. Child Lang.* 3: 1–12.

Olmsted, D. L. 1971. *Out of the mouth of babes*. The Hague: Mouton.

———. 1974. Review of N. V. Smith, *The acquisition of phonology: a case study. J. Child Lang.* 1: 133–138.

Oyama, S. 1973. A sensitive period for the acquisition of a second language. Ph.D. diss., Harvard University.

Palermo, D. S. 1973. More about less: a study of language comprehension. *J. Verb. Learning Verb. Behav.* 12: 211–221.

Papandrapoulou, I., and Sinclair, H. 1974. What is word? Experimental study of children's ideas on grammar. *Human Devel.* 17: 241–258.

Park, T-Z. 1970. The acquisition of German syntax. Unpublished paper. University of Bern, Switzerland, Psychological Institute.

Pavlovitch, M. 1920. *Le langage enfantin: acquisition du serbe et du francais par un enfant serbe*. Paris: Champion.

Penfield, W., and Roberts, L. 1959. *Speech and brain-mechanisms*. Princeton: Princeton University Press.

Pfuderer, C. 1969. Some suggestions for a syntactic characterization of baby talk style. Working paper no. 14, Berkeley: University of California.

Phillips, J. R. 1973. Syntax and vocabulary of mother's speech to young children: age and sex comparisons. *Child Devel.* 44: 182–185.

Piaget, J. 1967. Language and thought from the genetic point of view. In *Six psychological studies,* ed. D. Elkind. New York: Random House.

———. 1970. Piaget's theory. In *Carmichael's manual of child psychology,* 3rd ed., vol. 1, ed. P. H. Mussen. New York: Wiley.

———. 1972. *The child's conception of the world*. Totawa, N.J.: Littlefield, Adams and Co.

Pierce, J. E. 1974. A study of 750 Portland, Oregon, children during the first year. *Papers and Reports on Child Lang. Devel.* (Stanford University.) 8: 19–25.

Pierce, S. J., and Bartolucci, G. 1976. A syntactic investigation of verbal autistic, mentally retarded and normal subjects. Paper presented at First Annual Boston University Conference on Language Development.

Pitcher, E., and Prelinger, E. 1963. *Children tell stories*. New York: International Universities Press.

Porter, J. H. 1975. A cross-sectional study of morpheme acquisition in first language learners. Unpublished paper, Harvard University.

Premack, D. 1971. Language in chimpanzee? *Science,* 172: 808–822.

———. 1976. *Intelligence in ape and man*. Hillsdale, N.J.: Lawrence Erlbaum Associates.

Ramer, A. 1974. Syntactic styles and universal aspects of language emergence. Ph.D. diss., City University of New York.

Reichstein, J. 1964. Auditory threshold consistency in differential diagnosis of aphasic children. *J. Speech Hearing Disord.* 29: 147.

Remick, H. 1971. The maternal environment of linguistic development. Ph.D. diss., University of California, Davis.

Rheingold, H. L.; Gerwitz, J. L.; and Ross, H. W. 1959. Social conditioning of vocalizations in the infant. *J. Comp. Physiol. Psychol.* 52: 68–73.

Richards, J. 1971. A non-contrastive approach to error analysis. *English Language Teaching*. 25: 204–219.

Rosansky, E. J. 1976. Second language acquisition research: a question of methods. Ed.D. diss., Harvard University.

Rosch, E., and Mervis, C. G. 1975. Family resemblances: studies in the internal structure of categories. *Cognitive Psychol*. 7: 573–605.

Ross, J. R. 1967. Constraints in variables in syntax. Ph.D. diss., MIT

Rumbaugh, D. M., and Gill, T. V. 1976. Language and the acquisition of language-type skills by a chimpanzee. *Ann. N.Y. Acad. Sci*. 270: 90–135.

Rutter, M. 1968. Concepts of autism: a review of research. *J. Child Psychol. Psychiat*. 9: 1–25.

Ryan, J. 1973. Interpretation and imitation in early language development. In *Constraints on learning*, ed. R. A. Hinde and J. Stevenson-Hinde. New York: Academic Press.

Sachs, J.; Brown, R.; and Salerno, R. A. 1972. Adult's speech to children. Paper presented at the International Symposium on First Language Acquisition, Florence, Italy.

Sachs, J., and Devin, J. 1973. Young children's knowledge of age-appropriate speech styles. Paper presented at Linguistic Society of America, December.

Sapir, E. 1949. The grammarian and his language. In *Selected writings of Edward Sapir*, ed. D. G. Mandelbaum. Berkeley: University of California Press.

Savin, H. B., and Perchonock, E. 1965. Grammatical structure and the immediate recall of English sentences. *J. Verb. Learning Verb. Behav*. 4: 348–353.

Schlesinger, H. S., and Meadow, K. P. 1972. *Sound and sign*. Berkeley: University of California Press.

Schlesinger, I. M. 1974. Relational concepts underlying language. In *Language perspectives: acquisition, retardation and intervention*, ed. R. L. Schiefelbusch and L. L. Lloyd. Baltimore: University Park Press.

————. 1975. The role of cognitive development and linguistic input in language acquisition. Unpublished paper, Hebrew University of Jerusalem.

Schmitt, P. 1968. Deaf children's comprehension and production of sentence transformations. Ph.D. diss., University of Illinois.

Schöler, H. 1975. Verstehen und Imitation temporaler Satzformen. In *Zur Entwicklung sprachlicher Strukturformen bei Kindern*, ed. H. Grimm, H. Schöler, and M. Wintermantel. Weinheim, W. Germany: J. Beltz Verlag.

Seliger, H.; Krashen, S.; and Ladefoged, P. 1975. Maturational constraints in the acquisition of a native-like accent in second language learning. *Lang. Sciences* 36: 20–22.

Seligman, M. E. P., and Hager, J. L., eds. 1972. *The biological boundaries of learning*. New York: Appleton-Century-Crofts.

Selinker, L.; Swain, M.; and Dumas, G. 1975. The interlanguage hypothesis extended to children. *Lang. Learning* 25: 139–152.

Semmel, M. I.; Barritt, L. S.; and Bennett, S. W. 1970. Performance of EMR and nonretarded children in a modified cloze task. *Amer. J. Ment. Defic*. 74: 681–688.

Shapiro, T., and Huebner, H. F. 1976. Speech patterns of five psychotic children now in adolescence. *J. Child Psychiat*. 15: 278–293.

Shatz, M. 1974. The comprehension of indirect directives: can 2 year olds shut the door? Paper presented at Linguistic Society of America.

Shatz, M., and Gelman, R. 1973. The development of communication skills: modifications in the speech of young children as a function of the listener. *Monogr. Soc. Res. Child Dev.* 38, no. 152.

Shipley, E. S.; Smith, C. S.; and Gleitman, L. R. 1969. A study in the acquisition of language: free responses to commands. *Language* 45: 322–342.

Simon, N. 1975. Echolalic speech in childhood autism: consideration of possible underlying loci of brain damage. *Arch. Gen. Psychiat.* 32: 1439–1446.

Sinclair, H. 1971. Sensorimotor action patterns as a condition for the acquisition of syntax. In *Language acquisition: models and methods,* ed. R. Huxley and E. Ingram. New York: Academic Press.

Sinclair-de-Zwart, H. 1969. Developmental psycholinguistics. In *Studies in cognitive development,* ed. D. Elkind and J. H. Flavell. New York: Oxford University Press.

Skinner, B. F. 1957. *Verbal behavior.* New York: Appleton-Century-Crofts.

Slobin, D. I. 1966. Discussion of D. McNeill, Developmental psycholinguistics. In *The genesis of language,* ed. F. Smith and G. A. Miller. Cambridge, Mass.: MIT Press.

———. 1968. Imitation and grammatical development in children. In *Contemporary issues in developmental psychology,* ed. N. S. Endler, L. R. Boulter, and H. Osser. New York: Holt, Rinehart and Winston.

———. 1973. Cognitive prerequisites for the development of grammar. In *Studies of child language development,* ed. C. A. Ferguson and D. I. Slobin. New York: Holt, Rinehart and Winston.

Slobin, D. I., and Welsh, C. A. 1973. Elicited imitation as a research tool in developmental psycholinguistics. In *Studies of child language development,* ed. C. A. Ferguson and D. I. Slobin. New York: Holt, Rinehart and Winston.

Smith, N. V. 1973. *The acquisition of phonology: a case study.* Cambridge: Cambridge University Press.

———. 1975. Universal tendencies in the child's acquisition of phonology. In *Language, cognitive deficits, and retardation,* ed. N. O'Connor. London: Butterworth.

Snow, C. E. 1971. Language acquisition and mothers' speech to children. Ph.D. diss., McGill University.

———. 1972. Mother's speech to children learning language. *Child Devel.* 43: 549–565.

———. 1974. Mother's speech research: an overview. Paper presented at the conference on language input and acquisition, Boston.

Snow, C. E.; Arlman-Rupp, A.; Hassing, Y.; Jobse, J.; Jooksen, J.; and Vorster, J. 1974. Mother's speech in three social classes. Unpublished paper, University of Amsterdam.

Spreen, O. 1965. Language functions in mental retardation: a review. I. Language development, types of retardation and intelligence level. *Amer. J. Ment. Defic.* 69: 482–494.

Stevens, K. N. 1972. Segments, features and analysis by synthesis. In *Language by ear and eye: the relationships between speech and reading,* ed. J. F. Kavanagh and I. G. Mattingly. Cambridge, Mass.: MIT Press.

Stokoe, W. 1958. Sign language structure. In *Studies in Linguistics.* Occasional paper no. 8. Buffalo: University of Buffalo.

_____. 1972. *Semiotics and human sign languages*. The Hague: Mouton.

Strang, B. H. *Modern English Structure*. New York: St. Martin's Press.

Studdert-Kennedy, M. 1974. The perception of speech. In *Current trends in linguistics*, ed. T. A. Sebeok. The Hague: Mouton.

Svachkin, N. Kh. 1973. The development of phonemic speech perception in early childhood. In *Studies of child language development*, ed. C. A. Ferguson and D. I. Slobin, New York: Holt, Rinehart and Winston.

Taine, H. 1877. Acquisition of languages by children. *Mind* 2: 252–259.

Tallal, P., and Piercy, M. 1973. Developmental aphasia: impaired rate of nonverbal processing as a function of sensory modality. *Neuropsychologia* 11: 389–398.

_____. 1974. Developmental aphasia: rate of auditory processing and selective impairment of consonant perception. *Neuropsychologia* 12: 83–93.

_____. 1975. Developmental aphasia: the perception of brief vowels and extended stop consonants. *Neuropsychologia* 13: 69–74.

Tallal, P.; Stark, R. E.; and Curtiss, B. 1976. Relation between speech perception and speech production impairment in children with developmental dysphasia. *Brain and Language* 3: 305–317.

Tanouye, E.; Lifter, K.; and Bloom, L. 1977. Verb semantics and grammatical morphemes. Paper presented to the Biennial Conference of the Society for Research in Child Development, New Orleans.

Tashiro, L. 1971. On the acquisition of some non-comparative terms. Senior honors thesis, Stanford University.

Telford, C. W., and Sawrey, J. M. 1967. *The exceptional individual: psychological and educational aspects*. Englewood Cliffs, N.J.: Prentice-Hall.

Tervoort, B. 1961. Esoteric symbolism in the communicative behavior of young children. *Amer. Ann. Deaf.* 106: 436–480.

Thomson, J. R., and Chapman, R. S. 1975. Who is "Daddy"? The status of two year-olds' overextended words in use and comprehension. *Papers and Reports on Child Language Development* (Stanford University) 10: 59–68

Todd, G., and Palmer, B. 1968. Social reinforcement of infant babbling. *Child Devel.* 39: 591–596.

Tonkova-Yampol'skaya, R. V. 1969. Development of speech intonation in infants during the first two years of life. *Sov. Psychol.* 7: 48–54.

Townsend, D. J. 1976. Do children interpret "marked" comparative adjectives as their opposites? *J. Child Lang.* 3: 385–396.

Townsend, D. J., and Erb, M. 1975. Children's strategies for interpreting complex comparative questions. *J. Child Lang.* 2: 1–7.

Valian, V.; Caplan, J.; and deSciora, A. M. 1976. Children's use of abstract linguistic knowledge in an everyday speech situation. Paper presented at the First Annual Boston University Conference on Language Development.

Valian, V. V., and Wales, R. J. 1976. What's what: talkers help listeners hear and understand by clarifying sentential relations. *Cognition* 4: 155–176.

Velten, H. V. 1943. The growth of phonemic and lexical patterns in infant language. *Language* 19: 281–292.

Vernon, M. 1967. Relationship of language to the thinking process. *Arch. Gen. Psychiat.* 16: 325–333.

Vihman, M. 1976. From pre-speech to speech: on early phonology. Paper presented to the Eighth Child Language Research Forum, Stanford University.

Vorster, J. 1974. *Mother's speech to children: some methodological consider-ations*. Publications of the Institute for General Linguistics, no. 8. Amsterdam: University of Amsterdam.

Vygotsky, L. S. 1962. *Thought and language*. New York: Wiley.

Wales, R. J., and Campbell, R. N. 1970. The development of comparison and the comparison of development. In *Proceedings of Psycholinguistics Conference at Bressarone*. Amsterdam: North Holland.

Wanner, E.; Kaplan, R.; and Shiner, S. 1974. Garden paths in relative clauses. Unpublished paper, Harvard University.

Warden, D. A. 1976. The influence of context on children's use of identifying expressions and references. *Brit. J. Psych*. 67: 101–112.

Wason, P. C. 1965. The contexts of plausible denial. *J. Verb. Learning Verb. Behav*. 4: 7–11.

Webb, P. A., and Abrahamson, A. A. 1976. Stages of egocentrism in children's use of 'this' and 'that': a different point of view. *J. Child Lang*. 3: 349–367.

Weir, R. H. 1962. *Language in the crib*. The Hague: Mouton.

Weisberg, P. 1963. Social and nonsocial conditioning of infant vocalization. *Child. Devel*. 39: 377–388.

Wells, G. 1974. Learning to code experience through language. *J. Child Lang*. 1:243–269.

Wepman, J. M., and Hess, W. 1969. *A spoken word count (children–ages 5, 6, and 7)*. Language research associates.

Werner, H., and Kaplan, E. 1952. The acquisition of word meaning: a developmental study. *Monogr. Soc. Res. Child Dev*. 15.

Whitehurst, G. J.; Ironsmith, E. M.; and Goldfein, M. 1974. Selective imitation of the passive construction through modeling. *J. Exp. Child Psychol*. 17: 288–302.

Whitehurst, G. J., and Vasta, R. 1975. Is language acquired through imitation? *J. Psycholing. Res*. 4: 37–58.

Whorf, B. 1956. *Language, thought and reality*. Cambridge, Mass.: MIT Press.

Wickelgren, W. 1966. Distinctive features and errors in short-term memory for English consonants. *J. Acoust. Soc. Amer*. 39: 388–398.

Wilcox, S., and Palermo, D. S. 1975. "In," "on," and "under" revisited. *Cognition* 3: 245–254.

Williams, L. 1974. Speech perception and production as a function of exposure to à second language. Ph.D diss., Harvard University.

Wing, J. K. 1966. Diagnosis, epidemiology, aetiology. In *Early Childhood Autism*, ed. J. K. Wing. Oxford: Pergamon Press.

Wing, J. K., and Wing, L. 1971. Multiple impairments in early childhood autism. *J. Aut. Child. Schiz*. 1: 256–275.

Winitz, H. 1969. *Articulatory acquisition and behavior*. New York: Appleton-Century-Crofts.

Winitz, H., and Irwin, O. C. 1958. Syllabic and phonetic structure of infants' early words. *J. Speech Hearing Res*. 1: 250–256.

Witelson, S., and Pallie, W. 1973. Left hemisphere specialization for language in the newborn: anatomical evidence for asymmetry. *Brain* 96: 641–646.

Yoder, D. E., and Miller, J. F. 1972. What we may know and what we can do:

input toward a system. In *Language intervention with the retarded: developing strategies,* ed. J. E. McLean, D. E. Yoder, and R. L. Schiefelbusch. Baltimore: University Park Press.

Zhurova, L. Ye. 1973. The development of analysis of words into their sounds by preschool children. In *Studies of child language development,* ed. C. A. Ferguson and D. I. Slobin. New York: Holt, Rinehart and Winston.

Zufall, N., and Weiss, P. 1975. Selective verbal recall and comprehension in autistic children. Unpublished working paper, Harvard University.

Author Index

Abrahamson, A. A., 146
Anglin, J. M., 129–132, 138, 195
Antinucci, F., 158
Arboleda, C., 263
Asher, J., 214
Aug, R. G., 261
Austin, G. A., 35

Baer, D. M., 267–270
Baker, E., 125
Balfour, G., 142
Barritt, L. S., 254
Bartel, N. R., 254
Bartlett, E. J., 133, 137, 139, 141, 143
Bartolucci, G., 265
Basser, L. S., 162, 163
Bateson, M. C., 154
Bellugi, U., 71, 84, 96, 102–105, 167,
    182–184, 193–194, 197, 203, 206,
    238–242, 254
Bennett, S. W., 254
Berko, J., 46, 236, 254
Bernholtz, N., 50
Bernstein, B., 163
Bettelheim, B., 263
Bever, T. G., 20, 47, 117, 170, 181, 184,
    185, 187, 189, 217
Bierwisch, M., 126, 137, 142
Blank, M., 217, 223–224

Bloom, L. M., 47, 50, 51, 72, 76–79,
    81, 82, 99, 104, 128, 147, 202–203,
    241, 256, 261, 277
Blount, B. G., 193, 194, 195, 273
Bolles, R. C., 209
Bonvillian, J. D., 194, 204–205
Bornstein, M. H., 133
Bower, T. G. R., 122, 221
Bowerman, M. F., 72, 77, 80, 82, 128, 132,
    134, 252
Braine, M. D. S., 39, 70–71, 76–77, 79,
    179, 180, 277
Branigan, G., 50–51, 276
Brewer, W. F., 141, 143, 149
Bricker, D. D., 251, 267–269
Bricker, W. A., 251, 267–269
Broadbent, D. E., 214
Broen, P. A., 194
Brown, R., 22, 26, 46, 70–75, 78, 84–87,
    89–91, 96, 97, 102, 105, 106, 108, 109,
    128, 131, 136, 138, 146, 147, 153, 173,
    179, 184, 185, 190, 192–195, 197, 198,
    203–209, 224, 236, 252–254, 256
Bruce, D. J., 165
Bruner, J. S., 35, 146, 154
Bryen, D., 254
Buium, N., 198
Burling, R., 41
Burt, M. K., 93
Butler, B. V., 261, 265
Butterfield, E. C., 24, 29

304

Subject Index

Abnormal language, 228–271

Abstractness: of early rules, 75–82, 93; of early words, 130–132, 134

Acoustic phonetics, 12–16

Active learning, 3, 40–45, 209, 274–275

Adjectives: acquisition of, 133–143; and the derivational theory of complexity, 111

Adult-to-child speech, 192–198, 234–235, 241, 273–275

Abverbial phrases, 97–98

Ambiguity, 53, 63, 78–79

Animal communication, 2, 152, 173–176, 275. See also Chimpanzees, language in

Aphasia: traumatic, 31, 211–213; developmental, 244–249

Articles, 87, 154–156

Articulatory phonetics, 7–12

Autism, 85, 259–266

Auxiliaries, 97, 103–104

Awareness of language, 165–172

Babbling, 35–38, 45–46, 232–233

Bees, language of, 2, 175–176

Behavioral equivalence, 130–132

Billingualism, 92–93, 94, 210, 213–214

Biological maturation, 3, 37, 210–219

Case grammar, see Semantic relations

Categorical perception: in adults, 25–27; in infants, 28–30; in chinchillas, 30

Chimpanzees, language in, 2, 181–192, 275; Washoe, 182–185; Sarah, 185–191; Lana, 191

Cognition and language development, 75, 77–78, 82–83, 122–123, 130, 179–181, 220–227; of disordered children, 229, 264–265

Competence and performance, 5, 66–67, 116–117

Complexive organization of word meaning, 128–129, 132

Comprehension and production, 40–44, 51–52, 128–129, 162, 216, 218, 254, 270

Conceptual development: as a basis for language, 75, 77–78, 222–225; and word learning, 122–123, 130

Consonants, 7–9, 14–15, 25–30, 38–39, 41, 43–46, 216, 247–248; stop consonants, 8, 14–15, 25–30, 38–39, 41, 44, 247–248; fricatives, 8, 41, 44, 46; consonant clusters, 21–22, 43–44, 216; glides, 44–46; liquids, 44–46

Constituent structure, 56–66; in child speech, 95–99; as revealed in adult-to-child speech, 198

Constraints on language learning, 177–181, 210–227; biological, 210–219; linguistic, 219–220; cognitive, 220–227

Context: and the holophrase, 51–52; and semantic development, 147–148; freedom from, 152–153, 172; of language learning, 197–198

309